ions of Africa

The Civiliz

of Africa

A HISTORY TO 1800

Christopher Ehret

University of Virginia Press · Charlottesville

To my parents, who taught me that my kind was humankind

University of Virginia Press
© 2002 Christopher Ehret
All rights reserved
Printed in the United States of America on acid-free paper

First published 2002

9 8 7 6 5 4 3 2

LIBRARY OF CONGRESS CATALOGING-IN-PUBLICATION DATA

Ehret, Christopher.
  The civilizations of Africa : a history to 1800 / Christopher Ehret.
    p.   cm.
  Includes bibliographical references and index.
  ISBN 0-8139-2084-1 (cloth : alk. paper)—ISBN 0-8139-2085-x (pbk. : alk. paper)
  1. Africa—Civilization. I. Title.
  DT14.E36 2002
  960.1—dc21   2001005038

Contents

Illustrations

MAPS

TABLES

Acknowledgments

In putting this book together I owe thanks to many people. To the several anonymous reviewers of the manuscript, I am grateful for valuable critical comments and suggestions. For giving me permission to use their photographs to illustrate African history and cultures, I would like to thank Frances Cahill, Dr. William Cahill, Dr. Michael Goe, Lahra Smith, Professor Michael Morony, Dr. Serge Tornay of the Musée de l'Homme, Dr. Marie-Claude van Grunderbeek, and also Professor David Lewis-Williams and Dr. Benjamin Smith of the Rock Art Unit, University of Witwatersrand, and the San Heritage Society. I am most grateful, too, to Dr. Chapurukha Kusimba for his photographs of rare artifacts from the collections of the Field Museum, Chicago, and to him and the museum for letting me view their collections. Thanks are due also to Professor Merrick Posnansky for his photographs of important African archeological sites and for allowing me access to artifacts in his personal collection. My very special gratitude goes to the people who helped me at the Fowler Museum of Cultural History of the University of California at Los Angeles: to its director, Doran Ross, and chief curator, Mary Nooter Roberts, and above all to Farida Sunada for guiding me in how to discover relevant art and artifacts in the museum's collections; to Fran Krystok, collections manager, and her staff for locating the items I identified; and to Don Cole, senior photographer, for photographing them. They were all wonderfully helpful and a pleasure to work with.

Last and not at all least, I am grateful to my wife, Pat, an editor and technical writer, whose advice and critical perspectives helped me stay focused on my goal of writing a book intended to make the African past accessible to a wide audience.

The Civilizations of Africa

MAP 1 How big is Africa?

Africa is almost four times as large in area as the forty-eight contiguous states of the United States, shown here superimposed on the map of Africa. It is in fact bigger than the entire United States, all of China and India, and the whole continent of Australia combined.

1

Introducing Africa and Its History

Africa in a Global Frame

Africa lies at the heart of human history. It is the continent from which the distant ancestors of every one of us, no matter who we are today, originally came. Its peoples participated integrally in the great transformations of world history, from the first rise of agricultural ways of life to the various inventions of metalworking to the growth and spread of global networks of commerce. Bigger than the United States, China, India, and the continent of Australia combined, the African continent presents us with a historical panorama of surpassing richness and diversity.

Yet traditional history books, ironically, have long treated Africa as if it were the exemplar of isolation and difference—all because of a few very recent centuries marked by the terrible events of the slave trade. As key agents of that trade, many Europeans and their offspring in the Americas in the eighteenth and nineteenth centuries comforted and absolved themselves by denying the full humanity of Africans, and the histories they wrote so neglected Africa that in time it became accepted wisdom that Africa had no history, or at least no history worth mentioning.

That sad heritage continues to shape the envisioning of Africa today, not just in the West, but all across the non-African world and sometimes in Africa as well. As we begin the third millennium, it is now more than forty years since the teaching and study of African history, once upon a time a subject preserved only in black colleges in the American South, finally began to gain its rightful place in the university curricula of many parts of the world. An immense range of new knowledge of the African past has been built up by modern-day scholars, and the scholarly works of earlier times have been rediscovered. But even now these advances have made hardly a dent in Western folk understandings of Africans and the African past. Even historians themselves, involved these days in crafting courses and writing books on world history, find it profoundly difficult to integrate Africa into their global story, because they, too, grew up with those same folk understandings.

The story we tell here confronts exactly those issues. It presents the long history of Africans and their roles, at different times and in different parts of the continent, in agricultural innovation, in the creation and growth of larger and more complex societies and polities, in the development of new kinds of economic and social relations, and in the invention and spread of new ideas, tools, institutions, and modes of artistic and cultural expression. In myriad ways across the millennia, African developments connected and intersected with developments outside the continent, even as they followed their own unique pathways of change, and that part of the historical picture is traced out here, too.

Getting the Terms of Our Discourse Straight

In learning the story of the African past, students and scholars alike need to be especially sensitive to the problem of "loaded" terms, words that convey value judgments more than they communicate solid information. Scholars are trained early in their careers to watch out for and avoid such words or to use them with great care. But some loaded terms have so long been with us that they continue to be uncritically applied even by scholars who should know better. Historians in general tend to use in insufficiently examined fashion the word "civilization." The student of African history needs particularly to beware three other loaded terms: "tribe," "primitive," and "race."

"Civilization" and "Civilized"

Any book that, like this one, includes "civilization" in its title must confront the highly problematic nature of the term. Unfortunately, the most common applications of "civilization" both by historians and by the public are fraught with value judgments. Societies and peoples are only too commonly described as "civilized" or "uncivilized," or to "have civilization" or to lack it. To speak thus is to rely on mystification in place of substantive description and analysis.

What does it mean to be "uncivilized"? If it means, as its common colloquial use implies, to behave in a violent, disorderly manner and to act without the restraint of law or custom, then Europeans of the twentieth century, with their recurrent descents into genocide and pogroms, and those southern white folk of the early decades of the century who lynched black folk are among the most uncivilized people of history. But it is foolishness to distinguish societies as a whole by such a criterion. All societies have complex laws and rules of proper social behavior, whether written or oral, to which people are expected to conform, and a range of sanctions to be imposed on those who break the laws and rules. In that sense all societies throughout humanity's history have been civilized. Only during periods of breakdown of the social or political order does so-called uncivilized behavior predominate over civilized, and any society anywhere in time or place can potentially face such a breakdown.

Historians of ancient times fall into a related interpretive trap. They classify certain societies as civilizations and the rest as something other than civilizations. So general and uncritical is the acceptance of this practice by both the readers and writers of history that it may astonish the reader to learn just how insubstantial and inadequately grounded such a conceptualization is.

What in actuality are we dealing with when we apply the appellation of civilization to a particular society? In general terms the societies that have been called civilizations have stratified social systems and a significant degree of political elaboration and centralization, construct large buildings, tend to have towns or cities, and possibly but not necessarily have writing. Now the first appearances of societies of this kind were undeniably important developments in the overall course of history. The centralization of political power and the concentration of wealth in the hands of a few, as reflected in the fact of social stratification, allowed the wealthy to subsidize for the first time new kinds of specialized production. The ruling class in a "civilization" required servants and employed skilled artisans to fashion the outward material trappings of ruling status. The rulers could mobilize large labor forces for public works, and from the tribute they exacted from the common people they could support the efforts of full-time artists to produce "great" or at least monumental art. The ability of the wealthy to buy exotic goods encouraged the appearance of long-distance trade; the ability of the powerful to call up large military forces brought a new scale of warfare into being. Human beings ever after have had to deal with the repercussions of these two developments.

But when we take the shortcut of using the term "civilization" for such a society, we put at hazard our ability to gain a concrete grasp of what moved and shaped life in those earlier times. Whether we mean to or not, we convey to others the elements of mystification and uncritical approbation that inhere in the word. Only when we depict people and their lives and work in specific ways using specifically applicable terms, can we get beyond exalting, intentionally or not, what was, after all, no more than the special power of certain persons in certain societies to mobilize labor and glorify themselves. If these were societies with an urban component, let us describe them then as early, partially urbanized societies. If they possessed marked social and political stratification, then we should say as much in clear and specific fashion.

Relying on the term "civilization" unbalances our understanding of history as well. In most textbooks of ancient history and world history, what topics get the principal attention? The short answer is, "Civilizations." Those societies designated as civilizations are treated as if they were the centers of almost all innovation and of all the really important developments. They tend to be viewed, fallaciously, as culturally more complicated, artistically more accomplished, and technologically more advanced than those societies that are labeled as "noncivilizations." The fact that many key technological innovations in human history began, and much great art was produced, in other, less stratified, non-urban societies is glossed over. The fact that every early "civilization" took shape in a regional historical context of many interacting societies, large and small, is neglected, and so we construct a lopsided understanding of the history of the wider region in which that "civilization" took shape. We miss the many human accomplishments of lasting importance that originated in other places entirely. How peculiar, anyway, that today, in an era of democratic thinking, given to the idea of democracy for all people, we should continue in our history books to esteem so highly societies in which wealth and political power were monopolized by the few.

There is, however, another use of the term "civilization" that, if applied carefully, does have historical validity, and this is the meaning we will adopt in this work. What is this other meaning? Consider the phrases "Western civilization" and "Islamic civilization." In this context, the term "civilization" refers to a grouping of societies and their individual cultures, conjoined by their sharing of deep common historical roots. Despite many individual cultural differences, the societies in question share a range of fundamental social and cultural ideas and often a variety of less fundamental expectations and customs. These ideas and practices form a common historical heritage, stemming either from many centuries of close cultural interaction and the mutual diffusion of ideas or from a still more ancient common historical descent of the societies involved from some much earlier society or grouping of related societies. In our exploration of African history, we will encounter several key civilizations, far-flung groupings of culturally and historically linked societies, such as the Niger-Congo, Afrasan, Sudanic, and Khoisan civilizations. At times we will also use an alternative terminology, describing these historically linked culture groupings as cultural or historical "traditions."

"Tribes" and "Tribal"

The problems with the words "tribe" and "tribal" become overtly clear if we ask a series of questions. Why is it that, during the period of the Nigeria Civil War in the late 1960s, the more than 10 million Igbo people of southeastern Nigeria were called a tribe in all the newspaper articles dealing with the war, when the 200,000 Ruthenians (who reside in Slovakia, Poland, and Belorus) and the fewer than 400,000 citizens of Malta are called nationalities? Why was the war called a "tribal" war, anyway, instead of the civil war that it actually was? Why, time and again, do we see newspaper articles and news reporters on television add the qualifiers "tribe" or "tribal" to their descriptions of people and events in Africa? Why is Shaka, the famous nineteenth-century ruler, called a king of the Zulu "tribe" when he actually was the king of a centralized and militarily powerful state? Why are Africans in "traditional" dress said to be engaging in "tribal" dancing, when Europeans garbed similarly in the clothes of an earlier time are said to be performing "folk" dances? Why is the work of African artists, done in the styles of previous centuries, called "tribal" art? Is it not simply art fashioned by Africans? Why is a rural African man of today, who is more attuned to rural culture and less caught up in the modern-day African urban milieu, called a "tribesman"? Isn't he just a man, the same as any other?

Clearly "tribe" is an appellation Europeans have reserved for non-European ethnic groups and nationalities and most especially those of Africa. So pervasive was the use of "tribe" during the colonial era that even Africans themselves often unthinkingly use that word or its equivalent today when speaking English or other European languages. By "tribe" they translate words in their home languages that mean simply ethnic group or sometimes clan. But the English word conveys much more than that. For the native speaker of English, it takes only a moment of thought about a phrase such as "tribal dancing" to realize that we are being presented with a value judgment on the activity and the people involved in it. They are exotic, strange, acting perhaps a little out of control, culturally or technologically backward in comparison to us, and sometimes dangerous to boot.

"Primitive"

In a word, "tribal" people are "primitive." Once upon a time this term meant simply "primary" or "original." The members of the Primitive Baptist Church in North America, for example, still use the word in that sense. Through the naming of their church they make the claim that their religious practices faithfully reflect those of the original or "primitive" Christians of the first century AD. Anthropologists in the past have used the word to imply that the society they study is lacking in the kinds of complexity characteristic of a modern-day industrial society. But for all the rest of us, "primitive" conveys an unflattering picture of backwardness and lack of skill and accomplishment. It is a term that has no place in historical discourse (and it ought to be abandoned by anthropologists as well).

In any case there is no such thing as a primitive culture. Every culture, society, and people has historical roots reaching thousands and thousands of years back into the past, so that no one can be said to be primitive in the sense of being original. It is difficult as well to describe any pre-industrial society as consistently simpler or more backward than any other such society. Every human community has its areas of complex practice and intricate knowledge and expertise; every society has fields of knowledge and experience in which it is weak. A related point is that there is no such thing as a primitive language. Every language has a vocabulary of thousands of words, capable of expressing all the ideas and things that its human speakers know and feel and do, and an infinitely flexible grammar, able to convey all the nuances of human expression. So if we mean to say that a particular technology or a particular set of institutions is less complex in one society than another, then we need to say exactly that. If we see that the early form of an old practice or custom has been preserved by one people, but that the practice or custom has been modified in significant ways by another people, then again we must say simply that. The word "primitive" has no valid use for us.

"Race"

It probably will not be as immediately clear to the reader why "race" should be almost as suspect a term as "tribe" and "primitive." After all, race became in the twentieth century a bedrock element in human social self-conception all over the world. It has become a cultural and social reality. The germ of the modern idea of what constitutes "race" emerged in the developments of the sixteenth to eighteenth centuries, when Europeans began to distinguish, by means of certain visible, outward features of appearance, people subject to enslavement from those who were not.

Nevertheless, the concept of race as the English language uses the term today did not develop into a consistently applied set of ideas until nineteenth-century European thinkers made it so. Through most of the rest of human history and in nearly all parts of the globe, the *only* group distinctions people made were based on cultural and societal differences. People have always tended to be *ethnocentric:* human beings, in other words, commonly feel that the ideas and customs they grew up with and are familiar and comfortable with are better than the different and unfamiliar ways of societies other than their own. Competition, strife, and even hatred between different ethnic groups has often been present in human history. But racism as we understand it today—with its foolish, baseless, and evil claims of inborn and perpetual genetic differences among human beings—did not exist in earlier historical ages, in Africa or anywhere else.

What may surprise the reader most of all is that, for all its social historical salience, race can no longer be considered a valid scientific concept. In the terms of human genetic science, there is *no* such thing as race. The ancestry of every human being is made up of a unique set of thousands of genes. In any particular locality in the world, unless a great deal of immigration has occurred, the inhabitants will tend, on the whole, to share higher frequencies of the same genes with each other than they will share with people of more distant areas. But there are no hard and fast racial boundaries, and few significant differences, other than the mostly superficial elements of outward appearance, exist among the numerous human populations around the world.

So in this book we will encounter ethnic groups, societies, and peoples, but no tribes and no races. Civilizations for us will be historically linked groupings of peoples and societies, identifiable from their common possession of certain basic cultural ideas and social practices of ancient historical origin. We will view in specific ways the contributions and accomplishments of people all across Africa, and we will seek to set these developments into the wider context of contemporary developments elsewhere in the world.

Themes in History: What to Look For in Our Reading

A variety of recurrent themes crop up in the history of the civilizations and peoples of both Africa and other parts of the world. By seeking out such themes, we discover new ways to give connection and salience to the myriad of local and regional histories within Africa, different in their particulars but alike in the commonality of the human drives, aspirations, and abilities they express. Thematic perspectives enable us to identify the several key story lines in the immensely complex history of Africa, and these themes show us ways to weave the developments of Africa's past into the wider tapestry of world history.

A Theme Often Neglected: How People Got Their Food

The perhaps most lasting and powerful theme down through all of human history has been the matter of how people obtained their daily sustenance. From earliest times down to 10,000 BCE, all people everywhere gathered and hunted to get food. They practiced what we call gathering and hunting, or food-collecting, economies. The economies of those long-ago times were far from static systems. Both before and after 10,000, people in many different parts of the world brought into being innovative new systems of gathering and hunting. The greater productivity of these systems commonly led to the spread of the cultures associated with them. An example in New World history are the Clovis hunters of bison and other large-game animals, who created one such system around 13,000 years ago and spread their activities and culture widely across the central parts of North America. At least two of the early civilizations of Africa, the Afrasan and the Khoisan, spread out initially because of their mastery of effective new systems of gathering and hunting—the Afrasan all across the northeastern portions of Africa and the Khoisan across the eastern side of the continent.

Then sometime around 9000 BCE, peoples in several different parts of the world began slowly to shift to something truly new—to the domestication and deliberate raising of animals and plants as sources of food. They became farmers or what we sometimes call food producers. Sub-Saharan Africans in the southeastern Sahara regions and in West Africa were among both the earliest and the most important participants in the world in this fundamental realignment of human subsistence capabilities.

The shift to cultivation and herding had repercussions for the whole future course of social and political history in Africa and in each other part of the world in which that kind of changeover took place. At the most basic level, food production allowed people, over the long term of history, to produce more and more food from the same amount of land, a process that has continued down to the present. The ability to produce more food, in turn, allowed the gradual growth of larger local communities and of denser human populations overall.

Food production also gave to its practitioners a substantial productive as well as demographic advantage over neighboring peoples who remained entirely dependant on food collecting. Soon those who had taken up the new ways of subsistence began to expand their territories more and more widely. As they spread out, they progressively assimilated more and more of the neighboring gatherer-hunter peoples into their societies. In this manner the cultural traditions and languages of the first farmers and herders often spread across vast new territories. Their societies came to be part of widespread civilizations, consisting of many peoples, differing in individual elements of culture but holding in common an array of fundamental cultural ideas and practices and usually speaking languages belonging to the same family of related languages. In Africa, as we will learn, the historical roots of two of the major early civilizations of the continent, Niger-Congo and Sudanic, trace in large part back to the periods in which agriculture was invented.

Population growth, by creating larger local communities with more diverse individual interests, also pushed people toward new social and political adaptations for maintaining social cohesion and consensus. For a long time the resulting changes are likely to have remained small in scale and local in scope. Not until 5,000 or 6,000 years after the first food-producing economies were created did population densities in a few areas of the world, both within Africa and outside of it, finally grow great enough to allow the first states and socially stratified societies to take shape. But without the adoption of cultivation and herding neither the first states nor the world we live in today would have been possible.

Subsistence change remained a theme of recurrent importance down to the present in most parts of the world, not least in many parts of Africa. The addition of new crops has often increased the productivity of different environments and regions and so set off population growth and social and political change. New developments in agricultural technology repeatedly have had similar consequences. Time and again, as we will discover, new crops, new tools, new techniques, and new productive relations among people have shaped and reshaped the directions of historical change in Africa, just as they have elsewhere in the world. In the context of world history, we will learn, for instance, that Africans domesticated several major crops, most notably sorghum and cotton, of worldwide importance today, and that sorghum in particular spread several millennia ago from Africa to other parts of the world.

Themes in Social and Political History

Other thematic areas of recurring importance to our understanding of Africa in history include social structure and social institutions; political ideas and institutions; trade and commerce; towns and cities; technological change and invention; religion and its cultural, social, and political dimensions; art and music; and the diffusion of new ideas and things from society to society.

Among the issues of social history that will concern us are the ways in which different cultures divided up work between women and men and how the roles of women and men changed over time in different African societies. We will learn, for instance, of the ancient historical background of social institutions such as clans and lineages, so widely found in Africa, and about the changing political and social functions of those institutions over the course of history in different regions. *Matrilineal descent* systems, in which people trace their ancestry, for purposes of inheritance, through the clans or lineages of their mothers, were once common in Africa. Over the past several thousand years, however, these systems have been superceded in many parts of the continent by *patrilineal descent,* that is, by the tracing of inheritance only through one's father.

A great variety of leadership roles characterized the early civilizations of Africa, from clan ritual chiefs in some societies to no hereditary leaders at all among other peoples. When larger polities began to emerge in Africa, kings became the most common kind of institution around which Africans reconstructed the political order. But we will also learn that some Africans developed alternative forms of larger-scale political organization that were more democratic and inclusive in nature than kingdoms. Like governments everywhere, kingdoms in Africa rested on two conceptual pillars. They needed legitimacy— by that we mean a set of accepted ideas and institutions that justified kingship in the eyes of the people. And they needed a material basis, such as agricultural tribute or the profits of trade, that could adequately support the governing stratum of society. Yet the institutional and ideological bases of legitimacy could be exceedingly different in different parts of Africa. The material bases of kingly power also varied greatly from region to region, and even within one region or within one polity the economic underpinnings of the political system could change in significant ways over the course of time.

Trade, Commerce, and Towns

Trade and commerce took on a wide range of forms across the continent. During the past 3,000 years, growing commercial activity, instigated both from outside and deep within Africa, time and again provided part of the economic engine, along with agricultural innovation, driving the growth and centralization of political power and the rise of towns and cities. The reader will want to pay attention to the variety of products that fostered trade in different parts of the continent, to the methods and routes by which goods were transported, and to the often broadly parallel consequences of trade for social or political history in widely separate parts of the continent.

The earliest towns and cities in Africa developed before 3000 BCE, as early as anywhere in the world. The first cities, located along the Nile River, evolved as governing and ritual centers. Then, from about 1000 BCE onward, commerce grew into an equally and sometimes more important factor in the founding of towns and cities. Slowly, urban centers began to emerge here and there across the continent, first in the West African savannas and in the Horn of Africa and then during the past 2,000 years across progressively wider and wider parts of the continent.

What do we mean by town or city? For our purposes, the word "town" will refer to a center with a population in the range of 1,000–2,000 up to about 5,000–6,000 people. "City" will be reserved for larger urban centers, of greater than 5,000–6,000 inhabitants. "Villages" will mean smaller units of perhaps 100 up to 1,000 people; the term "hamlet" will apply to village-like settlements of typically fewer than 100 in population. Still another important kind of local settlement found in Africa was the neighborhood of scattered homesteads. This type of settlement, common for several thousand years in eastern parts of Africa, was characterized by a population range similar to that of a village, but its individual residences, unlike the clustered habitations of a village, were spread out over a number of square kilometers of land.

The defining population sizes of towns and cities seem very small by present-day standards, but they were typical of the great majority of urban centers in the pre-industrial eras of history all across the world. Small as such settlements appear to city-dwellers of today, their economic activities and political and social relations had effects on the social order that were qualitatively different from those of village life. The towns and cities were big enough and economically differentiated enough to support social stratification, and they were focal points of economic and political strength, dominant over the smaller settlements of the surrounding areas. In particular, the rise of a wealthy consuming stratum of society in the towns and cities, either as a ruling class or a merchant class or both at the same time, provided a growing local market for the wares of skilled artisans and other specialized occupations. Such wealthy classes tended also to employ household servants, further enhancing class differences.

Africans and Technological Innovation

In the history of technology, as we will discover, Africans south of the Sahara were active innovators and not, as they have often been depicted, the passive receivers of things invented elsewhere.

Africans in at least two different parts of the continent separately discovered how to mine, smelt, and work copper. Even more striking because it so conflicts with widely accepted ideas, Africans living in the heart of the continent appear independently to have invented the smelting and forging of iron. This development took place before 1000 BCE, almost as early as the Middle Eastern discovery of ironworking at around 1500 BCE in what is today Turkey, and more than 3,000 kilometers away from the Middle East.

There is now good evidence as well that another major development in world technology, the weaving of cotton, began separately in Africa much earlier than metallurgy. Its inventors were Africans who lived south of the Sahara along the middle reaches of the Nile River at around and before 5000 BCE. Another notable, ancient kind of textile making in Africa was the weaving of raffia cloth, a skill that apparently arose several millennia ago in West Africa.

The reader's attention will be drawn repeatedly in this book to the importance of technological themes in African history, and not just to developments in toolmaking or cloth manufacture. Changes in such diverse fields of endeavor as boat making, agricultural technology, and architecture were key elements in the overall panorama of history. We will learn, among other things, about the unique style of building in coral of the Swahili city-states; the great stone-walled structures of the capital city of the Zimbabwe kingdom, built without mortar yet still standing centuries later; and the wooden palaces of the

Mangbetu kings, which rivaled Japanese palaces and temples as the largest wooden structures ever built.

Religion in African History

Another thematic area of importance is that of religious history in Africa. Among the stimulating new ideas we will encounter is the fact that quite different religious traditions were practiced in ancient times by the peoples of the different early civilizations of Africa. We cannot say that Africans all believed such-and-such a thing, or that one or another ritual practice is "typical" of all Africa. Most interestingly, we will learn that two of the early African religions, those of the Niger-Congo and Sudanic civilizations, were distinctly monotheistic thousands of years before the idea of monotheism ever occurred to Middle Easterners or Europeans. We will discover also that the spread of religions can take place without formal missionary activity, and we will encounter in repeated instances the importance in African cultural history of religious *syncretism*—the blending together of ideas from different religious traditions.

And, by the way, we find no use for the term "animism" in this book. The indigenous religions of Africa took a variety of forms—monotheistic, henotheistic, nontheistic, and even polytheistic—about which we will learn more later. But none can properly be characterized as "animistic." Animism originated as a term among French scholars of West Africa, who sought to apply a less pejorative word than paganism to African systems of belief. But this terminology, besides failing to fit any particular African religion, does violence to historical reality: it lumps in an amorphous mass what are in actuality immensely different sets of ideas with distinctive consequences for the history of thought and culture in different parts of the continent.

Beginning about 2,000 years ago, "religions of the book"—that is to say, religions with fixed, written, sacred texts—began to reach parts of Africa. The first religion of this type to spread to the continent was Christianity, which took hold in parts of north and northeastern Africa in the first four centuries CE. After 640, a second religion of the book, Islam, began to spread south into the continent also. As we shall see, the encounter of the indigenous African religions with these introduced religions had a variety of repercussions for social and political history over the succeeding centuries. An interesting feature of these developments was the early importance of trade relations in spreading both religions.

Art and Music

We have much still to learn about yet another theme, the history of the arts in Africa. Nonetheless, we will at least touch upon a variety of important developments in the pages to follow. The ancient wood-sculpting tradition of the Niger-Congo civilization, for example, gave birth to notable flowerings of sculpture in other media during the past 3,000 years. Among the examples we will encounter are the fine works in terra-cotta of the Nok culture of the first millennium BCE in West Africa and of the fifth-century Lydenburg culture of South Africa. The most splendid accomplishments of this tradition are the brass sculptures of the Yoruba and Benin peoples, belonging to the past 1,000–1,500 years of history in West Africa, and the gold artworks of Akan artists, sculpted during the past 500 years.

As for the musical arts, we will learn a little about the development and spread of new kinds of instruments in Africa. But perhaps our most significant discovery will be that the kind of music people in the West tend to think of as typically African is in fact a characteristic only of the Niger-Congo civilization. We refer here to polyrhythmic music, strongly based on the use of percussion instruments—in particular, differently tuned drums. It is this style of music, brought to the New World by forced African immigrants between 1500 and 1800, in which lie the roots of gospel music, ragtime, and jazz, as well as rhythm and blues and its offspring, rock and roll, and the fast, active kind of social dancing that has now caught on across the world. The story of how these styles of music and dance took hold outside Africa is not a direct part of our history of Africa up to 1800. But the fact that they are fundamentally African in inspiration should be essential knowledge for any twenty-first-century inhabitant of our world.

Cultural Diffusion in History

Finally and most generally, we will learn that the dramas of history do not play out on closed stages. The ideas and the cultural and material developments of one region of Africa often spread to other areas—sometimes through the movements of people into new territories; sometimes through the spread of ideas through contacts among neighboring societies; and sometimes, especially during the last 2,000 years, through the long-distance travels of merchants. Societies that blended together in new ways the ideas, cultural practices, and technologies of other peoples frequently then embarked on their own markedly new and powerful directions of historical change. Equally important, African innovations, especially in agriculture, contributed in important ways to technological and economic interchange in other parts of the globe. Then as now, Africa's story has always been part of the common history of us all.

Africa and Human Origins

The First Hominids

Africa's centrality in the history of humankind, as a matter of fact, goes back to the very beginnings of the human lineage. It was the "Eden" of our own species and of all the species most closely related to us. Our story and theirs began about 8 to 5 million years ago in the forests of central and eastern Africa. In those regions there lived a particular species of ape, probably about the size of the chimpanzee and looking a bit like the chimpanzee, too. By 5 million years ago, the descendants of this species started to follow two distinct lines of evolutionary change. One line of descent remained closely tied to forest environments and gave rise over the long run of time to the modern-day chimpanzees and bonobos of the rainforests of central Africa. The other line of descent evolved into a new family of the great apes, the hominids, the very family to which our own species, *Homo sapiens,* belongs.

The hominids became strikingly different from the other apes in three crucial respects. First, and most crucial, they parted ways from their nearest relatives among the great apes by no longer living in forests but moving into the wooded savanna and bush country of eastern Africa and, in still later times, occupying as well the open grasslands of the eastern side of the continent. Second, they soon took on an upright posture and began to walk about on their two hind legs. Third, they developed fully opposable thumbs, giving them an enhanced potential for using and manipulating tools.

A variety of genera and species of hominids mark the fossil record of the periods between then and now. The most common genus of the time between 4 and 1.5 million years ago was *Australopithecus*. The Australopithecines, as we call the members of this genus, inhabited lands from as far north as the Red Sea coasts of the Horn of Africa to as far south as South Africa. They ate, it appears, an eclectic diet that included both plants and meat. A second notable early genus, called *Paranthropus*, diverged from the *Australopithecus* line of descent sometime after 3 million years ago. *Paranthropus* species had particularly robust skulls and massive chewing dentition, suitable for the grinding up of tough plant foods and thus indicating a rather different diet from that of the Australopithecines.

The First Toolmaking

Around 2.6 million years ago, a development fundamental to the future course of hominid history took place—one species began to deliberately fashion tools out of stone. The earlier members of our human subfamily had been little different from the other great apes in their intelligence or skills. No doubt, like our nearest modern-day relatives, the chimpanzees, they picked up sticks and sometimes stones and used them pry up or strike out at things. To that extent the earliest hominids were tool *users*. But they were not tool*makers*.

The first toolmakers, of 2.6 million years ago, appear to have belonged to a new species. The bones of this species show it to have been, physically speaking, little more than a somewhat more advanced Australopithecine. But because the shift to toolmaking was of such momentous importance, scholars use that event to mark the evolution of a new genus, *Homo*, out of the *Australopithecus* genus, and so they call the first toolmaking hominid *Homo habilis*. The tools of *H. habilis* belong to what we call the Olduwan industry. ("Industry" as used by archeologists of early humans refers to the kit of tools and the toolmaking techniques used by a particular human population.) This tool kit was rudimentary; it consisted simply of sharp flakes broken off of stones by striking them with other stones. The sharp flakes, however, could efficiently cut and skin even thick-skinned animals, and so the making of the Olduwan tools would have greatly facilitated the meat-collecting capabilities of their makers.

FIG. 1 Olduwan chopper tool

Olduwan implements were the earliest stone tools made by hominids, approximately 2.5 million years ago in the eastern parts of Africa. The original makers of these tools probably belonged to the species *Homo habilis*.

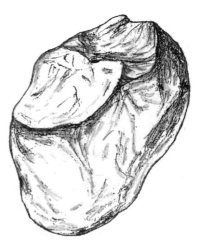

FIG. 2 Hand ax

This kind of tool was first made in Africa around 1.5 million years ago, probably by the descendants of *Homo ergaster*. The fashioning of the hand ax reveals a significant step forward in the evolving brainpower of the ancestors of human beings. Its shape shows that its makers had a picture in their minds of how the tool should look and made the tool accordingly. The hand ax shown here comes from South Africa.

Beginning about 1.8 million years ago, a second species of our human genus, *Homo ergaster,* appears in the fossil record. *H. ergaster* was markedly different from *H. habilis.* Whereas the *H. habilis* species was hardly more than three feet in height, *H. ergaster* was as tall as modern humans, and its body shape and full upright walking posture were much like those of modern humans.

H. ergaster at first made tools not significantly different from those of *H. habilis.* Then around 1.5 million years ago, another breakthrough took place. The first making of an entirely new type of tool, to which we give the misleading name "hand ax," appears in the archeological record of that time in eastern Africa. The hand ax, actually an all-purpose instrument for scraping, digging, and cutting, was the first hominid tool made to a regular preset pattern that must already have been present in the mind of its maker. Clearly a major transition in brainpower, the development of the ability to form mental conceptions, had taken place among the African descendants of *H. ergaster.*

The Triumph of the Genus *Homo*

Sometime before 1.5 million years ago, another first in hominid history was recorded—for the first time one of the hominid species migrated out of Africa and made itself at home across southern Asia. Until then, all the developments of hominid history had taken place within Africa and within the eastern parts of the continent in particular. The species that spread to Asia was closely related to, but distinct from, *H. ergaster.* We call this first Asian species *Homo erectus.* Because *H. erectus* left Africa more than 1.5 million years ago, its descendants continued to make flake tools and never adopted hand axes, as did the descendants of *H. ergaster.*

Some members of the genus *Australopithecus* survived for a few hundred thousand years after the migration of *H. erectus* 1.5 million years ago. But the toolmaking capacities of *H. ergaster* and its later descendants eventually allowed them to take over completely the ecological niches they had previously shared in Africa with *Australopithecus,* and this development gradually drove the Australopithecines into extinction. *H. erectus,* of course, moved into Asia, where there had previously been no hominids, and so it did not face the same kind of competition.

Between 1.5 million and 60,000 years ago, it now appears, several different species of the genus *Homo* evolved in different parts of the Eastern Hemisphere. Some were descendants of *H. ergaster* who spread from Africa into Europe and western Asia. In eastern Asia descendants of *H. erectus* probably long survived also. Down to 400,000 years ago and perhaps even later, hand axes remained the most common tool of the African members of the genus *Homo* and also of those members of *Homo* who expanded into Europe. Then, at some point between 400,000 and 200,000 years ago, a leap forward in toolmaking skills took hold among the evolving *Homo* species. The hand ax gradually dropped out of use, as a new technique of fashioning tools evolved in which the toolmaker first preshaped a stone core and then struck off tools of various shapes and uses from that core. From that time onward, differing tool styles began to appear in different regions.

There is, by the way, a no-longer-supportable opposing view that—from 1 million years ago down to the present—all the varieties of *Homo,* from the southern tip of Africa to the eastern tip of Asia, somehow, against all odds, continued to interbreed often enough to remain one gradually evolving species, all through that long span. Held by a declining number of scholars, this view is refuted both by DNA evidence and by our growing knowledge of human bone remains from different parts of the world. It is contradicted as well by everything we know about the patterns of evolution of the other widespread mammal genera, all of which over the same span of time diversified again and again into different species.

Homo Sapiens Enters the Scene

Of several species of the genus *Homo* that had come into existence before 60,000 years ago, the one that first pops into most people's minds is Neanderthal man, *Homo neanderthalensis.* How curious that is—because the most important new species of that era, the one we truly should think of first of all, was our own species, *Homo sapiens!*

Eurocentric thinking again is surely at work here. We now know that our particular species, *Homo sapiens,* evolved entirely in Africa. Yet most early work on human paleontology focused on discoveries in Europe of ancient bones and tools and was slow to accommodate new information from other parts of the globe. This is why Western folk imagination became so deeply imbued with the mysteriousness and romance of the extinct Neanderthal, which was, after all, an almost purely European species of *Homo.* Then, too, in the works of certain mid-twentieth-century writers who favored the idea of a million-year-long, multiregional evolution of a single human species all across the Eastern Hemisphere, one can detect, sadly, a more insidious tendency, a difficulty with accepting the idea that all of us might have a common, more recent African origin.

But the fact of the matter is that the species *Homo sapiens* had come fully into being more than 60,000 years ago, and it came into being entirely in Africa. Skulls found in African sites dating from 130,000 to 100,000 BCE were already almost fully modern in appearance. Except for a temporary advance of *Homo sapiens* into the far southwest corner of Asia between 100,000 and 70,000 years ago, it was not until after 60,000 years ago, and not until after 40,000 years ago in Europe, that any sites with modern human remains show up outside Africa. Instead, in both Europe and Asia, only more archaic species of *Homo,* such as the Neanderthal, are attested in the paleontological record of the period from 130,000 to 60,000 BCE.

DNA evidence gives us the same answer. Using both mitochondrial DNA, a kind of genetic material passed from mother to daughter, and Y-chromosome evidence from males, scholars have demonstrated conclusively that the greatest genetic diversity of *Homo sapiens* lies in Africa. Greater human genetic diversity exists in Africa for the simple reason that fully evolved *Homo sapiens* have been present on that continent longer than they have been anywhere else.

The evidence of toolmaking requires this conclusion as well. Two particular advances in tool technology, the making of bone implements and the shaping of backed blades, seem to be the characteristic accomplishments of the earliest modern *Homo sapiens* everywhere in the world. A backed blade, by the way, is one in which the back edge of the stone blade has been steeply chipped away. This steep back part provides a suitable surface for attaching the blade to

When?	What?
4.5 to 2.6 million BCE	Various hominids of the genus *Australopithecus* inhabit the eastern parts of the African continent.
2.6 million BCE	The first stone toolmaking industry, Olduwan, develops in eastern Africa; a new species of hominid, *Homo habilis,* is believed to have been the maker of these tools.
1.8 million BCE	A new species of hominid, *Homo ergaster,* is known in Africa in this period; a second, closely related species, *Homo erectus,* may have spread out of Africa into southern Asia not long after this time.
1.5 million BCE	The development of a new kind of stone tool industry, Acheulean, characterized most notably by the making of "hand axes," takes place in Africa; the inventors of this new kind of tool are thought to have been descendants of *Homo ergaster.*
800,000 to 600,000 BCE	The Acheulean tool industry spreads for the first time outside of Africa to the Middle East and Europe; several, as yet poorly known species of the genus *Homo,* descendants of the earlier African species *Homo ergaster,* appear to have been the makers of the Acheulean in Africa, the Middle East, and Europe.
90,000 to 60,000 BCE	In eastern and southern Africa the first fully modern *Homo sapiens,* the ancestors of us all, develop out of an earlier, archaic African species of the genus *Homo;* they are the makers of the first bone tools and backed blades, characteristic of all later human stone tool industries.
60,000 to 40,000 BCE	Fully modern *Homo sapiens* spread out of Africa, at first into the Middle East and southern Asia and then after 40,000 BCE into Europe and northern Asia (and eventually still later from Asia into the Americas), outcompeting and replacing all other species of the genus *Homo.*

FIG. 3 Time line of the descent of modern human beings

The stages reached in the development of toolmaking skills are noted at the relevant points in human descent.

a handle. The appearance of backed blades in the archeology marks, in other words, the crucial transition in human history to the regular making of efficient hafted tools, or tools with a handle. Both of these advances, in keeping with the African origins of modern humans like ourselves, appeared first in Africa, as many as 30,000–40,000 years before they occurred in other parts of the globe. Humans living in eastern Africa, according to recent discoveries, may have begun to make pointed tools from bone as early as 90,000 BCE. Other people living in southern Africa created the first backed blades at around 80,000 BCE. In Europe, by contrast, these innovations appeared no more than 40,000 years ago, brought in by the first true *Homo sapiens* (the Cro-Magnons) to arrive in that part of the world.

In other words, 60,000 years ago the ancestors of all of us had already been fully human for some thousands of years, and all those fully human ancestors of ours still lived on the continent of Africa. Only after that time did some of those Africans begin to spread out to other parts of our globe, giving rise to the whole rest of the world's populations and bringing about, both directly and indirectly, the extinction of all other species of the genus *Homo,* the Neanderthals among them. Exactly what our common African ancestors of those far-off times looked like is a matter for speculation. But what we can say with some assurance is that most of the superficial differences in outward appearance that

FIG. 4 Backed blades

This technological advance, a characteristic feature of the tool kits of the first modern humans, appeared earliest of all in the archeology of Africa, before 80,000 BCE and as many as 30,000–40,000 years before it turned up anywhere else in the world. This drawing shows three ways in which backed blades could be hafted, or attached to a handle, to make a variety of cutting, chopping, and scraping tools. The backed portions of the blades are depicted here in cross-section, showing how the blade was inserted into the wooden haft. Various kinds of mastic would have been used to attach the blade more securely to the wood.

exist among human beings today arose since then. We are all Africans, and it is time to come to terms with that lesson of history.

NOTES FOR READERS AND TEACHERS

Chapter 1 covers a number of topics that stimulate the rethinking of received ideas. Classroom discussions of the meaning and use of value-laden terms such as "civilized," "tribe," and "primitive" can be particularly enlightening and enlivening. Further issues for discussion include:

- What other "loaded" terms get applied to the history or culture of peoples in other parts of the world?
- Are there loaded terms with a positive slant that we use when talking about our own history?

Confronting the idea that race has a social and historical reality but lacks definable biological reality in human beings is especially intellectually challenging. It requires one to think closely about just what the social meanings and uses of the idea of race really are. It requires one as well to come to grips with the usually unexamined and often strongly held, but quite untenable, presumption that culture and biological ancestry always go hand in hand.

- What social purposes does the idea of race serve?
- In what kinds of specific historical circumstances does the idea of race take on meaning?

The discovery that the ancestors of all of us evolved into fully modern human beings entirely in Africa—that we were fully human before the ancestors of any of us left the continent—is another topic that can stimulate students and readers to take stock of the presumptions they bring to their reading. The scientific evidence in favor of this explanation is overwhelming. The development of new scientific dating methods in the past fifty years allowed scholars working with early human remains and tool kits in Africa to show that modern human skulls and tools typical of *Homo sapiens* occurred thousands of years earlier in Africa than anywhere else. Over the past two decades new developments in genetic analysis repeatedly confirmed the paleontological evidence that our direct human ancestors all lived in Africa as recently as 60,000 years ago.

There remain some scholars who continue to support multiregional origins for human beings. They believe that there was a single human species everywhere in the Eastern Hemisphere of the world for the past 1.8 million years and that over that whole long period, despite repeated ice ages and great geographical barriers, there somehow was enough interbreeding all across the 15,000 kilometers from the southern tip of Africa to the Pacific coast of Asia to keep those widely scattered populations a single species. Each human population, in this view, evolved in the particular part of the world in which it now lives. Despite the fact that every other widespread group of mammals diverged many times into different species over the past 1.8 million years, these scholars believe that the ancestors of human beings, against all odds, did not do so. Readers might wish to consider these ideas in the light of the following questions:

- What kind of idea of "race" informs the multiregional view of human origins?
- What might make the idea of multiple origins of human beings an attractive explanation to its proponents, even though skeletal, tool, and DNA evidence all disagree with it?

Two very readable works that present in accessible form the evidence and arguments showing not only that modern *Homo sapiens* like ourselves all originated in Africa but also that numerous separate species of hominids have existed over the past 1.8 million years, are the following:

Stringer, Chris, and Robin McKie. *African Exodus: The Origins of Modern Humanity.* New York: Henry Holt, 1997.
Tattershall, Ian. "Once We Were Not Alone." *Scientific American,* January 2000, pp. 56–62.

2

Africa before the Agricultural Age, 16,000–9000 BCE

Africa and the World: From Gathering to Farming

From 60,000 years ago down to the tenth millennium BCE, the peoples of Africa, like all human beings everywhere in the world in those times, and like their hominid ancestors of still earlier ages, obtained their food entirely by gathering wild plants and hunting wild animals. They were gatherer-hunters or, as we also say, food-collectors in economy.

Then in the very early Holocene—the most recent geological epoch, lasting from the eleventh millennium BCE down to the present—there appeared, separately and independently in three small regions of the world, a series of developments of immense importance for the overall course of human history. In those regions between 9500 and 7000 BCE, people began the first deliberate raising and nurturing of particular sources of food, both plant and animal—they took the first small steps toward creating food-producing, as opposed to food-collecting, ways of life. One of these regions lay in the Middle East, in the crescent of hill and plateau country with Mediterranean climate that stretches from Palestine and Syria eastward through southern Turkey and around into western Iran. A second center of earliest food production emerged in the tropical rainforest zones of southern East Asia. The third center of earliest agricultural invention lay in Africa, in the areas that today comprise the southern half of the eastern Sahara desert but in those days were lands of tropical and semitropical steppe and grassland vegetation.

Why did these developments begin where and when they did? Why were they of such momentous importance to the future directions of history?

The first question we can answer in at least broad terms. The last ice age, an epoch of worldwide effects, had only recently come to an end. The great glaciations, which spread more than 20,000 years ago across so much of northern Europe and northern North America, had by 10,000 BCE shrunk back till only the most northerly regions of the Northern Hemisphere, such as Greenland and parts of Alaska and Scandinavia, and high mountain ranges, such as the Alps and the Canadian Rockies, still maintained major ice packs. The smaller glaciers on the high equatorial peaks of Africa—Mount Ruwenzori, Mount Kilimanjaro, and Mount Kenya—had shrunk, too; and in many areas all across the globe, major climatic shifts had begun, changing in new and challenging ways the environments in which human beings lived. As a result, over a period of centuries, the kinds and availability of the wild foods people depended on changed, in some regions drastically.

The close of the ice age thus meant that people in many parts of the world increasingly had to seek out new kinds of food resources or pioneer new methods of obtaining sustenance. Most of the human societies of the time either found ways to adapt their older patterns of subsistence to the new situations or evolved new approaches to gathering and hunting that allowed them to persist as still more effective food collectors.

But in the southeastern Sahara, the Middle East, and southern East Asia, certain local communities of 9500–7000 BCE took these processes one step further: they began for the first time to add to their food resources by taking deliberate care of a few of their local animals and plants, tending and protecting them from the dangers of nature. In each area the early domesticates included animals—in the southeastern Sahara, the cow; in the Middle East, the sheep and the goat; and in Southeast Asia, the chicken. The food-producers of each of the three regions began also to cultivate a few of the important plants they had previously collected in the wild form. Among the peoples of the southeastern Sahara, it was the grain crop sorghum that gained first importance, while the Middle Easterners turned to the cultivation of wheat and barley, and the Southeast Asians to the domestication of rice and, perhaps later, the banana.

Between 8000 and 5000 BCE, peoples in at least three more distinct regions of the world moved separately and independently in the same historical directions. Two of these regions were located in sub-Saharan Africa; the third, which may have consisted of several interacting centers of plant domestication, lay in the Americas. In the woodland savannas of West Africa, local communities commenced the shift to a food-producing way of life before 6000 BCE by changing over from the collecting to the deliberate cultivation of several indigenous African species of yam. Probably almost as early in time, another group of African peoples, residing far away to the east, in high-rainfall areas of the Ethiopian Highlands, innovated a quite different agriculture based on utilization of the enset plant, which is similar in appearance to the banana plant. Still farther away, in Mesoamerica, the first Native American cultivation, of pumpkins, had emerged before 7000 BCE in northeastern Mexico. By 5000 BCE other crops, most notably maize ("corn" in American English), had begun to be added to the crop repertoire in other parts of Mesoamerica.

Why did these several groupings of peoples in disparate parts of the world respond in similarly distinctive manners, independently of each other, to the changing natural environments of the early Holocene epoch? That remains a question we cannot yet fully answer.

What we can do, however, is commence exploring the historical backgrounds out of which the first African food-producing societies emerged. We must first look more closely at the various worlds in which Africans lived during the several thousand years *before* 9000 BCE and at the differing food-collecting economies they practiced in those earlier times. From these considerations we may start to grasp the particular historical circumstances in which at least some of the earliest inventors of agriculture—namely the African communities residing 11,000 years ago in the southeastern Sahara—would have found it useful and worthwhile to add first animal raising and then plant cultivation to their existing subsistence activities. Similarly, we can then seek to understand the subsequent inventions of agriculture in West Africa and the Ethiopian Highlands and perhaps also gain some insight into the alternative, non-agricultural choices followed by African peoples outside those regions.

From the African cases we may in turn be able to draw wider lessons that can fruitfully reshape and deepen our understandings of human motivation and initiative in history. At the same time we will come to better see the fit of African history into the world history of those early eras.

Geography and Climate in African History

African Climate and Vegetation 18,000 Years Ago

In the earlier parts of the last ice age, before about 18,000 years ago, the African continent possessed a variety of climates not all that much different from those we know of today in Africa.

At the heart of the continent, extending on both sides of the equator to about five degrees south and five degrees north latitude, lay a zone of high precipitation. Rainfall, annually totaling more than 1,800 millimeters (70 or more inches), was spread throughout the year, except for a short dry period of one or two months. This rainfall regime supported a far-extended region of tropical rainforest occupying, as it does today, the central Congo Basin of equatorial central Africa as well as a belt of country extending up to 300 kilometers inland along most of the Atlantic coastal regions of West Africa. All across these regions, a dense cover of tall trees formed the predominant ecotype. In a few areas, where sandy soils prevailed, patches of savanna vegetation could also be found deep within the forest zones.

In West Africa to the north of the rainforest proper, and in the Congo Basin both to the north and to the south of the forest, lay regions with 1,300 to 1,800 millimeters (about 50 to 70 inches) of rain and a longer dry season of two to four months' length. Before human agricultural activity the natural vegetation of such areas would have been woodland savanna. This kind of environment is characterized by forest of less imposing size and density than the rainforest and with more interspersed areas of grass and bush.

Moving still farther north or south, one would have encountered successively less well watered lands. Immediately north and south of the belts of woodland savanna lay drier woodland savanna with 800 to 1,300 millimeters (about 30 to 50 inches) of precipitation. Farther north and south could be found still more open savanna, with dry deciduous woodland areas and 400 to 800 millimeters (15 to 30 inches) of rain a year. Next one would have reached steppe country with 150 to 400 millimeters of rain (6 to 15 inches) yearly. North and south of the steppe lands lay still more arid zones of desert steppe and desert.

The northerly African zone of steppe environment formed the long east-west belt of country known today as the Sahel. To the immediate north of the Sahel, then as now, lay the vast region of desert we call the Sahara. The Sahara in those times was an even more extreme desert than it is today. In contrast, the southern African counterpart of the Sahel and Sahara, the Kalahari region, for the most part actually consisted of steppe country, with only limited areas of desert steppe and true desert occurring along the Atlantic coast and the lower Orange River.

Finally, at the northern and southern extremes of the continent lay still another kind of climate regime. Here could be found two relatively narrow regions of subtropical Mediterranean climate, not unlike that of California, with modest yearly rainfall arriving principally in the cool season of the year. One region of this kind of climate extended across a considerable portion of North Africa; the other occupied coastal areas extending east from the Cape of Good Hope at the southern tip of the continent, in modern-day South Africa. (The vegetation zones of Africa before 16,000 BCE may not have been all that different from those for periods since 2000 BCE, shown on map 9 in chapter 4.)

The eastern side of Africa stood then, as it does now, outside the more general climatic pattern of the continent. Through most of the eastern areas, various kinds of savanna environments have long been the rule. Moist woodland savannas occurred in some areas around Lake Malawi and in several stretches of country along the Indian Ocean coast, while drier types of savanna prevailed across many of the intervening areas. Most of the vast stretch of land that comprises the interior regions of Somalia and northern Kenya, as is true today, was characterized by a still drier climatic regime with steppe vegetation, while areas of true desert covered parts of far northern Somalia.

In addition, the eastern side of Africa contains several major highland zones, which then as now were strikingly different in climate from the surrounding areas. The largest of these, the immense Ethiopian Highlands, covers a region larger than the whole of France. The region consists of a series of high hilly plateaus cut here and there by deep river gorges and valleys, and much of its varied terrain lies above 1,800 meters (5,900 feet) in elevation, with its highest peak reaching 4,620 meters (15,158 feet).

A second major highland region cuts across central and western Kenya, where its tallest peaks, Mount Elgon and Mount Kenya, reach heights, respectively, of 4,321 meters (14,178 feet) and 5,200 meters (17,058 feet). This highland zone extends southward into modern-day central northern Tanzania and includes such notable features there as the Serengeti Plains and Mount Kilimanjaro, Africa's highest peak at 5,895 meters (19,340 feet).

At the western edge of East Africa, stretching for 600 kilometers north and south along the modern boundary of Congo with Uganda, Rwanda, and Burundi, lies a third major area of highlands. Its highest peaks are Mount Ruwen-zori at 5,120 meters (16,791 feet), situated on the border of far western Uganda, and Mount Karisimbi in northwestern Rwanda, with its peak at 4,507 meters (14,786 feet).

High and cool and for the most part blessed with substantial yearly rainfall, these various highlands before 18,000 years ago (and more recently, as well) were home to extensive montane forests, principally between the elevations of 1,800 and 3,000 meters. ("Montane" describes highland environments in the tropics, cooler and wetter than the surrounding areas because of their higher altitudes.) Above 3,000 meters (9,800 feet), the forests gave way to cold moor-land environments, while grasslands occurred below the mountain forests, in highland areas of lesser rainfall, such as on the Serengeti Plains and in the great, long rift valleys that cut through each of the eastern African highlands.

The rift valleys were formed by long parallel fault lines left over from a pe-riod of intense geological activity from about 8 million to 5 million years ago. If the rifts had stayed geologically active, they would eventually have broken off the eastern side of Africa into a small continent of its own. Each rift region con-sists of long, narrow stretches of relatively deep valley, bordered usually on both sides by higher, mountainous lands. Volcanic activity associated with the rift-ing has further built up the height of the mountains around each rift valley. The floors of the rift valleys often lie at altitudes of 1,500 to 2,000 meters themselves, but the mountains on each side extend higher still. Three names are used for these features: Ethiopian Rift for the rift valley that crosses through the eastern and southern Ethiopian Highlands; Western Rift for the system of rift valleys that extends past Mount Ruwenzori for 1,500 kilometers along the west edge of East Africa; and Eastern or Kenya Rift for the Kenyan and northern Tanzanian example of this feature.

Map 2 is our master guide to locating these and other features of African geography. This map identifies the major mountains, basins, rift valley systems, rivers, lakes, and seas that will figure again and again in our story of the African past. Readers may wish to return to it from time to time for a geographical re-orientation. (One side point: one rift valley system of Africa, the long north-south Western Rift, is traced out by the curved line of lakes extending from Lake Rwitanzige on the north through Lakes Ruiru and Kivu to Lake Tanganyika on the south; there was not enough space to fit the words "Western Rift" onto the map.)

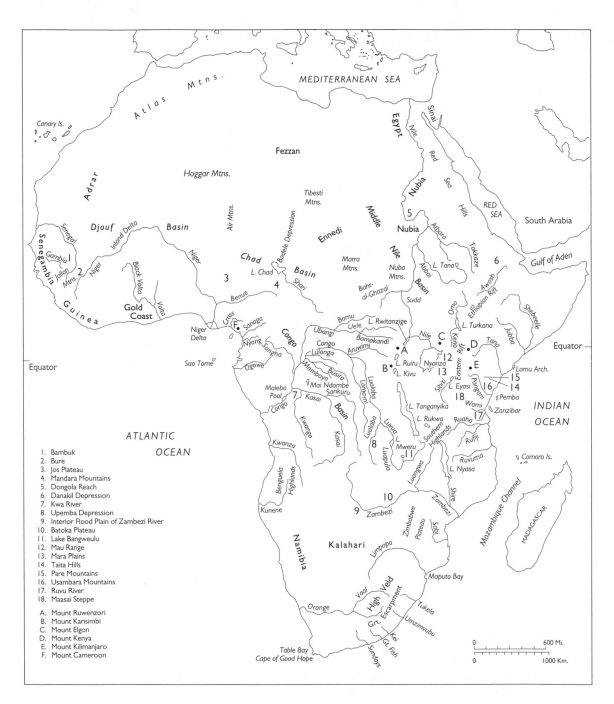

MAP 2 Africa: Rivers, lakes, mountains, and basins

1. Bambuk
2. Bure
3. Jos Plateau
4. Mandara Mountains
5. Dongola Reach
6. Danakil Depression
7. Kwa River
8. Upemba Depression
9. Interior Flood Plain of Zambezi River
10. Batoka Plateau
11. Lake Bangweulu
12. Mau Range
13. Mara Plains
14. Taita Hills
15. Pare Mountains
16. Usambara Mountains
17. Ruvu River
18. Maasai Steppe

A. Mount Ruwenzori
B. Mount Karisimbi
C. Mount Elgon
D. Mount Kenya
E. Mount Kilimanjaro
F. Mount Cameroon

Africa in an Arid Age, 18,000–13,500 Years Ago

Before 16,000 BCE, for reasons not yet clear, the climates of Africa passed through a period of major change, in which rainfall declined almost everywhere. The equatorial and West African rainforests shrank greatly, in most areas giving way to moist woodland savanna environments. The regions that had been moist savanna became lands of drier woodland savanna, while the dry open savanna zones declined to steppe, and the extreme desert of the Sahara expanded farther south into the former steppe lands of the Sahel. In northeastern Africa, the forests of the Ethiopian Highlands retreated in a great many areas, giving ground to expanding montane grasslands. Only in some parts of northern Africa did rainfall increase; there the Mediterranean climatic regime shifted southward into some parts of the Sahara desert, bringing with it Mediterranean grassland vegetation and fauna. It was a time of cooler climate as well, with daily Celsius temperatures averaging five or more degrees cooler than at present in some parts of tropical Africa, such that despite the decline in rainfall, the glaciers on the high equatorial peaks spread much farther downslope.

In response to these sweeping changes in climate, new ways of gathering and hunting began to take shape all across the African continent, with the peoples who created these new livelihoods expanding their territories at the expense of other peoples whose practices no longer fit well with the new conditions of life.

Four widely separated groupings of African peoples appear to have been the principal initiators of the successful new economies between 16,000 and 9,000 BCE: the Afrasans, the Nilo-Saharans, the Niger-Congo peoples, and the Khoisan. The Afrasans, so named because they spoke languages belonging to the Afrasan language family (also called the Afroasiatic family), were the makers, we believe, of a group of archeological cultures of that period, in which the collecting of wild grasses for food was a key element. The second important early cultural grouping of the time, the Nilo-Saharans, can be associated with what we can call the Middle Nile Tradition. A third key group, the Niger-Congo peoples, may have had archeological links to the West African Microlithic Tradition. The fourth cultural grouping consisted of the communities speaking languages of the Khoisan family; these early Khoisan peoples were makers of what we call the Eastern African Microlithic Tradition.

Their roles as the key economic innovators of the age led to the spread of each of the four distinctive cultural heritages across different large sections of the continent during subsequent eras of African history. Although the original

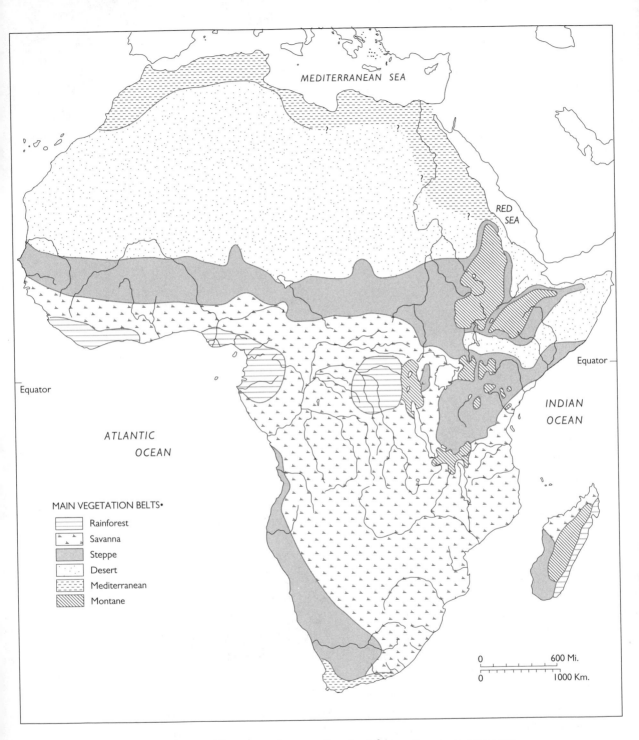

MEDITERRANEAN SEA

RED
SEA

Equator

Equator

ATLANTIC
OCEAN

INDIAN
OCEAN

MAIN VEGETATION BELTS•

Rainforest
Savanna
Steppe
Desert
Mediterranean
Montane

0   600 Mi.

0   1000 Km.

MAP 3 Climate and vegetation in Africa, 16,000–11,000 BCE

ideas, beliefs, and cultural practices of those traditions have, of course, been greatly reshaped by the thousands of years of historical change between then and now, one can still often discern the cultural debt of later African societies to the ideas and practices of those far-off days.

Afrasan Civilization

The Invention of Wild Grass Collection

Across an expanse of lands running from the region of the Nubian Nile eastward through the Red Sea hills to the northern Ethiopian Highlands—and probably not long after 16,000 BCE—an entirely new tack in gathering and hunting, unknown previously in the world, was taken by some of the peoples living in those regions. They began to use the edible parts of certain grasses for food. This new development in subsistence practices manifests itself in the archeological record as a collection of several archeological cultures, which have sometimes been grouped together as the Cataract Tradition. This name comes from the fact that the earliest known sites of this kind of food collecting lay in the areas between the cataracts, or waterfalls, of the Nile River south of Egypt. It appears that the first practitioners of the new type of economy depended in part on sedges, a kind of grass that grows typically in wetland areas. These "nut-grasses" produce tubers underground, which the first Cataract peoples ground into flour and used as food.

The excavated sites of the Cataract peoples consistently reveal communities whose most important stone tools tended to be of two kinds. Numerous grindstones evince the dependence of these peoples on wild grasses for much of the carbohydrate side of their diet. The wealth of medium-sized stone blades in their sites shows that in hunting wild game these peoples tended to rely on spears or other stabbing weapons rather than on bows and arrows. As long as the only grasses utilized were sedges, this economy had little possibility of expanding away from wetland areas along the Nile or in other scattered locales.

Afrasans and the Shift to Wild Grain Collection

But then, certainly before 11,000 and possibly as early as 13,000 BCE—the archeology does not provide sure evidence as yet on this—some of the Cataract peoples made a crucial further addition to their subsistence. They began to harvest the seeds of wild grasses other than sedges; they became collectors of wild grains. They gathered the wild grains, and they threshed and winnowed them for their seed just as the cultivators of domestic grains have done in more recent times. They then either roasted the whole grains or ground them on grindstones into flour, made dough from the flour, and baked the dough in the form of flat breads.

The particular Cataract peoples who invented this new way of using wild grasses spoke languages of the Afrasan (or Afroasiatic) language family. Just where these early Afrasans lived is not certain, but most probably their lands lay east of the Nile River, in and around the southern Red Sea hills and the northern edge of the Ethiopian Highlands. Now able to exploit the grasses that grew away from wetland areas, the Afrasans soon began to spread their ideas and subsistence practices far and wide across northeastern Africa.

The development of intensive wild grain collection was both a subsistence and a cultural breakthrough. First and foremost, it meant that Afrasan communities now had the ability to obtain a much greater quantity of food than before from the same amount of land. They could still pursue many of the activities of their ancestors; they could hunt the grazing animals that thrived in the grasslands and could still collect wild fruits, nuts, and the like. But to these resources they had added grains, an entirely new and additional source of calories for the diet.

Secondly, by thus enlarging their resource base, the Afrasans gained a long-term demographic advantage over neighboring societies in northeastern Africa that had chosen other, less productive responses to the changed climate and environment. Able to support more people on the same amount of land and thus able to slowly increase its population, the usual local community of Afrasan grain collectors would have been several times the size of the individual gathering and hunting bands typical among their neighbors. As many as several hundred people might have considered themselves part of the local Afrasan community.

Soon, too, the expanding Afrasan settlements would more and more have impinged on nearby lands, cutting into the resource base available to their various neighbors and creating a new kind of food crisis for those peoples. Such developments undoubtedly led to numerous instances of small-scale local conflict. We need to be quite clear, though, that probably nowhere in the world in those times did people fight large, violently bloody wars. That kind of behavior usually had to await the emergence of the first states thousands of years later. But when the expansion of an Afrasan community did lead to actual fighting

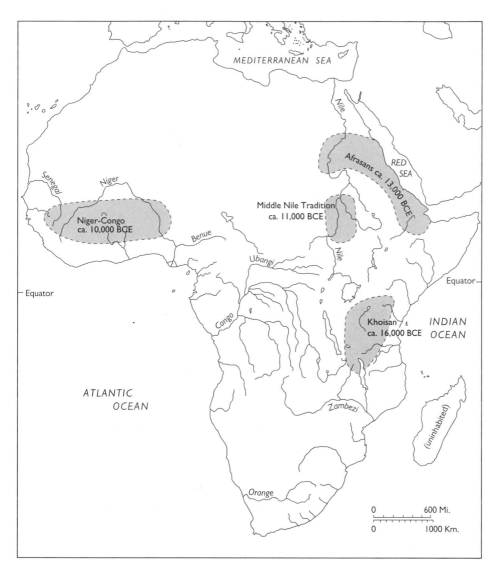

MAP 4 Proposed early lands of Afrasan, Middle Nile, Khoisan, and Niger-Congo traditions

over resources, the local advantage in numbers would recurrently have favored the Afrasans.

At the same time, the economy of the early Afrasans offered a way out of the food crisis that their expansion had brought about: the new economy carried with it the ideas and practices of wild grain collection. Faced with an expanding Afrasan presence in their territories, neighboring communities must frequently have found it most practical to assimilate to the Afrasan example—adopting wild grain collection, assimilating into the Afrasan societies over the longer term, and coming themselves to speak Afrasan languages. In short, the development of technology for wild grain collecting led in time to a far-flung spread of the culture, ideas, and languages of the Afrasan peoples who had pioneered that kind of economy.

The evidence of language shows that at least two groupings of communities arose early among the Afrasans. One of these, the Southern Afrasan peoples, have long been inhabitants of the Ethiopian Highlands. It was they who most likely adapted the ideas of wild grain collection to the cooler grasslands of that region sometime before 11,000 BCE. In contrast, the second group, the Erythraites, consisted of those Afrasans who continued to reside between the Red Sea and the Nile. Among the Erythraites the bow and arrow may have become an additional tool of importance in the eras after the initial breakup of the proto-Afrasan society. (We will encounter other instances of the prefix *proto-*, which in this context means "ancestral"; the proto-Afrasans were the original, ancestral Afrasan society.)

By the twelfth millennium BCE at the latest, wild grass and grain collecting had taken hold as far north as northern Egypt. One offshoot of this cultural complex, the Mushabian culture, then spread across the Sinai Peninsula from Africa into Palestine and Syria. There the Mushabian communities established themselves as neighbors of peoples belonging to the Geometric Kebaran culture, already long present in Palestine and Syria. Out of the interactions between these two cultures a new mixed culture, the Natufian, strongly committed to the practices of wild grain collection, then emerged between 11,000 and 10,000 BCE.

At each stage in the northward spread of these ideas, Afrasan-speaking communities, we suspect, were the prime movers in the resulting subsistence transformations. As we have seen, the Afrasan language family, contrary to widely held presumptions, originated not in Asia but in Africa, in the regions between the Nubian Nile and the northern Ethiopian Highlands. From there the early Afrasan societies expanded both southeastward into the Horn of Africa and northward up the Nile and the Red Sea hills. The arrival along the lower Nile of the ancient Egyptian language, a member of the Afrasan family, ultimately traces back to these northward movements. The earliest ancestral form of the Semitic languages, another subgroup of the Afrasan family, may have been brought into Palestine-Syria by the Mushabian communities; alternatively, some later, as yet archeologically unidentified movement of people may have taken Semitic from Africa into far southwestern Asia. Two other offshoots of the Afrasan family, the Chadic and Berber language groups, about which we will learn more in later chapters, moved westward after 9000 BCE from the farther eastern Sahara to parts of the central Sahara and North Africa.

Society and Customs of Ancient Afrasans

What sorts of social and political institutions existed among the early Afrasan wild grass and wild grain collectors? What do we know of their material culture? What kinds of beliefs did they hold? What can we say about their arts and musical traditions? Even in the current rudimentary state of our knowledge, these are questions to which we can begin to offer a few sketchy answers. Far removed in time as we are from those peoples, we cannot describe culture in detail for any of the particular Afrasan societies that resided in northeastern Africa between 16,000 and 9000 BCE. What does remain for our discovery today are a few of the broadly shared ideas, practices, and beliefs of those societies. But it is just those sorts of features of culture—shared by a wide variety of societies because of their common historical roots or because of millennia of cultural interaction and shared historical experience—that define civilizations. In this instance they define what we may call ancient Afrasan civilization.

(Table 1 at the end of chapter 3 presents summaries of the culture features commonly found, at the later period of around 5000 BCE, among peoples of the various African civilizations, including the Afrasan. Table 2, also at the end of chapter 3, lists peoples and societies dealt with in this book, arranged according to their language and historical relationships.)

Afrasan communities, from perhaps as early as the changeover to wild grain collection after 13,000 BCE, belonged to numerous clan-based communities. By a "clan," we mean a social grouping whose constitutional basis is its claim to a common descent from a founding ancestor who lived many generations earlier in time. Whether this claim to an often distant and diffuse kinship is real or fictive is not the point. Clans tend, in fact, more often than not, to include many people whose ancestors came from different backgrounds and were adopted into the group at different points in the past. What matters is one's ability to claim a particular clan descent and have one's claim accepted by other members of the clan. Afrasan clans from the beginning were most likely patrilineal.

Each Afrasan clan community was headed by a hereditary ritual leader. Among one major grouping of the Erythraite peoples, the Cushites, this religious leader was anciently called the *wap'er. (The asterisk signifies that this is what we believe the word's approximate pronunciation to have been.) We do not yet know the original Afrasan word for this office, although we suspect it was probably not *wap'er. But for the sake of convenience we will continue to use the Cushitic word.

The *wap'er was by no means a political chief, that is to say, a leader who was accorded significant political authority. Decisions affecting a whole clan probably were reached instead through extended discussion in large community meetings. If any secular leadership had to be authorized, as in the rare instance of war, it would have been temporary, sanctioned by the community only for as long as the emergency lasted. Still, the *wap'er must often have been able, because of his or her religious authority, to exert great influence on the course of community deliberations.

What kind of religious beliefs characterized the early period of Afrasan civilization? Because of the many thousand years of history that lie between then and now and, more significantly, because of the several major transformations in belief that have taken hold among Afrasan communities over the intervening millennia—all of which we will learn about in due course—it is more difficult to piece together the religious ideas of the ancient Afrasan Tradition than those of the other ancient African civilizations. Two key themes stand out, however.

First, the ancient Afrasans, it seems, centered their ritual observances around a clan deity. Each clan had its own particular deity to whom its members owed allegiance. The role of the clan *wap'er was to preside over the community rituals directed toward that deity and to act for the community as the intercessor and interpreter of the deity. This conception of spirit survived in later millennia as a relict feature of belief in two far separated regions where Afrasan-speaking peoples resided:

- among Omotic peoples in far southwestern Ethiopia, with it remaining the key focus of religion for some even today; and
- among certain of the ancient Semitic peoples of the Palestinian region, notably, but not only, the ancient Hebrews, whose god Yahweh was, in origin, as modern biblical scholars have shown, just such an ethnically restricted deity.

The ancient Afrasans, in other words, were neither *monotheists* nor *polytheists* in their conceptions of spirit. Their kind of belief system, in which a person gives allegiance to the community's own god while still accepting that other gods exist, is called *henotheism*.

A second theme with which all philosophy and religion must deal is the problem of evil. By that phrase we mean the only too common experience for us all—that the good can suffer and the evil prosper, that the rain falls on both the just and unjust. The ancient Afrasan worldview commonly attributed bad happenings to the activities of harmful spirits. All across the Afrasan-speaking world of later times, from the Omotic peoples to the Semites of southwestern Asia, this kind of belief can be found. The demons driven out of sick or mad people by Jesus were examples of this kind of spirit. The *jinn* of Arabic literature, as in the story of Aladdin's lamp, are the attenuated remnants of this ancient Afrasan view of evil.

One other custom, the circumcising of boys, very likely goes back to the earliest eras of the Afrasan cultural tradition, to well before 9000 BCE. Nearly universal among the later cultural heirs of the early Afrasans, circumcision probably originated as a ritual marking the passage of boys from juvenile to adult status. A comparable female genital cutting, clitoridectomy, was practiced widely among Afrasan societies of later times, but it was less universally known and most probably was a later development than circumcision. The early Afrasan grain collectors who moved across Sinai into Palestine, in all likelihood, brought the practice of male circumcision with them. The modern-day presence of this custom in Judaism and as a subsidiary cultural aspect of Islam—two religions started by people who spoke languages of the only Asian branch of Afrasan, Semitic—undoubtedly traces back to this ancient aspect of Afrasan civilization. Interestingly, the Afrasan-speaking societies in far southwestern Asia, unlike the rest of the Afrasans, began at some point to circumcise male children just after birth rather than in adolescence.

About the arts in the ancient Afrasan civilization, we can as yet say very little. Most of that small and uncertain knowledge concerns music and dance. Music probably followed a single melodic and rhythmic line. We suspect from the widespread cultural patterns of later Afrasan-speaking societies that early Afrasan dance performance principally used swaying body movements and various kinds of footwork. Drums were most emphatically *not* part of early Afrasan musical traditions. Stringed instruments, such as lyres, were widely used among later Afrasan peoples by the fifth to third millennia BCE, but

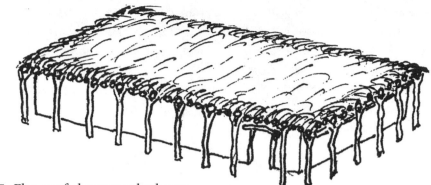

FIG. 5 Flat-roofed rectangular house

Depicted here is a particular version of this house style, built by some of the more recent cultural heirs of the early Afrasans, who lived in East Africa in the past 2,000 years.

whether such instruments can be traced back to the really early Afrasan societies, before 9000 BCE, is not yet known.

Nor is a great deal known as yet about the residential patterns favored by peoples of the Afrasan civilization. We suspect that at early periods, at least among the communities of the Erythraite group, the typical house is likely to have been rectangular in floor plan, with a flat roof. But how the larger community was laid out—whether, for instance, people might have lived in villages or in neighborhoods of scattered households—remains unclear.

Nilo-Saharan Peoples and the Middle Nile Archeological Tradition

To the west and south of the early Afrasans, in the region around the middle stretches of the Nile River, lay another distinctive grouping of peoples belonging to the era between 16,000 and 9000 BCE. Speakers of languages of the Nilo-Saharan family, they pursued a livelihood that included both the hunting of large game and a certain amount of fishing where the environment allowed it. Their toolmaking tradition, notable for the emphasis it placed on the fashioning of stone blades, has been called the Middle Nile Tradition (see map 4). The sizes and shapes of many of these blades indicate that the early Nilo-Saharans, like the Afrasans, used spears in their hunting. Not until much later times did bows and arrows appear among their descendants, and even then the preferred weapon usually appears to have remained the spear.

The environments in which the early Nilo-Saharans thrived differed sharply from those of their contemporaries, the Afrasans, and were separated from them by a wide stretch of then uninhabitable Sahara desert, extending 300–400 kilometers farther south than it does today. The Nilo-Saharan lands consisted of extensive plains, punctuated in several areas by isolated ranges of hills. Characterized by tropical steppe vegetation on the north and tropical deciduous savanna to the south, these environments provided the necessary grazing and browsing for the many species of antelope and other large herbivores on which the hunting activities of the Middle Nile peoples depended.

We know a good deal about the Nilo-Saharan cultures of the period after 9000 BCE, but little about them before that date. Our archeological information is confined to their stone tools, and the language evidence for those eras has yet to receive the kind of study it deserves. The residential patterns of the earliest Nilo-Saharans, the kinds of dwellings they built, their social institutions, and so forth—of these we have as yet little useful knowledge. Only in the matter of religion can we venture some conclusions about their cultural lives, and even these are tentative.

The early Nilo-Saharan communities, it is thought, held to a nontheistic belief system, similar to that known among a few modern-day Nilo-Saharan peoples, such as the Uduk, whose languages belong to the Koman branch of that family. In this religion spiritual power and spiritual danger do not reside in a deity but are expressed by an animating force. In the modern Uduk language this force is called *arum*. It is a force, concentrating in our livers, that makes us and animals alive; it is also the source of our anger, our fears, and our affections. Human beings restrain the *arum* within themselves through their receptive consciousness, called by the Uduk *kashira*, which is understood to reside in our stomachs. In the modern-day Uduk version of this belief system, there also exists disembodied *arum*, the residue of lives, animal and human, that have been lived in the past. The *arum* of people properly buried is reconstituted safely in communities underground. But there are also wandering *arum*, the residuum of people lost in the wild and never properly buried, and of animals killed by hunters. This animating force in its disembodied aspect, when not properly dealt with through ritual and religious observances, can be the source of danger and harm to people. Its effects, in other words, explain the problem of evil.

The longer-term historical significance of this ancient Nilo-Saharan Tradition lies in its contributions after 9000 BCE to the emergence of the Sudanic civilization. That civilization was built up by people who indeed spoke Nilo-Saharan languages, but who were to develop livelihoods and cultural ideas far different from those of their Middle Nile ancestors.

Niger-Congo Civilization

Early Niger-Congo Peoples and Their Subsistence Economy

Far to the west of northeastern Africa, in West Africa, the characteristic development of the period from 16,000 to 9000 BCE was the emergence, especially in the greatly expanded woodland savanna environments of that period, of a new tool technology, to which we may give the name West African Microlithic Tradition. The term "microlithic" describes a tool kit in which the typical stone tools are small, finely made points and other shapes, most of them no more than two or three centimeters in length. Most of the makers of the various varieties of this West African Microlithic complex probably belonged to societies speaking early languages of the Niger-Congo language family (see map 4).

From the beginning Niger-Congo hunters made and used the bow and arrow in their activities. We know this not yet directly from the archeology, but from the fact that an ancient word, *-ta,* for the bow can be reconstructed all the way back to proto-Niger-Congo, the language ancestral to all the hundreds of Niger-Congo languages spoken today. Bows and arrows are typically the weapons of microlithic toolmakers, and so this inference is not a surprising one. It seems also probable that the Niger-Congo hunters began developing poisons to be placed on their arrowheads fairly early, in this way considerably enhancing the effectiveness of their hunting.

From a relatively early period, a second major element of Niger-Congo subsistence was the intensive collection of wild yams. Indigenous yams, belonging to several species of the genus *Dioscorea,* were common plants of the open areas within the woodland savanna zones of West Africa. These plants, which form large edible tubers under the ground and whose leaves are suitable as greens, became a major source of carbohydrates in the diet, greatly increasing the productivity of food-collecting activities for the early Niger-Congo societies. (When North Americans use the word "yam," they mean a different plant altogether, the sweet potato, a crop domesticated long ago by Native Americans of South America.)

A third major element of early Niger-Congo livelihood was the pioneering of fishing technology. Fishing, which seems to us today such an obvious source of food, appears to have been first taken up by human beings in most parts of the globe between 16,000 and 9000 BCE, although it may have been practiced in the regions of the upper Nile River far more anciently than that. Niger-Congo communities may have been some of the first peoples to develop the technique of fishing by hook and line, their hooks having been carved from bone, shell, or hard wood. Another early fishing technique of Niger-Congo peoples may have been the use of special baskets to scoop unsuspecting fish from the water.

Niger-Congo communities, of course, pursued a wide range of other gathering and hunting practices. Various wild greens probably formed one important category of plant food for them, and they would have hunted a variety of game in the savannas and savanna woodlands.

Early Niger-Congo Society

In contrast to our relatively meager knowledge about the early Afrasan civilization, we know a good deal about the nonsubsistence portions of culture among the early Niger-Congo peoples. Some of these features we can trace back to the earliest Niger-Congo communities. Other characteristic features of Niger-Congo civilization emerged in later periods and then spread more widely.

Niger-Congo communities from an early period appear to have been clan based, with the clan in early times forming the primary wider social and political grouping of people. Descent was reckoned matrilineally, with goods and office inherited through one's mother or the brother of one's mother. We can therefore call early Niger-Congo descent groups matriclans; additionally, most probably they were matrilocal and uxorilocal. That is to say, women continued to live in their mother's villages, and when a man and a woman married, the man was expected to move to his wife's village, rather than the other way around. The man probably also had to perform bride-service for the bride's family—working and contributing for a time to the household of the bride's family—before being allowed to marry her. This custom remained a widely found feature down to recent times, turning up here and there all across the Niger-Congo parts of Africa wherever unstratified, egalitarian, and matrilineal social systems still persisted.

A hereditary position of clan chief seems to be an old feature of Niger-Congo clans. Although having community ritual responsibilities like the *wap'er* of Afrasan civilization, the Niger-Congo kin chief operated within an entirely different religious framework and sometimes had a degree of political authority not available to the *wap'er*. In the later agricultural eras, the chief was responsible, for instance, for allocating land to newcomers wanting to settle in the clan's or lineage's territory. The chief was also expected to adjudicate disputes within the community, to preside over community ceremonial occasions, and to act as a spokesperson in communal dealings with other people.

We suspect that Niger-Congo peoples from early times, like the Afrasans, practiced male circumcision as a rite of passage from child to adult status. In recent centuries this custom could be found in a great many Niger-Congo societies scattered as far west as Senegambia and as far east as Cameroon. How girls may have been initiated into adulthood in early Niger-Congo civilization is not yet known. A smaller number of Niger-Congo societies in West Africa did practice clitoridectomy in recent eras, but we remain unsure how old this custom may actually have been. There is no reason at present to think that circumcision among the early Afrasans had any historical connection to the presence of circumcision among the early Niger-Congo peoples.

The typical residential unit in early Niger-Congo civilization may have been a relatively compact village, containing probably somewhere in the range of 100–200 inhabitants. Typically, people belonging to one clan or to one particular lineage within the clan would have formed the core element in a village. It would have been their village. But attached to that core population would have been other people, especially the husbands from other clans who had married women of the village. The village might also include a few families or individuals who had moved from other areas and had been allowed to settle and become part of village life. If such people stayed on, over the long term their children or grandchildren would gradually come to be accepted as members of the local clan or lineage.

We cannot be sure about the layout of the earliest Niger-Congo villages, but one notable pattern became especially favored in the rainforest areas of West Africa after about the sixth millennium BCE. In this pattern the village consisted of a single street, with the houses set out along each side of that street. If such a village fronted on a river, then the riverbank area formed the street, and the village comprised a single row of houses on the side of the street away from the stream. The houses in these villages had a rectangular floor plan and ridge roofs covered with woven palm matting. (Figure 15 in chapter 3 shows an example of this kind of house.)

Technology and Artistry among the Early Niger-Congo Peoples

The Niger-Congo villages supported a range of skilled craft activities. Weaving techniques were especially well developed among Niger-Congo peoples by the sixth and fifth millennia BCE. Just how much earlier these skills can be traced back is not clear. Mats for sleeping and preparing food and a variety of baskets comprised the most notable woven items for everyday, practical use. As we have already seen, woven palm matting provided one favored kind of roofing material. The weaving of raffia cloth, a soft luxuriant textile fashioned from the fibers of the raffia palm, does not go back to the earliest periods of Niger-Congo history, but it became a widely diffused technology during the past 6,000 years. A probably much older Niger-Congo cloth-making technique that did not involve weaving was the fashioning of barkcloth. This cloth was made by removing and pounding out sheets of bark taken from certain species of trees.

Wood carving, using stone adzes and stone knives, was another well-developed field of village technology dating from early times. Before 6000 BCE, Niger-Congo peoples had become skilled boat builders, carving out from single large logs the canoes they needed for fishing and for traveling by stream through the forested areas.

Even earlier, the skills of the wood-carver created a particularly Niger-Congo contribution to world art history. From probably their earliest periods, Niger-Congo peoples carried on a powerful tradition of figure sculpture in wood. Almost everywhere the ideas of Niger-Congo civilization spread, wood sculpting spread, too, with the artists drawing on this tradition to develop and elaborate an immense variety of regional styles and expressive motifs. The artists of those times, it should be noted, were not alienated individuals pursuing their own tangents of self expression, but people who expressed themselves through the socially sanctioned forms and motifs of their community. It is important to note, by the way, that up until recent centuries, this has been the role of artists everywhere in the world, not just in Africa.

One rather personal art form also seems to go back to the earliest eras in Niger-Congo civilization. A particular kind of tight, intricate hair braiding, especially for women, remains a characteristic feature of adornment all across the vast areas of the continent inhabited today by peoples of Niger-Congo historical roots. In the past five centuries this kind of hair styling has been taken to the New World, where in the United States it is called cornrows.

In music and dance, too, Niger-Congo civilization gave rise to distinctive

FIG. 6 Chiwara sculpture, Mali

Artists working in the ancient Niger-Congo tradition of wood sculpture have evolved a great variety of styles and motifs all across the Niger-Congo parts of Africa. Chiwara, a stylized antelope, is a centuries-old type of wooden figure, most often sculpted in headdress form for ceremony and dancing in the Mali region. Its origins go back probably well before the period of the Mali empire. A number of other examples of Niger-Congo sculpture, not only in wood but also in terra-cotta and brass, are depicted in subsequent chapters.

types of expression. Percussion and polyrhythmic performance characterized both. From the earliest period of Niger-Congo history, drums were the characteristic instruments of Niger-Congo music. For at least the last several thousand years, highly developed types of drumming, involving drums of different pitches beaten simultaneously to different intertwining rhythmic schemes, have been a common and widespread feature of such music. What people often think of as typically African music turns out to be typically Niger-Congo music, quite different both in conception and fundamental forms from the musics of other African civilizations. In this music lie the historical roots of the modern-day genres of ragtime, jazz, and rhythm and blues, as well as rock and roll. Drum making, by the way, was another early important skill of the ancient Niger Congo woodworkers.

Dances were vigorous and energetic exercises, relying on multiple movements of the body much more than on footwork. In special dance performances at celebrations and festival times, elaborate masks and costumes, the facial parts carved from wood, were often worn by dancers. Here again we see the importance of the early Niger-Congo woodworking tradition.

Religion and Medicine in Niger-Congo Civilization

As for Niger-Congo religion, it proves useful once again to divide our considerations into two questions: how did Niger-Congo religion conceive of the realm of spirit, and how did it deal with the problem of evil?

FIG. 7 Tension drum and drumstick

The drummer played this particular early West African style of Niger-Congo drum by wrapping an arm around the middle of it and holding the drumstick with the other hand. By squeezing down with the arm on the strings running between the two ends of the instrument, the musician could raise the pitch of the instrument.

Niger-Congo religion recognized a series of levels of spirit. At the apex of the system, but of little direct consequence in everyday religion, there was God as a distant figure, who was the First Cause or Creator. This particular concept can with certainty be traced back to the sixth millennium BCE, and its historical origins appear to lie much further back in Niger-Congo history.

A second kind of spirit dwelt within a particular territory and was believed able to influence events there; we can call it therefore a territorial spirit. The domain of such a spirit might be a particular river, as among peoples living in an area, like the Niger Delta, abounding in rivers. Or its domain might be the drainage basin of a particular stream, as we know was true in the kingdom of Kongo 500 years ago, or some other definable expanse of land.

But the really crucial spirits for religious observance and ritual belonged to a third category. These were the ancestors. The ancestors were not worshiped; rather, they were venerated. They deserved and required respect and remembrance. They could greatly affect the lives of people here and now; and people prayed to them and made offerings to them. The ancestors came first to people's minds in times of crisis or of blessing.

In early Niger-Congo thought, evil had two principal causes. It could result from neglect of the ancestors or from the actions of an ancestor spirit who had been an evil or malicious person when alive. Or it could be due to the malice, hate, or envy of a living person, whose malicious will manifested itself in "witchcraft." By witchcraft we mean the use of medicines and spells to bring harm to others.

We must be careful in our use of the terms "witch" and "witchcraft" to translate the various words applied to this set of beliefs in the different Niger-Congo languages. For modern-day Americans, witchcraft conjures up Halloween images of ugly hags flying on broomsticks. In late medieval thought, a different, nastier image, of agents of the devil, was imposed on people, usually women, believed to be witches. Neither of these ideas has any validity for our understanding of Niger-Congo views. There was no devil in Niger-Congo belief systems. "Witches" were simply individuals driven by malice, hate, or envy, and they could be men or women. But the consequences of their activities could be dire indeed.

People in Niger-Congo civilization faced with undeserved evil happenings, with persistent or bad illness, or with personal or family misfortune turned for help to a kind of specialist, the doctor-diviner. Often called in English by the unsavory and inaccurate term "witch-doctor," this man or woman was in actuality a person knowledgeable about medicines derived from natural sources, some truly efficacious and some only thought to be, and a person skilled in reading people. (In the southern United States, the role of the conjure man or conjure woman had its historical roots in this Niger-Congo cultural position.) The job of the doctor-diviner was to divine the underlying cause of bad happenings—to diagnose whether the malice of an enemy or the failure to look properly after the ancestors was at fault—and to prescribe remedies. One of the remedies might be identifying and expelling the witch from the society; hence the English translation of the African words for this person as "witch-doctor."

Khoisan Civilization

Khoisan Peoples and the Eastern African Microlithic Tradition

A fourth major grouping of African societies of the period between 16,000 and 9000 BCE formed the Khoisan civilization. Spread in those eras from the southern edges of the Ethiopian Highlands in the north to the Zambezi region in the south (see map 4), the peoples of this cultural tradition spoke languages of a fourth African language family, Khoisan, and prospered by engaging in what can be described as eclectic types of gathering and hunting. They pursued a great variety of game, hunting small animals as often or more often than large ones, and they collected a great variety of wild plant foods, these latter resources actually providing by far the greater portion of their diet. Later on, during the seventh and sixth millennia BCE, Khoisan peoples spread their culture and language south and west of the Limpopo River, rapidly expanding all across the areas that today compose the countries of South Africa, Botswana, and Namibia (see chapter 3 for more on this era of history).

The various regional toolmaking styles practiced by the Khoisan can all be grouped together archeologically as the Eastern African Microlithic, or Wilton, Tradition. Almost all their stone implements, as befits a microlithic technology, were very small, consisting of small crescent shapes, points, and so forth. And like the otherwise very different makers of the West African Microlithic Tradition, the Khoisan communities from an early period came to depend on the bow and arrow in their hunting and independently developed a variety of arrow poisons to enhance their effectiveness as hunters.

Interestingly, one moderately large stone implement did have a notable presence in the Eastern African Microlithic tool kit. This item, consisting of a stone fashioned into a doughnut shape with a hole bored in the middle of it, was used as a weight on a digging stick. Its presence in the tool kit shows that the Khoisan peoples had begun to add edible tubers to their diet, bringing into use a new category of plant food.

The Eastern African Microlithic Tradition of the Khoisan may actually have begun to take shape before the era of drier African climates between 16,000 and 11,500 BCE. The specific antecedents of the Eastern African Microlithic Tradition can be traced back to toolmaking developments of as early as 20,000 BCE in what is today eastern Zambia. These changes, toward an increasingly microlithic tool kit, emerged initially, it appears, as an adaptation to that region's drier woodland savanna areas of 700–1,000 millimeters of rain a year, an environment with relatively low populations of larger game, and with few of the antelopes that congregate in large herds. By hunting a great variety of small animals and expanding the range of plant foods collected, the peoples who developed this approach more than overcame the deficiency of large animals.

In so doing, they fashioned an approach to gathering and hunting that was extraordinarily resilient and long-lived. The great shift to drier climates before 16,000 BCE appears, if anything, to have enhanced the viability of this kind of food-collecting economy. The willingness of Khoisan peoples, with their Eastern African Microlithic tool technology, to utilize all kinds of food resources made them equally well able to increase the productivity of food collecting in more open savanna and in steppe areas of eastern Africa, too. Armed with the new approaches, techniques, and attitudes, the Khoisan cultural tradition spread within a period of no more than 1,000 to 2,000 years after 16,000 BCE

FIG. 8 Bored stone weight for a digging stick

This kind of tool was made and used by peoples of the Eastern African Microlithic Tradition. Its presence in their tool kit shows that they had added a new type of food, plant tubers that grew under the ground, to their diet.

across much of the eastern side of Africa, from the Zambezi to the south edges of the Ethiopian Highlands.

Social Practices among the Early Khoisan

The local social and residential unit of the early Khoisan societies took the form of a band. Ranging in size usually from perhaps 25 up to 50 people, the band tended at its core to consist of a group of people relatively closely linked to each other by birth or marriage, although it might also include others not so closely tied. No formal structures of kinship, such as clans or lineages, appear to have existed; people reckoned their family connections bilaterally, recognizing both their fathers' and their mothers' families as equally important relations.

The band was a moderately mobile group, which in some regions needed to move its whole settlement to a different locale each season, but in other regions might not have reason to move at all. The typical settlement would have consisted of a loose arrangement of small hemispherical houses, each simple to build and therefore no great loss if one had to move and build again somewhere else. Judging from later practice, each band would have had a recognized territory in which it would have first rights at gathering and hunting. Depending on the climate, the territory could range from 400 or 500 up to 4,000 or more square kilometers especially in resource-poor areas.

Each band belonged to a wider grouping of neighboring bands speaking the same language. The yearly patterns of social interaction, the mobility of people, and the relative ease with which people could change from one band to another meant that such a grouping of bands might together cover a considerable expanse of land. Different bands would meet together at particular times of the year at places with dependable water and food resources, holding dances and trading the irregular surpluses of their gathering and hunting. These occasions were important for sustaining cooperative relationships with other bands and allowed people to establish wider circles of friends and acquaintances than their own small band. This social dimension was especially important for marriage, because people normally had to seek their matrimonial partners in other bands.

No hereditary leadership can be reconstructed for the early Khoisan peoples. The close kin connections within the band usually provided an adequate basis for cooperation in so small a group. Irresolvable differences, if they did arise, could often be relieved by some people's moving away to join another nearby band or to form a band of their own.

Arts and Religion in Khoisan Civilization

Music and dance in Khoisan civilization, as far back as we can trace, followed a single rhythmic beat. In dance, footwork had the key importance, and only restrained movement of the body took place. String instruments of several kinds were typical features of the Khoisan musical traditions during the last several millennia and may date to relatively early times. The single-string musical bow may have been the earliest such instrument played by the Khoisan, but four- or five-string instruments, which used hollow gourds as resonators, also appear to be of considerable antiquity among the Khoisan. Drums, however, were entirely unknown to Khoisan peoples before the last 2,000 years and were never used by them.

The Khoisan, like the earliest Nilo-Saharans, adhered to a nontheistic religious outlook. Their beliefs recognized the existence of an impersonal condition of spirit, a force that existed outside human beings as well as in some animals. In the thought of the particular Khoisan peoples who have lived in southern Africa since 5000 BCE, this force could be tapped by means of the trance-dance and used to heal sickness and to relieve social and individual stress and conflict. In this procedure a person recognized for special religious talents, a kind of shaman whom we may call a trance-healer, dances until he or she goes into a state of trance, which might last for many hours. The trance-healers were not full-time specialists, as were the doctor-diviners of the Niger-Congo civilization. If no trance dance was being performed, and that means the great majority of the time, the healer held no special position and engaged in the usual pursuits of everyone else, in hunting if a man and gathering if a woman, and in leisure-time activities.

This particular aspect of religion had a fundamental tie to the characteristic art form of Khoisan civilization, rock painting. This kind of artistry, its canvasses being the bare walls of rock shelters or caves, occurs widely through the old areas of Khoisan civilization, from Tanzania to Zimbabwe to Namibia and South Africa. Where suitable rock surfaces did not exist, as in the plains of central South Africa, the artists expressed themselves through rock engravings. The most spectacular and best preserved examples of rock painting, found in South Africa, have been shown by recent scholarship to depict the religious experiences of the trance-healers. The healers themselves, it seems, were the artists.

We cannot be certain that the practices of the trance-dance as found among the southern African Khoisan go back to the early times of Khoisan civilization. The often differing imagery and different emphases in the rock art outside South Africa tell us that the idioms and metaphors, even if not the fundamental themes, in Khoisan religion did change and develop over the long run of their history. The rituals of that religion, including the trance-dance, surely evolved also.

In far southern Africa a tradition of rock painting existed long before the spread of Khoisan-speaking peoples into those regions at around 6000 to 5000 BCE. The earliest known examples of this earlier tradition date to more than 26,000 years ago. How the later Khoisan rock art tradition and this older artistry affected each other remains to be studied.

Summing Up the Period 16,000–9000 BCE in Africa

The cultural foundations of two of the four major civilizations of later African history—the Afrasan and the Niger-Congo—were laid in the period between 16,000 and 9000 BCE. A third, Sudanic civilization, emerged after that period, but its historical roots in part trace back to the more ancient Middle Nile Tradition of the early Nilo-Saharan peoples. The fourth tradition of great importance since 9000 BCE, Khoisan, first began to take shape probably even before 16,000.

These were far from the only African peoples of those times. In South Africa and Namibia, other communities, known archeologically as the Albany culture, persisted as principally large game hunters until around the seventh millennium BCE, when their way of life was finally displaced by the eclectic gathering and hunting livelihood of Khoisan civilization. In the vast Congo Basin of western and central equatorial parts of Africa, another long-lived and distinctive cultural tradition predominated, represented in the archeology by the Lupemban and the later Tshitolian cultures. The peoples who created this tradition were the ancestors, we believe, of the scattered modern-day gatherer-hunter communities of that region, the BaTwa (commonly called "Pygmies" in European languages). We will have more to say about the BaTwa, in particular, in later chapters. But it was the Afrasan, Sudanic, and Niger-Congo peoples, and to a lesser extent the Khoisan, whose cultural heirs most powerfully shaped the later ages of African history.

Issues and Questions

Chapter 2 focuses on certain developments in livelihood and culture in Africa between 16,000 and 9000 BCE. One set of questions we may ask of these developments concerns the deep levels of historical cause and effect—the encounter of humans and nature. These questions relate directly or indirectly to subsistence, to how people got their food:

- In what notable ways did human beings of the period before 9000 BCE successfully deal with the different African environments?
- In what sorts of ways did the natural environments shape the choices people made?
- Why did some cultural traditions expand across vast new territories?

Answering these questions means learning about specific new developments of the period:

- What new successful approaches to acquiring food appeared in this period?
- When and where did they appear?
- What made them "successful"?

If we look to other areas of historical change, to matters of custom and belief, the questions we consider have a different focus, emphasizing the content and great diversity of the early African cultural traditions. Here readers may find it useful to take a comparative perspective:

- How did the three major early widespread African civilizations—Afrasan, Niger-Congo, and Khoisan—differ from each other and from early Nilo-Saharan peoples of the middle Nile in viewing the realm of the spirit and the problem of evil?
- How did they differ in their ideas of kinship and in the kinds of social and residential units they lived in?
- How did they differ in the kinds of individual roles of leadership and authority they each recognized?
- How did they differ in various aspects of material culture?

What is most difficult for us to do for the earliest periods is to capture a sense of the flow and movement that characterize all history. The evidence we most commonly uncover relates to the elements of life and custom that long persisted. So we must always try to ask the following question, even if we cannot always answer it:

- What kinds of change or development over the long term, large or small, can we discern in either customs or the material pursuits of life?

Further Reading

A selection of key resource articles on the historical periods in Africa covered in this chapter, and on the evidence and arguments relating to these eras, appears in a volume forthcoming in 2006:

Ehret, C. *African History and the Testimony of Language*. Oxford: James Currey Publishers, forthcoming.

Along with articles on early African language family and cultural history, this book includes articles that examine the correlating of archeological and linguistic evidence; the spread of Sudanic agriculture (relevant to chapter 3) and the history of the Nilotic peoples (relevant to chapters 4 and 5); the interactions of South Arabian settlers with Cushitic peoples in the Ethiopian highlands in the first millennium BCE (relevant to chapter 5); and the origins of markets around Mount Kilimanjaro (relevant to chapter 6).

Points of Contention

The idea of grouping together several of the early wild-grass-collecting cultures of northeastern Africa under the rubric of the Cataract Tradition can be a contentious issue. "Cataract" is used here as a loosely applicable term, implying the broad resemblances among the cultures of the region but not requiring one to accept that a single origin accounts for them all.

The old Western and Middle Eastern presumption that the Afrasan (Afroasiatic) language family originated in Asia can simply no longer be sustained, now that we have large amounts of first-rate data from the African branches of the family. But this newer evidence is still almost unknown to most scholars of the Semitic and ancient Egyptian languages, with the consequence that an unbalanced understanding of the family continues to prevail in many quarters. Unfortunately, the outdated view of Afrasan as having an Asian origin continues to affect not only popular thinking but also the interpretations of scholars in other fields, such as biological anthropology, who study Africa.

Some readers are disturbed by the idea that the Semitic and Egyptian languages are related, because they think such a relationship would make Egyptian an Asian language. Of course, that is not so. Semitic alone, among all the divisions of the family, consisted in earlier times of languages of the far southwest corners of Asia, spoken even then right next to Africa. All the rest of the divisions are entirely African, and the only reasonable interpretation of this evidence is that Semitic was a solitary Asian offshoot of the family, brought into Asia long ago by immigrants from Africa.

A related presumption, also widely held, that the Afrasan family of languages expanded because its speakers acquired livestock and cultivation, similarly turns out to be unsubstantiated, once the full evidence of the African languages is considered. We can indeed reconstruct back to the proto-Afrasan language a number of words dealing with the use of grasses as food in some form—words such as those for "flour" and "grindstone," among several others. But not a single proto-Afrasan word is diagnostic of cultivation. That is, there are no words that mean "to cultivate," "to weed," "cultivated field," or the like. Similarly, there are no proto-Afrasan words diagnostic of the raising of livestock. A few old root words for "sheep" or "goat" do appear in more than one branch of the Afrasan family, but a critical analysis of the semantic or phonological histories of each shows one of two things. Either the name for the animal spread by borrowing from one branch to the other—showing that the animal itself spread long after the proto-Afrasan period—or the word originally referred to a species of antelope and shifted to the meaning "sheep" or "goat" at some later point in history. The evidence, in other words, strongly requires the proto-Afrasan use of wild grasses for food, but it consistently shows that cultivation and herding arose in later times. A recent summary statement of these issues is found in the following: C. Ehret, S. O. Y. Keita, and Paul Newman. "The Origins of Afroasiatic." *Science* 306 (3 Dec. 2004): 1680.

The issue of whether the Khoisan languages can be demonstrated to belong to a single family remains contentious. I take the view that we will eventually be able to demonstrate this relationship in a satisfactory manner. The languages attributed to the Khoisan family share a number of similar deep features of structure and phonology, many unique to them, as well as more basic vocabulary words than is often recognized to be the case. But even without claiming certainty about the relatedness of the Khoisan languages as a whole, we would have to argue from the historical side that a common, long-lived, East African Microlithic cultural tradition persisted all across a large portion of the eastern side of Africa between about 16,000 and 3000 BCE, with related stone tool industries and artistic traditions.

One small, but diverse, set of related Niger-Congo peoples, the Kordofanian group, distantly connected in language to the rest of the Niger-Congo family, has been left out of our story here. The Kordofanian communities have resided for thousands of years in the Nuba Mountains of the southwestern Middle Nile Basin. Their location reflects a prior stage of history before the rise of the Niger-Congo civilization, possibly dating before 15,000 years ago. During this stage either the ancestral Kordofanian people diverged from their Niger-Congo relatives by moving eastward from West Africa, or else the ancestral Niger-Congo people diverged from the Kordofanian by spreading west to West Africa. How the Kordofanian group fits into the wider frame of African history will be an interesting problem for future historians and archeologists to consider.

3

Culture and Technology in Africa, 9000–3500 BCE

The Environments of Agricultural Invention

In the twelfth and eleventh millennia BCE, Africa again entered into a period of major climatic shift. Once more, after several thousand years of relatively stable climates, communities in many parts of the continent found their ways of subsistence challenged by the forces of nature. But this time the direction of climatic change was toward wetter climate regimes. Rainfall increased everywhere, and in one vast region, the Sahara, uninhabited areas became habitable by human beings for the first time in many thousands of years. Climatologists often refer to this period as the Holocene Climatic Optimum. The increase in rainfall developed in two stages.

At first, between about 11,000 and 9000 BCE, the climates in different parts of the continent became either like those of modern times or had somewhat greater amounts of rainfall than today. Rainforest vegetation began to spread again all across the Congo Basin and to expand farther inland behind the West African coasts. The savanna belt north of the forest advanced northward into former steppe country, while dry steppe vegetation itself commenced spreading north into the southern Sahara. From the north side of the Sahara, Mediterranean grassland and steppe spread at the same time farther southward into the desert. It was an era of warming as well, with annual temperature ranges across Africa becoming much like those encountered today, and as a result the glaciers of the high equatorial peaks, such as Kilimanjaro and Ruwenzori, shrank even as precipitation increased.

Then, between about 9000 and the early seventh millennium BCE, there ensued the peak period of this moist era. Rainforest expanded another 200 to 300 kilometers northward and southward into formerly moist woodland savanna.

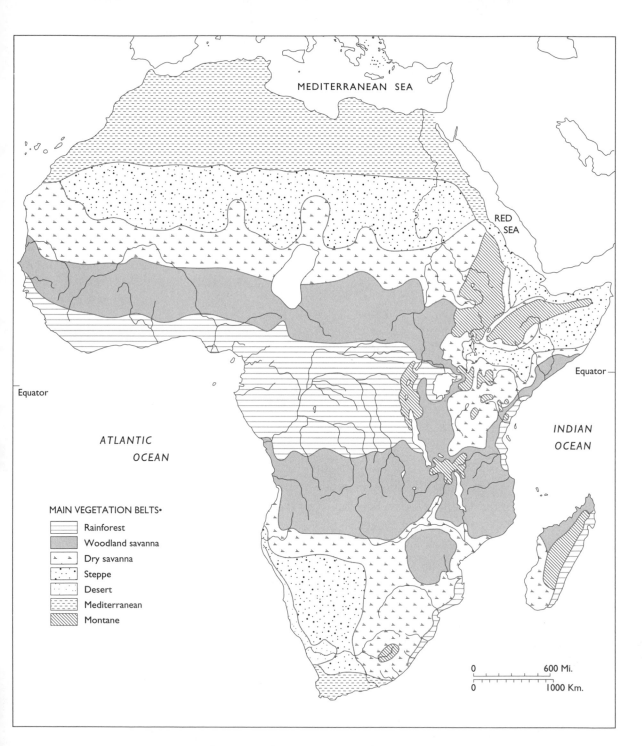

MEDITERRANEAN SEA

RED
SEA

Equator

ATLANTIC
OCEAN

INDIAN
OCEAN

Equator

MAIN VEGETATION BELTS·

Rainforest
Woodland savanna
Dry savanna
Steppe
Desert
Mediterranean
Montane

0   600 Mi.
0   1000 Km.

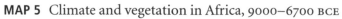

MAP 5 Climate and vegetation in Africa, 9000–6700 BCE

The woodland savanna belts shifted correspondingly farther north and south of the rainforest, and tropical steppe and grassland vegetation became established far into the Sahara region. East and west across the middle of the present-day Sahara desert, the tropical African steppe overlapped the southern edges of the subtropical steppe grasslands extending south from the Mediterranean Sea. New lakes appeared and old ones grew in size all along the southern edges of the Sahara region. Lake Chad in particular expanded into a huge body of water, Lake Megachad, half the size of the Caspian Sea. Perennial streams flowed out of the two central Saharan mountain ranges, Tibesti and Hoggar, where only dry channels exist today.

Inventing Agriculture: The Eastern Sahara, 9000–5500 BCE

The Beginnings of Food Production

The economic and cultural consequences of this climatic shift only gradually emerged. For up to 2,000 years after 11,000 BCE, most of the existing African approaches to gathering and hunting continued to be pursued successfully.

The reason is a simple one: the first effect of any rainfall increase is to enhance the growth and reproduction of plants and animals already present in a region. The new kinds of plant communities and their associated fauna advance across the region only slowly, over a period of centuries, in the wake of the increased rainfall because of the manner in which plants reproduce. Plants must first grow to maturity; annuals do this each year, but the dominant trees and bushes of a plant community may take several years to reach this stage. They then produce seed that the next year will allow the same plants to take hold anywhere from a few meters to a few kilometers away, depending on the ways their seed gets spread, whether by birds, wind, or some other force of nature. And so, each year, little by little, the new plant communities extend their range farther in the direction of the rain increase. Thus there tends to be a lag of centuries between the climatic shift and the subsequent vegetation change with which the real impact on human economies begins, and this lag was clearly present in Africa in the centuries following 11,000 BCE.

The development of greatest long-term effect on the course of African history, culminating in the first African invention of an agricultural economy, began between 10,000 and 9000 BCE. During that time certain Nilo-Saharan communities expanded their lands northward, following the slow advance of dry tropical steppe vegetation into the southern half of the eastern Sahara.

These particular Nilo-Saharans spoke what we call today the proto-Northern Sudanic language. The ethnic names they gave themselves have been lost from the historical record, and so we will term them simply the Northern Sudanians. They brought with them a version of the older Middle Nile Tradition specially adapted to the arid conditions in which they lived. The principal objects of their hunting, because of the relative rarity of larger game in such marginal environments, were the numerous hares that thrived in the sparse steppe grasslands.

With their expansion into that region, the Northern Sudanians came into close contact with the Erythraic communities, Afrasan in civilization, who resided east and north of them in the lands between the Nile River and the Red Sea. From that point onward, there began over 3,000 years of mutual interactions that greatly reshaped the directions of history across a large part of Africa.

One notable constant throughout this history was the correlation of ethnicity with climate. The great shift in rainfall belts after 11,000 BCE, as we have already seen, established two different climatic regimes in the eastern Sahara. Mediterranean grasslands advanced far south and became more extensive in the Red Sea hills, while to the west of the northern Red Sea hills, dry Mediterranean steppe vegetation extended as far as the southern parts of modern-day Egypt. In this regime, rainfall arrived in the cool season of the year, equivalent to the wintertime of the Northern Hemisphere. But from far southern Egypt southward, the tropical African steppe prevailed, its rains coming at the same time as the northern summer. Throughout the wet phase, Erythraic communities of the Afrasan cultural tradition resided in the Mediterranean environments, east and north of the climatic transition; Northern Sudanic peoples occupied the tropical steppe to the south. Cultural influences flowed both ways, and people must have interacted frequently and moved in both directions across this climatic transition, but their ethnic groups as a whole tended to spread out within the environmental zone they already occupied.

Agriculture and Technology in the Sahara

Nevertheless, because of the cultural interactions, several important economic and technological innovations crossed that climatic and cultural divide between 10,000 and 6000 BCE.

The first major economic consequence came early, some centuries before 9000 BCE. From their new Erythraic neighbors, the Northern Sudanians adopted wild grain collection, adding grindstones to their tool kits and thereby

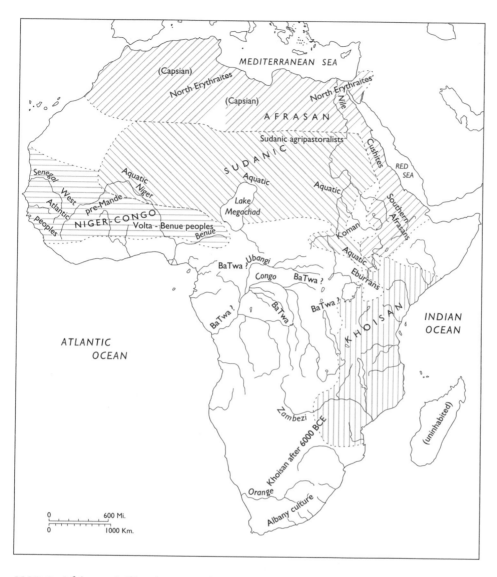

MAP 6 African civilizations, 9000–6700 BCE

greatly increasing the overall productivity of their gathering and hunting. But because the grass species of the tropical steppe were quite different from those of the Red Sea hills, the Sudanians reapplied the grain-collecting techniques to tropical African grasses. Such grasses included wild sorghum, fonio, and pearl millet.

At about the same time as their adoption of wild grain collection, the

Northern Sudanians made a particular breakthrough of their own of major significance in world technological history: they invented the first known pottery of the western and central parts of the Eastern Hemisphere. Before any Middle Easterners, and long before any Europeans, Sudanian peoples were making finely crafted pots. Only in Japan may an earlier ceramic tradition have appeared, and that Far East Asian invention had no impact beyond Japan until later.

Just how early pottery making emerged among the Nilo-Saharan-speaking peoples is not yet certain. All the earliest examples so far discovered belong to the period of 9000 to 8000 BCE. But the skill with which these pots were being made even then shows that the technology must already have existed among the ancestors of the Northern Sudanians for some centuries before that time. Sometime in the next 2,000 years after 8000 BCE, the idea of pot making began to be taken up by some of the Erythraic neighbors of the Sudanians. Before 7000 BCE, this technology had advanced over large parts of Saharan Africa, and by the seventh millennium pottery making began to appear in parts of western Asia as well.

The Northern Sudanic invention of pottery has some interesting consequences for Sudanian peoples' cuisines. In particular, from the beginning they prepared their grains differently from their Erythraic neighbors. Having pots, they could and did make porridge rather than breads from their flour. They may have learned from the Erythraites the techniques of collecting and processing wild grains as food, but they chose their own quite different way of cooking them. Porridge came to be used, as rice is in many Asian dishes, as the base component to which other foods could be added—gravies, meat, vegetables, cooking oils, and so forth. The invention of pottery, in other words, allowed the Northern Sudanians and their descendants to turn cereals into the basis for a potentially more varied and interesting cuisine.

Northern Sudanians and the Domestication of Cattle

The second major historical development in the regional subsistence economy probably came within a relatively few centuries of the Northern Sudanic adoption of wild grain collection. The extension of a Mediterranean climate south through the Red Sea hills quite naturally brought with it the fauna of the Mediterranean, including, most prominently, wild cattle. Around 9000–8000 BCE, some of the peoples living in areas to the west of the Red Sea hills, who may previously have hunted the wild cattle, began to tame and raise them for their meat. The first food production in Africa had begun.

In the available archeological evidence, the earliest bones of domestic cattle discovered so far turn up in sites that were, we believe, inhabited by Northern Sudanic wild-grain-collecting communities. These sites are located in the heart of the eastern Sahara, west of the Nile in areas that then lay just south of the transition from Mediterranean to tropical steppe climate. These were very dry areas lacking the year-round supplies of surface water essential to the survival of wild cattle. Only if the Northern Sudanians drove the cattle out seasonally, during and just after the rains, to the pastures and temporary ponds of what was then desert steppe and returned with them to the Nile in the long dry season could the cattle have survived in those regions.

The important point from the perspective of world history is that the domestication of wild cattle in the far eastern Sahara was one of probably three independent domestications of the animal. More than a thousand years later, a separate taming of cattle took place in the eastern Mediterranean and Middle Eastern regions. The third place in which cows appear to have been independently domesticated was India, probably again somewhat later than in Africa.

Slowly at first and then more rapidly, the adoption of cattle raising began to transform the culture and demography of the Northern Sudanians. Until perhaps 7000 BCE, Northern Sudanians grew in population and gradually expanded over a wider stretch of territories in the southern Sahara. In the process they diverged into two sets of communities: (1) a society we call the proto-Saharo-Sahelians, situated west of the Nile River, and (2) the pre-Kunama, residing perhaps east of the Nile in the steppe lands between the Atbara River and the Red Sea hills.

Society and Religion among the Northern Sudanians

The residential units of the Northern Sudanians, the archeology shows us, were small and ephemeral. They apparently built temporary settlements and supplemented their exploitation of the wild grain resources of their land with a transhumant kind of cattle raising, moving their herds about so as not to exhaust the scattered and meager pastures of their country. They reckoned descent matrilineally and probably belonged to territorially dispersed matriclans. This feature of social organization likely traces back even earlier in time, to the ancestral Nilo-Saharan peoples of the early Middle Nile Tradition before 9000

BCE, since it is characteristic of the Koman peoples, such as the Uduk (see chapter 2), and was an ancient feature among the Central Sudanians (as described later in this chapter). Both these groups are Nilo-Saharans in language, like the Northern Sudanians, but evolved along separate lines of historical descent out of the proto-Nilo-Saharan society.

The Northern Sudanians developed religious ideas strikingly different from the nontheistic beliefs we attributed (in chapter 2) to their ancestors in the earlier Middle Nile Tradition. Their Sudanic religion, as we will term it here, was monotheistic. At the core of the belief system was a single Divinity, or God. Divinity was identified metaphorically with the sky, and the power of Divinity was often symbolized by lightning. There was no other category of spirits or deities. In some more recent versions of the Sudanic religion, Divinity might choose to manifest itself to human beings in the form of seemingly particular, lesser spirits, but the followers of Sudanic religion understood those spirits to be just other guises of Divinity. The Sudanic belief viewed evil as a Divine judgment or retribution for the wrong that a person, or a person's forebears, had done in life. The ancestors passed after death into some kind of vaguely conceived afterlife, but they had no functional role in religious observance or ritual.

The Saharo-Sahelian Peoples and the Beginnings of Crop Cultivation

Sometime between 8000 and 7000 BCE, the Saharo-Sahelian descendants of the Northern Sudanian people set in motion an economic shift of even greater social and cultural impact: they began the first deliberate cultivation of at least some of the grains—sorghum may have been one—that they previously had gathered as wild. The timing of this development may have something to do with the still further increase in rainfall at this particular period. More rainfall meant more areas of the Sahara in which sorghum could be successfully grown and so would have made grain cultivation seem a less chancy venture than it would have been before. (Our knowledge of the next several thousand years of pre-Kunama history is virtually nil, so the remaining discussion focuses on the Saharo-Sahelians, who in any case seem to have been the major innovating group of peoples.)

The keeping of cattle had previously added considerably to the meat resources of the Northern Sudanic lands, otherwise poorly endowed with large mammals. But with cultivation the Saharo-Sahelians created a set of subsistence practices that gave them the potential, over the long run of history, to expand their food supply many times over and to support a growing population. We can call the set of crops and the cultivating practices pioneered by the Saharo-Sahelians "Sudanic seed agriculture" or just "Sudanic agriculture." The term "seed" is included to bring attention to the fact that the key crops of this agriculture were all propagated from seed. We sometimes also call the combined livestock-raising and cultivating practices of these peoples the Sudanic "agripastoral" tradition. Progressively over the period between 7000 and 5000 BCE, the Saharo-Sahelians and their descendants brought under cultivation new crops in addition to sorghum, domesticating more of the indigenous wild food plants of the region—first, before 6000 BCE, a variety of gourds and calabashes including the edible gourd, and then, by perhaps 5000 BCE, cotton, pearl millet, and watermelons.

The requirements of cultivation also changed the conditions of human settlement. The Saharo-Sahelians, in order to tend their fields more effectively, had to set down larger and longer-lasting settlements. Because they stayed all year in one place, they began to dig wells to provide water for their cattle and themselves through the long dry season, and they soon transformed the structure and layout of their residences.

By 7000 BCE the typical Saharo-Sahelian extended family resided in a large homestead surrounded by a thick thornbush fence. The area of ground thus enclosed acted as a cattle pen, protecting their animals at night from predators, principally lions and hyenas. The thorn pens also served as the location for their houses and the granaries in which they stored their cultivated grain. The Saharo-Sahelians built their houses according to a style that has since become widespread in the savanna and steppe parts of Africa—circular in floor plan with a conical thatched roof. The earliest granaries were dug into the ground. But after 5500 BCE, as Sudanian communities began to spread their agriculture southward, a different style of granary, consisting of a small house-shaped structure raised off the ground, widely replaced the older type.

Of the crops domesticated by the descendants of the Saharo-Sahelian peoples, cotton had the most far-reaching implications for world technological history. The archeological evidence from the eastern Sudan shows that spindle whorls of baked clay were being made in the heart of the Middle Nile Basin as early as 5000 BCE, during the same broad period that cotton was being domesticated in that region. In combination, these bits of evidence suggest that already cotton textiles of some sort were being woven in this region by around 7,000 years ago, as early as anywhere else in the world. The history of cotton

FIG. 9 Spindle whorls

The spinner of thread performed her task by spinning the cotton fibers with a spindle inserted through the hole in the middle of the whorl. Spindle whorls acted as stabilizing weights. The two shown here, one flat and circular and the other conical, exemplify the earliest known styles of African ceramic whorls, dating to 7,000 or more years ago in the eastern parts of the Sudan belt.

weaving in the Sudan region between the fifth and the first millennia BCE is something historians have yet to explore, and it is a gap in our knowledge that must be rectified. What is apparent even now, however, is that we can no longer assume that cotton textile technology, which attained such powerful economic importance farther west in Africa in the first and second millennia CE, reached the continent from anywhere else. We have strong reason instead to think that Africans of the northern Middle Nile Basin were the original source of the African versions of this technology.

The Aquatic Tradition of the Sudan, 9000–5500 BCE

Aquatic Food Collecting in the Sudan

If we are tempted to think that farmers and herders have an automatic economic advantage over gatherer-hunter peoples, then the success of an alternative way of life, based on aquatic food collection, all across the southern Sahara after 9000 BCE may give us pause. How did this alternative, quite successful economy arise? Between 11,000 and 9000 BCE in the savannas of the Middle Nile Basin, a number of societies, speaking Nilo-Saharan languages related to Northern Sudanic, found the climatic changes of the time favorable to their existing livelihoods. Unlike their Northern Sudanian kin, who had followed the spread of dry steppe into the southern Sahara, these other Nilo-Saharan peoples had stayed behind in lands that often became more productive for large game. Around and to the south of the confluence of the Nile and the Abbai Rivers, open savanna with scattered deciduous tree cover would have displaced formerly steppe vegetation. There in particular, the population of large gregarious game, including many species of African antelope, zebras, and buffaloes, may have significantly grown after 11,000 BCE. At the same time, increased stream flow in the region probably encouraged a growing attention to riparian resources, such as fish.

Around 9000 BCE this attention to river and lake sources of food gave rise to a powerfully productive new combination of aquatic-based gathering and hunting activities. The origins of this way of life probably lay among the earlier fishing peoples along the middle Nile River—peoples who spoke languages of the Nilo-Saharan family and whose earlier historical roots, like those of the Northern Sudanians, were to be found in the old Middle Nile Tradition. Because of its reliance on waterside food resources, we can call this new livelihood the Aquatic adaptation and call the cultures and societies associated with it the Aquatic Tradition. Taking advantage of the great increase in year-round streams and the numerous lakes created by the further increase in rainfall in the ninth and eighth millennia BCE, Aquatic peoples spread within a period of a several hundred years across more than 5,000 kilometers of Africa. They expanded west as far as the great Bend of the Niger River and the Hoggar Mountains of the east-central Sahara. They followed newly flowing rivers as far southeastward as Lake Turkana in what is today northern Kenya (see map 6).

Up until the mid-seventh millennium BCE, the Aquatic peoples were much more numerous and historically important than the Saharo-Sahelian herders and cultivators, and of the two ways of life, their economy would have been much more successful. The early Sudanic agricultural population densities would have been exceedingly low. To successfully feed a herd of cattle in steppe grassland typically requires many hectares of land per cow, and the areas suitable to early Sudanic cultivation would have been widely scattered. In contrast, the Aquatic communities concentrated around the great number of densely productive wetlands, and archeological findings indicate that they inhabited large encampments in some areas and may have built lasting villages in other areas.

To take a comparative perspective, we can say that the majority of the Nilo-Saharan communities of the ninth millennium BCE took advantage of the great expansion of aquatic environments during the early Holocene wet phase by adopting the Aquatic way of life. The Northern Sudanians began as a divergent minority of Nilo-Saharan communities who responded differently to these same climate changes. They differed because they pioneered a way to better take advantage of the drier and less favored environments away from the streams and lakes.

The Aquatic Tradition: Society and Culture

We understand a good deal about technology and subsistence among the Aquatic peoples and very little as yet about their nonmaterial culture. The Aquatic peoples are known especially for their bone harpoons, with which they speared large fish, such as the Nile perch, and hunted down hippopotamuses. They made a variety of other fishing gear, including probably fish traps and, in some areas, fishhooks formed out of shell. In the Sahara the lands of the

FIG. 10 Bone harpoon point

This implement was an important and typical tool of the Aquatic Tradition of Sudanic civilization. Depicted here is a style of harpoon point made for many centuries in the Middle Nile Basin regions. Typically such a harpoon was 13 centimeters or more in length.

Aquatic societies frequently intertwined with those of the Northern Sudanian agripastoralists, with the Aquatic communities living right along the larger permanent streams and lakes and the cattle raisers occupying the intervening areas away from the major bodies of water.

Most interestingly, the Aquatic peoples participated in the same invention of pottery as their Northern Sudanian neighbors, drawing on the same body of decorative motifs and the same techniques in their own pot making. In early human history, before the rise of stratified economies and specialist pottery makers, the particular decorative motifs and the placement of those motifs in pottery decoration normally were strongly tied to ethnicity. They were expressions of a people's social self-identification, rooted in the cultural history background of the particular society that used that decorative format. If a people adopted the idea of making pottery from someone else, they might keep some of the pot shapes, but they would soon substitute their own decorative arrangements for those of the other society. There is no more powerful indicator of the common historical roots of the Aquatic and early Sudanic agricultural peoples than the fact that they fashioned closely related pottery wares.

Environmental Change, 6500–5500 BCE, and the Spread of Sudanic Agriculture

Around the middle of the seventh millennium BCE, however, a lasting shift in the balance of advantage between the Aquatic economy and the still evolving Sudanic agriculture began to take shape. The fundamental factor in this shift was a 1,000-year interval of distinctly drier climate. Starting around 6700–6500, rainfall totals in many parts of the Sahara and Sudan underwent a period of abrupt decline, known as the Mid-Holocene arid phase. Lakes shrank, and many perennial rivers flowing out of the central Sahara must have changed back into seasonal streams, dry most of the year. Then around 5500 BCE more humid conditions returned; lakes refilled, and many rivers ran all year once again.

But by then the balance of advantage had changed for good. The Aquatic way of life retreated southward with the decline of the lakes and streams, persisting after 6500 BCE principally along the larger permanent rivers, such as the middle Niger and the Nile, and around such remaining lakes as the still quite large Lake Megachad. The Sudanic agriculture, adapted to steppe conditions, expanded in its place. When the second Holocene humid phase took hold in the second half of the sixth millennium BCE, Sudanic cattle raisers spread even more widely all across the Sahara. Other Sudanic farmers, with more even mixes of herding and cultivation, expanded both in the west, reaching as far as the Bend of the Niger, and in the east, where they advanced southward, deep into the Middle Nile Basin. The success of the agricultural economies was enhanced by a broadening of the crop repertoire of Sudanic cultivation. As we have learned, additional crops cultivated in Sudanic agriculture before the end of the sixth millennium included edible gourds, cotton, and possibly pearl millet and watermelons.

Sudanic Civilization: The Intertwining of the Sudanic Agripastoral and the Aquatic Traditions

Even in the ninth millennium BCE, the archeological remains of both the Northern Sudanians and the Aquatic societies can no longer be said to belong to the Middle Nile Tradition. Everyday lives and technology had changed by that point in fundamental ways. The domestication of cattle by the Northern Sudanians, and of grain crops by their Saharo-Sahelian descendants, and the adoption of a new gathering-hunting technocomplex by the Aquatic societies set in motion new directions of cultural change, as did their shared invention of ceramic wares. Together the Northern Sudanians and Aquatic peoples were the fashioners of a new, long-lived African historical tradition, Sudanic civilization. The geographical expansion of the Sudanic farming economy in the sixth millennium only further intertwined this already dual cultural heritage.

But although the Saharo-Sahelian languages between 6500 and 5500 BCE came gradually to prevail across the Sudan belt as far west as the Bend of the Niger, the original Sudanic duality of economies and social patterns did not entirely disappear. Along the middle Nile River, a region for which our exceedingly uneven archeological knowledge is strongest, a modified form of the Aquatic way of life continued to operate into much later times. Village-based societies emerged there in the sixth millennium, supplementing the fishing expertise of the Aquatic background with livestock raising and cultivation. We suspect that similar developments were taking place near the Bend of the Niger and around Lake Megachad. In contrast, away from the major bodies of water, especially in the eastern Sudan, communities mixing livestock raising with varying amounts of cultivation tended to predominate. The most common local political and social unit in such societies may have been the neighborhood of scattered homesteads, each within its thornbush fence, a pattern already characteristic among the original Saharo-Sahelian agripastoralists of the eighth millennium BCE.

On the other hand, a variety of common features took hold everywhere in Sudanic civilization. Most visibly, the building of round houses with conical roofs became the pattern all across the Sudan geographical belt. (Actually, this kind of house construction not only took hold among all the Sudanic societies but eventually spread as well to the Niger-Congo peoples of the savanna zones of West Africa.) The Sudanic monotheistic religion, centered on Divinity, emerged as the generally accepted belief system across nearly all of the Middle Nile Basin and probably among the Sudanic peoples of the Chad Basin as well. None of the early Sudanic peoples practiced either circumcision or clitoridectomy, but they did engage in another notable kind of bodily marking, the extraction in adolescents of the two lower incisor teeth. Unlike circumcision, this trait is visible in the archeological record. When archeologists encounter skeletons lacking the two lower front teeth, they have a useful marker for identifying the sites of Sudanic civilization.

Matrilineal descent was another feature that characterized early Sudanic civilization, of both the Aquatic and Sudanic agripastoral varieties, certainly in the Middle Nile regions and in at least parts of the Chad Basin. Whether this pattern prevailed in the farther west communities of this civilization in the seventh and sixth millennia BCE is less clear. Among most peoples of the Sudanic Tradition, patrilineal social relations replaced matrilineal reckoning of descent and inheritance at some point between the fifth millennium and the present day. Still, matrilineal ideas continued to hold their own in a number of societies in and around the Middle Nile Basin right down to the end of the second millennium CE.

Another practice among peoples of Sudanic civilization that probably dates back to this era was the use of horns both as trumpets and as instruments of warning or announcement. The interesting performance feature of this tradition was that the horns consistently were side-blown instruments. That is, the opening through which a person blew was placed not at the tapering end of the instrument, as in European or Middle Eastern styles of trumpets, but along the side of the horn. We can tell that Sudanic musicians originally fashioned their side-blown trumpets from the horns of animals, such as cows or antelopes, because they gave the wooden and metal trumpets of later eras similarly curved,

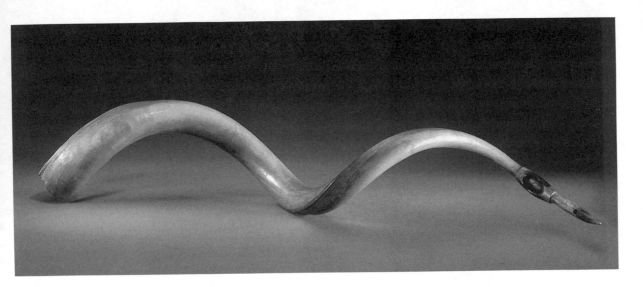

FIG. 11 Kudu horn trumpet

From a very early period, peoples of the Sudanic civilization used animal horns as instruments of warning or public announcement. One instrument of this type, developed probably about 3,000 to 2,000 years ago by certain northern East African peoples of the Sudanic tradition, utilized a hollowed-out horn of the kudu antelope. Note that the player of this trumpet blew into an opening located, not at the tip itself, but distinctively along the side of the instrument. Unlike their Middle Eastern and European counterparts, African trumpets were typically side-blown instruments, whether they were made out of wood, ivory, or actual animal horns. This recent example of a kudu trumpet comes from Southern Nilotic people living in Kenya.

horn-like shapes. The most eye-catching instrument of this type was an extremely long, curving, carved wooden trumpet, sometimes three meters or more in length and called *abu* by the Luo people of the upper Nile regions. Just how ancient this particular variety of horn may be is uncertain, but recent examples of this instrument occur among Sudanic peoples living as far apart as Lake Chad and the western side of Lake Nyanza (Victoria). The widespread use of the *abu* and its relatives suggests that its invention dates back at least several thousand years.

As we see from this historical and cultural summary, the Aquatic peoples did not disappear abruptly from history. Instead, they adopted new Nilo-

Saharan languages, belonging to the Saharan-Sahelian group, and they reformulated the mix of activities they carried out. Over the course of the sixth and fifth millennia BCE, cultivation provided an increasing proportion of daily subsistence everywhere, even in the villages along the Nile and in the Chad Basin. In the flooded savanna and swampland of the far southern Middle Nile Basin, the full Aquatic Tradition, we suspect, may have survived in some places as late as the third millennium BCE. But even there, beyond the direct reach of the expansion of the Sahelian peoples, Sudanic agricultural ideas and practices eventually spread by slow diffusion. At the same time a variety of other cultural elements became part of the common heritage of the Sudan belt of Africa, including such diverse customs as the extracting of the lower incisor teeth, the building of round houses, and the playing of side-blown horns and trumpets.

Inventing Agriculture: The Horn of Africa and the Northern Sahara, 9000–5500 BCE

Animal Domestication among Erythraite Peoples

The economic transformation of the ninth and eighth millennia BCE affected the Erythraites of the Afrasan civilization rather differently than it did the descendants of the Northern Sudanians. Living in the Mediterranean-like climatic conditions of the Red Sea hills, where wild cattle could thrive, the Erythraites may not have moved as quickly as their Northern Sudanian neighbors to full domestication, but rather may have built up their economies around the protecting of wild cows.

By the time the domestication of cattle began to take place, the Erythraites had long before diverged into several distinct peoples. One southern Erythraite society, the ancestral Cushites, came into being in a stretch of country that would have included the southern Red Sea hills and probably the far northern fringe of the Ethiopian Highlands. Several other Erythraite societies evolved among the communities that had previously taken the wild-grain-collecting economy northward into Egypt and the surrounding areas of the eastern Sahara. We can call these peoples collectively the "northern Erythraites."

Beginning about 9000 BCE, some of the northern Erythraite communities expanded farther westward in a movement across the northern Sahara that paralleled the contemporary Sudanian and Aquatic expansions to the south. Archeologists call the material remains of these northern Erythraites the Capsian Tradition. Just as the subsistence culture of the Northern Sudanians was an adaptation to the tropical steppe lands of the southern Sahara, the Capsian culture of the northern Erythraites was an adaptation to the subtropical Mediterranean steppe of the northern half of the Sahara (see map 7).

Another group of northern Erythraite communities, speaking a language ancestral to the later Semitic languages, moved northward at some point across the Sinai Peninsula and into the Palestine-Syria region of far southwestern Asia. Just when this movement of language and culture out of Africa took place is not yet known. One possibility, as we saw in chapter 2, is that the spread of the Mushabian culture from Africa to Palestine-Syria before 11,000 BCE brought about this development.

The extent to which any of the Erythraite societies of the eastern Sahara were involved, along with the Northern Sudanians, in the first domestication of cattle is still unclear. It seems probable that the practice of protecting wild cattle remained prevalent much longer among them than among the Sudanian communities. Farther north, the northern Erythraites may have extended protection to wild animals other than the cow. Among the ancestors of the ancient Egyptians, the early important protected animal may have been the pig. To the north, across the Sinai Peninsula, the Erythraite society whose cultural heirs in much later times were the Semites probably participated, along with their Middle Eastern neighbors, in first the protection and then the domestication of sheep and goats. The earliest speakers of another northern Erythraite group of languages, Chadic, probably lived at the southern fringes of the northern Erythraic speech territories, possibly fairly close to the early Cushites, and they seem initially to have put their emphasis, like the Cushites, on cattle.

These early economic relationships are reflected in part in the history of one key word found already in the ancestral Erythraite language. This word, *ɬoʼ (the letter ɬ sounds a little like *hl*), appears originally to have referred specifically to "cow" or perhaps to "protected animal" in general. In the ancestral Cushitic and Chadic languages it meant simply "cow." In the ancient Egyptian language, in contrast, it became the word for "pig," an animal domesticated in the Mediterranean regions, while in the early Semitic languages it came to mean to "sheep, goat (in general)," the early important domestic animals of the Levant, the lands bordering the eastern shores of the Mediterranean.

After about 7000 BCE the full domestication of cattle may have began to take hold in parts of the northern Sahara regions. Among the Erythraite peoples, who made the Capsian archeological cultures of those areas, domestic cattle were probably present by sometime in the seventh millennium, if not before.

In the southern Red Sea hills, the ancestors of the Cushites may conceivably have taken up cattle raising as early as the ninth or eighth millennium, not much later than their Northern Sudanian neighbors themselves had domesticated the indigenous wild cattle. Unfortunately we lack any archeological evidence from the region, so that remains an urgent topic for future research.

We owe the domestication of still another important animal, the donkey, to the early Erythraite inhabitants of the Red Sea hills region. Donkeys may have been tamed almost as early as cattle. The keeping of donkeys spread before 4000 BCE from Africa into southwestern Asia, where they replaced the onager, a related but difficult to domesticate equine, as the major beast of burden. Donkeys may also have diffused fairly early to some of the Sudanic agripastoralists, but the evidence is less clear on this point.

New Additions to Saharan Livestock Raising: Goats and Sheep

One new and significant addition to agricultural practice traveled in the opposite direction during this period. The raising of sheep and goats spread southward from Asia into northeastern Africa, diffusing across the lines of Erythraite cultural expansion. These two animals owe their domestication to a second independent invention of food production, in southwest Asia between 9500 and 8500 BCE, at about the same time as or slightly earlier than the Erythraite and Northern Sudanic domestication of cattle. The peoples of the western Asian center of agricultural invention followed a course of agricultural development broadly parallel to that seen in northeastern Africa. Like the Northern Sudanians, they domesticated animals, in their case the goat and the sheep, after 9000 BCE, while between 10,000 and 8000 BCE they brought under cultivation two formerly wild grains, wheat and barley, both belonging to their own Mediterranean subtropical flora.

Goats and/or sheep (archeologists often have trouble distinguishing their bones) may first appear in the African archeological record around 7000 BCE in sites of the Capsian Tradition and then between 7000 and 6000 BCE in some of the eastern sites of the Sudanic agripastoralists. The language evidence on sheep and goats agrees with the archeology and gives us additional information for regions not yet given adequate archeological exploration. The words used for the two animals in the Northern Sudanic languages tell us that both goats and sheep arrived in the southeastern Sahara only after the Saharo-Sahelian farmers had spread as far west as the central Sahara. Some of that language evidence is fairly specific in its implications. The two key words for "goat" in the

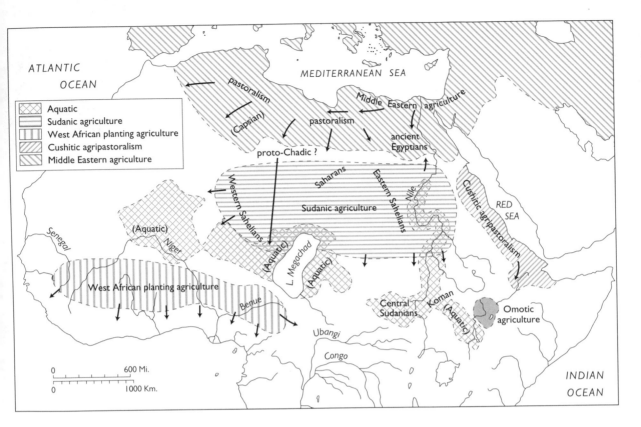

MAP 7 African agriculture, ca. 5500 BCE

Sahelian branch of the Saharo-Sahelian languages, *ay* and *nay*, are of Cushitic origin. In contrast, the word *tam*, "sheep," in the Saharan branch of Saharo-Sahelian came from an early form of the proto-Chadic language. Proto-Chadic, which is discussed below, was probably one of the northern Erythraite languages spoken by the peoples of the Capsian Tradition.

Taken as a whole, the different kinds of evidence indicate that sheep and goats spread through Sinai into Africa by or before 7000 BCE, first to far northeasterly groups of the northern Erythraite peoples. From there they diffused south down the Red Sea hills to the early Cushites and west across the northern Sahara to the Capsian peoples. These communities spoke languages ancestral to those of the Chadic and the Berber peoples of later historical eras. Sometime after 7000 BCE, the keeping of goats and sheep passed from the Cushites to the eastern Saharo-Sahelian communities and from the Capsian peoples to the western Saharo-Sahelian groups.

New Cultural and Economic Expansions: The Cushites

The full establishment of livestock-raising economies set off new population movements among some of the Erythraites. Many of the Cushites, now herders of goats and sheep as well as cattle, expanded southward into the northern and northeastern parts of the Ethiopian Highlands in the seventh or sixth millennium BCE. One branch, the Northern Cushites, continued to inhabit the southern Red Sea hills; their latter-day descendants are the Beja people of that region. But a number of distinct Cushitic societies took shape among those who spread into the northern Horn of Africa.

The history of these southern Erythraites provides an intriguing example of the spread of religion without the existence of either missionaries or religious writings. The religious beliefs of the proto-Cushites, probably as early as the seventh millennium BCE, came to blend two distinct religious traditions. The Cushitic system of clans with clan priest-chiefs, the *wap'er*, which derived from their ancient Afrasan cultural roots, still persisted as the basis of social loyalty and cooperation among the proto-Cushites, but the belief in a clan deity lost its salience. In its place, and no doubt as a result of their long association with the Northern Sudanic peoples to their immediate east, the early Cushites adopted the Sudanic concept of Divinity. They chose their own word for the new concept of spirit, expanding the meaning of the old Cushitic root word *waak'a* for "sky" to apply to both "sky" and "Divinity." The *wap'er* still had religious duties, but these duties came to be redirected toward Divinity. The Cushites retained the old Afrasan practice of attributing bad happenings to dangerous spirits, although they now sometimes also viewed evil as a Divine retribution.

New Cultural and Economic Expansions: The Chadic Peoples

A second major expansion of Erythraite peoples took place far to the west, in the Chad Basin, as early as the sixth millennium BCE. There the proto-Chadic society—who were by then the raisers, too, of cattle, sheep, and goats—extended their grazing lands southward through the central Sahara and into the Lake Chad Basin. The timing of this development suggests that it followed the Mid-Holocene arid phase of 6700–5500 BCE and the westward expansion of Sudanic agriculture.

As a result the proto-Chadic people assimilated goodly numbers of the Sudanic farmers and herders into their society and adopted the Sudanic agriculture as their own. We lack as yet the confirmatory archeology of this history, but the language evidence, consisting of the Chadic borrowing of even such a basic Saharo-Sahelian term as the word for "elephant" (proto-Chadic *g^yəwan* from old Nilo-Saharan *kowon*), shows us that the Chadic expansion must have incorporated many erstwhile Saharo-Sahelian peoples. The Chadic communities may have made one notable contribution all their own, the introduction of the donkey.

But what of the wider aspects of culture? Did Chadic peoples contribute new ideas to Sudanic civilization in other areas? Did they form a separate cultural tradition of their own? On the whole, the answers seem to be, first, that the Chadic societies adopted more from the Sudanic people than they gave, especially in agriculture and technology, but, second, that their social and political institutions long remained distinctive from those of Sudanic civilization. We will encounter Chadic peoples again in the events of the most recent 2,000 years of African history, but Chadic history between the sixth and first millennia BCE remains as yet unstudied by historians.

Agricultural Invention: Enset Agriculture in the Horn

A third independent invention of crop cultivation in Africa arose among certain Southern Afrasan communities of the Ethiopian Highlands, possibly as early as 6500–5500 BCE. A long sequence of historical developments, about which we have only the sparsest of information, lay behind the creation there of a distinctively different kind of agricultural economy, based on the raising of the enset plant. With the rise in rainfall after 11,000 BCE, tree cover spread over most of the highlands, gradually turning many former grassland areas into montane forest. As a result, probably even before 9000 BCE, many of the Southern Afrasan communities of the highlands, which had previously been collectors of wild grains, would have faced a declining ability to feed themselves. But somewhere in the region—we do not know exactly where—there resided a community or a set of communities that came across a truly different idea for obtaining food.

The resource they utilized to cope with the growing food crisis was not grain, not a tuber or root, not a seed or fruit, and not even the leafy greens of plants. They discovered instead that the interior part of the stem and the bulb of a certain large wild plant, when pounded up and cooked, provided a large and reliable supply of carbohydrates, the basic stuff of the diet—bland, it is true, but sufficiently nourishing and tasty when prepared with oils and condiments. This plant was the enset, which grows to a height of as much as five meters, looks almost exactly like a banana plant, and, in fact, is a relative of it. But unlike the banana, enset does not have a tasty fruit, only an edible inner stalk and bulb.

The further increase in rainfall between 9000 and 7000 BCE spread montane forest still more widely across the Ethiopian Highlands, with grassland areas probably persisting only along the northern and eastern fringes of the region. Now that the collection of wild grains was no longer a viable way of life in most highland areas, the reliance on enset may have begun to spread to most of the region. But we simply know too little at present about this time period in the Horn of Africa to be sure even of that.

Then, sometime in about the seventh or sixth millennium, one of the Southern Afrasan peoples, whom we call the proto-Omotic society, took a further major step. They turned to the deliberate cultivation of the enset plant. We do not know yet just what precipitated this shift in economy. One plausible explanation is that proto-Omotic people began the deliberate protection and nurturing of certain plants, among them the enset, in response to the modest decline of rainfall in their areas, occasioned by the Mid-Holocene arid phase of the seventh and sixth millennia. Enset quickly became the staple of the emerg-

FIG. 12 Enset

This drawing by the eighteenth-century traveler James Bruce depicts the above-ground portions of the plant. The Omotic peoples used the bulb and part of the inner stalk of the enset as food.

ing Omotic agriculture. Another early Omotic crop, of little importance today, may have been the Ethiopian species of the yam.

The origins of the proto-Omotic people appear to lie far to the south in the Ethiopian Highlands. Over the period of the sixth to fourth millennia BCE their descendants and cultural heirs expanded northward, spreading the enset agriculture and the Omotic languages widely across the southern, central, and north-central parts of the highlands.

Agricultural Invention: West African Planting Agriculture, 9000–5500 BCE

To the south of the Sahara, African peoples found other innovative ways to respond to the climatic shifts that emerged by 11,000 BCE. None of these at first entailed the adoption of agriculture but were instead approaches that enhanced the productivity of the wild environment.

In West Africa a variety of consequences was set in motion by the increased rainfall between 11,500 and 8000 BCE. All across a 300- to 400-kilometer-wide zone extending inland from the Atlantic coast, from Senegambia in the west to Cameroon in the east, woodland savanna was replaced by expanding rainforest. In Cameroon the spread of the West African forest zone connected up with the newly expanding equatorial rainforest of central Africa. The woodland savanna belt shifted northward into the previously open savanna areas of the southern Djouf Basin. In addition, stream flow increased, and more rivers than before ran year round.

The shift to still wetter climate in West Africa during and after the ninth millennium BCE had different effects in different areas. Increased river flow enhanced the possibilities for fishing, and the northward advance of woodland savanna opened up new areas favorable to yams. At the same time, however, many areas nearer the coast that were previously covered by moist woodland savanna began to be swallowed up by the expanding rainforest, in which there was too little direct sunlight to support the particular yam species favored by the Niger-Congo peoples.

But it was also the period in West African history in which a new African agriculture was invented. We do not know yet when some of the Niger-Congo communities commenced the shift to deliberate cultivation of yams, nor exactly where. The most probable answer is that the changeover began sometime around 8000 BCE and that the locales of the first yam agriculture lay in intermediate parts of the West African woodland savanna zone—in areas where the abundance of wild yams had declined with the spread of woodland conditions, but where a farmer's efforts in preparing the ground and planting and protecting the growing plants could effectively reverse that decline.

We can call this new and independent invention "West African planting agriculture," from the fact that the farmers reproduced their *staple* (most important) crops, the different types of West African yam, not by sowing seed, but by *planting* a part of the yam itself back in the ground. These early West African farmers by no means restricted their agricultural experimentation, however, to just yams. They domesticated one animal, the guineafowl, at probably an early stage in their development of food production. From an early period they also tended two tree crops, the oil palm and the raffia palm. The oil palm provided cooking oil from its nuts as well as palm wine from its sap; the raffia palm was another source of palm wine, and by the fourth or third millennium BCE its fibers had become highly valued by West Africans for the weaving of raffia cloth. In the woodland savannas of modern-day Nigeria and Cameroon, Niger-Congo communities brought under cultivation two major food plants grown from seed, black-eyed peas and voandzeia (an African groundnut), probably as

FIG. 13 Dance costume made from raffia fiber

This particular example, from the Ibibio people of southeastern Nigeria, reflects an old way of using raffia cloth among Niger-Congo societies.

early as the sixth and fifth millennia. Okra was still another quite early crop of Niger-Congo farmers, while the kola nut, a tree crop of the West African rainforest, became important later, in the last 3000 years BCE. The inventors of this agriculture, by the way, were women, who in pre-agricultural eras had borne the chief responsibility for the collecting of wild yams and other wild plant foods.

Gradually an important new development in technology took hold along with the new economy. Niger-Congo peoples began to make polished stone axes, in this way becoming able to effectively clear patches of woodlands and grow their sunlight-requiring yams and oil palms in more and more areas.

Livelihood and Culture History in Africa, 5500–3500 BCE

Themes in Society and Economy

The most important themes in the history of Africa between about 5500 and 3500 BCE revolve around the consolidation, elaboration, and spread of the several African agricultures. Everywhere that farming livelihoods took hold the human population began to grow, and the peoples who put these new modes of subsistence into practice began not only to grow in numbers but also to spread their cultures and languages widely across new territories. On the western side of the continent, the consolidation of the West African planting agriculture and new developments in stone tool technology set in motion new expansions of Niger-Congo peoples in West Africa, first across the whole of the woodland savanna belt and then southward into rainforest environments. In the drier zones to the north of the woodland savannas, the herders and cultivators who spoke the Saharo-Sahelian languages gradually built up the complexity of their Sudanic seed agriculture, both by domesticating more indigenous crops and by adding new kinds of domestic animals. At the same time, they embarked on expansions into a variety of new areas. In the Horn of Africa, notable new agricultural developments also took place, among them the creation of a third independent African agricultural system by the Omotic peoples of the Afrasan civilization.

But that was by no means all that took place between 5500 and 3500 BCE. In many areas, as new crops and animals were added to the existing agriculture, a growing proportion of the diet began to come from domesticated sources of food. In addition, a number of crops and animals that had originated in one or another of the African agricultures now spread to peoples practicing other farming systems, thus further contributing to agricultural elaboration. People in most areas grew more and more reliant on agricultural foods and less and less able to make due with wild foods if their crops or herds failed.

North of the middle of the Sahara, a more mixed picture of the history of agricultural change emerges. The northern Erythraites of those regions, who had earlier adopted the raising of goats, sheep, and cattle, began to combine herding with a cultivating system that had originated outside the continent. The Mediterranean climate of the northern regions, with its cool season rainfall, was not suited to the African grain crops of the Sudanic agriculture. In consequence, when cultivation first reached the far northern Sahara in the later 6000s BCE, its most important crops came not from the Sudanic cultivators to the south but from the Middle East. A Mediterranean variety of the Middle Eastern agriculture, with wheat and barley as its staples, emerged by the fifth and fourth millennia BCE among the descendants of the Capsian northern Erythraites.

Because of these varied and complex developments, by 3500 BCE most of Africa north of 5 degrees north latitude came to be affected to one extent or another by the arrival of cultivated crops and domesticated animals. Only south of that latitude did gatherer-hunter societies still remain undisturbed in their ways by the burgeoning shift to food production farther north.

Eastern Sahelian Peoples in the Middle Nile Basin

In the Middle Nile Basin, Sudanic agriculture spread southward after 5500 BCE, both east and west of the Nile. Peoples whose languages belonged to the Eastern Sahelian subgroup of the Saharo-Sahelians quickly emerged as the most prominent actors in the new southward spread of agripastoral pursuits. Over the sixth and fifth millennia, their descendants expanded progressively southward all across the central parts of the modern-day nation of Sudan, absorbing and assimilating formerly Aquatic peoples into their societies. Their farthest south outliers, by the fourth and third millennia, had reached the northern-most edges of East Africa.

In several parts of the Middle Nile Basin, the societies still dependent on food collecting lived in areas far enough away from the advancing Eastern Sahelian agripastoral peoples that they avoided being absorbed into those expanding communities. They were able to adopt the ways and means of food production in a less direct manner, through diffusion from the Eastern Sahelians. Readapting in this way to the new historical circumstances of the age, such societies began also to be able to grow in numbers and expand their territories and to withstand the competition of the Eastern Sahelians for the resources of the land.

Among such peoples of the Middle Nile Basin, the most notable for the course of later Eastern African history were the proto–Central Sudanians. Their lands in the fifth millennium BCE lay to the immediate south of the Bahr-al-Ghazal flood basin in the modern far southern Sudan Republic. The vocabulary evidence strongly intimates that proto–Central Sudanians descended from practitioners of the food-collecting Aquatic Tradition. Their possession of a root word *we for "harpoon," the typical instrument of the Aquatic economy, is an especially telling indicator of this kind of subsistence emphasis. The early Central Sudanians were probably matrilineal in their social organization. Although most Central Sudanic societies of more recent times have been strongly patrilineal, the oldest root word we can yet reconstruct in the Central Sudanic languages for "clan," *d'i, seems originally to have referred specifically to a matriclan.

Perhaps sheltered from direct early Eastern Sahelian agricultural impact by the then perennial wetlands of the Bahr-al-Ghazal and by tsetse-fly-infested areas, the proto–Central Sudanians were able to adapt slowly to the new ideas between about 5000 and 3500 BCE. They soon made the practices of grain cultivation into major elements of their own heritage. At the same time, they remained strongly committed to fishing and appear to have taken up the serious raising of goats and cows only gradually. Most Central Sudanians continued to reside in the Bahr-al-Ghazal region until much later. But one group, the early East Central Sudanian communities, moved south with their now mixed gathering, hunting, fishing, cultivating, and herding economy, into the lands immediately along the northern parts of the great Western Rift, possibly as early as 3500 BCE (see map 8).

The Cushitic Agripastoral Tradition

The period around the seventh millennium BCE marked the first spread, attested to linguistically but not as yet known archeologically, of another descendant grouping of the Afrasan Erythraite peoples, the Cushites, southward into the northern edges of the Ethiopian Highlands. From there various subdivisions of the Cushites pressed farther southward in the sixth and fifth millennia, into the north-central and eastern sides of the highlands. By the fourth millennium, two major long-term developments had overtaken the participants in this history.

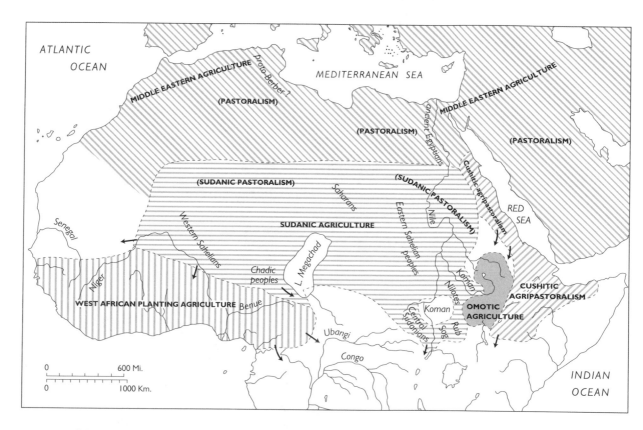

MAP 8 African agriculture, ca. 3500 BCE

One development was the Cushitic contribution of a fourth independent African cultivating tradition. As early as the sixth millennium BCE, the Cushites who moved into grasslands of Eritrea may have begun to switch from supplementing their diet with wild-grain collection to the deliberate cultivation of two indigenous highland grains, t'ef and finger millet. There is no reason to attribute the emergence of this core cultivating feature of the Cushitic agripastoral tradition to stimulus diffusion from either the Middle Eastern or the Sudanic agriculturists. Its vocabulary is entirely Cushitic, including notably the old Cushitic words *tankaws-* for "finger millet" and *tl'eff-* for "t'ef." The Mid-Holocene arid phase, 6700–5500 BCE, expanded the grassy areas and shrank the montane forest in the northern Ethiopian Highlands and along the Ethiopian Rift Valley. Perhaps the spread of grassland increased the attractiveness of grain cultivation for the Cushites. Alternatively, the decline of the wild grain resources, with the return to wetter conditions after 5500, may have been what pushed the Cushites toward cultivation.

The second long-term development was the spread, by stages between 5500 and 3500 BCE, of Cushitic peoples and cultures into all but the central and southwestern portions of the Ethiopian Highlands. As the Cushites expanded, they absorbed many of the former Omotic peoples into their societies. In parts of southern and south-central Ethiopia, these developments encouraged the incipient emergence of a new, more complex agricultural synthesis, which combined the raising of the enset of the Omotic agriculture with the grain crops and the domestic animals of the Cushites (see map 8).

Planting Agriculture Spreads into the West African Rainforest

Still another region of agricultural expansion in the period 5500–3500 BCE lay far to the west. There the West African planting agricultural tradition commenced spreading by about the fifth millennium BCE into the belt of rainforest that occupies the hinterlands of West Africa's Atlantic coast. A new expansion of Niger-Congo cultivating peoples into the forest set in motion this era of change. In the archeological record from modern-day southern Côte d'Ivoire

FIG. 14 Polished stone axes

The examples of this early West African Neolithic technology shown here come from sites in the modern-day countries of Ghana and Benin.

in the west to southern Cameroon in the east, this set of developments is revealed in the appearance of the new kind of Niger-Congo tool, the polished stone ax. Stone axes provided the means by which the incoming farmers could reshape the rainforest environment, specifically by cutting the trees and making the sunlit clearings required for the growing of yams and the tending of oil palms. During this same broad period of time, the manufacturing of pottery spread south from the Sudan belt and became a basic part of the technology of Niger-Congo peoples. Everywhere in these regions women seem to have been the early potters.

The particular Niger-Congo peoples who accounted for the agricultural settlement of the central and eastern parts of the West African rainforest and the Atlantic coast belonged to a group of peoples we call the Benue-Kwa. A number of societies notable in the recent centuries of African history, such as the Yoruba, Igbo, and Akan—societies to which many African Americans can trace their ancestry—are descendants of the Benue-Kwa settlers of the rainforest belt of the fifth millennium BCE (see map 8). The Bantu peoples, who carried the ideas of Niger-Congo civilization into the equatorial forest from the fourth millennium BCE onward (see chapter 4), also originated as an offshoot of the Benue-Kwa.

With these expansions of Niger-Congo-speaking peoples came the spread as well of a particular version of the Niger-Congo civilization into the West African rainforest. The early Benue-Kwa communities brought with them many of the older characteristic traits of the Niger-Congo culture: musical performance involving polyrhythms and drums, a religion centered on ancestor veneration and territorial spirits, and the ancient traditions of sculpture in wood and mask making. They were boat builders and fishing people and characteristically lived in single-street villages of rectangular, ridge-roofed houses with woven palm roofs. In those times they were still all matrilineal, with inheritance of goods or position coming through one's mother, not one's father. Clan chiefs, called *kumu,* of a religious but not as yet truly political kind existed among them, and the influence of such a priest-chief must rarely have extended beyond one or two villages.

Independence and Interconnection in Agricultural Invention

Although separate and distinctive in their inventions of cultivation, the Sudanian, Cushitic, and Niger-Congo worlds did not lack for elements of historical interconnection.

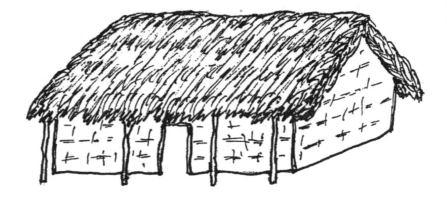

FIG. 15 Ridge-roofed rectangular house

Different varieties of this style of house have been built for probably the past 6,000 years or more by Benue-Kwa peoples of the Niger-Congo civilization.

At its onset more than 10,000 years ago, the keeping of cattle in northeastern Africa probably was a development shared between Cushites and Northern Sudanians, even if contributory in separate fashions to the growth and expansion of each set of peoples. The domestication of cattle, moreover, took place there first in all the world. From outside of northeastern Africa, goats and sheep arrived later, by about the seventh millennium, and were added onto the Sudanic and Cushitic agripastoral economies. At about the same period, the keeping of donkeys, domesticated probably by Cushites in the southern Red Sea hills, gradually became more widely practiced and spread northward toward the Middle East.

Among the Niger-Congo peoples in West Africa, the effects of the diffusion of agricultural items from one region to another made themselves felt in both similar and different ways. The raising of goats spread still farther south and began to be taken up by many of the Niger-Congo peoples as early as 6000 to 5000 BCE, and cattle became known in at least some of the Niger-Congo areas just as early. By 4000 BCE, more and more Niger-Congo communities, especially in the regions of modern-day Nigeria, were also beginning to adopt gourds from their Nilo-Saharan and Chadic neighbors to the north, even as their own crops, black-eyed peas and voandzeia, spread the opposite direction. By probably the later fourth millennium BCE these two crops could be found widely all across the Sudan belt of Africa.

Themes in the History of Culture, 9000–3500 BCE

Several notable developments in culture, belief, and the organization of society spread between civilizations during the founding eras of agriculture in Africa. The most notable regions for this kind of change lay in northeastern and Saharan Africa.

Developments in the History of Religion

One especially intriguing early development was the spread of the idea of a single Divinity or God, symbolically associated with the sky, from the Saharo-Sahelian peoples to their eastern neighbors, the Cushites of the southern Red Sea hills and the far northern Ethiopian Highlands. The Cushites did not discard the old Afrasan explanation of dangerous spirits as the principal cause of evil, but they did drop their earlier allegiances to clan deities in favor of a belief in one Divinity. The earliest Cushitic name for Divinity that has come down to us is *Waak'a. The *wap'er continued to be the central religious figure in the still clan-based societies of the Cushites, but as a mediator between the society and *Waak'a, rather than between the clan and its deity. Dating to sometime in the eighth or seventh millennium BCE, the Cushitic blending of the Sudanic concept of Divinity with beliefs drawn from their earlier Afrasan religion is the earliest instance of religious syncretism yet known in world history.

The fascinating thing about this historical episode is what it tells us about how religion can spread. In earlier ages, clearly religious ideas could diffuse from one set of peoples to another without the written texts or formal missionary activity that has seemed so essential to the establishment of the major religions of recent history. Just how and why the idea of Divinity struck a responsive chord in the Cushites of those long-ago times is something we do not yet know, and may never. Interestingly, this kind of religious belief did not penetrate beyond the Cushites into the Omotic parts of the Ethiopian Highlands. The old henotheistic Afrasan religion of clan deities in very much its original form continued to hold the allegiance of the Omotic peoples for several thousand years to come.

Cultural Interactions in the Middle Nile Basin

Another major area of the blending of cultural backgrounds lay in the Middle Nile Basin and the Sahel zone of the southern Sahara. The latest of the early

African civilizations we describe here, the Sudanic, took shape during three millennia of close interactions between two widespread sets of the peoples—the Nilo-Saharan-speaking Northern Sudanian and Saharo-Sahelian peoples, with their Sudanic agriculture, and the probably Nilo-Saharan-speaking societies of the Aquatic Tradition. Their common historical background is evident in their making of related styles of pottery between 9000 and 7000 BCE. The culminating stage of the emergence of a common Sudanic civilization fell between 6500 and 5500. During this time the Saharo-Sahelian peoples, in response to the environmental opportunities opened up by the first period of declining rainfall, spread their agripastoral economy and their languages more widely southward and westward across the Sudan belt.

The duality of origins for the Sudanic cultural tradition never completely disappeared from history. Despite sharing many of the most fundamental features of culture, such as the monotheistic Sudanic religion with its focus on Divinity, the peoples of the Sudanic civilization followed two diverging tendencies in several areas of culture, notably in their political and residential patterns. One variety of Sudanic society, with its earlier roots probably in the Aquatic Tradition, has tended to live in villages and give political allegiance to what we call Sudanic sacral chiefs or sacral kings. Many of the early large kingdoms of the Sudan drew inspiration from this side of the Sudanic Tradition. Peoples of the second tendency have resided down through history in neighborhoods of scattered homesteads and have usually had no chiefs at all, instead relying on the small-scale democracy of the neighborhood meeting of adults. The Nilotes, of whom we will have more to say in later chapters, are the best known example of this variety of Sudanic civilization.

Sudanic Influence on Egypt

Most interesting of all, there arose during the period of the sixth to fourth millennia BCE an influential new zone of cultural interchange between the different African civilizations. Its heartland lay in the northern Middle Nile Basin, inhabited by Saharo-Sahelian peoples, and so we call it the Middle Nile Culture Area. But its cultural reach extended northward down the Nile into predynastic Egypt. To understand the consequences of this era of cultural interaction for the origins of ancient Egypt—and to do justice to the seminal contributions of the Saharo-Sahelians—we need to turn our attention back in time, to the long historical interplay out of which Egyptian culture gradually developed.

Over the long run of northeastern African history, what emerges most strongly is the extent to which ancient Egypt's culture grew from sub-Saharan African roots. The earliest foundations of the culture that was to evolve into that of dynastic Egypt were laid, as we have already discovered, by Afrasan immigrants from the general direction of the southern Red Sea hills, who arrived probably well before 10,000 BCE. The new inhabitants brought with them a language directly ancestral to ancient Egyptian. They introduced to Egypt the idea of using wild grasses or grains as food. They also introduced a new religion. Its central belief, in the efficacy of clan deities, explains the traceability of the ancient Egyptian gods to different particular Egyptian localities: originally they were the deities of the local communities, whose members in still earlier times had belonged to a clan or a group of related clans.

In later times, from roughly the seventh to the fifth millennium, the now Afrasan-speaking population of Egypt faced two directions in its acquisition of agriculture. Because of their suitable soils and their dry Mediterranean climate, the pre-dynastic Egyptians adopted two staple crops, wheat and barley, and the use of the plow under influences stemming from the ancient Middle Eastern center of agricultural invention, with its similarly Mediterranean climate. During the same period, however, they gained two animals—the cow, of *major* cultural importance, and the donkey—and several secondary crops, including gourds and watermelons, from the Sudanic agriculture of the Saharo-Sahelians to their south.

By the sixth or fifth millennium, Egypt began to be drawn into the Middle Nile Culture Area of its southern neighbors, the Eastern Sahelian peoples. Already in the fifth and early fourth millennia, new fluctuations in climate began to push more of the human population of the eastern Sahara into areas with good access to the waters of the Nile, and along the Nile itself the bottomlands began for the first time to be cleared and farmed. In the changing climatic situation of the times, the river increasingly became a line of cultural linkage between far-flung areas.

From the Middle Nile Culture Area, Egypt gained, during the centuries before 3500 BCE, new items of livelihood other than just crops and animals. One of these new adoptions was a kind of cattle pen. Its Egyptian name *s3* (earlier **sr*) can be derived from the Eastern Sahelian term **sar* for the pen's thornbush fence, indicating that the word referred to the old Saharo-Sahelian style of cattle pen. The Egyptian word *pg3*, "bowl," a borrowing of Nilo-Saharan **pokur*, "wooden bowl or trough," reveals still another adoption in material culture that most probably belongs to this era. The ties of Egypt to its southern neighbors are evident, too, in the archeology, which shows that, in the fourth millennium BCE, a string of mutually interacting cultures extended along the Nile southward from southern Egypt for an as yet unknown distance into the Middle Nile Basin.

One key feature of classical Egyptian political culture, often assumed to have begun in Egypt, can be strongly linked to the southern influences of this period. We refer here to Sudanic sacral chiefship, which entailed, in its earliest versions, one especially salient custom, the sending of servants into the afterlife along with the deceased chief. The roots of later Egyptian "divine" kingship lay in this Sudanic innovation. If we were able to travel back in time to visit the areas along the middle Nile and Egypt in 3500 BCE, we would discover there a long-extended region of sacral chiefdoms and tiny sacral kingdoms. This long belt of small polities would have encompassed both the Eastern Sahelian communities to the south along the river and their southernmost Egyptian-speaking neighbors on the north.

Persistent Gatherer-Hunters: The Southern Third of Africa

Historians know much less as yet about the southern third of Africa between 6000 and 3500 BCE. Across those regions a number of much older gathering and hunting cultural traditions prevailed. The southern parts of Africa thus held much the same kind of relation to developments elsewhere in the continent that farther northern and northwestern Europe and northern Asia held to events in the rest of the Eurasian land mass. They were areas where the agricultural transformation arrived late, where highly successful food collecting adaptations could long hold their own (see maps 7 and 8).

All across the Congo Basin lived the BaTwa peoples (commonly called "Pygmies" by Westerners). Next to nothing is known about them before the third millennium. They had their own distinctive musical tradition, with flutes and whistles as their important musical instruments and with styles of dance that emphasized footwork. Just how they carried on their gathering and hunting activities before they entered trade relations in the third millennium with incoming Bantu farmers, a topic for the next chapter, remains to be studied by historians and archeologists. The eastern outliers of BaTwa culture reached into the then heavily forested lands of present-day Rwanda and Burundi.

Through most of the rest of eastern Africa, the Khoisan Tradition predominated. The two exceptions to this pattern lay along the shores of Lake Turkana, where the Aquatic civilization took root after 8000 BCE and lingered on until the fourth millennium, and in the Kenya Highlands, where the distinctive gatherer-hunter communities of the mountain forests, the Eburrans, continued to persist right through the period. We do yet not know what the wider cultural connections of this particular group of peoples might have been. The Eburrans began, though, to come under a strong and long-lasting Khoisan influence, evident in their gradual adoption of more and more tools of the Eastern African Microlithic kind well before 3500.

The Khoisan civilization, about which we know much more, entered into a new period of expansion in southern Africa at around the seventh millennium BCE. In the archeology this development shows up in the spread of what archeologists call the Wilton culture, an offshoot of the old Eastern African Microlithic Tradition of the Khoisan peoples. The expansion of Wilton culture took in most of far southern Africa, from southern Mozambique on the east to Namibia on the west. It brought an end to the Albany culture and its emphasis on the hunting of large game. In its place, the Wilton culture introduced the eclectic gathering and hunting practices and the microlithic tools of the Eastern African Microlithic, previously not found farther south than Zimbabwe (see maps 6–8).

On the whole this expansion of culture must have had only a minor demographic impact. The older populations of southern Africa adopted a new kind of tool kit and a new set of food-collecting practices, and they took up Khoisan languages in place of their earlier languages (no evidence remains of what the relationships of those previous languages were) and many of the culture features of the Khoisan Tradition.

But their descendants continued to practice an ancient rock art tradition, the finest and longest-lived such art in the world. The oldest known rock paintings in southern Africa date to 26,000 years ago; the most recent, to the last few centuries. In contrast, until recent discoveries in France, the earliest Paleolithic cave paintings known from Europe were made barely over 20,000 years ago. The southern African paintings tended as well to be finer work than their European counterparts, better conveying movement and perspective. The 32,000-year-old cave paintings discovered in the 1990s in southern France finally provide us with European examples of rock art that are on a par in quality with those found in ancient southern Africa, similarly able to show movement and perspective. (As an exercise in looking at the world from a different perspective, readers might want to ask themselves why Western newspapers and other media gave so much coverage in 1995 to the newly discovered European cave paintings. Why do we hear nothing about the ancient southern African rock art?)

Africa 9000–3500 BCE in the Context of World History

The parallels between the courses of change in Africa in the period 9000–3500 BCE and contemporary developments elsewhere in the world are striking. The key factors, which even then had begun to set in motion a fundamental redirection of the overall trajectory of human history, were the several independent inventions of food production in different parts of the world. In these developments Africans, as we have seen, were major players.

The three earliest agricultures anywhere in the world emerged between 9500 and 8000 BCE in three distinct parts of the Eastern Hemisphere. One of these was African; it originated among the Northern Sudanian peoples and perhaps secondarily among the southern Erythraic ancestors of the Cushites. A second agriculture was located in southwest Asia. Its originators probably spoke languages of one of the Caucasic families, but later on the ancestors of the Semites took up this particular economy, too. The third agriculture came into being in southern East Asia; its makers spoke languages belonging to the Austronesian and probably other branches of the Austric macro-family.

One of the three earliest agricultures, contrary to what scholars used to think, began with the domestication of a wild animal. In the eastern Sahara, that animal was the cow. The Saharo-Sahelian descendants of the Northern Sudanian cattle raisers cultivated sorghum, apparently before the end of the eighth millennium. In southwestern Asia, in contrast, cultivation of crops, wheat and barley, came first, in the tenth millennium, with the raising of goats and sheep dating a thousand or more years later. In southern East Asia, rice and perhaps Asian yams and later bananas are believed to be among the early cultivated crops. The DNA evidence suggests that chickens were the early domestic animal of southeast Asia; whether it was domesticated as early as the first plant cultivation is unclear, but it may have been just as early.

Between 8000 and 5000 BCE, a variety of other regions entered into the history of plant and animal domestication. Three of these new centers of agricultural innovation lay in Africa, two of them in the Horn of Africa. The Cushites of the drier northern Horn, already heirs to the eastern Saharan domestication of cattle, began between about 6000 and 5000, we believe, to cultivate two highland Ethiopian grains, t'ef and finger millet. In the forested zones of the central and southern Ethiopian Highlands, an entirely different kind of agriculture, based on the enset plant, took hold among Omotic peoples by perhaps around the sixth millennium BCE. Far across the continent, in the woodland savanna belt of West Africa, a third agriculture of still different inspiration arose among Niger-Congo peoples. This agriculture, the West African planting tradition, evolved possibly as early as 8000 and surely before 6000 BCE.

Food production may have had an independent inception in up to six other regions of the world as well. As many as three separate inventions of agriculture can be traced in the Western Hemisphere. The earliest was initiated by the domestication of pumpkins and chilies in northeastern Mexico at around the eighth millennium. The heartland of this agriculture shifted southward by about the sixth millennium, when maize (corn) and beans were brought into cultivation in the better watered southern Mexican and northern Central American region. A second American agriculture was invented in the Andean highlands. Its key early crop was potatoes, and it was there that the most notable domestic animal of the Americas, the llama, was raised. A third center of agricultural invention may have been in the tropical lowlands of South America, with manioc and American yams as major crops. Two other early centers of agriculture can be proposed for eastern parts of Asia, one in north China, based on millet, and the other on the island of New Guinea. It also now appears possible that food production began separately, too, in India, with an independent domestication there of the zebu type of cattle as early as the eighth or seventh millennium BCE.

The powerful lesson we learn from this information is that we can no longer view southwestern Asia as the central shaper of the directions of history that lead down to our world of today. The Middle East, so long treated by scholars as if unique and seminal for world agricultural origins, was in fact just one of at least seven and possibly ten or more independent centers of agricultural invention that arose between 9500 and 5000 BCE, scattered across distant parts of the globe. A large number of peoples in different parts of the world created the basic economic underpinnings—the different kinds of agriculture—that led to the growth of population and the expansion of the various cultural traditions responsible for those new directions of historical change.

Sub-Saharan Africans were key instigators. Four separate systems of crop cultivation arose in that one continent. Just one such system emerged in the Middle East, and none at all in Europe. Agriculture reached Europe only later, from the Middle East. Some African crops, most notably sorghum, eventually became important all over the world, and many other plants, such as watermelons, black-eyed peas, gourds, and okra, have gained wide use as secondary crops. One African animal, the donkey, spread early to Asia and played an essential role in communications and transport in the early urban societies of southwestern Asia in the fifth to third millennia BCE.

Even more notably, a still more ancient, wholly African invention—a set of techniques and tools for using wild grasses for food—dates to around 16,000–13,000 BCE and laid the basic foundations for three different later creations of grain-based agriculture. In nearly all of the Old World outside of East and Southeast Asia, the development of cultivation rested ultimately on that one foundation. The Saharo-Sahelian sorghum raisers of the eighth millennium BCE built on that heritage, as did the first Cushitic farmers in domesticating t'ef and finger millet.

The third agriculture that grew from these African roots was southwest Asian. The idea of collecting wild grains did not spread from Africa into Palestine, Syria, and the fringes of Turkey and Iran until about the eleventh millennium BCE. Only after that idea took hold there did it become possible for the inhabitants of those southwest Asian regions to take the further step of domesticating their own suitable wild grains, wheat and barley. This they did 1,000 years later, in about the tenth and ninth millennia. Only later still, when the wheat- and barley-based agriculture of southwest Asia diffused westward through Europe between 6500 and 4000 BCE, did the various European peoples finally become caught up, too, in the consequences of the agricultural transformation. In this they became indirectly the heirs, like the ancient Middle Eastern civilization, of a subsistence invention that began among Africans thousands of years before.

We have also seen that a key technological invention, pottery, emerged first among peoples of the Northern Sudanian background in Africa and did not appear among peoples of southwestern Asia until 2,000 or more years later. Whether the knowledge and making of pottery diffused from the Northern Sudanians or their Saharo-Sahelian descendants to the Afrasans of northeastern Africa and from them into the Middle East or were separately developed in western Asia remains an issue that archeologists have not yet adequately addressed. The lag of as much as 2,000 years between the African invention of pottery and its appearance in the Middle East certainly makes the possibility of the diffusion of ceramic technology from Africa a conjecture worthy of further investigation.

Between 6500 and 3500 BCE, the diffusion of the different African agricultural systems within the continent brought peoples of the different traditions into increasing agricultural contact. As we have seen, these contacts led to the adoption, for instance, by Niger-Congo peoples of goats and cattle and also crops of Sudanic origin. More important for world history, other crops domesticated by the Saharo-Sahelians in their Sudanic agricultural system spread outside of Africa during this era. The Sahara was as yet no barrier; the full drying out of its climate was not to take place until later. At least four Sudanic crops diffused widely outside sub-Saharan Africa before the end of the period: sorghum, which eventually became important as far away as north China (and, in the past five centuries, in the Americas as well), castor beans, and two different species of gourds. Other African crops reached Asia probably somewhat later; these included pearl millet, found in India, watermelons, and black-eyed peas.

From the Cushites of the Red Sea hills and the Horn of Africa came two other early domesticates. The donkey, a crucial animal for communication and trade, spread to southwest Asia probably before the fourth millennium BCE. In addition, finger millet took on considerable importance in later times in India, but it is not clear yet how early its spread there took place.

The agricultural influences were, of course, not all one way. Two important animals, the sheep and the goat, were domesticated in the Middle East and were adopted early by African herding peoples. A more restricted zone of Middle Eastern influences lay in northern Africa, where the climate favored the southwest Asian and Mediterranean grains, wheat and barley, over the Sudanic grains.

But outside of those North African areas, the predominant direction of the spread of invention before 3500 BCE was out of Africa. From the wider perspective of world history, in the three millennia between 6500 and 3500, sub-Saharan Africa was a net exporter of agricultural innovations and technology—of crops, such as sorghum, castor beans, and gourds, of an important domestic animal, the donkey, and conceivably also of the technology of pottery making. Just two animals of non-African origin, the goat and the sheep, became established widely in sub-Saharan Africa during that era.

To sum up, the peoples of Africa as a whole followed courses of historical change before 3500 BCE that broadly paralleled the key trends of other parts of the world. As late as the fourth millennium, much of the land area of the world, in Africa as well as in Eurasia and the Americas, was still occupied by gathering and hunting peoples. But already between 9500 and 5000 BCE major new economic orientations had begun to take shape in several parts of the globe, and by the fifth and fourth millennia more and more of the world had come into the sphere of those changes. During that span of time, independently of each other, some African peoples, just like some Asians and some Native Americans in those eras, took up new approaches to subsistence. In the process, they created the various early agricultural systems. Africans from several parts of the continent were among the instigators, in other words, of the fundamental reshaping of human livelihoods that agriculture has brought to human history.

NOTES FOR READERS AND TEACHERS

Issues and Questions

The period between 9000 and 3500 BCE was marked in Africa by a wide range of major new developments, both in economy and in society. We know more about the changes that took place in material and cultural life in this period than in earlier times, and because these changes were varied and numerous, we can far better convey the flow and movement of history.

A major new factor of growing importance in Africa was agriculture, including both livestock raising and the cultivation of crops. A range of questions on this topic present themselves:

- Why do people begin to domesticate animals or crops in the first place? (The answer is not that it makes life or work easier!)
- What does environment have to do with the kinds of agriculture that different peoples invented in Africa?
- What sorts of effects does the adoption of livestock raising or the cultivation of crops have on other aspects of history?
- How was it that for 2,500 years the Aquatic gathering and hunting way of life was able to successfully outcompete Sudanic agriculture? Why did the balance of advantage between the two ways of life finally shift?
- Into what parts of the continent did the various African agricultural systems spread over the period 9000–3500 BCE? Were there different stages to this history?
- Which African civilizations and peoples invented and spread each of the agricultures?

- Which crops and domestic animals were original in each agricultural system, and which were added later?

Chapter 3 also introduces us to a fourth African civilization, Sudanic, in addition to the other three, Afrasan, Niger-Congo, and Khoisan, already broached in chapter 2, and to two major technological innovations of Sudanic peoples, the invention of pottery (ceramics) and the beginnings of cotton spinning and weaving. Among the questions that teachers and students may wish to pursue are the following:

- How and when did Sudanic civilization begin to take shape, and why do we say that it had a dual origin?
- What notable features of custom and belief characterized early Sudanic civilization?
- In what various ways was the invention of pottery significant?
- Why was the invention of cotton weaving an important development in human history?
- What kinds of relations did the pre-dynastic Egyptians and the Sudanic peoples of the Middle Nile Basin have with each other?

The many new developments in economy, society, and technology in Africa between 9000 and 3500 BCE prompt us to raise questions, as well, about Africa's place in world history and about African contributions even before 3500 BCE to change outside the continent:

- In what ways did developments in Africa between 9000 and 3500 BCE parallel or not parallel the courses of change on other continents?
- What were the notable contributions of Africans before 3500 BCE to world agriculture or to technology?
- What cultural or economic contributions spread the other way, from Asia into Africa, before 3500 BCE?

Points of Contention

Certain historical interpretations in this chapter rest on recent findings, with which other scholars may find reason to disagree. The evidence, in particular, for the correlation of the Northern Sudanians and their Saharo-Sahelian descendants with the first Sudanic cattle raisers and cultivators was published only in 1993:

Ehret, C. "Nilo-Saharans and the Saharo-Sudanese Neolithic." In Thurstan Shaw, Paul Sinclair, Bassey Andah, and Alex Okpoko, eds., *The Archaeology of Africa: Foods, Metals and Towns*, pp. 104–25. London and New York: Routledge, 1993.

The archeological findings relating to these developments were recently brought up to date in another publication in 1998. This restatement of the archeology presents a story that, if anything, matches even more closely than before with the linguistic portrait of early Sudanic food production:

Wendorf, Fred, and Romuald Schild. "Nabta Playa and Its Role in Northeastern African Prehistory." *Anthropological Archaeology* 20 (1998): 97–123.

TABLE 1 The Major Civilizations of Africa: Typical Features of Culture, ca. 5000 BCE

	Niger-Congo	Sudanic	Afrasan	Khoisan
Language family	Niger-Congo	Nilo-Saharan	Afrasan (Afroasiatic)	Khoisan
Kinship and social institutions	matrilineages; in some regions possibly matriclans composed of several lineages	clans, originally matrilineal	patrilineal clans	bilateral reckoning of relationships, without lineages or clans
Local community	village	village in many areas; also neighborhood of scattered homesteads, especially in eastern Sudan belt	village in many areas; also neighborhood of scattered homesteads, especially in the Horn of Africa	mobile band
Leadership roles	lineage priest-chiefs	Sudanic sacral chiefs in many areas, especially Nile and central Sudan; no hereditary chiefs in parts of eastern Sudan	clan-chiefs with ritual responsibilities (*wap'er*)	no hereditary leadership
Livelihood	West African planting agriculture; fishing, hunting, and gathering	Sudanic agriculture; fishing along lakes and major streams	agriculture (Cushites: cattle raising, t'ef, finger millet cultivation; Omotic peoples: enset cultivation; Egypt and North Africa: beginnings of livestock raising, wheat and barley cultivation; ancestral Chadic society: Sudanic agriculture)	eclectic gathering and hunting

	Niger-Congo	Sudanic	Afrasan	Khoisan
Notable tools and weapons	bows and arrows; stone axes/hoes and adzes	spears; digging poles and sticks for farming	bows and arrows; spears; digging poles and sticks for farming	bows and arrows; weighted digging sticks
Specialized crafts	weaving (mats, raffia cloth), barkcloth making; basketry; woodworking (boat building, mask making, etc.); after about 5000 BCE, pottery making	pottery making as early as 9000 BCE; carving of wooden bowls, troughs; boat making; basketry; leather working; cotton weaving in eastern Sudan	leather working; pottery after 6000 BCE?	[uncertain]
House styles	rectangular, gable-roofed houses (especially in rainforest areas)	round houses with cone-shaped roofs	rectangular, flat-roofed houses in most areas; round houses among Omotic peoples	hemispherical dome-shaped houses
Principal visual art	sculpture in wood	[uncertain]	rock painting, engraving (Sahara)	rock painting, engraving
Music and dance	polyrhythmic, percussion-based music; drums; dance involving multiple body movements	horns, string instruments used from relatively early times	string instruments; dance may possibly have involved swaying body movements and footwork	string instruments; dance in which footwork was most important
Features of religion and medicinal belief and practice; religious and medical roles	Creator God; ancestor spirits; territorial spirits; evil caused by individual malice or by neglect of duties to ancestors; diviner-doctors; priests of territorial spirits	Divinity; evil caused by Divine judgment or retribution; herbal healers; prophets (people who feel called by Divinity to divine the causes of evil or to act as mediators between people and Divinity)	henotheism (primary belief in the particular deity of one's own community, while also accepting existence of other such deities); evil often caused by dangerous spirits	nontheistic belief in the existence of a condition of Spirit or Power underlying existence, which can be tapped with the trance-dance; what was believed to cause evil is uncertain; trance-healers (shamans)

TABLE 2 Linguistic Groupings of African Societies

I. AFRASAN PEOPLES
Southern Afrasans
- Omotic peoples
  - Kafa
  - Bench
  - Nao
  - Ometo

Erythraites
- Cushites
  - Northern Cushites (Beja, Medjay)
  - Agaw
  - Eastern Cushites
    - Highland Eastern Cushites
      - Hadiya
      - Dawaro
    - Dullay
    - Lowland EasternCushites
      - North Lowland East Cushites (Afar)
      - Baz
      - Omo-Tana
        - Jiiddu
        - Soomaali
          - Maxay (Dir, Isaaq, Darood)
        - Ajuraan
        - Garree
      - Konsoromo
      - Oromo
      - Konso
  - Southern Cushites
    - Ma'a (also Gumba?)
    - Dahaloans
    - Rift Southern Cushites
      - Tale
      - Iringa
      - Kw'adza

Northern Erythraites
- Ancient Egyptians, Copts
- Berber peoples
  - Kabyle
  - Libyans
  - Znaga
  - Tuareg
  - Nasmonians?
  - Garamantes?
- Chadic peoples
  - Hausa
  - Wandala
- Semitic peoples
  - South Arabians (Saba')
  - Ethiopic groups (Amhara, Ge'ez)
  - Arabs

II. NILO-SAHARAN PEOPLES
Koman peoples
- Uduk

Central Sudanians
- East Central Sudanians
  - Balese, Mamvu
  - Medje-Lombi (Mangbetu)
  - Moru, Madi, Lugbara
- West Central Sudanians
  - Bongo-Bagirmi
    - Bagirmi
    - Bulala
    - Sara

Northern Sudanians
- Kunama
- Saharo-Sahelians
  - Saharans
    - Zaghawa
    - Bodele group
      - Tibu (also Garamantes?)
      - Kanuri (Kanem, Bornu)

- Sahelians
  - For (Darfur)
  - Western Sahelians
    - Songay
    - Maba (Wadai)
  - Eastern Sahelians
    - Meroites?
    - Ta-Seti people?
    - Nubians
      - Nobadia
      - Alodia
    - Daju
    - Sog
    - Rub
  - Nilotes
    - Western Nilotes
      - Jii (Jyang [Dinka], Naath [Nuer])
      - Luo, Ocolo
    - Eastern Nilotes
      - Ateker
      - Maa-Ongamo
        - Ongamo
        - Maa (Maasai)
    - Southern Nilotes
      - Kalenjin
        - Marakwet
        - Sirikwa
      - Tato (Datoga)

III. NIGER-CONGO PEOPLES
Mande peoples
- Bozo
- Marka
- Manding (Mali, Segu, Kaarta)
- Soninke (Wagadu, Jaara)
- Susu
- Mende

West Atlantic peoples
  Wolof (Jolof)
  Fula (Takrur)
  Temne
  Dyola
  Gola
Kru
Gur peoples
  Mossi
Ijo
Adamawa and Ubangian
  peoples
  Nzakara
  Ngbandi
  Zande
Benue-Kwa peoples
  Volta-Comoe
    Guang, Dagomba
    Akan
  Ga, Dangme, Krobo
  Benin
  Yoruba (Ife, Oyo)
  Igbo
  Ibibio
  Akpa
  Igala
  Nupe
  Dahomey
  Bantu peoples
    (Nyong-Lomami)
      Boans
      Nyali
    (Sangha-Nzadi)
      Mongo
      Kuba
      Bolia
      Teke (Tyo)
      Loango
      Kongo

Savanna-Bantu
  Western-Savanna Bantu
    Kimbundu (Ndongo,
      Matamba, Ndembu,
      Mbwila, Imbangala
      [Kasanje]; Jaga?)
    Ovimbundu (Bie)
    Lunda (Rund)
    Lwena (Luvale, Luchazi)
    Southwest-Bantu
      Mataman, Herero,
      Ovambo, Humbe
    Luyana (Bulozi)
  Central-Savanna Bantu
    Lubans
    Luba
    Kanyok
    Songye
    Kaonde
    Botatwe (Ila, Tonga,
    Lenje)
    Sabi (Bemba, Bisa,
    Lala, Lamba, Nsenga)
  Mashariki Bantu
    Kaskazi peoples
      Lakes Bantu
        Kitara
        Bunyoro
        Buganda
        (BaGanda)
        Nkore
        Buhweju
        Mpororo
        Luyia
        Burundi
        Rwanda
      Takama
      Upland Bantu
        Thagiicu
        Gikuyu

        Kamba
        Segeju
        Daiso
        Chaga
        Ugweno
      Northeast-Coastal
      Bantu
        Seuta (Shambaa)
        Ruvu
        Doe
        Sagala
        Asu
        Sabaki
        Mijikenda
        Swahili
      Rufiji-Ruvuma
      Bantu
        Yao
      Rukwa peoples
      Njombe peoples
      Muteteshi people
      Salumano people
    Kusi peoples
      Nyasa (Nyanja,
        Chewa; Malawi)
      Makua
      Shona-Sala
        Sala
        Shona
        Toutswe?
      Southeast-Bantu
        Venda
        Nguni
          Zulu, Xhosa,
          Mpondo
        Sotho
          Rolong
          Kwena,
          Kgatla

**Culture and
Technology
in Africa**

IV. KHOISAN PEOPLES

Hadza
Sandawe
Southern Khoisan
  Taa-Kwi
  Ju
  Khwe
    Kwadi
    Khoekhoe
      Cape-Orange Khoekhoe
        Cape Khoekhoe
        Chochoqua
        Inqua
        Gqona
      Orange-River Khoekhoe
        Nama
        !Ora

V. OTHER PEOPLES

BaTwa (original language affiliations unknown)
Eburrans (recent descendants: Okiek: Kalenjin-speaking since around 800–1000 CE)
Albany culture peoples (language affiliations unknown)
Malagasy (Austronesian language family)

4

Diverging Paths of History: Africa, 3500–1000 BCE

Africa in Comparative Historical Perspective

In every inhabited continent except Australia, the characteristic developments of the period between about 3500 and 1000 BCE included the spread of agricultural ways of life to more and more regions, the growth of more complex agricultural traditions, the emergence of the first states, the appearance of early, precommercial cities, and, in technology, the development of metallurgy. Africa, Eurasia, and the Americas at the beginning of the era each contained regions of already long-established agriculture, as well as regions of resilient hunting and gathering life.

One major African climatic development with important consequences for human beings took place in this period: between 2600 and 2000 BCE, the long Holocene wet phase, the "Holocene Climatic Optimum" as we have called it, finally came to an end. The most powerful impact of this climatic shift was on peoples of the Sahara, a region that became extremely arid and in many areas virtually uninhabitable. More than 1,500 kilometers wide, the Sahara, previously a crossroads of cultural and economic influences, became for centuries a barrier between sub-Saharan Africa and the rest of the world. But as we will discover, the consequences of this change were not limited to the Sahara.

Farther south, in the woodland savanna and rainforest zones that surround the heart of Africa, the impact of the climate shift was less profound. The zones of more open savanna, with mixed grassland and trees, expanded a bit at the expense of the woodland savanna. The northern and southern margins of the forest gave way here and there to woodland savanna conditions. But on the whole, it took human agency since 1000 BCE, manifested in the clearing of land for crops by farmers and the cutting of timber for building, firewood, and charcoal,

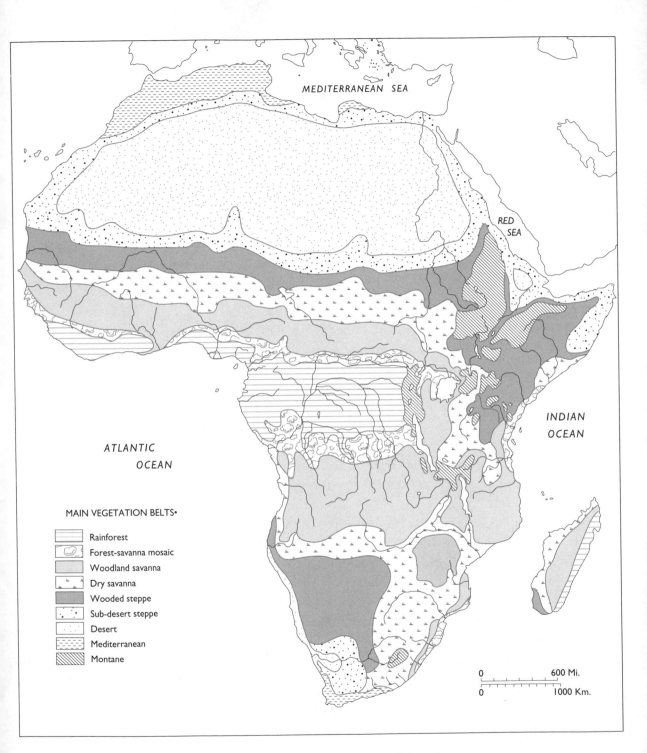

MAIN VEGETATION BELTS•

	Rainforest
	Forest-savanna mosaic
	Woodland savanna
	Dry savanna
	Wooded steppe
	Sub-desert steppe
	Desert
	Mediterranean
	Montane

MEDITERRANEAN SEA

RED SEA

ATLANTIC OCEAN

INDIAN OCEAN

0   600 Mi.

0   1000 Km.

MAP 9 Climate and vegetation in Africa after 2000 BCE

to turn the borderlands of the rainforests into savanna interspersed with gallery forests along the rivers and to change the woodland savannas into open country. (On this topic, we will have more to say in later chapters.) For most of sub-Saharan Africa during the period between 3500 and 1000 BCE, the density of farming populations remained quite low, and nature still dictated the appearance of the land more than humans did.

In certain limited areas of the African continent, population concentrations began, before 3000 BCE, to reach the kind of density that could sustain the emergence of states and towns. But through most of the continent, population densities remained low, even as agricultural ways of life spread more and more widely. They remained low because Africa is an enormous continent. Unlike the even bigger Eurasian landmass, with its large expanses of land uncultivable or nearly so because of climate or terrain, much of Africa in 3500 BCE was potentially arable or, at worst, grazeable land. Almost the whole southern 40 percent of the continent still remained untouched by the spread of agricultural economies. One of the issues we will consider in this chapter concerns the wider implications of this kind of demography for political history.

By 3500 BCE, agricultural peoples, as we have already learned, predominated in most parts of Africa as far south as five degrees north latitude. The second half of the fourth millennium was marked by several new advances of the agricultural frontier. Then between 3000 and 1000 BCE, these initially modest advances gave rise to a series of agricultural transformations that encompassed the greater part of the equatorial belt of Africa. It was a multifaceted period of change with respect to both the historical background of the peoples involved and the variety of agricultural practices they brought with them into their new lands.

The play of these differing historical circumstances brought into being sharply contrasting courses of cultural and economic change across Africa. In a few regions, a greatly increased social and political complexity emerged. But in most areas, the nonstratified and more democratic social expectations of the early African civilizations were powerfully reinforced, and small-scale political and social units remained the norm, even as agriculture spread farther and farther across the continent.

The Spread of Agriculture into Central Africa

Peoples and Crops

From West Africa there came a new spread of the West African planting tradition. In about the late sixth or the early fifth millennium BCE, two groups of Niger-Congo peoples had brought the West African planting agriculture into Cameroon and the far western edges of the present-day Central African Republic. One of these groups consisted of the easternmost Benue-Kwa societies; the other group was the Adamawans.

The eastern Benue-Kwa and Adamawan peoples of the fifth millennium

FIG. 16 Pende mask

Niger-Congo peoples for thousands of years have made masks for ritual and celebratory dancing. The example shown here is a modern mask from the Pende, a Niger-Congo people of the Savanna branch of the Bantu living in the southern Congo Basin. Masks of this type were used by the Pende in rituals of healing and in male rites of initiation.

spread across a mix of environments, from woodland savanna and grassland in the north to rainforest in the south. They raised yams and oil palms and kept goats and guineafowl, and they fished and also hunted and gathered wild foods to round out their subsistence.

Between 4000 and 3000 BCE, the agriculture of these eastern Benue-Kwa and Adamawan peoples grew more varied. They began to cultivate new crops, including black-eyed peas, voandzeia, and at least one kind of gourd. By this period also, peoples living in the woodland savanna zone of West Africa had developed their own breed of small cattle, resistant to cattle sleeping sickness. This development allowed some of the Benue-Kwa and Adamawan communities to begin keeping a small number of cows. And as we learned in chapter 3, pottery by this time had become a regular part of the technology of Niger-Congo peoples.

Bantu Peoples in the Far Northwestern Equatorial Rainforest

The most southerly of the eastern Benue-Kwa communities settled in areas where rainforest predominated over woodland savanna. By the early fourth millennium BCE, one group of the Eastern Benue-Kwa, situated in the region of the Sanaga and Nyong Rivers in modern-day southern Cameroon, formed the distinct society we call the proto-Bantu. Like their Benue-Kwa relatives to the west in southern Nigeria and farther north in Cameroon, the proto-Bantu were a "Neolithic" people, who used polished stone axes to clear small areas of woodland or forest for their crops. Similarly, they were boat builders and sculptors in wood, and they lived in villages and built houses with rectangular floor plans and ridge roofs of sewn palm thatch. They carved masks to be worn at public festivals and dances, and although they believed in a remote Creator God, they normally directed their prayers to their ancestors and to local territorial spirits.

Each village belonged to a particular matrilineage, although other people, allied or related by being married to the villagers, would reside there also. At the center of village affairs stood the *mu-kumu,* a lineage priest-chief, whose tasks included presiding over community rituals and probably also acting as the moderator of village meetings and community decision making and as the spokesperson in community dealings with other villages.

The people in such a village saw themselves as part of a mutually recognized wider grouping of many villages, which they called *-lungu.* This word derives from a proto-Bantu verb, *-lung-,* meaning "to join by tying." The metaphor

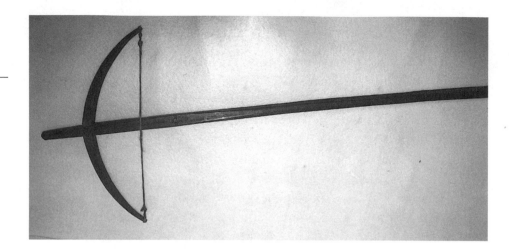

FIG. 17 Arbolet

The BaTwa may have been the inventors of this African type of crossbow, widely used in the equatorial rainforest regions.

encoded in the word shows that even though the earliest Bantu people based their rights in the local village community on kinship, they saw their wider society or ethnicity as a joining together of separate kin groups—as something mutually entered into rather than imposed by birth.

The Bantu of the fourth millennium BCE, with their Neolithic tools and economy, by no means had southern Cameroon all to themselves. They had settled in a country already inhabited by forest-based hunting and gathering peoples, the BaTwa, commonly called "Pygmies" in European languages. But the early Bantu were selective in their use of environment. Rather than directly challenging the forest, they first sought out open areas along the streams and open patches within the forest where soils were of kinds that did not favor heavy tree growth, and only gradually in later centuries did they clear new areas. As a result, vast reaches of rainforest remained available down to recent times to support the older ways of life of the BaTwa.

From the beginning of their encounter, the Bantu and the BaTwa entered into trade relations. The archeology of the earliest stages of this encounter in the fifth and fourth millennia reveals that the BaTwa acquired pottery and polished stone axes through trade with their Bantu neighbors and used these axes alongside stone tools of their own making. From the BaTwa, the Bantu gained new knowledge of the rainforest environment and obtained forest products, such as honey and the meat and skins of wild game. The BaTwa may have been the inventors of a particular African kind of crossbow, the arbolet, of lasting importance in the economy of forest hunting.

Early Southward Movements of Bantu Peoples, 3500–2000 BCE

During the fourth millennium, one small grouping of Bantu appear to have taken up a new waterside environmental niche along the Atlantic coast and to have extended their settlements southward as far as the mouth of the Ogowe River. For another several hundred years, the rest of the Bantu communities continued to gradually expand their territory and strengthen their mastery of the rainforest world into which increasingly they moved. By 3000 BCE, the lands of these communities covered a variety of areas around the Nyong River and lower Sanaga River in southern Cameroon.

Then, in the first half of the third millennium, for reasons we do not yet know, a relatively rapid and far-flung expansion of the Bantu began. Bantu settlers passed eastward out of the Nyong River country, crossing first into the areas drained by the upper tributaries of the Sangha River and then following those rivers southeastward toward the confluence of the Sangha with the Congo River. But their expansion did not stop there. Several communities at the forefront of this advance moved progressively farther upstream along the Congo itself, reaching as far east as the confluences of the Lomami, Aruwimi, and Congo Rivers by the end of the millennium. Because these settlements extended from the Nyong all the way to the Lomami, we can call this period of expansion the Nyong-Lomami era. The fullest extent of the Nyong-Lomami expansion was accomplished by several Bantu societies, among them the Boans and the ancestral Nyali, who followed the Aruwimi River still farther east, practically to the northeastern edges of the rainforest. The boat-building skill of Bantu-speaking artisans surely goes far toward accounting for the ease and relative rapidity with which the various Nyong-Lomami communities followed the rivers eastward, even if it does not explain why their expansion began in the first place.

The early Bantu settlers of the equatorial rainforest brought most features of their agricultural way of life along with them. They continued to focus their cultivation on yams and oil palms, and goats and guineafowl remained highly important food sources. In addition, they were skilled at fishing. Cows did not prove adaptable to the equatorial rainforest, however, and although some of the Nyong-Lomami communities continued to raise three seed crops—black-eyed peas, voandzeia, and a species of gourd—these must have often proved to be unreliable sources of food in rainforest conditions, except perhaps in the rare patches of savanna within the forest.

In many parts of this new environment, the Bantu had also to develop a special technique of cultivation. The soils in the parts of Cameroon settled by their Benue-Kwa ancestors tended to be relatively rich and deep in comparison with most of the soils of sub-Saharan Africa. Thousands of years of volcanic activity around Mount Cameroon had contributed to the enriching of these soils. But the equatorial rainforest region, into which the early Bantu moved, was characterized in many areas by lateritic soils, relatively high in iron content but poor in the nutrients needed by cultivated plants. If such soil is left bare, heavy rains can rapidly leach out the nutrients it does contain. Worse yet, when beaten by direct tropical rains, lateritic soils can turn into a rock-hard surface, uncultivable for generations to come.

The Nyong-Lomami farmers, who, by the way, were the women of the society, therefore put together a set of techniques that preserved soil fertility and protected it for future use. The men were called upon to clear away trees and other large vegetation, but much of the litter of clearing was left lying about on the surface, so that the rain would not strike the ground directly. The women then made narrow slices into the soil, inserting into these notches the cuttings from which their new crop of yams would grow. The tool they used to cut into the soil may have been the polished stone ax, the same tool used to make the clearing in the first place.

By the later third millennium, one grouping of the Nyong-Lomami peoples, a cluster of communities we call the Sangha-Nzadi, initiated a second major period of expansion. Again the ease of river transport seems to have been a crucial element. The original Sangha-Nzadi society emerged among those Nyong-Lomami who had settled along the lower course of the Sangha River. From there, the later Sangha-Nzadi communities spread mostly downstream along the Congo River as far south as its juncture with the Kwa River, although a number of groups broke off toward the west, traveling up several east-flowing streams into the upper Ogowe River country.

New Bantu Settlements, 2000–1000 BCE

In the early second millennium, a third stage in this long process of expanding Bantu settlement began to emerge. The impetus for this new spread came from one of the more northerly of the Sangha-Nzadi societies, and it was a different kind of expansion in one notable way: it began a sort of "filling-in" expansion.

That is to say, these communities moved especially into areas away from the main rivers and skipped over by the earlier Bantu settlements of the third millennium.

There are two intriguing features to this period of gradual expansion of the territories occupied by Bantu food-producers. One was that the Sangha-Nzadi communities spread across the rainforest at its narrowest point, and as a result the lands of the most southerly Sangha-Nzadi now began to overlap into the high-rainfall woodland savannas just south of the forest. This environment was more naturally suited to the yam and oil palm of the early Bantu than was the rainforest and much more appropriate for the raising of black-eyed peas and voandzeia. In addition, one particular subset of the Sangha-Nzadi communities soon took advantage of the new environmental possibilities and of the presence of still more river routes to launch a new, even more extended, expansion of their own. Who were these people? Their name for themselves has been lost to history, but modern-day scholars call them the ancestral Savanna-Bantu because their later descendants spread all across the southern savanna belt and eventually into the varied savanna and montane environments of eastern Africa.

The details of that story belong to the next chapter. What matters here is that the ancestral Savanna-Bantu society took shape somewhere near the confluence of the Kwa and Congo Rivers, in an area characterized at least in recent times by a major northward bulge of the savanna belt. In those times, around 2000 BCE, this area would still have been covered with rainforest. By probably no later than the middle of the second millennium, a number of the Savanna-Bantu communities began to move out eastward into new lands, most of them following, we suspect, the Kasai and then Sankuru Rivers upstream from the confluence of the Kwa with the Kasai. By 1000 BCE, the eastern outliers of this expansion had reached the west side of the great Western Rift, almost 1,200 kilometers east of the Kwa confluence, and several societies had begun to take shape across that stretch. The farthest east outliers of this expansion were the Mashariki people, whose country lay near the Western Rift and whose key role in later African history will engage our attention in the next chapter.

From one viewpoint, the successive expansions of the Nyong-Lomami peoples and their Sangha-Nzadi descendants, and then of proto-Savanna-Bantu, may seem to merge into one ongoing process. Each stage tended to form a further wave of advance, overlapping with the previous stage and carrying a similar combination of agriculture, fishing, and tool technology into new territories previously occupied only by gatherer-hunters. And each stage in this history brought into new areas the multiple use of the environment engendered by the trade and coexistence of the Bantu farmers with the autochthonous BaTwa gatherer-hunter peoples.

But significant differences of opportunity or motivation must have existed, too, because at each stage just one of the emergent new societies took the lead in the next era of emigration outward. The rest continued to remain mostly within more restricted territories. Why this should be so is unclear. The two periods of expansion among the Sangha-Nzadi communities in the third and early second millennia BCE both originated somewhere in the areas around the Sangha-Congo confluence. Was this a region of especially vibrant, cross-flowing cultural and economic stimuli in the later third and early second millennia? The last stage, the expansion eastward of the proto-Savanna-Bantu in the middle and later second millennium, began in another area of numerous intersecting rivers and environmental diversity as well. Could there again have been special economic conditions at work in this history? On the other hand, perhaps the expansion of Savanna-Bantu communities was encouraged by the simple fact that no competing farming populations occupied the lands, well suited to yam-based planting agriculture and to fishing, that lay beyond them to the east.

Culture and Society in Early Bantu History

We know in broad terms how the cultural lives of the early Bantu peoples of western equatorial Africa were carried out but little as yet about the myriad of lesser changes in culture that must surely have taken place over the period from 3000 to 1000 BCE. The Nyong-Lomami peoples and their Sangha-Nzadi descendants continued to live typically in villages of a few hundred inhabitants at most. They carried with them the older Niger-Congo practices of laying out the village along one main lane and building rectangular houses with ridge roofs made of tightly woven palm matting. They traced their descent matrilineally, as had their still earlier Niger-Congo forebears in West Africa. Each village would have been principally the abode of one particular matrilineage, although other people related by marriage or allied through close friendship would also have been found among the village's inhabitants. The recognized ritual and political head of each lineage was the *mu-kumu*, the priest-chief. His or her responsibilities centered around maintaining beneficial relations through ritual observances between the local community and its ancestor spirits.

Although people recognized larger societal groupings, *-lungu, to which their own village belonged, they followed no higher political or ritual authority than their own *mu-kumu. Such ethnicities would therefore have consisted of loose regional groupings of villages, tied together by common language and customs and by marriage alliances and trade. As communities moved out into new areas, and dialect differences increased, new *-lungu would time and again have taken shape out of the old.

We know only a little as yet about the life cycles of individuals in these communities. Boys were circumcised and initiated into relatively informal age-sets during their adolescence. Historians know this because they are able to reconstruct the original Bantu word for such an age-set, *-kula, and an early verb for circumcision, *-tib-. The noun *-kula, interestingly, derives from a verb *-kul-, "to grow, mature," and that allows us to infer that age-sets were formed of boys who had reached puberty. Age-sets were community-wide institutions, and their members would have been called upon by the village or the *mu-kumu from time to time to undertake group tasks for the community, such as clearing paths. In the Savanna-Bantu society of the later second millennium, a series of observances lasting as much as several weeks surrounded the circumcision and initiation of boys. These observances included the seclusion of the boys in a circumcision camp, masked dancing, the ritual marking of the boys with white clay, and probably other rituals. How much farther back in time various of these customs might have been practiced has not as yet been studied, however.

Girls were not circumcised, but they did go through two major rites of passage before being considered as full adults by their society. Interestingly, marriage was probably not one of those major passages. Instead it appears that girls at puberty were first initiated into the status of *mw-ali, or young woman. (This term derives from another verb meaning "to grow," *-al-, so it has the same implication of reaching puberty as the verb *-kul- had for boys.) Whether initiation was undertaken by the village as a whole or was handled by the girl's extended family is not yet known. A young woman continued to be a *mw-ali until her first child was born; the rites associated with the birth of that child constituted her second passage, into the status of a full adult woman. Marriage took place, but it may have been a weak bond, and it certainly was not at all the defining event in a woman's life that it commonly is, for instance, in Western societies. Rather, childbearing, which enhanced the size and therefore the strength of the matrilineage and the village, was the key event. In keeping with the centrality of matrilineal concerns in a woman's life, marriage generally would have been matrilocal. In other words, after marriage a woman usually continued to live in her family's village, and the man moved in with her.

By late in the period 3000–1000 BCE, several new complexities in social organization had taken shape especially among the southerly rainforest Bantu societies. In some areas two levels of kin relations had emerged. In addition to the older institution, the matrilineage, a new wider kin grouping, the matriclan, to which a large number of localized matrilineages would belong, came to be recognized. Larger villages appear to have become common, too. Such a larger village would include several matrilineages, each inhabiting its own small ward of the village and each with its own *mu-kumu. When one group of people in the village moved away to form a new community, their matrilineage would form the basis for the new village. In this way, matriclans often came to consist of a number of matrilineages dispersed over a considerable area.

At the far south, the ancestral Savanna-Bantu people of the second millennium BCE had a still more complicated system: they practiced a kind of double descent, combining elements of both matriliny and patriliny. Matrilineal relationships continued to be the key to a person's social position and inheritance, and matrilineage and matriclan allegiances remained the basis of where a person resided. But Savanna-Bantu communities also recognized descent from fathers by forming patrilineages. Just what social purpose the patrilineages may have served and why and when they might have arisen in the first place are not yet known, however.

One new wrinkle in political and ritual roles also emerged late in the period and among just one grouping of the Savanna-Bantu. Probably not long before 1000 BCE, a new position, the *mw-ami, with the same kind of responsibilities as the *mu-kumu but over a wider group of people, began to be recognized among the farthest east of the Savanna-Bantu societies, who at that period of history had moved into the areas between the Lualaba River and Western Rift. The *mu-kumu remained the ritual head of the matrilineage, while the *mw-ami appears to have taken on that role for the matriclan.

Ubangian Peoples of the Eastern Woodland Savannas

To the north of the Bantu, across the woodland savanna zone immediately north of the equatorial rainforest, a parallel and roughly contemporary expansion of a different set of Niger-Congo farming peoples, the Ubangians, carried the agricultural frontier eastward. Like the early Bantu, the Ubangians raised yams, tended oil palms, and kept goats and guineafowl, and like the Bantu also, they brought with them many of the customs and practices of their earlier Niger-Congo heritage, such as barkcloth making and canoe building.

Very poorly studied as yet, the early history of the Ubangian peoples is far less well known than that of their Bantu-speaking contemporaries. The ancestral Ubangian society emerged in about the fourth millennium BCE. It was formed by an eastern offshoot of the Adamawan peoples, who not many centuries before had brought the West African planting agricultural tradition into north-central Cameroon and the far west parts of today's Central African Republic. The first major spread of the Ubangian farming communities, dating to the third millennium, advanced, like the contemporaneous spread of the Nyong-Lomami peoples, principally eastward along river routes, in this case up the Ubangi River and its major eastern tributaries, the Uele and Bomu Rivers. A second expansion of Ubangian peoples, in the second millennium BCE, shows similarities also to developments of the same era among the Sangha-Nzadi Bantu peoples to the south. In particular, the Ubangian communities involved in this second period of population movement seem to have engaged in "filling-in" movements. In other words, they tended to settle in areas that had not been favored by their Ubangian forebears of the third millennium.

Cultivation and Herding Come to Eastern Africa

Southern Cushites and the Spread of Agripastoral Livelihoods

Far to the east, in the plains and highlands of central East Africa, the southward advance of the agricultural frontier took a sharply different form. There, in the centuries after 3500 BCE, a mixed agriculture with grain crops and livestock raising took hold. An Erythraite people, whom we call the Southern Cushites, were the instigators of this period of economic transformation.

The ancestral Southern Cushitic society emerged as a distinct people in the later fifth and early fourth millennia. They formed the southernmost grouping among the Cushitic peoples who, as we have seen, spread around the northern and eastern sides of the Ethiopian Highlands between 6000 and 3500 BCE. But the Southern Cushites soon began to move into a sharply different kind of environment and to enter into a radically different set of intercultural contacts from those of their forebears.

What first made the Southern Cushites of 3500 BCE distinctive was their move out of the cool tropical highlands of Ethiopia and into the hotter low-

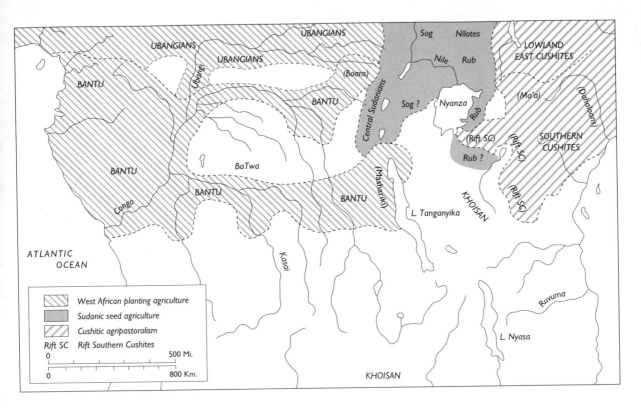

MAP 10 Expansion of the African agriculture frontier, 3500–1000 BCE

lands that lie to the east of Lake Turkana in modern-day northern Kenya. There they could still graze their cows, sheep, goats, and donkeys, but the cultivation of crops was another matter. Many of the Southern Cushites cultivated little at all in the new environment, and when they did cultivate, they found it more profitable to adopt three crops already present in the Sudanic agriculture of neighboring peoples to the west—sorghum, black-eyed peas, and voandzeia. They continued to raise the finger millet of their Cushitic ancestors, but probably only in wetter, cooler locales.

The second distinctive feature of the history of the Southern Cushites in the fourth millennium BCE was their ethnic neighborhood. In moving south out of the Ethiopian Highlands, the early Southern Cushites entered into an entirely new set of relations with other peoples. To their immediate west, around Lake Turkana itself, lived some of the last representatives of the old Aquatic civilization. Just to the northwest, across the Omo River, lay the countries of cultivating and livestock-raising Eastern Sahelian peoples, such as the Rub. From these societies, we suspect, came the Sudanic crops adopted by the early Southern Cushites. The building of the old Saharo-Sahelian style of round, thornbush livestock pens by Southern Cushites of more recent centuries also probably goes back to this era of Eastern Sahelian influences.

Equally important to the Southern Cushites of the fourth millennium were the Khoisan-speaking communities into whose lands the Southern Cushites directly moved. The Cushites probably depended on trade with these people for much of the honey from which they made their one fermented drink, mead. The Khoisan also appear to have influenced Cushitic technology to some extent, most notably in bow and arrow making. Most surprising was the adoption by these early Southern Cushites of new words from the Khoisan for the numbers four (*haka) and five (*ko'an). The reason this is surprising is that people usually adopt new words for their numbers only from economically dominant neighbors, and yet here the Cushites rather than the Khoisan seem to have been the dominant partners. This unusual situation suggests that we have much more still to learn about the earliest period of relations between the Khoisan and the incoming Southern Cushites.

Society and Culture among the Southern Cushites

Despite the importance of neighboring peoples for changes in their subsistence economy, the Southern Cushites in other respects of culture remained very much the heirs of the older Afrasan civilization. They long continued, we suspect, to build their houses according to a rectangular, flat-roofed plan. In hilly country, they dug a flat plot for the house into a hillside, and in some cases the bank at the back of the plot formed the lower part of the house's back wall. They also maintained the ancient Cushitic customs of circumcision and clitoridectomy.

Their religious beliefs centered around *Waak'a, "God" (or "Divinity"). This term, as we learned in chapter 3, originally connoted both "God" and "sky," and this tells us that the early Southern Cushites continued to hold to the Sudanic concept of Divinity, adopted by their proto-Cushitic ancestors several thousand years before. At the same time, the Southern Cushites recognized a lesser category of spirits from whom danger or harm could come. They maintained the older clan basis for local social and residential groupings and recognized the mediating role of the hereditary clan head, the *wap'er, in communal and religious matters.

Between 3500 and 1000 BCE, the Southern Cushites spread first over a considerable portion of modern-day Kenya and then into central northern Tanzania. Three major groupings of Southern Cushitic communities evolved out of these expansions. The Ma'a came to occupy the areas that extend from the Turkana Basin of the north as far south as the central parts of the Kenya Rift Valley. The Olmalenge archeological culture of those regions can be attributed to them. The Dahaloans formed across a scatter of lands, from the eastern side of the Kenya Rift to the northern Kenya coastlands. Their archeological culture is as yet unidentified. The Rift Southern Cushites constituted the southernmost populations, with their lands centering on the vast plains that extend from present-day south-central and southwestern Kenya into northern Tanzania. Their archeological remains belong to the culture we call Oldishi.

Everywhere they settled, the Southern Cushites continued to coexist with gatherer-hunters. As time passed, more and more of these food-collecting communities gave up their older languages, most often belonging to the Khoisan family, and began to speak Southern Cushitic tongues in their stead. Today, only two Khoisan languages, Sandawe and Hadza, are still spoken in East Africa. In the Kenya Highlands, the Ma'a and Rift Southern Cushites entered into especially close relations in the second millennium BCE with the Eburran gatherer-hunters of the montane forests, of whose earlier cultural connections little is

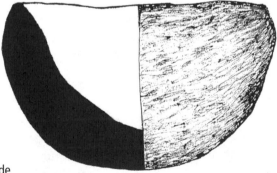

FIG. 18 Stone bowl

Depicted here is one among several styles of this artifact, fashioned by Southern Cushites, Southern Nilotes, and Eburran peoples in East Africa from about 3000 BCE down to the beginning of the first millennium CE, after which time this practice ceased. The left side of this drawing presents a cross-section of the bowl, showing the relative thickness of its wall (in black). The bowls were hewn generally out of different kinds of lava; they were small, usually around 20–30 centimeters across. How they were used is mostly unclear to us. In a number of instances we know them to have been among the grave goods interred in human burials.

known. One of the notable cross-cultural sharings that emerged in this period was the making of stone bowls by both the Cushites and Eburrans.

Even when East African food-collecting communities adopted Southern Cushitic languages, most of them continued to hold strongly to their own economic pursuits, often exchanging their products for those of the Southern Cushitic herders and cultivators but in the end still depending on the collection of wild plants and hunting of game to sustain themselves. The remarkable persistence of the old eastern African hunting and gathering economies in the face of the ever-growing presence of food producers all about them is a topic we shall return to in later chapters.

The Middle Frontier: Early Agriculture in the Upper Nile Region

Between the Bantu farmers of the equatorial rainforest and the Southern Cushitic herders of farther East Africa lay the third major zone of agricultural expansion of the period 3500–1000 BCE, the upper Nile region. Several peoples took the lead in advancing the agricultural transformation into these areas, all of them bearers of one version or another of the Sudanic tradition of mixed cultivation and livestock raising.

Central Sudanian Farmers and Fishers of the Western Rift

Along the great Western Rift, communities belonging to the eastern branch of the Central Sudanians were the key actors. As we discovered in chapter 3, the early Central Sudanians of the Bahr-al-Ghazal region appear to have been cultural heirs of the Aquatic Tradition of Sudanic civilization. They adopted grain crops in about the fifth millennium BCE and gradually took up the raising of goats, cows, and sheep from their Eastern Sahelian neighbors to the north. At the same time, they maintained their older emphasis on the use of wild aquatic resources, especially on fishing, and they collected wild yams, among other wild plant foods.

In the third millennium, the East Central Sudanians spread southward into the series of rift valleys, lakes, and mountain ranges that form the Western Rift zone—into a complex of differing environments side by side, from savanna to montane forest to open grasslands. To their west, beyond the line of mountains and plateaus that rim the western side of the rift, lay an even greater environmental divide. There the higher elevations of the Western Rift dropped away to the lowland rainforests of the Congo Basin.

The Central Sudanians moved south at first into areas in and around the Western Rift itself, where sorghum could be grown and some cattle raised. Their adoption of finger millet as a new grain crop, probably a bit before 1000 BCE, added to their mastery of that kind of environment. A native of highland areas, it grew better than sorghum in many of the areas where the Sudanians lived. How far south this first stage of expansion reached is not yet known for certain, but the probable answer is that its southern fringes extended into the basin of Lake Kivu.

But already by the third millennium BCE, the variety of subsistence approaches followed by the East Central Sudanic communities—and their familiarity with differing, nearby environments—had encouraged their experimentation with new mixes of crops and wild foods. The Mamvu-Balese society, for instance, turned to the cultivation of yams, the gathering of forest plants, and fishing. Armed with these new features of culture, they were able as early as 2000 BCE to resettle to the west, in several far northeastern parts of the equatorial rainforest. A similar course of economic adaptation was followed by the forebears of the Medje-Lombi branch of the East Central Sudanians, although their spread west into the forest may belong to later centuries (see map 10).

The dating of these developments makes it possible that the practices of yam cultivation diffused eastward to the Mamvu-Balese and Medje-Lombi from the early Boan communities. These Bantu people, as we previously learned, had also settled in the northeastern equatorial rainforest by or before 2000 BCE. On the other hand, the evidence of old Central Sudanic agricultural vocabulary suggests that yams were a more ancient food source among the Central Sudanians. Might the Sudanians themselves, then, have domesticated African yams independently of the Niger-Congo peoples? It is a problem we cannot yet solve, but one that will greatly interest future historians.

Early Farmers of the Upper Nile

To the east of the Central Sudanians, in today's far southern Republic of Sudan and far northern Uganda, two other peoples, the Sog and Rub, carried the agricultural frontier southward. Both peoples spoke Eastern Sahelian languages, and both raised sorghum as their staple food crop and kept cattle, goats, and probably sheep.

Our information on the Rub is a bit better than it is for the Sog. The Rub certainly raised gourds of more than one kind. They built granaries of the style that became popular among Eastern Sahelian peoples by possibly as early as the

FIG. 19 Hut granary

The example shown here, in a style common among Western Nilotic peoples, is situated next to a round cone-roofed house. This kind of granary, in the shape of a miniature round house on short stilts, became widely used in the past 5,000 or more years in the southern Middle Nile Basin and in East Africa.

fifth millennium, consisting of a small round hut, sitting on several short posts that raise it off the ground. They kept their livestock within the round kind of thornbush pens invented much earlier by their Saharo-Sahelian forebears. Scholars suspect that several other Sudanic crops were grown by both the Rub and Sog, but lack the evidence as yet to prove their case.

We know almost nothing about the history of each of these Eastern Sahelian peoples before 2000 BCE. The earlier roots of the Sog society, current scholarship indicates, go back to the northwest, to the earlier proto–Eastern Sahelian people whose lands lay in the Middle Nile Basin, west of the Nile and north of the Bahr-al-Ghazal. The ancestors of the Rub moved south at an undetermined date, probably following, in contrast, the eastern side of the Middle Nile Basin into far northeastern Uganda. By the last thousand years BCE, the lands of the Sog society extended southward to the east of the Western Rift as far as modern-day southwestern Uganda, while the Rub peoples inhabited sections of today's far southeastern Sudan, eastern Uganda, and the east side of Lake Nyanza.

Both the Rub and Sog were challenged in the second millennium BCE by the arrival from the north of another group of Eastern Sahelian agricultural peoples, who were new to the region. These new peoples, the Nilotes, may have become a factor in part as a result of the end of Africa's Holocene wet phase in the third millennium. In the southern Middle Nile Basin, the important consequence of the drying of the climate was a shrinking back of the swampy conditions that had prevailed for the previous 6,000 to 7,000 years all across the vast plains that surround the confluence of the Bahr-al-Ghazal and the Nile River. Even today this whole stretch of country, known as the Sudd region, is often subject to flooding in the rainy season. The Western Nilotic peoples, the Dinka and Nuer, who currently inhabit the region, retreat at such times, with their animals and possessions, to the many isolated low ridges that rise above the flood levels. Once the flood season is past, the land again affords good grazing and farming.

This kind of use of the Sudd region and the surrounding flatlands of the southern Middle Nile Basin became possible only in the second millennium, after the drying of the African climates had taken place and the danger of flooding had become seasonal rather than year-round. The Nilotes, who had previously resided in the eastern Middle Nile Basin north of the Sudd zone, then spread south into the lands newly opened up to the grazing of cattle and the cultivation of Sudanic crops.

Beyond the Agricultural Frontier: South-Central and Southern Africa

Our knowledge of developments for the period 3500–1000 BCE in the parts of Africa south of the advancing agricultural frontier is as yet sketchy. Throughout the majority of these regions the old Khoisan cultural tradition remained strong, and most peoples continued to depend on eclectic gathering and hunting for their basic sustenance. The societies of southern Africa in those centuries did not live in some timeless past, any more than did people anywhere else in the world, but the details of their histories are unfortunately still mostly inaccessible to us. A few interesting developments nevertheless stand out.

In the far upper watershed of the Congo Basin, one society living in and around the swamplands of Lake Bangweulu in these centuries embarked on a more specialized kind of food collection centered around extensive fishing. We are not sure of the earlier historical affinities of the Bangweulu communities.

Their country lay within what in those times would have been woodland savanna, so their more ancient connections may have been to the Khoisan peoples east and south of them. Alternatively, they may have been a southerly offshoot of BaTwa gatherer-hunters of the areas of the Congo Basin north of them. Their focus on fishing served them well, and their descendants have continued to form a distinctive population in the region down to recent centuries.

Another notable new development in fishing dating to these times took place hundreds of kilometers to the south, along the coasts of modern-day Natal-Kwazulu and the Transkei region. There local Khoisan communities in around the second millennium BCE began to build stone dams along the shore to enhance the productivity of fishing. During a high tide the rising seawater would fill in the areas behind the small dams. As the tide receded a few hours later, the water would filter out between the stones, stranding fish in the shrinking pools of water behind the dams and making them easy to find and catch. This innovation had a lasting importance, and as late as the twentieth century coastal communities continued to repair and use these structures.

Neither did ethnic and linguistic boundaries remain static across southern Africa. The most notable population shifts may have taken place in the middle Orange River Basin. There a period of very arid climate starting around the fourth millennium BCE brought about exceptionally low densities of human population. With the return of somewhat better conditions in the second millennium, a new expansion of the southern Khoisan, or Taa-Kwi, communities spread all across this region of plains and mountains, greatly reshaping the distributions of culture and people. In the centuries after 1000 BCE, it was artists from the Taa-Kwi communities who were responsible for the last great flowering of the old southern Africa rock-painting tradition.

Sahara, Sudan, and the Horn of Africa, 3500–1000 BCE

North of the regions into which agriculture was newly spreading between 3500 and 1000 BCE, an even more varied array of historical developments took place. New, more complex agricultures took shape in the Horn of Africa. Far to the west, in the Aïr Mountains, the first sub-Saharan African invention of metallurgy took place. As we have just seen, in the third millennium BCE, during the final decline of the long Holocene wet phase, Sudanic agriculture spread still farther south, into areas, such as the Western Rift and Uganda, that had formerly been too wet for many of its crops. The Sahara at the same period became a largely inhospitable desert, able to support significant human populations only in a few areas, notably in the Tibesti, Aïr, Ennedi, and Hoggar mountain ranges. New grazing lands opened up in the northern Chad Basin, as Lake Megachad gradually shrank to become the Lake Chad we know today. Meanwhile, in the northern Middle Nile Basin, neighboring Eastern Sahelians and Afrasan peoples responded to the new environmental pressures by joining in a series of developments that created the first African states and towns. We now move on to take a closer look at each of these developments.

New Ways of Life in Northeastern Africa

Agricultural Elaboration in the Horn of Africa

The period from 3500 to 1000 BCE in the Ethiopian Highlands was marked by the continuing expansion of Cushitic populations. During this era the group of Cushitic peoples known as the Agaw established themselves across large parts of the northern and north-central highlands. At the same time, Eastern Cushitic communities newly expanded their cultivation and herding into a wide range of areas all through the eastern parts of the highlands. The consequences for agricultural history were varied.

In the northern and central Ethiopian Highland zones, Agaw peoples settled in areas of mountain forest well suited, once they had cleared back the trees, to their indigenous grain crops, finger millet and t'ef, and to new crops recently adopted by them, wheat and barley. We have more to say about these two grains later in this chapter.

The southward expansion of Agaw communities took them into lands previously inhabited by Omotic peoples. Over the centuries, the Omotic communities were gradually absorbed into the expanding Agaw societies, until eventually all of the highlands as far south as the Abbai River (Blue Nile) and as far southwest as the far upper Awash River had become part of the Agaw world (see map 10).

The drying of the climate only further consolidated this trend of history. Drier conditions made it easier for Agaw farmers to clear back the montane forests for the open kinds of fields their grain crops required. At the same time, lower rainfall made the cultivating of the moisture-loving enset plant of the Omotic farmers a more risky business. The incoming Agaw communities brought with them a built-in advantage: their grain crops offered an effective alternative to the raising of enset, no longer a truly viable crop in the northern

Ethiopian Highlands. Enset plants are still grown here and there today by Agaw peoples, but as decorative plants set about the entranceways to homesteads, and not as sources of food.

Still farther south in the highlands, a different kind of encounter between Omotic and Cushitic peoples took place. The Eastern Cushites, as we have learned, had moved southward well before the end of the wet phase. They were able to do so because they followed the line of drier climate that characterized the Ethiopian Rift Valley, which cuts diagonally southward through the eastern and southeastern parts of the highlands. In the grasslands of the rift valley floor, they could raise their cattle, goats, sheep, and donkeys, and along the sides of the valley they could plant their fields of finger millet. (T'ef seems to have been an unimportant crop among them.) Their neighbors in the higher, forested areas all around the rift were Omotic cultivators of enset.

As the climate became markedly drier in the third millennium BCE, a new kind of agricultural adaptation took shape. One subgroup of Eastern Cushitic communities, whom we call the Highland Eastern Cushites, moved into the areas all along the western side of the rift that had formerly been solely the lands of Omotic farmers. Out of this encounter, a new blend of peoples and culture began to take shape. By the later second millennium BCE, at least two new societies had emerged, mixing people of Cushitic and Omotic ancestry. One spoke the ancestral Highland Eastern Cushitic language. The other spoke an Omotic language, Ometo. The agriculture of these two peoples also revealed their mixture of backgrounds: each people cultivated enset, with finger millet as the crop of second importance. Each also included an important element of cattle raising coming from the Eastern Cushitic side of their ancestry.

Agricultural Intensification in the Ethiopian Rift Valley

By the second millennium BCE, a still more notable course of development, an intensification of agriculture, was taking shape in the rift valley areas of southern Ethiopia. The initiating event in this skein of technological change was the instituting of irrigation works, undertaken first, it appears, by the ancestral Highland East Cushitic people. The slopes of the rift valley, where they lived, were especially well suited to this kind of innovation. Many small streams flowed down to the plains from the higher elevations, and it was relatively easy to turn water from the streams into irrigation furrows that would carry the water by gravity flow to nearby fields.

Just when the Highland East Cushites first began to build these works is as

FIG. 20 Cairn

Ancient Cushitic peoples, especially the Eastern and Southern Cushites, built stone burial cairns over the interment sites of prominent people, in eras even before the Highland Eastern Cushites and their neighbors began constructing stone terraces and walls. The example shown here, from near the Taita Hills in Kenya, was probably the work of the Mbisha Southern Cushites, who resided in East Africa around 2,000 years ago.

yet uncertain, but most probably the period of the new changes fell in the centuries around 2000 BCE, coincident with or not long after the development by the North Highland and Ometo societies of their mixed enset and grain cultivation. The drying of the climate at that period meant that, even in the higher areas above the rift valley floor, additional water might be needed if enset cultivation was to retain its central role in the economy of the household.

Along with irrigation, some of the communities involved in creating the new technology developed a more specialized use for their cattle—as sources of manure for their fields. This innovation allowed them to cultivate the same fields again and again and thus avoid having to soon dig new irrigation furrows or extend old ones to new, more distant fields.

But more than just the digging of irrigation furrows and the use of manuring was involved in these developments. Because the fields to be irrigated lay on steep hillsides, the Highland East Cushitic farmers began to build terraces to stave off the erosion of their lands. The earliest terraced fields may have been supported simply by earthen embankments. But early on, probably well before 1000 BCE, the irrigation farmers of the southern Ethiopian Highlands increasingly turned to building stone-walled terraces, a much more effective and long-lasting kind of support than earthen embankments.

Stone became, in fact, a building material with many uses all across the region. Homestead walls came to be built of it, and people frequently used stone to construct the foundations and bottom parts of the walls of their otherwise wooden, thatched-roofed houses. A new kind of stone-walled, round ritual enclosure, in which sacrifices to the clan deity were made, became common in the region. In some areas people also laid stone pavements on the main pathways between settlements or between settlements and fields.

Alongside these practical uses, stone in megalithic form also took on a ritual and artistic importance in this era among the peoples of the southern rift valley regions of Ethiopia. Megaliths are huge stones placed upright, usually for ritual purposes or to convey ritual meanings. Stonehenge in England is a famous example of a megalithic monument belonging to the same time period, although in a different part of the world. In southern Ethiopian history, two particular uses of megaliths have been noted. One practice was to place freestanding tall stones on the burial grounds of clan priest-chiefs; the other was to insert such megaliths into the stone walls of the sacrificial enclosures. Exactly when these practices first took hold is as yet unclear. Although they surely date back to the second or possibly the third millennium BCE, archeological research will be required if we are to pin down the origins of these developments any closer than that.

Armed with the new agricultural technology, the Highland East Cushites by the middle of the second millennium BCE began to expand north and south, clearing new lands for cultivation all along the sides of the rift valley. As they spread into new lands, their technology attracted the attention of their neighbors, and in several areas these neighboring peoples fully adopted both the purely agricultural features and the building techniques of the new technology. The two notable examples of secondary adoption of the new technology are the ancestral Ometo, the Omotic people who lived on the western side of the rift valley, and the early Dullay, an Eastern Cushitic people who around 1500 BCE lived in the southern parts of the Ethiopian Rift Valley, in the basin of Lake Abaya. As a consequence, both the ancestral Ometo and the ancestral Dullay societies grew in importance and may even have begun to expand their territories by the close of the second millennium.

Out of these new developments in agriculture there began to emerge an ethnically linked dual economy. Highland East Cushites, Dullay, and Ometo peoples, with their focus on terraced irrigation agriculture, centered their settlements on the mountainous areas adjacent to the Ethiopian Rift Valley. The plains and grasslands along the rift valley floor and at the southern edge of the Ethiopian Highlands, in contrast, became the domain of two groups of Lowland Eastern Cushitic peoples, the Konsoromo and the Omo-Tana. Both of these groups continued to emphasize the older Cushitic agripastoral economy of livestock raising supplemented by grain cultivation. In time they adopted the Sudanic grain sorghum as their principle crop, while trading livestock to the farmers of the mountainsides for other foods and other kinds of grains.

Agricultural Intensification in the Ethiopian Rift: Cultural Effects

These developments in economy were not without repercussions for social and political history. Population must have grown overall in the rift valley areas of the Ethiopian Highlands between 3500 and 1000 BCE. But more to the point, in some areas the densities of population must have increased, in particular in those areas where the new kind of intensive cultivation came to be practiced. Denser populations create pressures on the older institutions of social cohesion and community decision making. At such times, social or political institutions that include more people, or have more formal structure, tend to emerge. The most common kind of response to demographic pressures in early historical eras all across the globe is for states to form, and we will return to this theme later in this chapter, when we discuss the northern Middle Nile Basin and Egypt.

In the Ethiopian rift region, however, a sharply different way of providing wider social cohesion—a cycling age-set system—came into being no later than sometime in the second millennium BCE. This institution appears to have arisen first in the Konsoromo society. Age-sets, as we learned in our discussions of Bantu history in the equatorial rainforest region, are groupings formed of adolescent boys who have gone through a common rite of passage together, one that has bestowed upon them the status of young adulthood.

A cycling age-set system is an especially complex and formalized version of this kind of institution. In a cycling system, each age-set is given a particular name, and that name is one of a regularly repeating cycle of names. Each successive group of boys initiated takes the next successive name on the cycle as the name for their age-set. Among the Konsoromo, the original cycle in the second millennium BCE apparently consisted of eight age-set names. A new group of adolescent boys would be initiated in a ceremony held approximately every eight years. When the last name on the cycle had been used, the next initiated age-set would take the first name of the cycle and so start the process over again.

An additional feature of the old Konsoromo age-set system was its division of the eight age-set names into two "generation" sets, one consisting of the first four names of the cycle and the second comprising the second four names. A young man was required to be initiated into an age-set belonging to the opposite generation set from that of his father's age-set.

How did this kind of age-set system create a wider social cohesion? It did so because the individual age-sets in this region were recruited, not from a single village or neighborhood, but from a number of local communities that considered themselves part of a common society. The boys of these localities, at the crucial period of their adolescence, when their basic allegiances and self-images were being formed, would be taken together as a group through a demanding and painful series of rites (circumcision was originally, it appears, part of the ceremonies). For the rest of their lives, they would then be age-mates, sharing a common age-set name and owing common responsibilities of hospitality and loyalty to each other. In this way, even after they returned to their individual villages or neighborhoods, a wider intercommunity network of cooperative relationships, useful in times of both peace and war, was built up. With each initiation of a new age-set, these links were reasserted and reinforced.

Farther to the west of the rift valley, in the southwestern parts of the Ethiopian Highlands, the end of the Holocene wet phase made much less difference for agricultural practices. Annual rainfall amounts remained high there, with yearly totals of as much as 2,000–3,000 millimeters (80–120 inches) in some areas. All across the region, the Omotic enset agriculture continued to predominate and does so even today; and Omotic speaking societies remained solidly entrenched across the landscape of history. The old Afrasan religion of the clan deity remained strong, and the position of a clan priest-chief, the *t'et'-, an Omotic version of the Afrasan hereditary clan head, continued to hold religious authority and, sometimes, a secular authority as well.

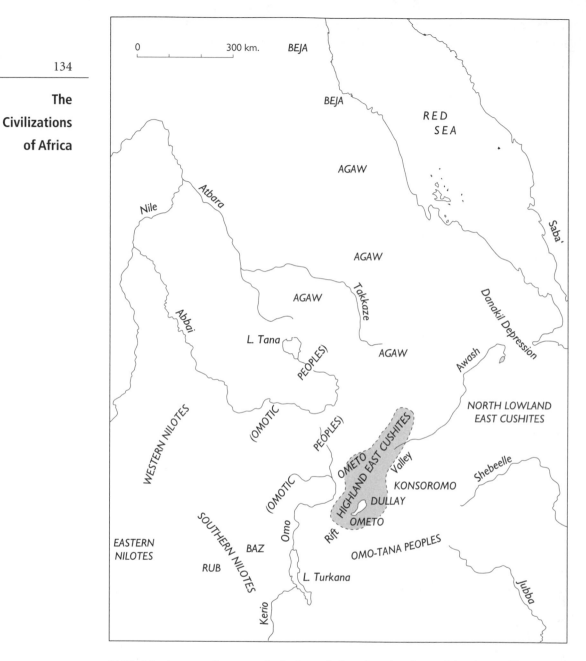

MAP 11 Areas of terraced, irrigated farming in the Ethiopian Rift region, ca. 1500–1000 BCE

Wheat, Barley, and the Plow in Northeastern Africa

There remains to be considered one other, overarching set of agricultural developments, dating to the period 3500–1000 BCE, that eventually came to affect nearly all of the Ethiopian Highlands. By sometime in the fourth or early third millennium, a new group of crops and a new technology, of Middle Eastern origin, began to make their appearance in the Ethiopian Highlands. Two notable grains, wheat and barley, along with a new cultivating tool, the plow, spread south apparently from Egypt via the Northern Cushitic people of the Red Sea hills and probably during the fourth millennium BCE. As we have seen, the early Agaw of the northern edges of the highlands may have been planting these grains and using the plow by around 3000 BCE.

Between 3000 and 2000 BCE, this new knowledge diffused to the Eastern Cushites of the central highlands, and from them it spread to other peoples as far south as the southern Ethiopian Rift Valley. In these areas the new additions to tools and crops further enriched the emerging intensive agriculture of mixed enset and grain cultivation of that region. Barley, for instance, proved to be a crop easily adapted to the coolest, highest farming areas, and in time it displaced finger millet as the most important grain among many of the enset-cultivating peoples.

Certain particular features of the environment and of climatic history explain why these crops and the plow were able to spread to the Horn of Africa but nowhere else in sub-Saharan Africa. Both wheat and barley had their origin in the eastern Mediterranean and far southwest Asia. They were therefore crops of a climate characterized by a cool rainfall season and hotter dry season; a cool rainy season allowed them to sprout, but a hot wet season would not. The Red Sea region had that kind of climate as long as the Holocene wet phase lasted, and so wheat and barley were able to spread farther south to the Red Sea hills sometime after their appearance in Egypt in the sixth millennium. The Ethiopian Highlands, because of their altitude, always had a cool rainy season, and so the two crops could easily spread still farther south, into that region as well. In the second millennium BCE, after the end of the wet phase, the climate of the Red Sea hills became much too dry for wheat or barley cultivation, and the role of that region as an intermediary in crop diffusion came to an end.

The spread of plows to Ethiopia depended on another factor, the presence of rich topsoils, deep enough to be suitable for plow cultivation. Across most of

Africa, plows were never adopted. A reason often given is that, because of disease, draft animals to pull the plows, such as oxen, could not survive in the rainforest and in most woodland savanna environments.

But there is another more important set of considerations that affects the great majority of sub-Saharan African climes. Most African topsoils are too shallow, their fertility is too low, and the tropical evaporation rates are too high for them to be dug deep and turned over in the way that a plow does. If land is plowed, the nutrients that exist in the soil may be rapidly leached out by the rains. In dry times, the winds may blow away too large a proportion of the shallow topsoil. (Winds also remove topsoil from plowed land in the United States, but there the top layer tends to be much deeper.) In addition, turning over the soil increases the amount of earth bared to the sun and air and thus enhances the drying out of the soil, so that the crops might wither more easily if the rainy season is a meager one.

In the rainforest and wetter woodland savanna zones, an even more potent factor militates against plowing. There lateritic soils widely occur. These soils, as already mentioned, turn to a hard stone-like surface if beaten by direct tropical rainfall. Only generations of regrowth of rainforest can break up this tough surface and turn it back into soil. A full clearing of the ground in the forest even without digging it up, let alone plowing it, can endanger the future fertility of the land.

Crops and Metals in West Africa

Copper Workers of the Aïr Mountains

The first metalworking in Africa, involving copper and its alloys, appeared in two widely separated areas. The earliest of all was in Egypt in the second half of the fourth millennium BCE. Egypt formed part of a wider sphere of metallurgical innovation that included the adjacent areas of southwestern Asia and the eastern Mediterranean. It was from this wider region that copper and bronze spread eventually to western and northern Europe.

The second appearance of copper working in Africa began in the Aïr Mountains of the far southern Sahara, just north of modern-day Nigeria, at around 3000–2500 BCE. There is no clear evidence that this development owes its origin to influences coming from the north across the Sahara. By this time the wet phase was nearly over, and the Sahara had become more and more a hindrance to human interaction. The archeological discoveries in Aïr indicate, in fact, that the technology did not appear there fully developed, as would have been the case had it come from somewhere else, but evolved in situ between the early third millennium and the middle of the second millennium BCE. The Aïr peoples at first utilized "native" copper, naturally occurring outcrops of relatively pure metal. Between 2500 and 1500 BCE they experimented with different shapes of furnaces for smelting copper ores, finally settling on a lasting furnace style around the middle of the second millennium CE. The Aïr region, in other words, appears to have been one of several different areas of the world in which copper working was independently invented.

We must digress a moment here to put the discovery of metals into a wider world historical context. The Middle East together with Egypt forms the best known of the several areas in which metalworking originated, but it was far from being the oldest. The earliest copper users of all were the people who made the Old Copper culture of the American Great Lakes region, dating to around 6000 BCE. Copper also seems to have been used before contact with Europeans or

FIG. 21 Ethiopian style of plow

The thin pole extending to the left is the stilt, or plow handle, held by the farmer. The beam, the thicker pole extending to the right, attaches to the yoke around the necks of the team of oxen that pull the plow.

other outsiders by Alaskan and Yukon Natives, although how far back that acquaintance goes is not certain. In addition, copper along with gold and silver was an ancient part of the technological heritage of the Meso-American peoples. A sixth area of possible independent development of copper working may have been in east Asia. One characteristic distinguishes the activities of the Old Copper people and the Alaskans: they each made use of copper outcroppings, whereas the other early peoples of the metal age took the further technological step of learning to smelt copper ores to obtain their metal.

Who the people were who initiated the smelting of copper in the Aïr Mountains is not entirely clear. The chances are, however, that they spoke a language the closest relative of which is the modern Songay language of Niger. Megalithic burial sites associated with the copper workers indicate that the emergence of five competing polities, apparently chiefdoms or small kingdoms, accompanied this technological development. A great number of small cemeteries, marked by both rectangles and circles of stones, have been found, dating from about 2000 down to 700 BCE. But five of the cemeteries are exceptionally large, containing over a hundred monuments apiece, and each appears associated with a different territory in the Aïr region. The production of copper and the resulting new scale of trading relations, it seems, encouraged new concentrations of wealth and the political power in and around the Aïr Mountains. As we will learn in the next chapter, copper soon came to play an even wider role in the rise of commerce and states in West Africa after 1000 BCE, and it had, as well, a key part in the history of West African art in the first and second millennia CE.

Agricultural Innovation in West Africa

In West Africa as a whole, the 2,500 years between 3500 and 1000 BCE saw no major transformations. Agricultural practices continued to evolve, and population to grow, and the end of the Holocene wet phase seems to have set off a period of ethnic and agricultural shifts. But the rise of the first towns and states lay in the future.

Several new crops came under cultivation in West Africa either early in the period or perhaps a bit before 3500. In the forest zone, okra and the kola tree are among the possible new domesticates of this period. The kola nut, as we will discover, became a mainstay of West African commerce in more recent times.

The most important of the new crops was African rice, *Oryza glaberima*.

Begun, we believe, by Niger-Congo farmers who spoke languages of the Mande group and lived around the Inland Delta of the Niger, rice cultivation spread south from there, up the Niger River and into the rainforest regions along the Atlantic coast that extend from Senegambia to the Gold Coast. The adopting of rice by coast dwellers triggered off a period, not yet satisfactorily dated, of complex technological innovation aimed at taking advantage of the ebb and flow of the tides up the estuaries of the many rivers. Much later, enslaved Africans would bring this technology across the Atlantic to South Carolina, where their skills and knowledge made possible the colonial prosperity of coastal Carolina in the eighteenth century.

In the third millennium BCE the end of the final stage of the Holocene wet phase forced a variety of adjustments upon peoples inhabiting the middle belt of West Africa. By middle belt, we refer here to the zone of country stretching across West Africa that consisted, during the wet phase, mostly of woodland savanna, but that evolved toward more open savanna as the climate got drier. For the farmers, this shift meant putting more emphasis on seed crops of Sudanic origin and relying less on yams and other crops of the West African planting tradition.

In many areas, the transition probably came relatively easily, since some of the Sudanic plants had already been widely adopted as supplementary crops by Niger-Congo farmers between 6000 and 3500 BCE. The decline of the climatic "optimum" had, after all, been uneven. It began in the seventh and sixth millennia with the first drying of the climate across the continent during the Mid-Holocene arid phase. Several times in the 3,000 years after 5500 BCE, rainfall increased for a period of centuries, declined, and then increased again, before the final decline of the third millennium. In many sub-Saharan regions the end of wetter climates was not an abrupt disaster, but a time of adjustment.

Nonetheless, in a couple of regions, major new ethnic shifts seem to have coincided with the final emergence of the climatic regimes that have lasted down to the present. In both instances, it appears that Niger-Congo peoples whose forebears had long inhabited the drier northern edges of the woodland savanna belt were the instigators. It can be supposed that their ancestors, though belonging to the Niger-Congo civilization, were peoples who must long previously have had to shift to an economy that more consistently relied on Sudanic crops. In the basin of the Volta River, for example, a major new culture complex, Kintampo, characterized by reliance on Sudanic crops, spread widely in the second millennium. The makers of this new archeological tradition may have spoken languages of the Gur subgroup of Niger-Congo languages. West of the Volta Basin, an agricultural changeover of even wider historical repercussions took place. There the Mande group of Niger-Congo peoples spread between 3000 and 1000 BCE all across the regions that make up the upper drainage basin of the Niger River. It was their early southward expansions that most probably carried the practices of African rice cultivation from the Inland Delta of the Niger southward toward the Atlantic coast of West Africa.

New Developments in the Chad Basin

In the middle of the Sudan belt, in the Chad Basin, Sudanic agricultural practices also took wider hold in the aftermath of the decline of rainfall after 2500 BCE. The Chadic peoples spread more widely around the shrinking southern shores of Lake Megachad, carrying the cultivation of sorghum and other Sudanic crops into areas previously under water. They expanded as well more widely southward, into regions such as the Mandara Mountains and the Jos Plateau, where the more open savanna environments highly favorable to seed agriculture and livestock raising had begun to replace earlier woodland savanna and forest conditions. In those regions the advancing Chadic communities frequently incorporated former Niger-Congo peoples into their societies, spreading a new ethnic identification along with the Sudanic agriculture.

Lake Megachad as a whole only very slowly turned into the Lake Chad we know today. In the northern Chad Basin, for as much as a thousand years after 2000 BCE, the Bodele Depression remained a land of lakes and extensive wetlands interspersed with gradually growing expanses of steppe grassland. As land suitable for grazing expanded, people speaking what we call the proto-Bodele language moved in from the adjacent Tibesti region. The speakers of this language were descendants of the Saharo-Sahelian people (see chapter 3) who had brought Sudanic agriculture as early perhaps as 6500 BCE into the areas around the Tibesti Range. In place of the Aquatic way of life still practiced around the shores of the shrinking lake, the proto-Bodele communities established a strongly pastoral agriculture, cultivating sorghum and other Sudanic crops where rainfall or seasonally wet soils allowed it, and everywhere herding cattle, sheep, goats, and donkeys. We lack direct evidence as yet that Sudanic sacral chiefs or kings existed in the proto-Bodele society, but their descendants in the later first millennium CE strongly held to this political ideology, and it seems not at all improbable that sacral rulership was an inheritance from the proto-Bodele period.

Specialized Production and Early Market Relations in West Africa

In at least two regions of West Africa, we suspect, local communities already began to specialize in the production of goods for trade in the period 3500–1000 BCE. The significance of these developments for longer-term history is that they laid the foundation for more multifaceted types of commerce in subsequent eras. They also created the conditions for the first emergence of an important kind of trading institution, regular local markets, which grew into the fundamental units of West African trade and commercial relations.

Along the lower Niger River and particularly in the coastal Niger Delta region an intra-regional trade exchanging the products of the river and sea for the products of the land evolved early, because two different environments existed there side by side. Within the delta itself, inhabited by the Ijo people, water-logged land and inundated forest predominated, and farming in most areas was simply not possible. All around the landward sides of the delta, in contrast, lay the West African rainforest, inhabited by various peoples of the Benue-Kwa branch of the Niger-Congo family. The forebears of the Ijo, though belonging also to Niger-Congo civilization, had lived in the delta, it appears, since before the Benue-Kwa expansions in the fifth millennium brought the full-fledged West African planting agriculture into the rainforest zone. The Ijo persisted as a distinct people in the face of this expansion, probably for the simple reason that they lived in a watery environment into which the agriculture of the Benue-Kwa communities could not easily penetrate.

The establishment of rainforest agriculture in the areas around the edges of the coastal delta of the Niger River opened up new possibilities for the Ijo. Cultivated foods became available to them through trade with their neighbors. The Ijo lived along the numerous bayous of the delta, rich in fish, and so they became, if they were not already, fishing specialists, catching and drying or salting fish and trading this product for yams and other goods of the peoples of the nearby rainforests. The Ijo, because of their direct access to the seashore, became the producers as well of salt and of shells for the inland trade.

In later centuries people in this region attended regular markets to carry on trade, traveling to different market locations on different particular days of a (usually) four-day market week. The market system there clearly goes back a long time into the past, beyond the reach of our usual kinds of historical evidence. We strongly suspect, but cannot yet prove, that its origins lie in the growth of regular trading relations across the Niger Delta region, between 3500 and 1000 BCE.

Far to the west and far inland, in another region of bayous and wet soils, similar forces were at work. In the middle Niger region, in and around the Inland Delta of the Niger River, the decline of rainfall in the third millennium BCE created the conditions for an even more significant growth of productive specialization and trade. As the climate dried out, the areas along the middle Niger River became, to an extent not true before, an environment sharply distinct from the surrounding plains. Away from the river, steppe and dry savanna environments took hold, with few perennial streams and few pools of water that lasted through the long dry season. But along the river and its various channels, and especially therefore in the Inland Delta of the Niger, the permanent availability of extensive surface water and wet soils and of high groundwater levels under the less wet soils mimicked many of the conditions of an earlier, wetter time.

The sharply contrasting kinds of subsistence production available in the contrasting, adjacent environments encouraged, earliest of all, the development of specialized fishing by people living in the Inland Delta, who turned full time to the catching and drying of fish for trade to other people. Their descendants in later times, the Bozo, who speak a Mande language of the Niger-Congo family, describe themselves in their historical traditions as the primordial inhabitants of the region.

A second response to the changing climatic conditions of 4,000 to 3,000 years ago was the immigration of another people, the Marka, also apparently of Mande origin, out of the surrounding area and into the Inland Delta. While the Bozo dominated the bayous of the Niger, the Marka took up residence on the wet soils between the bayous, becoming specialist farmers of African rice.

This first age of productive specialization, as it took shape before 1000 BCE in and around the Inland Niger Delta, had a strong ethnic component. The Bozo traded fish; the Marka, rice. They exchanged these products with each other, and they each traded their primary product to other peoples residing outside the delta, receiving in return such subsistence items as sorghum and the meat of livestock along with other goods of the steppe not readily available in the delta, such as leather. We suspect, but again cannot yet prove, that the first regular marketplaces of the middle Niger region came into being during this time. After 1000 BCE, as we shall learn in chapter 5, new kinds of specialization, involving the production of manufactured goods, built this intra-regional trade into a far-flung web of interregional commerce.

Lands of States and Towns: Nubia and Egypt

Sources of Political Growth and Social Stratification

Throughout the two and a half millennia between 3500 and 1000 BCE, small-scale democratic political and social organization continued to prevail in the Horn of Africa and across much of the rest of the continent (as well as in most other parts of the world in those times). Many of the social and cultural patterns established among the early Cushites and the Omotic communities spread, with only a little change, as these peoples took up residence across an increasing portion of northeastern Africa. A new social and political institution, cycling age-sets, did come into being in response to new kinds of population concentration in the Ethiopian Rift Valley region. But only along the Egyptian and Nubian reaches of the Nile River did states and strongly marked class formation appear in Africa before the first millennium BCE.

Why was this so? What distinguished the rest of Africa from Egypt and Nubia—and from the ancient Middle East, where states also arose early—and made sub-Saharan Africa more like Europe, where states were similarly late in appearing? The key element, it can be proposed, was that each of the African agricultural traditions initially took hold across an area that comprised just a small portion of the lands readily adaptable to its crops. Enormous areas of the continent lay potentially open to the spread of each kind of agriculture. The uneven decline of the African climatic optimum in the 3,500 years after 6000 BCE set in motion a retreat of rainforest and an expansion of all kinds of savanna that only further increased the amount of land suitable for the sub-Saharan Africa agricultural traditions. The early African farmers and herders had so much more country into which they could expand their way of life that thousands of years were to pass in most parts of the continent before their populations would attain densities sufficient to provide material support for states or to engender the scale of competition for scarce resources that could generate social stratification.

Egypt and Nubia grew in density of population much earlier, during the fifth and fourth millennia BCE, because of their opposite environmental predicament during the fading centuries of the climatic optimum. As climatic conditions alternately declined, improved, and declined again, the arable and water-containing soils for their agriculture more and more came to be restricted to the bottomlands along the Nile River, while everywhere else around them lay an increasingly arid desert. Population pressures thus rose rapidly and dramatically, especially in Egypt, even before 3000 BCE. (The interspersing of arable riverine lands with desert similarly helped just as early to create areas of notably greater population concentration in the Middle East; and there, too, states had begun to emerge before 3000 BCE.)

How does growing population density encourage the emergence of class differences in a society and the formation of states? As population pressure increases, a common consequence is a growing competition and conflict over the available resources. The existing institutions of society—which arose in times when small, local social units were the rule, and easy access to resources was available for all—lack rules and customary laws adequate to address the new problems. In the turmoil of such times, the men (or sometimes women), such as the clan-chiefs, who already hold culturally recognized roles of authority in society, are particularly well situated to apply the sanctions and social influence of their positions in new ways. Those among them who have the necessary ambition and talents take the central role in establishing new rules for unequal access to resources. In so doing, they consolidate new kinds of political and social positions for themselves, as chiefs or kings in a new, layered social order.

The Historical Roots of Nubian and Egyptian Kingship

In Nubia and Egypt, the older Middle Nile Basin institutions of Sudanic sacral chiefship evolved by these processes into the earliest kingships. As we already saw in chapter 3, a variety of evidence shows us that Egypt in the early fourth millennium BCE formed the northern outlier of a wider region of cultural interaction, the heart of which lay to the south among Sudanic peoples of the northern Middle Nile Basin. By 3500 BCE, a cultural world of sacral chiefdoms and petty sacral kingdoms was gradually coming into being in Nubia, and the ideas that undergirded these social formations also took hold in the far south of Egypt. Recent archeological work shows that this political and cultural outlook then spread from southern Egypt northward into Lower Egypt after perhaps 3300, culminating in the establishment of a unified Egypt around 3100 BCE.

For a while between 3400 and 3200 BCE, the most powerful of the small states may have been Ta-Seti, actually located in the northern Nubian stretches of the Nile, just south of Egypt. The pictorial documents left by its kings reveal

Ta-Seti's claim to having conquered and ruled over Upper Egypt for a time. The kingdom had strong connections both up and down the Nile. Imported items from as far north as the Syria-Palestine region turn up in the grave goods of the rulers. At the same time, Ta-Seti appears to have formed the northern outlier of the Middle Nile Basin culture area of Sudanic civilization. The affinities of the locally made pottery of the kingdom show its people to have belonged to a wider span of related Sudanic societies extending at least as far south as the confluence of the Abbai and the Nile, 800 kilometers away.

By the thirty-second century BCE, the power and wealth of Ta-Seti was in steep decline. The balance of power had shifted to the rulers of Upper Egypt, with its much more extensive areas suitable for farming and much greater concentrations of population. It is tempting to see the first moves toward Egyptian unification in the south as, at least in part, a response to earlier attacks from Ta-Seti, but other factors must have been involved as well. Sometime around 3100 BCE the Upper Egyptian rulers brought all of Egypt under one rule. The final blow for Ta-Seti came when the First Dynasty king Aha sent his forces southward to destroy the last remnants of the kingdom.

The unification of Egypt in the late fourth millennium completed the social and political transformation of the country. The sacral chiefs of the Middle Nile Basin culture area became the divine kings of Egypt, who as late as the start of the Third Dynasty still required actual human beings to be sent along with them into the afterlife. As part of the same historical drama of unification, the separate local deities of Egypt's predynastic Afrasan religion were co-opted into a new religious synthesis. They became gods in a newly polytheistic religion, a religious unification of the country that paralleled its political unification and gave the formerly independent small polities of Egypt an ideological stake in the new state.

An interesting light is thrown on how a sacral leader becomes a divine ruler if one looks at this religious context. South of Egypt, under the monotheistic Sudanic religion, the later kings of Nubia and other states of the Sudan belt of Africa retained their sacral aspects but could never become viewed as gods themselves. In contrast, in Egypt, where political unification changed henotheism into polytheism, it was possible by the time of the Third Dynasty for a king to convert the claim of sacred status into a claim of being included among the gods. We can therefore speak of divine kingship in relation to Egyptian culture, but only of sacral kingship within the context of Sudanic civilization itself.

Political History along the Lower Nile

The centuries from 3500 to 1000 BCE in Egypt are generally thought to comprise six main historical periods. The long predynastic era, in which a string of independent local polities, each with their own principal deity and probably their own rulers, occupied a different stretch of the Nile, came to an end by about 3100. The later nomes, the administrative units into which Egypt was divided, probably preserve these older, once-independent political divisions.

Between 3100 and 2300 BCE came the period of the Old Kingdom. The rulers of the Third and Fourth Dynasties, from around 2900 to 2500, consolidated and brought new elaboration to the royal ideology of divine kingship. The most striking outward material sign of these changes in Egyptian thought was the development of pyramids as the proper form for a royal tomb. For the Third Dynasty kings this kind of monument took the form of the step pyramid. The Fourth Dynasty rulers began the building of true pyramids. The three enormous and justly famous pyramids built at Giza were the burial places respectively of the second king of the dynasty, Khufu, and of his son and grandson. Khufu's pyramid is still the most massive building constructed in history. But the effort involved in raising the great pyramids must have stretched the social and material support systems of kingly power to the limit, for no later pyramids come near to matching them in size or grandeur.

In any case, a rebalancing of power between kings and subjects appears to have taken place after the Fourth Dynasty. The growing influence of certain

FIG. 22 Queen's pyramid, Old Kingdom

This smaller pyramid stands in the foreground of the great pyramid of Menkaure (Fourth Dynasty).

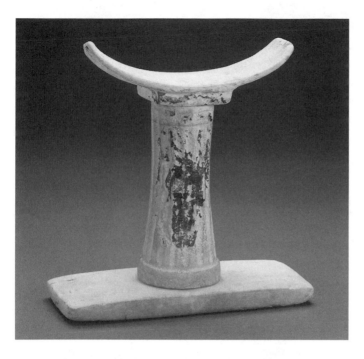

FIG. 23 Alabaster neckrest, later Old Kingdom

Neckrests, originally carved out of wood, most likely were invented by Middle Nile Basin peoples of the Sudanic civilization before 5000 BCE. This kind of artisanry spread north to Egypt, probably during the interactions of Egyptians with Middle Nile cultures of the fifth and fourth millennia BCE. The fashioning of wooden neckrests also diffused from Sudanic peoples to the Cushites of the Horn of Africa and, either during or after the first millennium BCE, far south to the Bantu societies of the southern savanna belt south of the equatorial rainforest. People used neckrests rather like pillows, to rest their heads while reclining.

priesthoods seems evident in increased temple building. Wealth became more widely distributed among the provincial ruling class, and during the Sixth Dynasty provincial governors, especially in Upper Egypt, seem to have gained increasing autonomy. Royally sanctioned long-distance trade continued to be important from the Third Dynasty down through the Sixth Dynasty. The kings' agents traveled not only regularly around the eastern Mediterranean but less regularly southward along the Red Sea to a land called Punt, located on the north coast of the Horn of Africa, and also overland up the Nile to the smaller Sudanic kingdoms of Nubia.

The long rule of the fifth king of the Sixth Dynasty, Pepi II, marks the effective end of the Old Kingdom. Attaining the throne at six years of age, Pepi II had a reign conventionally reckoned at ninety-four years, the longest known rule of any king anywhere. But under the surface appearance of unity, the devolution of power to the provinces proceeded apace during Pepi's lifetime, and at his death the Old Kingdom came apart. After that there followed a time of weakness and disunity, known as the First Intermediate Period, lasting from about 2280 to the first half of the twenty-first century BCE.

Then from around 2060 to the 1780s BCE came a new period of Egyptian unity, known as the Middle Kingdom. The Egyptian kings of this era seem particularly to have focused their attentions on building up the economy of their country and on establishing their dominance of the routes leading south into Nubia. These actions included building Egyptian fortifications south of Egypt in Lower Nubia and establishing some degree of colonial rule, at least for a time, over the Sai kingdom of that region. Farther south the Egyptians set up regular trade relations with Sai's southern neighbor, the kingdom of Kerma, about which we will learn more shortly.

The collapse of the Middle Kingdom in the early eighteenth century BCE was followed by the Second Intermediate Period. In the last third of the century a people of Asian origin, known as the Hyksos, invaded and conquered the Nile Delta and from that base exerted their power and influence in less direct ways over other parts of Egypt. They deeply affected military practice in the country by introducing from southwestern Asia the horse, the chariot, and body armor.

Then, in the early sixteenth century BCE, there began a new resurgence of Egyptian power and unity, known as the period of the New Kingdom. The alternative name for this time in Egyptian history, Empire Period, captures just how different this era was from the earlier times of Egyptian unity. The Egyptian reaction to Hyksos rule, which gave rise to the Eighteenth Dynasty, took a powerfully military form from the beginning. Ahmose I, the founder of the new dynasty, broke the power of the Hyksos by pursuing them north into Palestine and penetrating with his forces as far north as Phoenicia. He then turned his forces farther southward into Nubia than Egyptian armies had ever penetrated before, carrying his conquests as far south as the Third Cataract and the borders of the Kerma heartland. But it remained to his grandson Thutmose I to complete the conquest of Kerma itself between 1530 and 1520 BCE and to his great-grandson Thutmose III to consolidate Egyptian hegemony and influence in Palestine and Syria.

A number of interesting characters people the story of the ruling class in the New Kingdom. One of these was the ambitious Queen Hatshepsut, who ruled just after Thutmose I. She commissioned a number of important building projects and reinstituted the trade to Punt, which had lapsed for several hundred years. Another intriguing individual was Amenhotep IV, who later took the name Akhenaton and tried to change Egypt over to a new religion, with a single God, symbolized by Aton, the sun's disk. Did influences from the much older monotheism of the Sudanic civilization of the lands south of Egypt have anything to do with this abortive effort at religious change? There is no reason at present to think so, but it remains an intriguing speculation.

Egypt retained its empire on through the thirteenth century BCE. Its power extended as far north as Lebanon during the sixty-seven-year reign of Rameses II, whose treaty with the Hittite empire of Anatolia set the boundaries between the two spheres of power. After the death of Rameses' successor the power and influence of Egypt again waned. It lost its Asian possessions, and Nubia regained its cultural and political independence. Egypt persisted usually as a single state after 1100, although with not infrequent changes of dynasty and with periods of considerable internal disunity.

The Kerma Kingdom

Farther south of Egypt, smaller sacral kingdoms remained the common pattern for several centuries following 3000 BCE. By the late third millennium, however, political power along the Nubian stretches of the Nile appears to have been consolidated into two larger states, the Kerma kingdom with its capital at the city of Kerma along the Dongola Reach of the Nile, and a second, smaller kingdom with its capital at Sai between Kerma and Egypt. Sometime probably in the eighteenth century BCE, Kerma conquered the Sai kingdom and took over the whole of the Nubian Nile. How far south the rule of Kerma extended is uncertain. The indirect indications of archeological excavations are that its territories may have stretched almost to the confluence of the Nile and Abbai (Blue Nile) Rivers. If so, it was a very large kingdom indeed, not much smaller than the later Meroitic empire.

We know little as yet about the history of this kingdom. It was a Sudanic sacral state, though. That, at least, is clear, because the archeological excavations of royal burials at its capital city show that servants were buried along with the king. Kerma's heartland in the Dongola Reach of the Nile contained the most extensive and best farmland between Egypt and the more central parts of the Middle Nile Basin far to the south. The capital city lay at the northern end of the

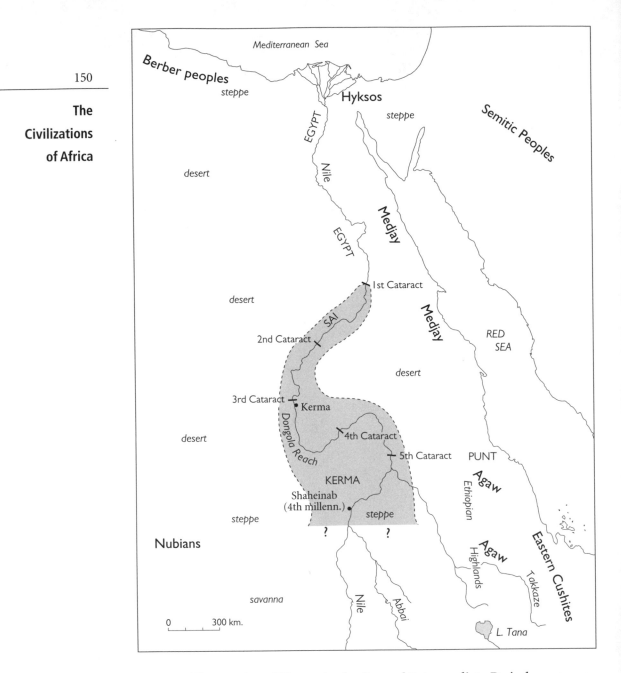

MAP 12 The empire of Kerma in the Second Intermediate Period, ca. seventeenth century BCE

Dongola Reach just south of the Third Cataract. This location was one of clear strategic importance. River-borne traffic had to debark here and go by land around the cataract. By controlling the land around the cataract, the state of Kerma could interdict, if it wished, any movement up and down the river.

Some scholars have argued that the location of Kerma city indicates the kingdom's dependence on trade with Egypt to the north, but it is just as probable that defensive concerns dictated the city's placement. To control the land around the Third Cataract was to be able to concentrate one's forces at the one narrow point of easy access that an army coming from the north was most likely to follow. In any case, as with Egypt in those times, surely Kerma's growth and power ultimately rested not on trade, even though trade was important, but on the capacity of its lands to sustain a concentrated population and the abilities of its rulers to draw tribute in kind and in labor service from the general populace.

In the later sixteenth century BCE, the resurgent power of the New Kingdom in Egypt, as we have already learned, brought the independence of Kerma abruptly to an end and ushered in a long era of Egyptian colonial rule over the Nubian stretches of the Nile. How independence came again to the region is a topic we will take up in the next chapter.

Urban and Rural Life along the Nile

The fourth millennium BCE was the time of the emergence not only of the first African states but also of the first towns in Africa, a development that took shape along the Nile in both Nubia and Egypt. Nearly everywhere in the world, the first towns developed around the political or the religious centers of the society. In the case of the sacral chiefdoms and kingdoms of the Middle Nile Basin and pre-dynastic Egypt, towns were both political and religious centers at the same time. Towns attracted population, because power and influence resided there, and access to position and wealth could be gained through service to the royal or hieratic leadership.

Trade goods came to these early towns because they had larger potential markets. But whether in Egypt, or Kerma, or elsewhere in the world, the earliest towns were not commercial centers in their own right. Local produce might be brought in by farmers and traded to people living in the town, but socially valuable products, such as ivory or ostrich feathers or precious metals, tended to be a monopoly of the ruler. By controlling access to such commodities, and

FIG. 24 Pillars and roof beams, mortuary temple of Rameses II

This picture illustrates features of the architectural and building technology available to the artisans and builders of the New Kingdom period of Egyptian history.

by appointing royal agents to acquire them, a king or chief kept control over the redistribution of prestige goods and used that control to reinforce and enhance royal power. Capitalism had no place in the economic order of the earliest states and towns.

Neither did taxation as we know it exist in the early state. Kings were owed tribute and labor from their subjects. In Old Kingdom Egypt of the third millennium, slavery certainly already existed. But the three great pyramids at Giza were more probably built by "free" labor, that is, by subjects of the king who pursued their own lives for a majority of the year, but also owed labor service to the king. The same kind of labor no doubt was used in the Kerma kingdom, too, to build the monuments of its capital city.

Along with towns and, above all, sacral kingship came class formation. For the first time, significant stratification of a society emerged. In the pre-commercial towns of Nubia and Egypt, as centers of ritual and governance, two strata would have emerged at the first stage. At the top would have been a king and the king's court, made up of the ruling family and those who had built status and wealth for themselves by successfully offering their service to the king. Court society itself, we suspect, would have drawn many of its recruits from the chiefly families of former independent chiefdoms or petty kingdoms incorporated into the larger state. In time, three other classes emerged: a priestly stratum, probably at first only in Egypt, as religious activities became increasingly specialized; a class of skilled artisans who worked for the king and court or the hieratic class; and a slave class, as warfare between states began to produce captives. Outside the towns resided the great bulk of the population of the state, farmers all, whose chief obligation would have been yearly tribute to the king, paid in farm produce and labor service, in return for being able to reside under the protective powers of a sacred ruler.

A great variety of skilled artisans worked in the Egyptian towns and sometimes in the countryside as well: boat builders, stoneworkers, wood carvers, builders, linen weavers, jewelers, coppersmiths, and many others. The history of textile weaving in ancient Egypt, in particular, throws an interesting light on the sorts of effects social preference can have on technology. Cotton—despite its use by Sudanic peoples in the northern Middle Nile Basin in the third and second millennia BCE (and its importance as a crop today in Egypt)—seems to have bypassed the ancient Egyptians as it spread wider in Africa. Egyptian royalty and upper-class consumers throughout the Old, Middle, and New Kingdom periods valued and wore only linen, a kind of cloth woven from the fibers of flax, a plant domesticated in earlier times by Middle Eastern farmers. Ancient Egyptian cultivators as a result planted flax but, as far as we can tell from the records, raised no cotton at all.

North African Steppe and Desert Peoples, 3500–1000 BCE

The Nile Valley of 3500 to 1000 BCE formed a unique historical environment within northern Africa. Away from the river, in the steppe and desert lands that covered most of these regions, human populations were far more widely and sparsely scattered, and state formation and urban life remained unknown before the first millennium BCE.

Immediately east of Egypt and Kerma, in the Red Sea hills region, lived people called the Medjay in the ancient records. We believe they may have spoken an early version of Beja, the modern-day Northern Cushitic language of the southern half of the Red Sea hills. Inhabiting lands that after the close of the Holocene wet phase were unsuited to cattle or cultivation and marginal even for the raising of goats and sheep, the Medjay must have eked out a meager existence. Greatly impoverished in comparison to the ancient Egyptians, they raided the settlements of the Nile from time to time, and in later periods Medjay men often hired on as mercenary soldiers of the Egyptian kingdom.

West of Egypt a narrow strip of Mediterranean steppe climate extended along the southern shores of the Mediterranean Sea as far as present-day Tunisia. From there to the Atlantic Ocean, in the regions known today as the Maghrib—consisting of most of Tunisia and the northern parts of modern-day Algeria and Morocco—a much wider band of both Mediterranean savanna and steppe extended 300–350 kilometers southward before giving way in the south to the arid desert of the Sahara regions. From the sixth to the fourth millennia BCE, these areas supported Afrasan-speaking populations—descendants of the Capsian peoples—who raised sheep, goats, cattle, and donkeys. Gradually over the period they increased their reliance on the cultivation of grains and other crops. Because they lived in a Mediterranean climatic zone, their most important crops tended to be of Middle Eastern rather than sub-Saharan origin. Wheat and barley, we suspect, were the staples, but such Sudanic crops as gourds may also been adopted early by the farmers of these regions.

By the third and second millennia BCE, further new elements of technology were taking hold among these North Africans. In several areas the knowledge of copper working, coming from Egypt or from across the Mediterranean, may have become important a bit before the second millennium. In addition, the weaving of wool garments from the hair of goats and sheep, an important craft among North African peoples during the past 2,000 years, may actually have begun at this period in time, earlier than is usually thought to have been the case.

Sometime in the latter half of the third millennium, one Afrasan people of the Maghrib region, whom we call the proto-Berber, began a far-flung expansion. The repercussions of their population movements extended from as far west as Morocco to as far east as Egypt. Why this period of Berber expansion took place when it did remains unknown. One highly speculative possibility is that refugees from the Sahara, forced out of their lands by the final decline of the Holocene wet phase during the middle of the third millennium, set off a period of social turmoil and readjustment in North Africa, which culminated in this first era of Berber expansion.

But whatever its causes, its consequences for ethnic realignment were profound. Across almost the whole of North Africa, Berber-speaking societies

FIG. 25 Berber polished stone amulet

The example shown here comes from the Tuareg people, who have inhabited the Hoggar region for at least the past 1,000 years. But this kind of artifact, because of its fashioning from a material of bygone eras, stone, likely preserves a style of ornamentation going back to the earliest eras of Berber culture, before 1000 BCE.

came to predominate by the early second millennium BCE. On the east, Berber raiders, operating out of the oases to the west of the Nile Valley, attacked Egypt on a number of occasions in the twenty-first and twentieth centuries BCE. The consolidation of royal power in the Middle Kingdom eventually reestablished peace on Egypt's western borderlands, in part by giving some of these Berbers employment in the Egyptian military forces. Far to the southwest, another Berber society, the ancestral Znaga, formed the western outlier of this expansion. They spread through the western Sahara, where a dry steppe environment persisted as late as the early first millennium CE, settling there in the second millennium BCE as the northern neighbors of the westernmost Niger-Congo peoples. Raisers, we suspect, principally of goats and sheep, the ancestral Znaga became the suppliers of animals and animal products to the wider networks of the exchange of primary goods emanating, by the late second millennium, out of the Inland Niger Delta region.

Africa, 3500–1000 BCE: What Have We Learned?

If we look back across the whole range of developments in Africa between 3500 and 1000 BCE, we see a continent whose history paralleled in most respects the historical patterns on other continents. Agriculture in a great range of varieties had become the basis of the domestic economy over two-thirds of Africa, just as similar livelihoods had become widely spread in Europe, Asia, and the Americas. In the southern portion of the continent, hunting and gathering still held sway, as it did in different forms in the northern regions of Asia, the farther north of Europe, the northern parts of North America, and the southern reaches of South America. The first smelting of metals—in particular, copper—developed in sub-Saharan Africa during this 2,500-year period, just as it did in parts of Asia and Europe and separately in Meso-America. More specialized production for trade took shape in several areas of the continent. And, in parallel fashion to peoples in the Mesopotamian region of southwest Asia and in almost the same time period, Africans in both Nubia and Egypt participated in the kinds of historical developments that led first to concentrated population growth on favored farming lands and then to the emergence of the first states, to pre-commercial towns, and to class societies.

Notes for Readers and Teachers

Issues and Questions

Chapter 4 takes us into an era of African history in which a variety of distinct regional historical trends emerged. Four developments especially stand out in this period in different parts of the continent:

1. the advance of the agricultural frontiers much farther southward in the center of Africa
2. the rise of the first African towns and states in the northern Middle Nile Basin and along the Egyptian Nile
3. the earliest smelting of metals on the continent in Egypt and separately in the south-central Sahara
4. new developments in agricultural technology in the Ethiopian Highlands

Here are some questions students and teachers may wish to consider in seeking to consolidate and focus their knowledge:

- Which groups of peoples carried agriculture southward into the central belt of Africa?
- Which agricultural traditions did each of these groups take with them, and into which regions did each spread?
- What kinds of relations developed between the expanding agriculturists and the gatherer-hunter peoples in those regions?
- What influences spread from one African agricultural system to another during this period?
- What were the several notable developments in agricultural technology that took place in the Ethiopian Highlands between 3500 and 1000 BCE, and which peoples and regions were involved in these changes?
- Two kinds of occupational specialization arose in this period of history—(a) in the production of certain kinds of foods for trade in parts of West Africa and the Congo Basin and (b) in the production of manufactured goods in the Middle Nile Basin, Egypt, and the Aïr Mountains region. What kinds of social and/or political effects, if any, did these economic developments have in each region?
- Why should states and towns have arisen first along the Nile in the Middle Nile Basin and Egypt?
- What kinds of institutions and ideology (legitimization) characterized the earliest African states?
- What were the material bases of kingly rule in the earliest African states?
- What kinds of functions did the earliest towns and cities serve?
- Why do we think that copper metallurgy was independently invented in the Aïr Range in the third and second millennia BCE?

Issues

There is general agreement that the Bantu language group underwent a succession of early branchings and thus that Bantu populations passed through several stages of advance into and across the equatorial rainforest belt before eventually reaching eastern Africa. Nearly all studies, back to the late 1960s, reached this conclusion, even though applying a variety of approaches and evidence. A summing up of this work can be found in:

Ehret, C. "Bantu Expansions: Re-Envisioning a Central Problem of Early African History." *International Journal of African Historical Studies* 34 (2001).

A single group of collaborating linguists initially took an alternative view—that Bantu divided into two primary branches, one western and the other eastern. One historian of Africa, Jan Vansina, follows that lead in his own writings. The most recent work by this group, however, presents a more nuanced understanding of the evidence:

Bastin, Yvonne, André Coupez, and Michael Mann. *Continuity and Divergence in the Bantu Languages: Perspectives from a Lexicostatistic Study.* Tervuren, Belgium: Musée royal de l'Afrique centrale, 1999.

This book offers eight different historical scenarios, all but two of which posit several successive early branchings of Bantu, so that there seems now to be broad agreement across the board.

For an encompassing synthesis of the early history of Bantu-speaking communities in the equatorial rainforest regions, the reader can turn to:

Klieman, Kairn. *"The Pygmies Were Our Compass": Bantu and Batwa in the History of West Central Africa, Early Times to c. 1900 C.E.* Portsmouth, NH: Heinemann, 2003.

Klieman lays out the Nyong-Lomami and Sangha-Nzadi stages of early Bantu expansion, evokes the intellectual and cultural perspectives of the early Bantu-speaking societies, and depicts the subsequent "filling-in" of the rainforest zone by Bantu speakers. She presents us with the first-ever treatment of the BaTwa communities as key, long-term historical actors in these events.

The evidence on early African copper metallurgy is usefully surveyed in:

Holl, Augustin F. C. "Metals and Precolonial African Society." In M. S. Bisson et al., eds., *Ancient African Metallurgy.* Walnut Creek, CA: Altamira Press, 2000.

On a different note, the case for tracing Sudanic sacral kingship back to an ancient sacral chiefship of early Sudanic civilization has been reprised in:

Ehret, C. "Sudanic Civilization." In Michael Adas, ed., *Agricultural and Pastoral Societies in Ancient and Classical History.* Philadelphia: Temple University Press, 2001.

The distinctive early feature of this complex, the burial of servants to accompany rulers into the afterlife, evoked historically shared ideas about death already deeply imbedded in Middle Nile culture 5,000 years ago. In contrast, human sacrifices in the royal ritual of some recent Niger-Congo-speaking kingdoms, such as Benin and Dahomey, belonged to a quite different conceptual system. They were just that, sacrifices, propitiating gods or invoking sacred power, and not statements about life after death.

5

An Age of Commerce, an Age of Iron: Africa, 1000 BCE to 300 CE

Africa in World History, 1000 BCE to 300 CE

Commerce and Iron

Two key developments characterized the long-term histories of both Africa and Eurasia during the centuries between 1000 BCE and 300 CE. One of these was the spread of ironworking technologies over most of the Eastern Hemisphere. The second was what can be called the Commercial Revolution. The coming of the "Iron Age" has long been viewed as an epoch of special importance in the technological history of humankind. The Commercial Revolution, in contrast, has remained almost unnoticed, and yet its consequences for the overall course of world history were ultimately greater than those of the adoption of iron.

As the effects of these two developments spread wider, the peoples of Africa passed through their own varied regional histories. Just as in Asia and Europe, so also in Africa the Commercial Revolution created new, more direct links of the continent to disparate parts of the world. Just as elsewhere, the development of iron metallurgy in Africa led to radical changes in toolmaking. All in all, however, factors and forces internal to Africa still predominantly shaped the course of events across the continent. We will turn our attention to the regional trends and themes of African history in the body of this chapter. But first we must look more closely at just what the two developments of world historical consequence, the "Iron Age" and the Commercial Revolution, were and what they portended, both inside and outside of Africa.

The encounters of Africans with these two transforming sets of developments showed both significant parallels to and significant differences from the experiences of Asians and Europeans. To grasp just how alike or different the consequences were in Africa, we must now examine the Iron Age and the Commercial Revolution. What actually took place? How did events play themselves out in different regions of the world?

The Anatolian and Central African Origins of Iron Technology

Ironworking nearly everywhere in the Eastern Hemisphere spread by diffusion from people to people and from region to region. With the knowledge that comes from hindsight, we can see that the transition from the use of stone or copper to the use of iron in toolmaking was essential to many kinds of later

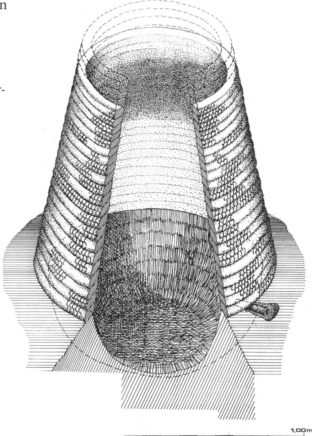

FIG. 26 Central African iron-smelting furnace

This particular drawing presents the archeologist Marie-Claude Van Grunderbeek's reconstruction of a furnace from the tenth to the fifth century BCE that she excavated in the modern-day country of Rwanda.

1.00m

technological developments. Most notably, the Industrial Revolution of the nineteenth century would have been inconceivable without the availability of iron.

But we should not make the mistake of projecting our modern-day expectations back into the past. The initial spread of iron did not have anything like the kind of impact that the Industrial Revolution had. The importance of iron and ironworking technology grew as the availability of iron increased, and its availability increased only as the smelters and forgers of the metal, the smiths, gradually expanded their production, and as people gradually accumulated more iron goods. Only rarely did the possession of iron technology by itself become, over the short run, the central factor in social or political change.

For half a century, historians have presumed there was a single origin the world over for ironworking—the time and place: somewhere in Anatolia (modern Turkey) by or before 1500 BCE. Certainly the evidence is strong that, at least throughout Europe, in North Africa, and in the Middle East and India, iron technology spread from that Anatolian center of invention.

But the story of iron has its own special African twist. Africa south of the Sahara, it now seems, was home to a separate and independent invention of iron metallurgy. The smelting of iron appears to have already been established well before 500 BCE in two parts of sub-Saharan Africa—in northern Nigeria and Cameroon and, far away to the east, in the African Great Lakes region. In the western Great Lakes ironworking was practiced, in fact, from as early as 1000 BCE. Equally early sites of ironworking lay 2,000 kilometers to the northwest, in the areas just south of Lake Chad. In other words, ironworking was an established technology in both those regions several centuries *before* iron became regularly available in Egypt and North Africa. How could that be so, if African ironworking had actually diffused south from the ancient Middle East? In addition, significant differences in early African iron-smelting technology distinguish it from that of the Middle East and so further make the case for an independent African invention of ironworking. The historical significance of this shift in basic tool technology is an issue that we will return to later in the chapter.

To sum up the available evidence, iron technology across much of sub-Saharan Africa has an African origin dating to before 1000 BCE. The earliest African practitioners of ironworking may have lived somewhere between the Chad Basin and the Great Lakes region, perhaps in what is today the Central African Republic. The subsequent history of the spread of iron in West Africa outside of northern Nigeria remains to be explored, but it seems to have become widely established in the west by the later first millennium BCE. To the east and south of West Africa, ironmaking spread out from the Great Lakes region between 500 BCE and 200 CE. One direction of its spread was westward, from society to society, across the Congo Basin to the Atlantic coast. The other major direction of spread carried the knowledge of iron to the far southern shores of the continent by the beginning of the first millennium CE.

In just one region of sub-Saharan Africa, the Horn of Africa, did the first knowledge of iron apparently come instead from the Middle East, before the African invention of ironworking reached that area. This introduction of iron from outside the continent reflects the effects of the other contemporary major world historical development of the age, the Commercial Revolution.

Understanding the Commercial Revolution

The Commercial Revolution began as no more than a subplot running through the drama of Middle Eastern and eastern Mediterranean history. Its roots lay in the development, from somewhere around or a bit before 1000 BCE, of a new approach to carrying out long-distance trade. In the third millennium BCE, such trade had generally been controlled by rulers and, in Mesopotamia, perhaps also by corporate religious groups. In Egypt it was carried out by agents of the king and took the form of expeditions capitalized by the court. These kinds of long-distance trade probably predominated through most of the second millennium.

By the start of the last thousand years before the onset of the common era, however, there are increasing indications of the growth of a new form of long-distance trade, carried on by trading parties of lesser scale than an expedition. The early prominent factors in this trade were the Phoenician city-states. From around the eleventh century BCE onward, they extended their trading connections initially westward through the Mediterranean Sea by settling colonies along the shores of that sea, including, most notably, the city of Carthage in today's Tunisia. In the eighth century the Greek city-states began to imitate the Phoenician example, establishing colonies of their own and rapidly becoming equally powerful commercial factors in the Mediterranean, soon spreading their settlements and influences north to the Black Sea as well.

Along with the growth of sea-borne commerce, a second new, major direction of expanding long-distance trade in the early centuries of the first millennium BCE passed overland from Phoenicia and Israel to southern Arabia. After the fourth century BCE, the regular sea routes of commerce spread farther afield, reaching India via the Persian Gulf and the Red Sea, and before the beginning of the common era extending well down the East African coast and expanding east from India to encompass western Indonesia.

The key to the long-range historical importance of these commercial developments was the fundamental shift they occasioned in the social economy of trade. Increasingly a new class emerged in the societies of the eastern Medi-

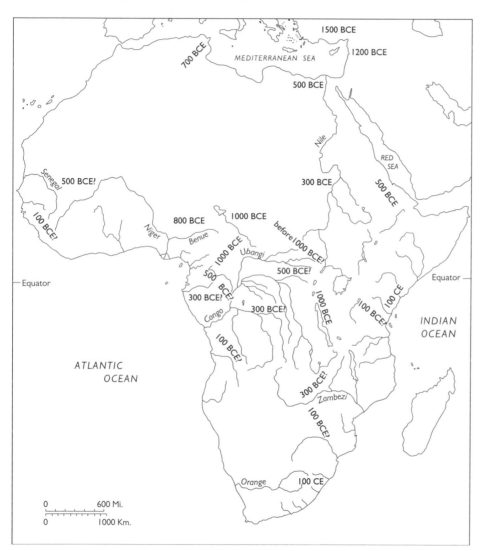

MAP 13 The spread of ironworking in Africa

terranean region, composed of people who specialized in carrying on commerce; for the first time in history a class of merchants came into being. The emergence of this class was probably gradual and slow. For a long time the major capitalization of commercial ventures must still have come from kings and people wealthy in land. Merchants initially were people who carried on trade for others. As late as the later Roman Empire of the fourth century, wealthy landowners in the western regions must often have provided capital for commerce, even if the actual organizers and instigators of trade tended to be people of not so great wealth. But in the Levant, real merchant capitalist enterprise increasingly took shape. Wealthy merchants able to outfit ships emerged in time; less wealthy merchants, in the manner of Sinbad in the later Arabian Nights stories, could band together to hire a captain and ship to carry them to their destinations.

Now, merchants have a different relation to trade than do agents of a king who seeks luxury goods for ostentatious display, expressive of his exalted position in society, and for redistribution to his loyal clients and lords. Merchants serve a more eclectic clientele, and they must compete for markets and for products. They do not have a single, powerful consumer to satisfy. If they are to continue over the long run to profit and to be able to maintain or expand their economic position, they will from time to time be forced to seek out new goods to buy and new places to sell the products they bring with them. The natural long-term tendency of merchant-run trade is thus a recurrently expanding trading network and a progressive growth in the variety and quantity of goods traded.

Social and Political Consequences of the Commercial Revolution

Because of the Commercial Revolution, a variety of other processes and developments new to human history first appeared in the first millennium BCE.

For the first time the planting of colonies in distant lands became possible. The Phoenician settlements in the central and western Mediterranean, such as at Carthage in North Africa, and the slightly later establishment of Greek colonies are early examples. The movement around mid-millennium of South Arabians across the Red Sea and their settlement in the far northern Ethiopian Highlands marks the subsequent spread of this sort of commercial consequence to the Horn of Africa. In the third and second millennia BCE, a state such as Egypt might colonize areas outside its heartland, as in Nubia. But this colonization comprised military outposts and ethnic settlements that were planted to hold the contiguous territories of a land empire, not distant localities far separated from the home country.

The Commercial Revolution constructed the economic basis as well for a new kind of town or city, an urban center that above all serviced trade and was home to the crafts and occupational specializations that went along with commercial development. The urban locations of earlier times commonly drew trade simply because their populations included a privileged stratum of elite consumers. But such towns had arisen in the first place as political and religious centers of the society. They attracted population because power and influence resided there, and access to position and wealth could be gained through service to the royal or priestly leadership.

The natural political manifestation of the Commercial Revolution was the city-state, by which we mean a polity, relatively small in population and territory, centered around a single commercially based city. The domains of such a state usually included a swath of surrounding rural land as well as the city itself, but the city was the hub of all important economic activities and the focus of its citizens' allegiance and cultural identification.

Empires and territorial kingdoms still rose and fell in the regions affected by the transformation in exchange relations, and their rulers often had the power to rule over the nearby city-states. But in the last analysis that power still rested on their mastery of extensive areas of land and people. An empire or large territorial state could exert control over a city-state because it could muster much larger military forces out of its much larger population.

When the effects of the commercial transformation reached a region, kings and emperors soon lost their ability to treat trade as a royally capitalized and instigated activity, intended to preserve the commodities of trade as the perquisites of immemorial power and position. Instead their policies shifted toward controlling access to the products of commerce and to ensuring security and other conditions that attracted and enhanced the movement of goods. No longer could kings rely on agriculturally sustained and religiously based claims to an ability to protect their lands and people; now they also had to overtly support the material prosperity of their people vis-à-vis other societies.

Rather than exerting a monopoly over prestige commodities, as Egyptian kings of the third and second millennia had done, and redistributing such commodities in ways designed to reinforce the allegiance of their subjects and enhance the awesomeness of their position, rulers turned to the taxation of trade and to the creation and control of currency. More and more they relied on trade

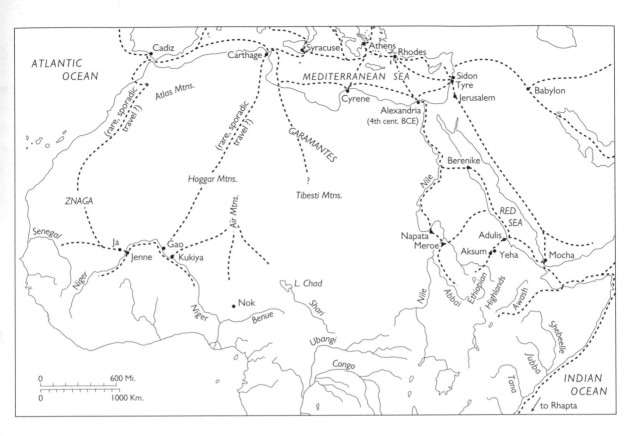

MAP 14 Routes and entrepots of commerce in Africa in the last millennium BCE

duties and other revenues to support the apparatus of the state. It was no historical accident that the first coinage in the world began to be minted in eighth-century Anatolia and that the use of coins rapidly spread with the expanding Commercial Revolution. The material bases and the legitimizations of state authority as we know them today had begun to take shape.

The Commercial Revolution tended also to spread a particular pattern of exchange. The early commercial centers of the Mediterranean most characteristically offered manufactured goods—purple dye, metal goods, wine, olive oil, and so forth—for the raw materials or the partially processed natural products of other regions, such as the tortoiseshell and the frankincense and myrrh of the northern Horn of Africa, or the wheat of the Black Sea ports. As the Commercial Revolution spread, this kind of exchange tended to spread with it. The more recently added areas of commerce provided new kinds of raw materials or new sources for familiar products of the natural world. The longer established commercial centers—which might themselves formerly have lain at the margins of this transformation—produced, or acted as middlemen in the transmission of, manufactured commodities. India, for instance, had developed by the turn of the era into a major exporter of its own cotton textiles as well as naturally occurring materials, such as gems of various kinds, and at the same time its merchants were the middlemen of the silk trade. But African markets continued mostly to provide raw materials. Already in the first millennium BCE, in other words, one thread in the fashioning of modern Africa's patterns of exchange with the other regions and of its less competitive position in the world economy was being spun—long before the eras to which modern scholarly theory has credited Africa's "underdevelopment."

Finally, because of the Commercial Revolution, long-distance lanes for the diffusion of ideas, practices, and things emerged. No longer did innovations and influences spread only from community to neighboring community or because of the expansions of ethnic and language frontiers. Crops, technology, and religion, as well as the valued commodities of the trade, might spread in a short span of time to new and distant areas. The establishment of Christianity in Aksum in the fourth century CE, for instance, owed a great deal to the major commercial connections of the Aksum kingdom with the largely Christianized Levant of that period. Two and three centuries before that, at the period of the Han Dynasty in China and the early empire in Rome, a few goods, notably silk cloth, had begun to move overland through various hands, all the way from China to the Mediterranean. Thus did the events of even distant regional dramas of world history begin for the first time, in small ways, here and there, to connect up, all because of the Commercial Revolution.

The social and economic consequences of the Commercial Revolution, then, opened a new era for all of human history, an era still with us today. Its spreading and evolving consequences formed the world we know. Slowly, exceedingly unevenly, the developments it set in motion built up a common stage for the playing out of human history. Bit by bit over the centuries between then and now, more intricate links were forged between the multiple regional dramas of earlier eras, eventually replacing them with the inextricably tied-together world of the twenty-first century.

European expansion during the final six centuries of the common era did not by itself alone create the modern world economy that underpins our interdependent world. Rather it extended a set of developments that were begun in the Levant by the Commercial Revolution of the first millennium BCE and that were perpetuated and gradually expanded by other peoples, especially Arabs and Indians, across the intervening centuries. European expansion was possible in the first place only because the commercial framework for creating a truly worldwide movement of goods and people was already in place by the fourteenth century CE. The western and southwestern Europeans had the good fortune in the fifteenth and sixteenth centuries to have had the perceived material needs, the requisitely presumptuous outlook toward the rest of the world, and the kinds of seaward locations that allowed them to take full advantage of the times. But they also accommodated themselves to the relations of trade that other commercially minded peoples had already constructed over the more than 2,000 previous years, and they directly tapped the knowledge and expertise of such peoples in their early commercial expansions.

The Rise of "World" Religions

The first millennium BCE saw the first appearance of one other factor of great importance in the long term for world history—of religions that claimed universal validity for their particular beliefs. These religions—among them Zoroastrianism (the religion of the "Magi"), Buddhism, and Judaism and its sister religion Samaritanism—all traced themselves back to prophetic, founding figures. Two more religions of this kind emerged in the first millennium CE, both of them with earlier roots in the Judaic-Samaritan Tradition. The first was Christianity, tracing itself to the teachings of Jesus, who lived in Galilee and Judaea in the eastern Roman Empire at the beginning of the first millennium CE. The second was Islam, preached by Muhammad in Arabia in the early seventh century CE. Both these latter religions, along with Buddhism, were especially given to missionary fervor in spreading their ideas.

The new kind of religion based itself on fixed sacred texts. These texts soon came to be written down and so took an aura, at least in the eyes of believers, of unchangeable truth. Because of the claims of such religions to universal validity, backed up by fixed sacred writings, for the first time in human history it became possible for people to persecute other people simply for believing differently. For the first time, it became possible for people to fight destructive wars of religion against other human beings for not having the "right" beliefs.

The powerful effects of the "world" religions in history during the past 2,500 years may obscure to us the extent to which their importance was contingent on another historical development of a quite different kind, the Commercial Revolution. Without the far-reaching economic links created by the growth of commerce in the first millennium BCE and early first millennium CE, human beings of those centuries would not have traveled great distances, carrying their ideas as well as their goods to people far away. Buddhism spread to southeast Asia and to east Asia along the ever-widening links of trade in those centuries, by sea in the eastern Indian Ocean and by land on the Asian continent. Christianity, as we will learn in the next chapter, was carried initially through the Red Sea by merchants to the kingdom of Aksum, and the spread of Islam in West Africa in recent centuries, as we will discover in the next several chapters, can similarly be attributed most of all to merchants' activities.

In the period before 300 CE, however, these new currents hardly affected Africans. Christianity gained some adherents both in Egypt and farther west in North Africa in the second and third centuries. But nearly everywhere on the continent religions continued to spread as they always had—by the shifting of cultural and ethnic boundaries and the cross-cultural interchange of ideas between peoples. African societies, not yet given to claiming universal, timeless truth for their beliefs, remained open to new ideas in religion and to the creative fashioning of new religious syncretisms in their cultural interactions with their neighbors. The idea of killing and dying merely because of religious differences long remained a concept alien to most of the continent.

But we have said enough on the wide-ranging factors of world history after 1000 BCE. We must now set about the task of laying out the particular themes and issues of African history between 1000 BCE and 300 CE. How the "Iron Age" or the Commercial Revolution impinged on that history will emerge as we proceed through our task.

Eastern Africa in Its Classical Age

Throughout the eastern side of Africa, from the African Great Lakes region at the north to the southeastern coasts of the continent, an immense realignment of culture and language took place in the centuries between 1000 BCE and 300 CE. It was a classical age for eastern African history in much the same sense that the Greek and Roman eras were viewed as a classical age by the later Europeans. Like the Mediterranean classical age, it was marked by the coming together of different cultural traditions and the emergence of new beliefs and new technologies. The new cultural complex fashioned in eastern Africa's Classical Age then spread to a much wider set of regions, laying the cultural foundations on which most of the societies of greater eastern Africa were to build for the next 1,500 years.

The Formative Age: The Early Mashariki Bantu and Their Neighbors

The initiating events of the Classical Age of eastern Africa took place in the African Great Lakes region during the early and middle centuries of the first millennium BCE. At around 1000 BCE, at the threshold of the Classical Age, the peoples of this region viewed their world from a variety of cultural and economic perspectives. Cultivation and some raising of livestock characterized the economies of the Central Sudanians of the Western Rift region and the Sog and Rub peoples of the northern and northeastern parts of the Great Lakes region. Southern Cushites, largely but not solely pastoral in economy, occupied areas to the east of the Great Lakes, in central Kenya and in northern Tanzania. All around and among these various peoples lived numerous other, smaller communities, which still centered their livelihoods on the hunting and gathering of wild food resources and maintained the ancient Khoisan cultural tradition.

Into that mix of economies and cultures, a major new ethnic element, the Mashariki Bantu, began to intrude from the west at a date around or not long after 1000 BCE. Their arrival at the western edge of the Great Lakes region initiated a long period of economic and cultural change and ethnic shift that spread

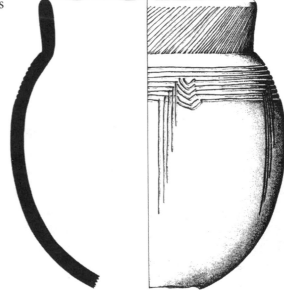

FIG. 27 Chifumbaze ceramics

The pot depicted here represents the Urewe variety of the Chifumbaze archeological tradition, made by Mashariki peoples living in the African Great Lakes region, and dates to about 2,000 years ago.

across much of the Great Lakes region in the middle centuries of the first millennium BCE.

The first millennium BCE saw also the establishment of iron technology throughout the African Great Lakes. But it was the early Mashariki Bantu, with their resoundingly different approaches to livelihood and cultural expression, who gradually became the prime movers in a radical realignment of society, economy, and ethnicity. Beginning in the Great Lakes region, that realignment was eventually spread by later Mashariki peoples all across eastern and southeastern Africa, from Uganda to Natal. In the early and middle centuries of the first millennium BCE, however, the Mashariki communities, although gradually growing in population and in social and economic importance, continued to occupy a more restricted historical landscape. The heartland of the founding era of Mashariki settlement lay in areas adjoining the great Western Rift, that long run of mountains and rift valleys extending north and south along the western edge of the Great Lakes region.

The initial penetration of Mashariki communities into the region took place probably along a broad front to the immediate west of the Western Rift. Precisely when this occurred is not known, but most probably it was at the beginning of the first millennium BCE. This settlement set in motion a variety of cultural interactions of Mashariki Bantu with Central Sudanic and Eastern Sahelian societies, and two areal groupings of Mashariki communities, the Kaskazi and Kusi, began to take shape. From the beginning the Kaskazi and Kusi may have consisted of clusters of communities that spoke several slightly differing versions of what was still a single Mashariki language.

Sometime before 500 BCE, the Kaskazi cluster of communities expanded farther eastward, probably principally into areas that would have included parts of modern-day Rwanda and Burundi. The pottery of the Chifumbaze Tradition found in Rwanda, and dating as early as the tenth to seventh centuries BCE, most probably belongs to this period. The Kusi cluster of communities, located in more southerly parts of the Western Rift region during the Middle Mashariki period, perhaps around Lake Tanganyika, probably grew in population and territory in a similar manner. They remained in contact with the developments affecting the Kaskazi peoples, but no longer in so direct a fashion.

Technology and Cultural Expansion in the Classical Age

The expansion of the Mashariki Bantu settlements triggered a wide range of new developments. First and foremost, Mashariki people began to open up large new areas to farming. The Central Sudanians had previously used the plains and the edges of the montane forest along the Western Rift. The Sog and Rub societies had relied particularly on more open savanna for their livestock and their grain crops. But in the early centuries of the first millennium BCE, large areas of the Great Lakes were still covered with forest. To the Mashariki communities, who had come from the high-rainfall, wooded regions of the Congo Basin, these areas offered a familiar kind of environment, attractive to their settlement.

Their choice of places to settle had two further probable consequences. Unopposed in the forested areas by established farming communities, the Mashariki populations are likely to have entered into a period of accelerated population growth, a common consequence elsewhere in world history when mature cultivating economies have intruded into lands previously occupied by purely food-collecting peoples. Secondly, their expansions would gradually

FIG. 28 Three-legged stools

The first of the two stools shown here is a unique woven variety of this item of furniture, made by BaTwa people. The second stool, from the Pakot, a Southern Nilotic people of Kenya, exemplifies the original technique—of carving the stool from a single block of wood. This technology developed before the first millennium BCE among peoples of the Sudanic civilization living at the south of the Middle Nile Basin.

have overwhelmed and eliminated independent hunting and gathering as a viable economic option, not only because of population growth among the Mashariki communities but also because the Mashariki people supplemented their farm-produced foods with hunting, fishing, and collecting on a considerable scale. In other words, they would have competed strongly for resources with the previous gathering peoples.

At the same time, a wider regional process of technological shift gradually began to take hold, as the knowledge and practice of ironworking spread among the peoples of the western Great Lakes. It appeared first among the Central and Eastern Sudanian communities, possibly before 1000 BCE. Before midmillennium, iron had become common among the more northerly Mashariki communities as well. Gradually, it can be expected, the adoption of iron drove into disuse the different stone toolmaking traditions of each of these sets of peoples, much later in some areas than in others.

Up to mid-millennium, these developments built up an irregular patchwork of different cultural and economic approaches to life in the western Great Lakes region, with sizable areas of Mashariki settlement interspersed, especially in the Western Rift zone and just to the east of there, with Central Sudanic and Sog territories. The interactions across ethnic lines created a new body of widely shared technological knowledge, not only of ironworking but also, especially among the Mashariki communities, of agricultural practices quite different from those they had brought with them into East Africa. As yet, however, the new agricultural knowledge had had little practical effect. Local economic orientations probably still largely coincided with ethnicity before 500 BCE.

Over the second half of the first millennium BCE, this patchwork of culture and economy began to break down. A number of particular features of material culture of Sudanic or Cushitic origin gained wide currency among the Bantu-speaking societies. Increasingly, it seems probable, Mashariki communities gave up their old style of rectangular, ridge-roofed houses in favor of the round, conical-roofed houses of the Sudanian societies. By late in the millennium, new developments in woodworking technology, notably the making of carved wooden stools, usually with three legs, and of beds with intertwined rope or wood-slat mattresses, had been adopted all across the region. Iron took on increasing importance in toolmaking even before the fifth century BCE, and the knowledge and practice of ironworking also began to spread out of the Great Lakes region, westward to Bantu peoples of the Congo Basin and to the more southerly Kusi communities of the Mashariki Bantu.

Meanwhile, the faster growth of Mashariki populations had shifted the demographic advantage away from the earlier farming societies. The Mashariki communities spread into more and more areas, and as a consequence the Central Sudanic and Sog people progressively began to be assimilated into the societies of their Bantu-speaking neighbors.

The pace of human-induced environmental change must also have increased in several areas, as a number of the Mashariki began adding grain cultivation to their agriculture, adopted new agricultural tools such as the long-handled digging stick and the iron hoe, and consequently started practicing a more extensive clearing of land. In the areas along the south or southwest of Lake Nyanza, this clearing of land by Mashariki communities may have already helped, as early as 500 BCE, open the way to the settlement for the first time of specialized cattle raisers, the Tale Southern Cushites, in the region. The Tale people were a western offshoot of the Rift Southern Cushites who inhabited the plains of north-central Tanzania. The clearing of the land would have had the effect, unintended by the Mashariki cultivators, of making available much more land for grazing animals and thus would have encouraged the spread of the Tale people with their cattle.

By about the fourth or third century BCE, the converging effects of these several different developments set off a new series of events. Population growth in more and more areas began to threaten the ability of the Mashariki to sustain, unmodified, the long-fallow yam-based agriculture that their ancestors had brought with them into western East Africa in the early parts of the millennium. One response, to add grain crops and increase the portion of the diet obtained from cultivation, had already been taken by some Mashariki communities. This step probably helped fuel the wider spread of Mashariki peoples within the African Great Lakes region. The adoption of sheep by various Mashariki societies during the same centuries and, where environment allowed, of cattle contributed a further increment to subsistence productivity. Increased livestock raising added another factor, grazing, that helped along the sustained decline of forest.

A second response was a more drastic one: to move entirely out of the western side of East Africa and to seek out suitable environments far afield in which to pursue the old livelihood or to carry on a mixture of yam raising and grain cultivation. This option was taken up particularly among the Kaskazi communities to the southwest of Lake Nyanza and among the Kusi groups residing still farther to the south. Thus began the events that mark the inception of the Later Classical Age of eastern Africa—the far-flung expansions of Bantu societies that within a period of three or four centuries, from perhaps 300 BCE to 100 CE, scattered Mashariki peoples from the coasts of Kenya at the north to the woodland savannas of Malawi and Mozambique and to the varied environments of Zimbabwe, Natal, and the Transvaal at the south.

With a now mixed agricultural heritage that blended Sudanic and West African agricultural traditions, Mashariki communities showed themselves able to adapt to a great variety of farmable environments. They became the chief expanders of the African agricultural frontier southward to the southern edge of the continent.

With them spread many ideas and practices rooted in the ancient Niger-Congo civilization of West Africa, the cultural tradition responsible for the creation of West African planting agriculture. Whole suites of social and religious ideas and of cultural practices unknown in eastern and southern Africa before 1000 BCE, and often in sharp conflict with the earlier cultural norms, had become by the fourth century CE the common heritage of communities spread from Uganda and Kenya to Natal and the Transvaal—in religion, the centrality of ancestor observances; in philosophy, the problem of evil understood as the consequence of individual malice or of the failure to honor one's ancestors; in music, an emphasis on polyrhythmic performance with drums as the key instruments; in dance, a new form of expression in which a variety of prescribed body movements took precedence over footwork; and in agriculture, the preeminence of women as the workers and the innovators.

In East Africa, Kaskazi communities were the instigators of these cultural shifts. Beginning probably as early as the second or first century BCE, several Kaskazi peoples relocated themselves at the southern and eastern edges of East Africa, far away from the Great Lakes region. A group we call the Upland Kaskazi moved 500 kilometers away, from the southern side of Lake Nyanza clear to the Pare and Usambara Mountains. Between then and 300 CE, they added new settlements in the coastal areas near modern-day Mombasa and on the southern slopes of Mount Kenya. A few of the Upland communities may even have moved farther north, to settle along the lower Jubba and Shebeelle Rivers in what is today the country of Somalia. Kaskazi people of the Northeast-Coastal group established themselves in the same centuries in the areas south of the Upland communities, near the Ruvu and Wami Rivers. Several other

Kaskazi societies moved southward, settling in the highlands all around the northern end of Lake Nyasa. Among them were the groups we call the ancestral Rufiji-Ruvuma, Rukwa, and Njombe.

With few exceptions, the Kaskazi peoples in the beginning sought out forested or woodland savanna country to settle. The Upland communities passed right across the dry central grasslands and steppe of East Africa to the tropical montane forests found in the Pare and Usambara Mountains and also on Mount Kenya. The Upland settlers on the coast took advantage of the belt of high-rainfall, wooded country along the immediate coastal hinterland of the Indian Ocean, as did their more southerly neighbors, the ancestral Northeast-Coastal Bantu. Similarly the Rufiji-Ruvuma, Rukwa, and Njombe, in settling 2,000 years ago at the north end of Lake Nyasa, all moved initially into wooded and forested lands. In all the areas, these various Kaskazi peoples were able to maintain key elements of the West African planting agriculture of their Bantu ancestors, although in many areas they would also have supplemented the growing of yams with the raising of grains. In some regions livestock, including cattle, gradually gained in importance among them as well. In the drier west-central parts of East Africa, several of the Kaskazi peoples, deeply influenced by their Southern Cushitic neighbors, even adopted the flat-roofed rectangular style of house as their own.

The Khoekhoe and the Spread of Food Production to Southern Africa

In southeastern Africa, both Kaskazi and Kusi peoples were instrumental in spreading the ideas and practices of the Classical Age of eastern Africa. In Zambia in the final two or three centuries before the common era, Kaskazi communities played a key role. Elsewhere in the southeastern parts of the continent, Kusi peoples were the principle spreaders of the new cultural ideas and the new agricultural economies.

But Kaskazi and Kusi peoples were not alone in initiating those developments. Far to the south of East Africa proper, in the lands around the middle Zambezi River, the economic developments of East Africa's Classical Age began to have a limited and indirect impact even before Mashariki peoples reached that region. We are not at all clear on how or just when these influences reached south of the Zambezi River. What we think may have happened is that a group of Eastern Sahelian–speaking peoples, formerly resident in the Great Lakes region of Africa, moved south with their livestock, possibly around the middle of the first millennium BCE, into the "Corridor" region between Lake Tanganyika

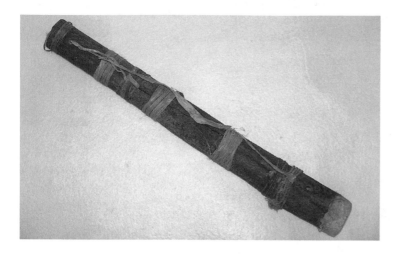

FIG. 29 Khoisan bark quiver, South Africa

Bows and arrows continued to be the chief weapons not only of Khoisan gatherer-hunters but also of the cattle- and sheep-raising Khoekhoe peoples right down to recent centuries, and this style of quiver was common among them.

and Lake Nyasa. From there, some moved farther south with their animals toward the middle stretches of the Zambezi. Across the river in what is today northeastern Botswana, a Khoisan people, the Khwe, adopted sheep and cattle from that Eastern Sahelian community, probably already by the fourth or third century BCE.

Combining sheep and cattle raising with their older hunting and gathering pursuits, the Khwe began to grow in number. Their herds grew even faster, and as a result the descendants of the Khwe had to seek out additional grazing lands to be able to feed their stock. One group, the Kwadi, expanded westward toward northern Namibia and far southern Angola. A second people, the Khoekhoe, spread southward, first into parts of the northern Transvaal and then, by the first century CE, to the south coast of Africa following the Sundays River. Between 100 and 300, some of the Khoekhoe communities expanded from there west to the Cape of Good Hope, while others moved eastward across the Kei River.

It would be wrong to see the early expansions of the Khoekhoe and of the Kwadi in northern Namibia as merely the taking over of gatherer-hunters' lands by more successful herders. Each cultural spread was as much a spread of an economic frontier as of people. As often as not, the new economy would have advanced because the people ahead of the economic frontier saw the advantages of the new mixed hunting and herding adaptation, accepted it, and made it their own. In the process, they merged into a common society with Khoekhoe or Kwadi groups who had initially brought the livestock into new areas. The languages of the Khoekhoe and Kwadi, because they were the means of communication associated with the new kind of economy, became the languages of the newly forming societies.

The growth of herder populations surely had consequences for the social and political order. Only for the Cape Khoekhoe, however, can even a partial picture of this history as yet be sketched out. From the meager preservation of bits of the Khoekhoe oral tradition, it appears that the growth and spread of the early Cape and Orange River communities led to a replacement of the bilateral, noncorporate reckoning of kinship found among their Khwe ancestors with a patrilineal, segmentary system.

As the first step in this process, we can hypothesize, the small set of close relatives by birth and marriage, who had formed the core of the earlier local Khwe gathering-hunting band, evolved into a more formal patrilineage around which a significantly larger herding band coalesced. At the same time, an older, informally recognized Khwe position of semi-hereditary band headman evolved into a more formal position of lineage-chief. The earlier typical food-collecting band, comparative cultural evidence suggests, probably had consisted of no more than twenty to thirty-five or forty people; the larger local herding band among the Khoekhoe came normally to comprise a hundred or more.

In such a larger community the nearest kin connections of many of its members must often have lain several generations back into the past. No longer could an informal, common knowledge of extended-family relationships be counted on to provide a sufficient social glue for the band, and no longer could group decision making be left to an informally reached consensus. Moreover, the spread of the economic frontier southward meant that many new people began to be incorporated into the society, people lacking previous kin connections to other members of the society. The development of formal patrilineal kin groups provided a means for incorporating such people into a recognized social unit. It provided a new constitution for social allegiance among the early Cape-Orange Khoekhoe. The lineage-chief evolved in tandem with this development into a leader able to act as the moderator over community meetings and as the enunciator, and thus also the major shaper, of the legal and political decisions that emerged from such meetings. This level of development was probably common to all of the Khoekhoe-speaking societies and may have taken place among the Kwadi as well.

In time, as the herding community continued to grow in population, the original lineage-based band would successively break up into a number of bands, each now forming a separate lineage-based local residential unit, but each also recognizing its common historical connection and considering its core patrilineages to belong to the same wider clan grouping. For the Cape Khoekhoe this second stage in the growth of social and political complexity probably began to emerge as early as their settlement near the southern coasts of South Africa, at around the beginning of the common era.

As the Cape Khoekhoe expanded farther eastward and westward in the first several centuries CE, still larger political groupings eventually emerged among them, each viewed by its members as a multiclan chiefdom. These polities comprised several clans that could trace their origins back to one earlier clan, which itself had developed out of a group of related patrilineages. The paramount chiefs of such a multiclan chiefdom were the chiefs of the senior clans within the polity. Seniority was based in this case on the historical claim of the senior clan that it was the original kin group from which the other clans of the chiefdom had split. The chiefs of the individual clans of the polity, including the historically senior clan, in turn apparently filled the roles of lineage-chiefs over the senior lineages of their respective clans.

If the evidence of seventeenth-century practice is any guide to fourth-century culture (and it may be a very weak guide at best), the chiefs of the larger chiefdoms had more a potential than practical authority over the populations of their polity. In day-to-day affairs their influence and authority tended to be exerted at the level of their own lineage and secondarily at the level of their clan. Only now and then would issues have arisen that would have brought into effect their roles as the adjudicators of interclan disputes or as the war leaders in conflicts with other chiefdoms. They had little if any role in communal religious observances. Their historical claims to chiefly ancestry and their ability to maintain a fitting degree of personal wealth in livestock appear to have been the fundamental pillars of their authority and influence.

Kusi and Kaskazi Bantu and Their Neighbors, 200 BCE to 300 CE

Already in the third and second centuries BCE, even as the Khoekhoe type of mixed herding and gathering-hunting economy began to spread south toward the eastern Cape regions, the first few Mashariki communities began to push into the northern parts of southeastern Africa. Belonging to the Kaskazi branch of the Mashariki Bantu, these communities settled in parts of central and eastern Zambia and in western Zimbabwe. Those who established themselves in Zambia made what the archeologists call the Muteteshi and Salumano cultures. A third group, who moved into western Zimbabwe, we call the Bambata people.

What is different about these communities when we compare them to other Mashariki of those times is that they already had added the major component of cattle raising to their economies. And that is perhaps not surprising. The Muteteshi, Salumano, and Bambata communities moved, after all, into the drier savanna areas that we suspect may have been the routes, a century or two earlier, of the spread of livestock south to the Khwe of the northeastern Kalahari region. The Bambata people, in particular, would have been the close neighbors of many of the early Khwe communities.

Then, by around the first century BCE and the first century CE, a still more important expansion of Mashariki Bantu communities into southern Africa got under way. Belonging to the Kusi branch of the Mashariki, these communities spread in the next 300 years across most of the higher rainfall areas of southeastern Africa.

Five major groupings of Kusi peoples took shape during this period. Around the areas on the immediate west side of Lake Nyasa could be found the ancestral Nyasan society. Across the Zambezi River, the better-watered parts of the Zimbabwe Plateau became home to the Gokomere communities, who may possibly have been a southern offshoot of the ancestral Nyasan society. To the east of Lake Nyasa and north of the Zambezi resided the ancestral Makua society, while farther south, in the coastal plain of what is today southern Mozambique, lay the lands of the ancestral Southeast-Bantu people. Finally, in the expanse of country running from the modern-day Transvaal south into Natal, could be found still another set of Kusi peoples, the ancestral Sala-Shona.

Even more strongly than the Khoekhoe and Kwadi expansions, the settlement of Kusi communities, wherever it took place in southern Africa, began to undermine the ability of the Khoisan gatherer-hunters to maintain an autonomous economic presence in the same regions. The Kusi peoples supplemented their farming with gathering and hunting and so, like the Khoekhoe and Kwadi, would have competed for food resources with Khoisan gatherer-hunters.

But the early Kusi may have held an even more important advantage of immediate and continuing effect. They settled in relatively compact villages, and those villages became manufacturing centers for the areas around them. The most important manufactures, new to southern Africa, would have been iron and iron tools. The villagers also made pottery, and it is clear from the archeological record that this pottery was often traded to neighboring gatherer-hunter bands. We suspect that a variety of other products, such as wooden stools and containers, baskets, and calabash containers, which were more perishable and so more difficult to find in the archeology, were also produced and exchanged by the village societies.

The people all about the village had only raw materials to offer in return. Hunters had hides and ostrich eggshells to trade, while the Khoekhoe would have been able to offer leather and domestic animals as well in exchange for the products of the village. The village would therefore have tended to be the focal point of inter-ethnic relations, a magnet to the countryside around it, much in

FIG. 30 Carved wooden neckrest, Zimbabwe

This kind of artifact appears to have originated among Sudanic peoples of the Middle Nile Basin. It may have been adopted in the Great Lakes region by some of the early Mashariki Bantu from their Eastern Sahelian neighbors and then taken south by the expanding Kusi peoples in the late first millennium BCE, or it may have diffused south somewhat later in time. In subsequent eras the making of neckrests spread all across the savannas south of the equatorial rainforest and even to a few of the rainforest communities (see also fig. 23).

the manner of a medieval European town. The hunters and herders had to come to the village to obtain the things they wanted or needed, and the Bantu tongue of the village would have become the language of inter-ethnic contact. If and when village expansion encroached on lands of the neighboring communities, the habits of previous contact and language use already favored an accommodation in which Bantu ethnicity would prevail.

Changes in Kinship and Chiefship among the Kusi and Kaskazi

An interesting apparent consequence of the scattering of Kaskazi and Kusi communities across east and southeastern Africa was a decrease in the scale of their political and social organization. Among most of these peoples, the double descent system of their Savanna-Bantu and early Mashariki ancestors, consisting of matriclans and matrilineages and less important patrilineages, ceased to operate and was replaced either by consistently matrilineal kinship or else, in some areas, such as among the Great Lakes Bantu, by patrilineal reckoning of descent. The two-level kinship structure of the ancestral Mashariki society, with clans and lineages, persisted among those Great Lakes communities, although shifting to a patrilineal basis. But in many of the distant areas of new settlement, we suspect, the new Kaskazi and Kusi communities may at first have reconstituted themselves around just one level of kinship, the clan.

The clan groupings that took shape in the distant new lands of settlement must often have been of heterogeneous origins. In the older Mashariki social ideology, clans had constituted named groupings of people identified with particular localities. The Mashariki expansions at the turn of the era from BCE to CE would rarely have involved large, clan-sized groups of people. Instead, the expansions, time and again, must have thrown together in a new, distant locality smaller groupings of families of different clan and regional origins. In this situation, the familiar kinship idioms the settlers brought with them would have predisposed them to view themselves as members of the same clan, simply because they now inhabited the same territory. As the new community grew, the earlier inhabitants of the region would also be incorporated into the emerging society. Sometimes the indigenous people would have joined one of the newly created clans. At other times, they would have been treated as if their herding or hunting band formed a clan of its own, and in this way would have been assimilated as a group into the new Kaskazi or Kusi society.

Similarly, the two corresponding levels of early Mashariki chiefship generally failed to survive the expansion of communities into new and distant lands. Among the ancestral Njombe, for example, chiefship seems to have been reconstituted on a new basis, with the heads of the earliest Kaskazi families in the region claiming chiefship by right of their being the first settlers. Among a number of other societies, the office of the *mu-kumu, or lineage priest-chief, persisted, although not that of the *mw-ami, or clan priest-chief; and the idea of the chief as the "owner" of his or her people and the importance of the chief in initiating the yearly rites of planting and harvesting also retained a wide acceptance.

Why chiefship should have become less complex is not hard to understand. The kin chiefs' powers depended on their relationships with the ancestors of their communities, and in the early Mashariki belief system those ancestors resided where the community had long resided. To leave the home village was to leave the lands where a chief had an established relationship with the ancestors buried there. The smaller unit, the lineage or a large part of it, was a community sufficiently compact to be able to move often over a long distance together. In those cases, the chiefship of the lineage, the *mu-kumu, might be able to reestablish itself in the new lands by undertaking rituals of conciliation with the ancestors of the previous inhabitants. But the whole clan and *mw-ami role could not so easily be carried long distances. Almost everywhere, therefore, that the new Kaskazi and Kusi expansions went in the centuries between 200 BCE and 300 CE, a lesser complexity of kin chiefship thus came into being than had been known among their Mashariki forebears before 200 BCE.

Because of this history, only among the Lakes Bantu societies, who remained in the Great Lakes region, did the position of the *mw-ami survive. Interestingly, though, the *ba-kumu (plural of *mu-kumu) of that region as early as possibly the fourth or third century BCE had ceased to be recognized as lineage heads and had been relegated to the role of doctor-diviners. A new class of chiefs, the *ba-kulu, instead became the local kin group leaders under the *mw-ami. We do not know for sure just what was going on in this case. One plausible explanation is that the *ba-ami (plural of *mw-ami) among the Lakes communities had been able to take on a new level of political authority by around 300 BCE, so that they were able to remove the competing authority of the *ba-kumu and replace it with the new subordinate position of *ba-kulu, appointed to their positions by the *ba-ami.

New Developments in Religious Thought

At two points in the final millennium before the common era, significant modifications of religious beliefs apparently also came into being in certain parts of eastern and southern Africa.

The first of these developments appears in the wide adoption by Kaskazi peoples in the Middle Mashariki period, which extended from about 700 to 500 BCE, of a new word for "God," *Mu-lungu*. This new term derived from an older Bantu verb, *-lung-*, "to become fitting, become straight." This derivation tells us that during the first half of the first millennium BCE, many of the Kaskazi communities took up an additional conceptualization of the Creator God of earlier Bantu religion as the one who put things in their proper order. This view might superficially seem similar to the concepts of Divinity we attribute to the Eastern Sahelian neighbors of the early Mashariki, the Sog and the Rub, who saw Divinity as the source of Divine judgment or retribution for wrongdoing. But the metaphor encapsulated in *Mu-lungu* is probably no more than an extension of the older Bantu conception of God as Creator to include the creation of the right order of being as well as the outward material world in which human beings find themselves. From all the rest of the indications available to us, the older Bantu conception of the Creator as a remote figure seems still to have been present among the Mashariki in the middle of the first millennium BCE.

An even more significant shift in religious ideas, but of less geographically wide impact, began about 1000 BCE in one part of East Africa. Rift Southern Cushites, including the ancestors of the Tale people, seem to have innovated a new kind of celestial metaphor for their concept of Divinity. The old Southern Cushitic word for "God" or "Divinity" was *Waak'a*, which also meant "sky." The Rift communities replaced this word with a new term, derived from their word for "sun." The change did not mean that they actually identified Divinity as the sun or as a sun god, but rather that they had begun, for reasons as yet unknown, to view the power of the sun in their daily lives as a more apt way of symbolically expressing the power of Divinity in nature.

Then in the period 800–500 BCE, this new Southern Cushitic conceptualization of Divinity spread wider, to the Southern Nilotes. This society, which formed one of the branches of the Eastern Sahelian Nilotes, moved southward around the ninth century from the Lake Turkana region and settled in the highlands west of the Kenya Rift Valley. After 500 BCE the Southern Nilotes diverged into two societies, the Kalenjin and the Tato, with the Tato moving still farther south to the Mara Plains. In both regions the Southern Nilotes came under the influence of Rift Southern Cushites who already resided in those regions, and among the new features of culture that they adopted from the Southern Cushitic inhabitants was the new idea of Divinity.

Then, toward the end of the first millennium BCE, this same new conception of Divinity spread still farther, to a number of the Kaskazi Bantu communities, who at that time were settling along the eastern and southern sides of Lake Nyanza. There they were neighbors of the western Tale Southern Cushites and also of the Tato branch of the Southern Nilotes. Their adoption of the sun metaphor is apparent in their reapplication of the ancient Bantu term for "sun," *Li-uba,* as a new word for their "Creator God," replacing the term *Mu-lungu* adopted a few hundred years earlier. Underpinning this name change was a new importance for God in the religious rites of the community and a view of God as a more actively accessible form of spirit than had been allowed for in the earlier Mashariki and proto-Bantu religion.

The interesting feature of this particular religious change was that the linkage of Divinity and the sun was very much a regional, cross-cultural development. It appeared first among the West Rift Southern Cushitic peoples, possibly no earlier than around 1000 BCE. These peoples included the various Tale communities, who lived at that period all across the Mara Plains, and other, closely related Southern Cushites in the nearby Mbulu Highlands of north-central Tanzania. The subsequent spread of this conceptualization in the second half of the first millennium BCE encompassed a large contiguous stretch of country extending northward from the Mara Plains to Mount Elgon—all lands of the Southern Nilotes by the fifth century BCE—and westward at the same time from there to the southern shores of Lake Nyanza, where Tale Southern Cushites lived and several early Mashariki communities had settled. Among all the peoples of that wide region, whatever their cultural roots or language affiliations, the same religious idea took hold. And that raises intriguing issues about the causes and the dynamics of religious change in preliterate eras, issues that remain to be explored by historians.

The Commercial Revolution and Its Consequences in Eastern Africa

The Later Classical Age of eastern African history coincided with the first period of encounter between East Africans and the Commercial Revolution. Long-distance overseas commerce reached the Indian Ocean coast of Africa during the late centuries of the first millennium BCE. It directly affected only a limited number of East Africans, but its indirect repercussions spread in time right across the continent.

One notable trading emporium, Rhapta, came into being at the coast before the first century CE and continued to be an important port town as late as the third or fourth century. Apparently the only really major trading port on the Indian Ocean seaboard of Africa, it lay most probably, from the descriptions we have of it, somewhere along the northern or north-central coast of present-day Tanzania, possibly near the present-day Tanzanian capital, Dar es Salaam. Its archeological remains have yet to be discovered. The local inhabitants of the region imported glass beads and iron goods, such as spears, axes, knives, and small awls, brought south by visiting South Arabian and eastern Mediterranean merchants, while exporting ivory, rhinoceros horn, and tortoiseshell.

Like Carthage, which was founded by Phoenicians on the Mediterranean coast of Africa, Rhapta originated as a trading settlement closely linked to outside commercial interests, in this case South Arabian merchants. Rhapta and its trade are reported in the first century CE to have been under the purview of the

FIG. 31 *Mtepe*

East African sailors were already building this kind of boat in the first century CE, nearly 2,000 years ago, along the coasts of present-day Kenya and Tanzania.

governor of Mapharitis, a province in the Himyaritic kingdom of Yemen in Arabia. The taxing and regulating of the trade along the coast and at Rhapta were farmed out to merchants from the South Arabian port city of Mocha, whose priority in the coastal trade had been established some time previous to the first century CE. Many of these merchants had married women from the Rhapta area and spoke the local language as well as their own South Arabian tongue. The majority of the local people, at least during Rhapta's halcyon days from the first to the fourth centuries, would probably have been Mashariki communities speaking a language we call Northeast-Coastal Bantu (see map 14).

The first-century CE merchants' guidebook, *Periplus Maris Erythraei*, tells us that the locals made "sewn" boats, an apparent early reference to the cord-sewn plank boat, the *mtepe*. East African coastal boat builders continued to construct this kind of seagoing craft as late as the nineteenth century. The merchants' guide also reports the use of dugout canoes at Rhapta. Dugouts were an ancient craft of Bantu-speaking societies and their Niger-Congo ancestors, and their use would be consistent with the placing of the earliest Northeast-Coastal Kaskazi communities around Rhapta. The *mtepe* style of boat is of uncertain origin. It may have been a partly local invention, but more widespread Indian Ocean ideas of boat technology probably contributed to its design.

The people of the region around Rhapta are said to have behaved "each in his own place, just like chiefs." They belonged, in other words, to the kind of small, local, independent communities that would have been typical of the early Kaskazi and Kusi societies.

Distant Repercussions of Commerce: Interior Africa

The new kind of trade had only a restricted direct impact on the eastern Africans during its heyday, from around 300 BCE to 300 CE. But the development of the wider Indian Ocean networks of commercial interchange had much further-reaching consequences for eastern African participation in two of the broader trends of world history in those times, agricultural elaboration and technological change. These consequences eventually extended to a far larger portion of the eastern and southern African populations, although such wider effects belong on the whole to later times, after the fourth century CE.

The sea trade itself, by offering iron and iron goods at the coast, provided an alternative access to metalworking technology, separate from the knowledge of iron that spread out contemporaneously from the Great Lakes region, which the Mashariki expansions brought to the coast at the turn of the era. The arrival of the Commercial Revolution, in other words, helped to link up the technological inventiveness of interior Africa with the parallel trends in metallurgy outside the continent.

In addition, with the founding of Rhapta in the last few centuries BCE, the new kind of town, as above all a commercial center, came also to eastern Africa. But Rhapta apparently long remained an exotic flower in the eastern African economic environment, apparently unable to survive the downturn in world commerce of the fifth to seventh centuries CE. Only in the ninth and tenth centuries CE, with the rise of the Swahili city-states, long after Rhapta had disappeared from the historical stage, can the commercial town be said to have truly taken root in the East African coastal milieu.

The Commercial Revolution had one other set of ramifications for eastern Africans of the early first millennium CE, set in motion by a different kind of long-distance colonizing movement. The colonists in this instance, of Indonesian origin, did not apparently come, like the South Arabians, for the purpose of setting up a commercial colony. But just why and how they did come to the continent remains unclear.

The evidence in the language of their modern Malagasy descendants, consisting of early word borrowings from a Mashariki tongue, shows that they first settled for a time along the coast of Tanzania or Kenya. They arrived there between the first and third centuries CE. They most probably traveled to their destination along the then developing sea lanes of the Indian Ocean, first following those connecting Indonesia with India, and then passing from India across to the shores of East Africa. In about the third or fourth century, having probably already intermarried to some extent with the local East African peoples, the forebears of the Malagasy sailed farther south and crossed over the Mozambique Channel to Madagascar, then uninhabited, and laid the basis for the modern-day Malagasy populations of that island.

The Indonesians had an impact exceeding what their small numbers might be expected to have imparted. They had such an effect for one interconnected pair of reasons—they came from a region with a wet tropical climate similar to that found along the Tanzanian shoreline and parts of the Kenyan coast; and they brought with them not only food crops well adapted to that climatic regime but for the most part crops reproduced by planting rather than sowing of seeds, notably Asian yams, taro, bananas, and sugarcane. Moreover, they arrived in the second to third centuries CE, when Northeast-Coastal and other

Mashariki communities, who already practiced a strikingly similar agriculture, had begun to establish themselves in the immediate hinterlands of the Indian Ocean seaboard.

These Bantu-speaking peoples—with their planting agriculture of West African origin, in which indigenous African yams may still have been the preferred staple of the diet—would thus have been able to rapidly add the Asian yams to their crop repertory. Sugarcane, taro, and bananas probably also were adopted relatively early in the first millennium CE by the Bantu communities of the coastal hinterlands. The consequence for these groups would have been a fairly rapid enrichment in the variety of their diet. Their encounter with influences arriving along the Indian Ocean sea lanes thus helped to bring about an even more productive and successful agriculture than had already been created by their forebears' synthesis of Sudanic and West African practices just a few centuries before, in the later centuries of the first millennium BCE.

Because these Asian crops had been domesticated in environments much like those found in many parts of tropical Africa, a few of them eventually spread inland far beyond the areas of direct contact of coastal East Africans with the Commercial Revolution. They had reached the continent in the newer historical fashion, via a long-distance lane of diffusion created by commercial contacts. But within the continent, where the effects of the Commercial Revolution were not strong until much more recent centuries, the new crops diffused the old-fashioned way, from community to neighboring community wherever the climate allowed. And for the most part the wider spread of the crops, because it was slow and uneven, belongs to a subsequent period of history, from the fifth to the tenth centuries, dealt with in chapter 6.

As an example, the banana appears to have spread by two routes during the centuries before 1000 CE. In northern Tanzania and southern Kenya, the crop moved inland from the coast to become strongly established in the Pare Mountains, around Mount Kilimanjaro, and in the Mount Kenya region only toward the end of the first millennium CE. In northern Mozambique, in contrast, the banana may have diffused inland to Malawi centuries earlier, advancing through the wetter climate zones of that region and then through far western Tanzania all the way to the Great Lakes by probably around 1,000 years ago. Even before then, a second arm of this movement probably passed northward through eastern Congo, then westward through the equatorial rainforest, and eventually into the better-watered parts of West Africa, before 1000 CE.

In the equatorial rainforest, the adoption of the banana has been argued to

FIG. 32 "Thumb-pianos," or lamellophones

The first instrument shown here typifies the complex, metal-pronged mbiras made by Shona musicians of southeastern Africa. The second instrument, from West Africa, has bamboo prongs and a simpler layout. It gives us an idea of what the earliest lamellophones may have looked like before the invention of iron-pronged thumb-pianos (mbiras) in the lower Zambezi regions 1,500 years ago and before the spread of this new type across the Congo Basin as far as West Africa.

have revolutionized the productive capacities of the local Bantu agriculture after 300 CE and so allowed new directions of social and political history to emerge in later centuries. The same kind of case has been made for the banana in several areas of East Africa, such as around Kilimanjaro and in Buganda and Bukoba along Lake Nyanza, and this is a theme we will consider in later chapters.

Another notable enrichment of the eastern and southern African diet that probably owes to the Indonesian influences of the first three or four centuries

CE is the introduction and spread of the chicken, a domesticate of southeast Asian origin. The keeping of chickens spread first into the eastern side of East Africa. It then diffused southward, after the expansion of Mashariki Bantu groups into southeastern Africa, and westward at the same time into the Great Lakes region and from there west across equatorial Africa. Whether the chicken reached West Africa from the equatorial regions or from other directions remains as yet uncertain.

One additional domestic animal that may owe its presence in parts of central eastern Africa to the Indonesian settlers is the pig. Raised by a number of Mashariki communities in the regions surrounding the lower Zambezi, the pig has an uncertain antiquity, however, in the region. An alternative introduction, by much later Portuguese intruders in the sixteenth century, is thus possible. But the great importance of the animal among the Malagasy and among their Indonesian forebears makes its introduction during the first millennium CE by the early Malagasy much the more probable answer.

Interestingly, the influences of the ancestors of the Malagasy on developments within Greater Eastern Africa extended into matters musical as well as agricultural. At least one instrument, the xylophone, today widely found in tropical Africa, had its clear historical antecedents in Southeast Asia and Indonesia. The xylophone seems most probably to have spread first from the southeastern coasts of Africa westward via the Zambezi region toward Angola and southern Congo. Its establishment in southeastern parts of the continent postdates the use of an indigenous eastern Africa musical instrument, the thumb-piano (or mbira). We know this because in several instances older names for the mbira were reapplied to the new instrument. The spread of the xylophone farther west across the continent, to the forested parts of West Africa, belongs to periods after the third or fourth century CE.

The mbira as we know it today originated in southeastern Africa in the early first millennium CE. The instrument in its simplest form consists of keys in the form of prongs attached to a resonance board. Various Benue-Kwa people, including the Bantu, built lamellophones, instruments ancestral to the mbira, with the prongs of bamboo or palm, probably much earlier than 2,000 years ago. But then, in the first half of the first millennium CE, musicians in one or more of the Kusi societies of southeastern Africa invented a new and more resonant kind of mbira with iron prongs. It is an instrument that requires considerable skill and training to play successfully, and its use has greatly enriched the musical traditions of many areas.

Western Equatorial Africa: Social and Economic Repercussions of Agricultural Expansion

Farming, Fishing, and Trade in the Rainforests

To the west of eastern Africa, in both the northern and southern savanna belts and in the rainforest, new expansions of Niger-Congo languages and cultures took place during the period from 1000 BCE to 300 CE. In many cases, these expansions accompanied the further spread of the agricultural frontier into new areas. Ironworking took hold, too, all across these regions before the end of the period, and in the savanna zones new agricultural developments gave added impetus to the establishment there of farming ways of life.

North of the rainforest, in woodland savannas of what is today the Central African Republic, new expansions of Ubangian peoples were under way. The early Ubangian movements eastward in the third and second millennia BCE had established a number of Ubangian societies along the Bomu and Uele Rivers and their tributary streams as far east as the western edge of the southern Middle Nile Basin. These communities practiced the West African planting agriculture with its yams and oil palms. Like the contemporary Bantu to the south, they made major use of river resources, by fishing and building dugout canoes, and they also hunted. Between 1000 BCE and 300 CE, these communities increasingly began to clear new lands for cultivation in areas well away from the major streams, lands previously left to the older gatherer-hunter peoples.

Two kinds of consequences arose from these developments. One was a growing incorporation of the former gatherer-hunter peoples into the expanding Ubangian societies. By 300 CE, only in southern areas, where Ubangian people lived in the rainforest as neighbors of the forest Bantu, did autonomous BaTwa communities of gatherer-hunters continue to persist alongside the farming peoples. A second consequence of the spread of Ubangian farming into areas away from the streams was the development of specialized fishing economies among those Ubangians who continued to reside along several of the major rivers. As the farming Ubangians exchanged farm produce for fish with the riverside communities, a new basis for extended and more complex trade relations began to slowly emerge in the region.

Within the rainforest itself, the 1,300 years between 1000 BCE and 300 CE were marked in several regions by a similar spread of Bantu-speaking agricultural communities into areas skipped over by the earlier age of Bantu settlement between 3500 and 1000 BCE. The biggest of these secondary expansions began just about 2,000 years ago, with the spread of the ancestral Mongo society into the heart of the Congo Basin. Following the various tributaries of the Lulonga, Busira, and Momboyo Rivers eastward from the areas south of the Ubangi-Congo confluence, Mongo communities by the early second millennium CE had come to occupy nearly the whole of the interior of the basin, from the middle Congo River on the north to the Sankuru River at the south.

A similar spread, but one that instead went westward, involved the Boan peoples. Descendants of Nyong-Lomami Bantu communities who had settled in the third or second millennium in the northeastern equatorial rainforest, the Boans began a succession of new expansions around the middle of the first millennium BCE. These expansions carried the Boans first northward to the southern edge of the northern savanna belt and then westward, spreading the older-style, minimally intrusive planting agriculture of their forebears into the regions lying between the middle Congo on the south and the Uele River on the north.

Previously, in the early centuries of the first millennium BCE, the northeastern rainforest had developed into a zone of varied cross-cultural encounter. The ancestral Boans, a Bantu-speaking society, occupied the lands around the upper Bomokandi River. Two quite different groupings of Central Sudanic-speaking farmers, the Mamvu-Balese and Medje-Lombi, resided to the east and the west, respectively, of the proto-Boans. To the north lay the lands of several Ubangian peoples with a cultivating economy. All through the region, BaTwa communities coexisted with the farmers, hunting the game and gathering the wild food of the rainforest.

The characterizing development of the centuries from about 500 BCE onward was the long-term, slow expansion of the Boans. In the early stages of their spread the Boans had particularly close interactions with the Mamvu-Balese and assimilated considerable numbers of these Central Sudanians into their societies. The early Mamvu-Balese must have had a strong impact on the development of Boan culture during this period. But just what these influences were has not yet been studied by historians.

By the early first millennium CE the major trend of Boan expansion shifted northward into the territories of the Ubangian peoples. The Boans contributed one particularly notable cultural influence that spread widely among the Ubangian peoples of the Uele and Bomu River areas. The Boan version of the ancient Bantu rites of male initiation and circumcision was eventually adopted all across those regions. The causes and course of this wide cultural diffusion are still unclear. Just how early this influence spread is also at question, although most probably these customs began to be adopted by Ubangian peoples during the initial period of expansion of Boan peoples northward into the eastern Ubangian lands, from about 2,000 to 1,500 years ago.

The BaTwa: Autonomy or Dependence?

A fascinating feature of developments within the equatorial rainforest itself is the extent to which the BaTwa gatherer-hunter communities in most areas were able to maintain their cultural and economic autonomy, even in the midst of an expanding agricultural world all about them. Clearly, large areas of forest must have remained in their possession, and as the work of Professor Kairn Klieman has shown, BaTwa peoples again and again in history reasserted their historical and cultural distinctiveness. The contrast with savanna regions in this respect is sharp, for in the northern savanna belt the Ubangians and, in

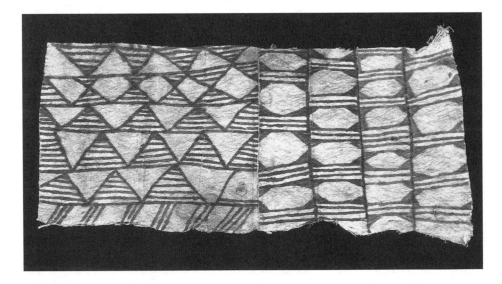

FIG. 33 Barkcloth

Making barkcloth is an ancient technology among Niger-Congo peoples. The particular example shown here, though, was made by BaTwa people of the northeastern parts of the Congo Basin. Whether the BaTwa adopted this technology after 3000 BCE from their Bantu-speaking Niger-Congo neighbors or may earlier have made barkcloth themselves is not yet known.

most of the southern savannas, the Savanna-Bantu relatively rapidly assimilated the former gatherer-hunter peoples of those regions. Only in the rainforests did the BaTwa preserve their autonomous communities down to recent centuries.

On the other hand, we should not mistake their autonomy for some kind of absolute independence. From the beginning of Bantu settlement in the rainforest in the fourth and third millennia, BaTwa peoples entered into close trade relations; and these relations introduced them early on to polished-stone tool technology and to pottery, among other things. By the last 1,000 years before the common era, BaTwa communities must often have relied as well on a mixture of food resources—those they themselves hunted and gathered, together with cultivated foods they obtained by trade from their agricultural neighbors.

A side effect of these close economic ties was the adoption over time by the BaTwa—depending on who their neighbors were—of either Bantu, Ubangian, or Central Sudanic languages. Their original languages are all now extinct and therefore unknown to us.

Culture Change in the Southern Savannas, 1000 BCE to 300 CE

In the southern savanna belt, a variety of societies evolved out of the ancestral Savanna-Bantu society. As we learned in chapter 3, the Savanna-Bantu had by around 1000 BCE scattered out along the southern edges of the rainforest in a long eastward-extending chain of communities. The farthest east of these groups, the Mashariki, then entered into a series of important roles in later eastern African history. But what about the Savanna-Bantu societies of the western regions?

Just west of the early Mashariki peoples, in the areas around and to the east of the middle Lualaba River, several groupings of Savanna-Bantu communities had emerged by about 1000 BCE. Two of these, the ancestral Sabi and the ancestral Botatwe, have had a lasting historical importance because of their role in the southward spread of agriculture and in the later culture history of east-central Africa. Toward the end of the first millennium BCE and in the first four centuries CE, the Sabi and Botatwe both moved southward and settled in adjacent parts of what is today the Katanga Province of Congo, the Sabi apparently along and to the east of the upper Lualaba River and the Botatwe to the west of the river.

In that region, though remaining distinct societies, the two peoples shared in a strongly linked set of cultural developments. Most notably, the early Sabi shifted to a solely matrilineal reckoning of descent and inheritance, and among both societies communal female initiation ceremonies became perhaps their central social rite. They maintained two rites of passage for women, the first at the onset of puberty and the second at the birth of the first child. In these rites, we suspect, they retained much earlier Bantu practices (see chapter 4), widely lost elsewhere. Male initiation became unimportant, and the rituals of male circumcision disappeared entirely from use. During the same period, both the ancestral Sabi and ancestral Botatwe languages created a new prefix, *na-, which was added to the words for social offices and occupations; this prefix identified female holders of those positions. Clearly, an important consolidation of female gender roles was coming into being in those centuries, in which women were, if anything, strengthening their position in society.

A second significant development of this Sabi-Botatwe cultural world was the emergence of a new conceptualization of the old Creator God of Niger-Congo religion. In both the ancestral Sabi and the ancestral Botatwe languages, a new word for "God," *Leeza, began to be used. Its derivation from a verb meaning "to nourish" reveals a shift away from the older concept of a distant Creator to a view that saw God as a more active and supportive force in human life. Professor Christine Ahmed has proposed that, because nurturing is commonly linked to women's roles in culture, this theological shift in part mirrored the general accentuating of female roles under way in those centuries in the ancestral Sabi and Botatwe societies.

To the west of the Sabi and Botatwe, another early Savanna-Bantu people, the ancestral Lubans, carried the agricultural frontier southward into the region between the middle Kasai and upper Lomami Rivers. By the close of the first millennium BCE, four descendant societies were taking shape in different parts of that region. In the north, near the Sankuru River, lay the lands of the ancestral Songye society, while the ancestral Luba, Kaonde, and Kanyok peoples could be found across the areas west and south of the earliest Songye. We know as yet little about the early cultural changes among these communities, but in later centuries some of these peoples, notably the Luba, would become key players in the rise of the earliest states in the southern savannas.

Still farther west lay the lands of the Western-Savanna peoples. In the early first millennium BCE, the ancestral Western-Savanna groups at first would have been located just south of the lower Congo River, in areas where rainforest and woodland savanna were interspersed. By the second half of the millennium, the Western-Savanna communities had begun a wide expansion along two fronts.

One direction of new settlements moved southeastward into the uppermost watershed of the Zambezi River; the other line of advance went more directly southward through the highland areas of today's Angola. In the first two or three centuries CE, one group of the Savanna-Bantu moved even farther south, following the Zambezi River into the area of moist soils that make up the interior floodplain of the Zambezi, in the far southwest portion of modern-day Zambia.

Agricultural Change and Expansion in the Southern Savannas

The early stages of expansion of both the Luban and the Western-Savanna peoples took place in areas of high-rainfall woodland savanna, where the older planting agriculture of their Bantu forebears could continue to be practiced easily and successfully. But by the close of the first millennium BCE, the new agricultural developments among the Mashariki Bantu of eastern Africa started to diffuse rapidly westward across the savanna region. From the western edges of the African Great Lakes region, the raising of finger millet and sorghum spread into the woodland savanna areas, first to the Sabi and then to the Botatwe and Luban peoples, and finally from them all the way west to the Atlantic coast and the mouth of the Congo River by early in the first millennium CE. In the first four centuries CE, sorghum and pearl millet spread, too, across the drier savanna farther south, from the Kaskazi communities of eastern and central Zambia and the Kusi peoples of southeastern Africa to the southernmost Western-Savanna communities of the Zambezi floodplain.

Several important domestic animals new to these regions further enhanced the range of potential food resources available for the rainforest and savanna societies of equatorial Africa. Sheep were widely adopted in both the rainforest and savanna zones during the first millennium BCE. They seem to have reached western equatorial Africa in this period by several routes of diffusion. One route of the spread of sheep raising followed down the Congo River, coming ultimately from the Central Sudanic peoples of the far northeastern equatorial rainforest; a second route passed more directly south from the Chad Basin into the western rainforest and beyond into Angola; a third introduction of sheep passed from the western Great Lakes region to the Luban peoples; and still a fourth line of the diffusion of sheep keeping lay along the northern edges of the Kalahari region. In this latter region, the early Khoekhoe and Kwadi communities were the transmitters of sheep to the later-arriving Bantu societies. The keeping of domestic pigs may have spread southward, too, in this era from West

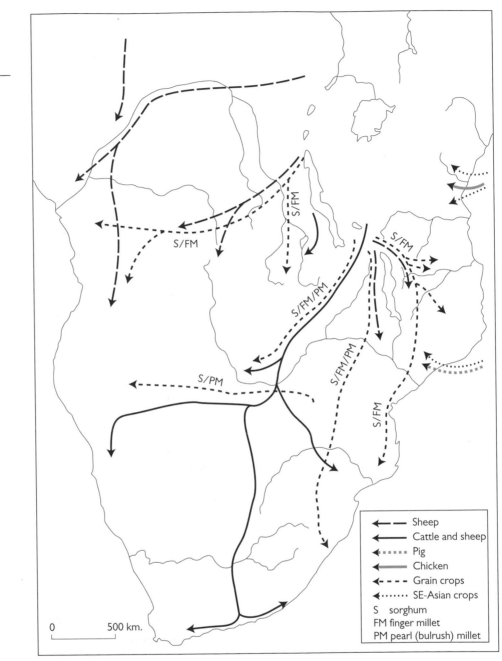

S/FM

S/FM

S/FM

S/FM/PM

S/PM

S/FM/PM

S/FM

	Sheep
	Cattle and sheep
	Pig
	Chicken
	Grain crops
	SE-Asian crops

S   sorghum
FM finger millet
PM pearl (bulrush) millet

0   500 km.

MAP 15 The spread of new crops and animals in the southern half of Africa,
300 BCE to 300 CE

Africa and become a widely practiced addition to the household economies of a large number of societies in both the rainforest and the western parts of the southern savanna belt.

Last but not least, the keeping of cattle also diffused westward early in the first millennium CE from the Mashariki Bantu of eastern Africa eventually as far as the Atlantic coast. Because the woodland savanna areas harbored tsetse flies, and thus cattle sleeping sickness, the knowledge of cattle diffused to these regions irregularly and often only centuries later, after sufficient woodland had been cleared to lessen the danger of sleeping sickness. Only in the southern, drier parts of the southern savanna belt, bordering on the Kalahari, did cattle keeping become a well-established practice among Savanna-Bantu societies during the first four centuries CE. Interestingly, in most western areas of the southern savanna zone the practice of milking cattle was never adopted, even where large numbers of cattle were raised in later times. Only the southern-most of the Western-Savanna societies, the Southwest-Bantu people, who had settled around the lower Kunene River, made milking an important source of food.

Ironworking in Western Equatorial African History

On top of these various developments came the spread of iron technology. The first stage of this changeover in technology took place sometime before 500 BCE, when knowledge of the smelting and forging of iron spread west to the Boans, under the influence, it appears, of both the Central Sudanian and the Kaskazi Bantu inhabitants of the Western Rift. From the Boans, ironworking then spread down the middle Congo River to the Ubangi confluence. From there, by or before 300 BCE, this technology spread south toward the mouth of the Congo, more directly west toward the Atlantic via the Ogowe River Valley, and up the Sangha River toward Cameroon. In Cameroon this spread of iron-working would soon have reached areas where the knowledge of iron had already been established for several centuries. A second line of the spread of ironworking seems to passed up the Lualaba to the Botatwe and Sabi peoples sometime between 500 and 100 BCE, and from them westward via the Sankuru and lower Kasai Rivers toward the lower Congo River region. Finally, between about 200 BCE and 300 CE, a third line of the spread of ironworking technology passed from the Kaskazi and Kusi Bantu of east-central Africa through the southern savanna belt and from there northwestward to the lower Congo, where all three lines of the spread of iron eventually crossed each other.

Ironworking took hold gradually in most regions and, perhaps for that reason, did not usually convey a sudden great economic or technological advantage to its makers. But its appearance in the various regions of western equatorial Africa did have serious long-term economic consequences. Some areas, because they had better iron ore resources, grew into important producing areas of iron and iron tools. Because the easiest routes of travel, particularly in the rainforest, were the rivers, the iron products of these regions frequently were carried by boat to distant markets. The older kinds of trade, for instance, in fish or in stone for stone toolmaking, began to be supplemented by an increasingly important trade in metal, and often the older fishing specialist communities grew into collections of allied trading villages, selling their own fish and acting as middlemen in the metal and other trades between distant places.

Several especially important centers of this new volume and variety of trade had already emerged by 100–300 CE. Two of these, which continued for centuries to be important junctures of trade, were the Ubangi-Congo confluence, where the long-distance trade of the two rivers merged, and the Ogowe River, which for many centuries provided the major connecting linking between the western and central parts of the equatorial rainforest. A third area, which gained particularly great importance after 1000 CE (see chapter 6), lay along the lower Congo River, above and below the Malebo Pool.

Commerce, Merchants, and States: Northeastern Africa

In the northeast portions of Africa, all across what are today the countries of Egypt, Sudan, Eritrea, Ethiopia, and Somalia, the period between 1000 BCE and 300 CE was similarly a time of great ferment and change. The age of iron gradually took hold in technology everywhere through these regions. Commerce penetrated directly into the northern portions, sometimes into places where states had long existed and sometimes where states and towns now for the first time came into being. In the southern portions of northeastern Africa, new kinds of government arose, and newer as well as older kinds of agricultural invention spread more widely.

Egypt and the Commercial Revolution

Egypt from the twelfth century BCE onward ceased for the most part to intervene directly in the affairs of neighboring regions. Historians often argue that the military adventures of Rameses II in southwestern Asia greatly undermined the economic capacities of Egypt, bringing an end to its period of military might; and this conclusion may well be true for the decades immediately after Rameses' reign. But it does not explain why Egypt never again successfully aspired to empire and why from the eighth century onward it repeatedly fell under the rule of outside powers—the Napatan kingdom between 751 and the 650s BCE; the Assyrians in the middle 600s; the Persians in the later sixth and the fifth centuries and again between 341 and 332; Alexander the Great from 332 to 323; after him, the Ptolemies from 323 to 30; and finally the Roman empire after 30 BCE.

A large part of the answer surely lies in the persistence in Egypt of a conservative kind of political economy. Even as late as the third century BCE under the Ptolemies, royal power through most of the long length of the country still rested on the right of divine kings to redistribute goods and property to the landed and priestly upper classes and, through this means, to exert a centralized control over the land, the people, and the disposition of the products of the land. With this kind of social formation still strongly in place, economic transactions in imported prestige goods could continue to be channeled through the court and regional authorities and used to enhance and maintain the system, just as had been true from the time of the earliest state building along the Nile. Geography assisted the old ruling class in keeping the Commercial Revolution at arm's length. Because the new kind of trade impinged directly on the country only at the far north, commerce could easily be channeled through a few central entrepots under royal control—in the Ptolemaic period, Alexandria on the Mediterranean coast especially served this kind of purpose.

One result was that an indigenous merchant class involved in long-distance commerce did not appear in Egypt until much later times. When we first begin to hear of such merchants in the country in the seventh century, they are Phoenicians or Greeks operating under the aegis of the Pharaoh. As a result also, the potentially advantageous developments of the age were often late in reaching Egypt. Most notably, ironworking did not fully take hold there until the sixth and fifth centuries BCE, at least 700 or 800 years after it had become important in the adjacent lands of southwest Asia. In other words, while nearby areas in Asia and the eastern Mediterranean grew in economic and material potential, Egypt not so much declined as stayed the same.

The Rise of the Napata Kingdom

The first major challenge to Egyptian independence, though, came not from the north but from the south, from the Dongola Reach of the Nile. Egyptian colonial rule, which had crushed Kerma in the sixteenth century BCE, became and remained a pervasive force throughout that region down through at least the fourteenth century. The initial withdrawal of direct Egyptian authority from Dongola Reach may have begun in the thirteenth century, when Rameses II transferred so many of the resources of Egypt to his efforts to conquer and hold the lands beyond Sinai in far western Asia. In any case, by the eleventh century, Egyptian rule over the Nubian stretches of the Nile was clearly something of the past, and the older Sudanic cultural traditions of the region soon began strongly to reassert themselves in all realms of life, from pottery manufacture to politics.

In the ninth century, a new major kingdom took form, with its center along the Dongola Reach. Its capital was the town of Napata, and we give that name also to the kingdom as a whole. In 750 BCE, under its fourth known king, Peye ("Piankhi"), Napata launched an invasion of Egypt; and in the next several years Peye, claiming to be the protector of the traditions of Egypt and allying with the priesthood of Amun in Thebes, was able to establish his rule over the southern portions of the country. Under Peye's grandson, Taharqa, the Napatan dynasty extended its control in the early seventh century over most of the country. Rebellion in northern Egypt and the Assyrian invasion and conquest of the country finally brought Napatan rule to an end in the middle of the century.

After the 650s, Napata history entered another era of which our knowledge is sketchy. From archeological work it is now evident that while the capital of the kingdom, Napata city, as well as the royal burial grounds of Nuri, lay along the Dongola Reach, the Napata kingdom had expanded well to the south. Its additional territories, lying along the Nile between the Fourth Cataract and the confluence of the Abbai and Nile Rivers, extended south of the Sahara Desert into areas of annual rainfall capable of supporting steppe vegetation. At least one other major city in the kingdom, Meroe, appears to have been founded even before the seventh century near where the Atbara River joins the Nile, and there may have been other such early towns in the southern regions yet to be excavated by archeologists.

Three potentially advantageous features characterized this southern portion of the Napata kingdom. First, it was an area which, because it received a regular yearly rainfall, had the potential to support a larger population and a more diversified agricultural base than the restricted belt of irrigated farmlands of the Dongola Reach. Secondly, it seems to have been a region affected fairly early by the establishment of ironworking, apparently introduced from the south. Thirdly, the stretches of the Nile around the town of Meroe lay in and near to regions in which could be found a number of the products that came to be valued in the Mediterranean world during the Commercial Revolution. Moreover, the evidence is strong that Meroe carried on the old cotton-weaving tradition of the Middle Nile Basin and soon became a manufacturing and exporting center for cotton cloth. The southern areas of the kingdom had, in other words, productive capacities that allowed them to benefit from the commercial trends of the age. The Dongola Reach, in the old heartlands of the state, lacked many of these capacities and so became something of an economic backwater.

Napatan Kingship Relocates to Meroe

Sometime between 640 and 300 BCE, the advantages of the southern areas led to a major shift of power in the Napatan state—the capital and the center of government moved south to the city of Meroe. From that point onward, historians call the state by a new name, after its new capital, the kingdom of Meroe. Exactly when this shift took place is uncertain, but it may have happened in the later seventh or early sixth century. For a long time after the shift of the political capital, the rulers of Meroe continued to be buried along the Dongola Reach at Nuri, in the old royal burial grounds. Not until 324 BCE did the kings and queens begin to be interred at Meroe itself. Napata remained, however, an especially important and, at times, a relatively autonomous province of the kingdom throughout its later history.

The high period of Meroitic power and influence lay in the centuries between 300 BCE and 100 CE. New directions of change in Egypt and the eastern Mediterranean came to play an essential part in the prosperity of Meroe during this period. After the death of Alexander the Great in 323, his conquests, which included Egypt, were divided up among his three leading generals. In this division, the rule over Egypt went to Ptolemy, whose descendants formed the last dynasty of independent ancient Egypt. The Ptolemaic period in Egyptian history lasted down to death of the final ruler of that dynasty, Queen Cleopatra, in 23 BCE.

Ptolemy and his immediate successors were quick to consolidate their hold over Egypt by molding their rule to fit in with traditional Egyptian views and ideology. At the same time, however, their own roots lay in the Hellenistic world of the eastern Mediterranean, with its wide-ranging cultural and commercial connections. So the Ptolemies from the first were aware that if they were maintain and strengthen their political base, they would have to build the

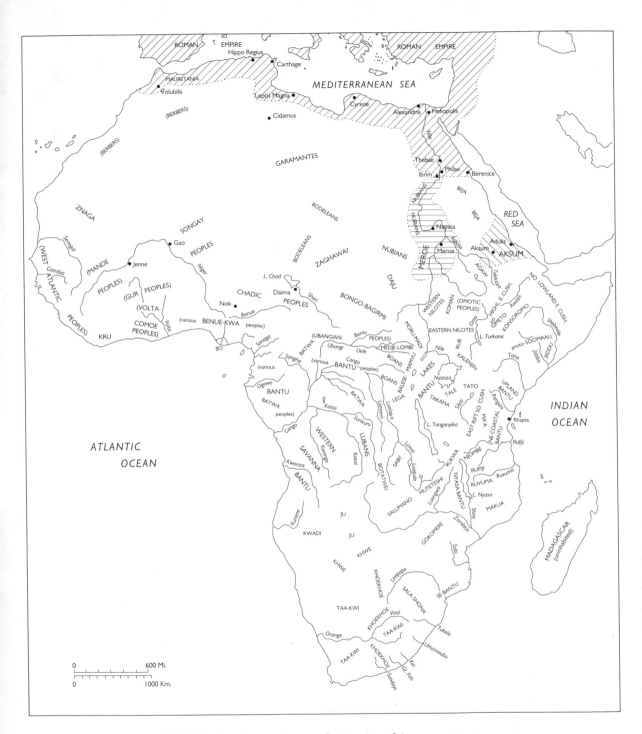

MAP 16 Peoples, states, and cities in Africa, ca. 100 CE

commercial strength of their country. For this reason they welcomed merchant activity. They also subsidized the opening up of the Red Sea to seagoing commerce, gaining for the first time a regular Egyptian participation in the new era of trade with northeastern Africa and the Indian Ocean.

The Ptolemaic development of commerce in the Red Sea had the immediate consequence for Meroe of providing regular outlets for Meroitic products. The city of Meroe lay less than 400 kilometers from suitable ports on the Red Sea coast, and soon a variety of products began to move to these ports from Meroe and its sister towns along the Nile. Some goods, such as iron, were produced in the urban areas, and other items, such as tortoiseshell and ostrich feathers, in the hills between Meroe and the Red Sea. Still other products, including gold and ivory, came from areas farther south in the Middle Nile Basin.

The cities of Meroe grew into significant manufacturing centers during these centuries. They produced cotton cloth for the trade. Meroe city itself became the leading iron-producing locale in the northern Middle Nile Basin. Its ironworks supplied local needs, military and domestic, and probably also provided iron and iron tools for regional trade with the surrounding peoples of the Middle Nile Basin.

The Meroitic kingdom through most of its history, we suspect, had a two-sector economy, manifested in two kinds of social structures. On the one hand, it had an urban population located in a number of towns along the Nile, the most important of which was the city of Meroe itself. In these cities resided the king and a class of government officials. The fact that a number of towns existed, not just a single capital city, suggests that more than government functions accounted for the existence of urban centers. Most probably, some sort of indigenous merchant class had come into being in the towns. In addition, weavers, iron smiths, potters, masons, and other skilled artisans plied their trades, as the Meroitic state built up its thriving economy. Below these strata would have come the servants and laborers, including probably slaves. These working folk would have formed the majority of the society and carried out much of the heavy and menial labor of urban life.

Outside the cities a different kind of society and economy would have prevailed. Divided into an uncertain number of provinces, rural areas would still have been populated, as they had been for several thousand years, largely either by people with mixed herding and cultivating economies or, in drier areas, by communities relying principally on livestock raising. Some of these communities would have had no more government than was provided by a local community assembly of elders. Others gave allegiance to sacral chiefs, but otherwise the only experience of a higher state authority would have been periodic encounters with Meroitic provincial government.

In one large rural area, however, we do have evidence that the Meroitic government exerted a more continuous and direct control. In the steppes to the east of the Nile, just south of the Atbara River, the Meroites built and maintained large earthen diversion dams across the beds of seasonal streams. As archeologists have noted, these engineering works would have created reservoirs providing water for livestock during the long, nine-month dry season of that area. What they have not always noted is that the dams would also have allowed recessional irrigation of fields to be practiced. In recessional irrigation farming, one plants crops in the wet soils left behind as a stream or other body of water shrinks in the dry season. By this means, both the meat and grain supplies available to the urban populations of Meroe along the Nile would have been considerably enhanced.

Culture, Economy, and Ethnicity in Meroe

The kingdom of Meroe had a multi-ethnic population. The people in towns such as Meroe city, and probably the people of the Dongola Reach, spoke the Meroitic language. In the southern areas a variety of Eastern Sahelian languages of the Nilo-Saharan family were spoken. In the dry steppe lands immediately west of the Nile lived transhumant livestock-herding peoples who spoke Nubian languages. Farther south, the Meroitic domains at their widest probably included parts of the Nuba Mountains region, where other Eastern Sahelian peoples, such as the early Daju, could be found. Eastward, on both sides of the road to the Red Sea, lay the country of the most northerly Cushitic people, the Blemmyes, who were probably the same people as the Medjay of the ancient Egyptian records. Their modern-day descendants are the Beja of the Red Sea hills regions.

The Nubians played an especially important role within the Meroitic domains. The first millennium BCE appears to have been a period of low population along the stretches of the Nile between Egypt and the Meroitic heartland. But from the third century BCE, two newly significant populations appear in the historical record of those areas. To the north of the Dongola Reach were the Nobadae, possibly already settled there for some centuries. In the Dongola Reach itself, the Makurians, a Nubian society previously living as herders of livestock in the steppes to the west of Meroe, became the dominant population, and their language replaced Meroitic as the spoken language of the Dongola countryside. The Makurians, in particular, may have been encouraged by the Meroitic kings to settle as a buffer population, responsible for the defense of these territories from threats coming from Ptolemaic and Roman Egypt to the north. They provide an example, not uncommon in world history, of a pastoral transhumant population attracted to the more productive lands and the material wealth of a neighboring, strongly sedentary and partially urbanized society.

During the next several centuries, other pastoral Nubian peoples continued to inhabit the steppes that extended westward from Meroe and the Nile River. They seem not to have emerged as a threat to the stability of the kingdom until its era of decline after 100 CE.

Throughout the lands of the Meroitic kingdom and probably earlier in those of the Napatan kingdom, the prevailing belief system remained the Sudanic religion, with its one Divinity or Spirit, associated with the sky. Faced with the Egyptian idioms with which religion was cloaked in the Napatan writings, scholars have often presumed that Egyptian polytheistic religion took hold in the Dongola Reach and in Meroe during its heyday. But the striking feature of the known Napatan written observance of religion is that it most commonly evoked a single Egyptian god, Amun. What seems more probable on the face of it is that the Napatan priests were using an Egyptian idiom, prestigious because of the earlier experience of Egyptian colonial rule, but they accommodated it to an indigenous conception of Spirit—that they saw Amun as a particular manifestation of Divinity rather than as a separate god. The lesser extent to which a few other Egyptian gods appear in the Napatan record suggests that they may have been understood as additional manifestations of the power of Divinity in life, again a belief in keeping with earlier Sudanic religious ideas.

The same case can be made for religion in the Meroitic kingdom, where again one named deity predominates in the record: Apedemak, symbolized in sculpture by a lion figure. Like the Eastern Sahelian peoples of the rural countryside of the kingdom, the people of the cities most likely were adherents of the old Sudanic religion, but with additional idioms and subsidiary beliefs influenced by Egyptian religion.

There remains a great deal still to be learned about the history of kingship in Napata and Meroe. In overall ideology, though, they were clearly Sudanic sacred polities. In particular, although relatively few royal graves have been excavated, enough cases are known to make it evident that the old Sudanic practice of burying people along with the ruler, to accompany him or her into the afterlife, was a fairly common part of the funeral observances. The burials of the rulers of Napata and Meroe must have been awe-filled events, hedged about with sacred symbols and ritual. In Napatan times, there came first a ceremonial voyage of the body up the Nile from Napata to Nuri, and at all times the burial site itself was commemorated by an inscription and a small pyramid, reflective of lingering Egyptian influences. In the Meroitic period in particular, it is clear that the *Kandake* (from which our name *Candace* comes), or queen, was also an uncommonly powerful figure, often able, as we learn from Greek and Roman documents and from the Meroitic monuments themselves, to act as the full-fledged ruler of the kingdom and in such cases to be buried with full royal ritual.

The earliest written records of the Napata kingdom were set down in Egyptian, but by the final three centuries before the common era, the Meroites had begun to write their own language. From that point, Meroitic became the written language of government and religion in the kingdom. We believe it to have been a Nilo-Saharan language, probably belonging to the Eastern Sahelian branch of that family. Unfortunately, although scholars know the phonetic values of the Meroitic alphabet, they do not know the meanings of most of the words, and so they have not yet properly deciphered the language. That task remains an important scholarly project for the future.

Aksum and the Commercial Revolution in the Horn of Africa

Southeastward from Meroe, in the northern parts of the Horn of Africa, related historical factors were at work during the first millennium BCE, but the contexts and contours of change in the Horn differed significantly from those in the northern Middle Nile Basin. In the northern Ethiopian Highlands, as we have seen, plow agriculture had begun to take hold among the Agaw peoples by as early as the fourth millennium BCE. By 1000 BCE, a great variety of grains, including wheat, barley, t'ef, and finger millet, characterized the crop repertory of the highlands Agaw communities, while sorghum growing and livestock raising provided the staples of the diet among those who lived on the lower slopes of the highlands.

The bulk of the population of the northern Horn lived in highland areas. In the sparsely populated coastlands and the northeastern areas of the Horn, the North Lowland Eastern Cushitic society followed a variety of more pastoral livelihoods, raising cattle and some grains in the higher areas and relying on goats and sheep in the dry, hot lowlands. Farther north, in the very dry Red Sea hills region, the ancestral Beja society followed a similarly varied set of strategies, raising goats and sheep in most areas, but also cattle in some southerly locations with more rainfall, and probably relying on streambed runoff after the rare rains to sustain small, temporary grain fields in a few localities.

The consequences of the Commercial Revolution reached this region indirectly via South Arabia. Already by the tenth century BCE, merchants had begun to travel overland down the western side of Arabia, from the Levant to South Arabia. The visit of the queen of Saba' (biblical "Sheba") to Jerusalem in the reign of Solomon in the early tenth century CE was surely above all a diplomatic trip, meant to consolidate these emerging trade links. Two key products in this trade were frankincense and myrrh, both extracts of plants that grew in lowland areas of South Arabia. The discovery by South Arabian merchants that both plants also grew just across the Red Sea, in the northern Horn of Africa, encouraged them from 500 BCE onward to strongly expand their commercial activities into those regions. The modern-day reader may get some idea of just how valuable these two trade commodities were in the Levant by considering the legend of Jesus' birth, in which frankincense and myrrh together with gold make up the three supremely valuable gifts brought by the wise men.

The South Arabian merchants quickly discovered that the Horn of Africa had much more of value to offer them than just frankincense and myrrh. They soon began to trade with the local inhabitants for rhinoceros horns to be ground up for potions and medicines and for ivory and tortoiseshell, valued for their decorative uses.

The social and political consequences of commerce were quite different in the Horn from what they were in Meroe. No state structures capable of overseeing or constraining the activities of the merchants existed among the Agaw peoples of the far northern Ethiopian Highlands. Instead, the South Arabians would have dealt with a variety of local *wambers,* the old ritual clan chiefs of Agaw culture, and with the clans or groupings of clans that recognized the *wambers'* ritual authority. The foreign merchants would also have encountered a mixture of lowland and highland environments almost identical in climate to those in South Arabia. Finding it easy to move across the Red Sea, they began to set up their own lasting settlements. Marrying the daughters of important local people, such as the *wambers,* may have been among the tactics the South Arabians used in consolidating and securing good economic relations with the inhabitants.

Even though the South Arabians, as the evidence of both human genetics and language shows us, formed only the tiniest of minorities in the overall population, their settlements gradually became the focus of a sweeping political reorganization of society. Their trading sites grew into towns that attracted goods from all around them, and as a result the South Arabians' language became the medium of commercial activity and inter-ethnic communication. We know from the archeological record that at least one such town, Yeha, had already become important in the fifth century BCE, and probably there were others. The South Arabian merchants also brought with them political institutions and ideas of kingship that had long been established in southern Arabia. These political practices at first had effect only in the South Arabian trading towns. Outside the towns, the older Cushitic clan polities, loosely tied by their allegiance to particular *wambers,* must still have prevailed as independent social and political groupings.

In the third century, an added stimulus to commercial activity came into the region, as the Ptolemaic rulers of Egypt sought to build up their own sphere of commercial relations in the Red Sea. One of the consequences of the new level of competition for the products of the Horn of Africa was the development of a string of small ports along the African shores of the Red Sea, extending from the modern-day Egyptian coast in the north to the shores of present-day northern Somalia. Another development probably closely connected to these commercial initiatives was the resettlement of one group of merchants of South Arabian ancestry. These people moved from the older towns, such as Yeha, and relocated themselves in the upper Awash Valley. This valley, lying at the eastern side of the Ethiopian Highlands, offered an easy route of access deep into the central highlands and also southward along the Ethiopian Rift Valley and so opened up new sources of African products for the Red Sea trade.

How the commercial activities of these South Arabian–speaking merchants fared between 300 BCE and early in the first millennium CE and what kinds of relations they may have had with the Highland Eastern Cushitic peoples of those areas are as yet unknown. What we do know is that their dialect of the South Arabian language gradually began to be adopted by a significant number of the local peoples of the area. By the first or second century CE, this language, which we call proto–South Ethiopic, had become the language of a new society, its territories extending across the northern end of the Ethiopian Rift Valley and into the adjacent highlands on each side of the rift.

The most fascinating aspect of this history was its social outcome: the

FIG. 34 Wooden cow or camel bell

The item shown here comes from Soomaali livestock raisers living near the city of Harar in Ethiopia. Although this particular piece was probably made in the nineteenth century and was likely worn by camels, it shows us what the original cowbells of the Horn of Africa would have looked like in the second or first millennium BCE, before knowledge of camels or of iron had reached the region. The originators of cowbells are likely to have been the more pastoral Lowland Eastern Cushitic peoples, who lived in the areas along the north and east sides of the Ethiopian Highlands and in the Ethiopian Rift Valley. The Maa-Ongamo, a Nilotic people, took cowbells south to the Kenya Rift Valley region in about the eighth to tenth centuries. A forged iron example of this kind of bell, made by a Maasai smith, appears in fig. 47.

proto–South Ethiopic society became and remained culturally Highland Eastern Cushitic in all but its language. In religion, in clan structure, and in its household economies, the people of this society carried on many practices anciently associated with the Cushites. The South Ethiopic language adopted numerous words from the Highland Eastern Cushitic language spoken by the ancestors of the majority of the people who made up the new society. Some members of the emerging proto–South Ethiopic society may have long continued to specialize in commerce, but that remains a matter to be explored by future historical studies.

Society and Culture in Aksum

In the northern Ethiopian Highlands, the growth of commercial competition set in motion by merchants of Ptolemaic Egypt engendered a different kind of development in the final three centuries before the beginning of the common era, a trend toward political consolidation. The culmination of this trend was the formation of the kingdom of Aksum. We are still uncertain of the dating of that event. But before the middle of the first century CE, this kingdom, with its capital at the city of Aksum, had come to control most of what is today the country of Eritrea as well as the areas of northern Ethiopia as far south as the middle Takkaze River (see map 16).

In commercial matters, the rise of Aksum represented a new centralization of the flow of international trade and a damping down of the competitive forces at work in the Red Sea regions in the last three centuries before the common era. A key tactic in Aksumite commercial policy from the first to the seventh century CE was the maintenance of a single major coastal entrepot, Adulis. Restricting the activities of foreign merchants to Adulis allowed efficient collection of the trade duties that supported the state and its military power.

The major road in the country led from Adulis to the city of Aksum, although secondary routes passed through other highland towns. Aksumite merchants and hunters followed still other paths of trade deep into the interior, apparently even beyond the Takkaze River, where obtaining ivory was a principle objective. By the sixth century CE, the routes to the southwest may have brought another product, gold, to the north from as far away as the Abbai River at the eastern edge of the Middle Nile Basin. But whether that connection was yet in existence by the second or third centuries CE is not yet known.

The collection of duties on the trade provided kings with the revenues to support military campaigns and to afford the splendid outward trappings of power. Aksum as the capital became a particular center of monumental building, including among its many large buildings a multistory royal palace. The towns became centers as well of artistic endeavors, supported probably most often by royal patronage in Aksum, but perhaps also by regional authorities and rich merchants in provincial towns. The most imposing works of art were the enormous steles, or pillars, of Aksum, the largest of which stood over 30 meters tall.

A sharp social dichotomy between town and country probably characterized the kingdom of Aksum, much as it did Meroe. In city and town, a multilayered social formation had evolved early, probably already incipient in the city-state of Yeha of the fifth century BCE. The language of the towns and of commerce was Ge'ez, a language derived from that of the immigrant South Arabians who had founded Yeha. At the top was the court or, in provincial towns, the government authorities. A merchant class, a class of artisans and skilled workers, and a majority stratum of servants, including probably some slaves, constituted the remainder of the urban population. Outside the towns, the older ethnic and clan connections still guided day-to-day affairs. Agaw continued to be the language of the countryside all through the central parts of the kingdom.

Very little is known as yet about the various accommodations that must have been made between the state and its culturally diverse subjects. An Aksumite provincial administration of some sort existed. From later records we know of a "governor of Agaw," whose responsibilities extended over the Agaw-speaking region to the south of Aksum, between the capital and the Takkaze. This region was especially important economically, because of the large elephant herds, with their ivory, that lived in the wilds of the Takkaze gorge. Aksum, it appears, ruled such outlying parts of the kingdom by exacting tribute and other duties from communities that otherwise remained largely autonomous in handling their own day-to-day affairs. In the Agaw-speaking areas, this kind of relationship would have allowed a continuing importance for the *wambers* in local matters and as liaisons between local communities and provincial authorities.

The continuing importance of the old Agaw religion, centered on Divinity associated with the sky, was apparent in different ways in the towns and in the countryside. All through the Agaw-speaking rural areas, the power of Divinity was invoked at local shrines, located in recesses hewn by natural forces or human effort out of the rock of precipitous mountainsides. This appears to have been an ancient practice of Agaw peoples, but lacking as yet any archeological work on such shrines, we remain uncertain just how far back before the Aksumite period this custom goes.

In the capital and other towns, in contrast, a religious syncretism, a combining of ideas from different religions, took place. The polytheistic ideas of the South Arabian merchant settlers held center place because they provided the ideological backup for the kind of kingship that was established in their merchant towns and was carried on in the Aksumite kingdom. The royal invocation in Aksum of an important religious symbol new to northeastern Africa, the crescent moon, reflects the salience of these religious importations. But at the same time, the South Arabian god of the sky, because of the Agaw influ-

FIG. 35 Aksumite stele

The most striking monuments of the city of Aksum in the first several centuries CE were huge steles, the tallest of which was more than 30 meters high.

ences, became transformed in Aksum into the chief god of the pantheon, essential to the expression of the king's power.

Politics and Trade in the Kingdom of Aksum

The foreign policies of the kings of Aksum recurrently expressed two central aims, to control the African outlets of the Red Sea trade and to bring the South Arabian land routes of the trade into the Aksumite sphere of influence. In practice, these policy goals were attained by conquest of the Red Sea coastlands as far north as the southern Red Sea hills and by episodes of Aksumite invasion and rule over parts of South Arabia. The successful establishment by the middle of the first century CE of Adulis as the single major port of Aksum on the Red Sea reflects the first stage of implementation of such policies. From documents dating to the fourth century, it appears that Aksumite rulers succeeded in spreading their power and influence north along the Red Sea hills and into parts of South Arabia during the second and third centuries CE.

The rise of Aksumite power appears to have had severe consequences for Meroe. Aksum's gaining of control over the Red Sea outlets would have restricted the access of Meroites to their accustomed markets. There are indirect indications that the new strength of Aksum led, in time, to an increasing diversion of the products of the Middle Nile Basin, such as exotic skins, ivory, and gold, directly into Aksumite hands, bypassing the Meroitic stretches of the Nile. Meroitic influence seems to have receded rapidly after the first century CE. After 100 we no longer hear of Meroe in the documents of the Roman world, whereas Aksum comes to be considered by the Romans as the third great power in their known world, along with their own empire and the empire of the Parthians and, later, of the Sassanids in Persia. We know from records found at the Meroitic fortress Ibrim on the borders of Egypt that Meroe's rule persisted along the Nile for another two centuries, even if it was now a less significant player in northeastern African history.

But by the 340s, when King Ezana of Aksum sent a major military campaign into the old territories of Meroe, all that seems to have remained of its former grandeur were a number of impoverished towns. From the borders of Egypt to as far south as the city of Meroe itself, Nubian-speaking kingdoms were the newly emerging political forces in the region.

Developments in the Southern and Eastern Horn, 1000 BCE to 300 CE

Several older themes continued to work themselves out in the history of the regions of the Horn east and south of Aksum's sphere of influence, while new courses of change also appeared in a number of areas.

In the Ethiopian Rift Valley region, the technologies of irrigated, terraced agriculture and of building in stone spread to still more areas during the last thousand years before the beginning of the common era. The most notable spread of this whole complex of ideas and practices accompanied the expansion of the group of Omotic peoples known as the Ometo. Beginning about 500 BCE, a number of Ometo communities moved across the southern Ethiopian Rift, spreading into a succession of new territories in the far southeastern portion of the Ethiopian Highlands. Gradually between 500 BCE and 300 CE, the Ometo implanted the new technological complex and their language and culture across this region. In the process they diverged into a large number of different Ometo societies. The initial stages of this expansion passed right through the heart of the old Highland East Cushitic territories, splitting the Highland East Cushites into separate northern and southern communities, and assimilating large numbers of former Highland East Cushites into the several emerging new Ometo societies.

Over the same centuries, it seems clear, a number of individual features of this technological complex spread westward into the heart of the Omotic-speaking regions of southwestern Ethiopia. In a few of the western Omotic areas, irrigation and terracing were adopted, although for the most part the much higher rainfall there obviated the need for these particular techniques. Of much wider impact was the adoption of the use of cattle manure and of the grain crops barley and, to a lesser extent, wheat. On the whole, however, the old enset-based agriculture solidly maintained its dominant position in the economy all across the southwestern Ethiopian Highlands.

The first millennium BCE probably also marked the emergence in the southwestern Ethiopian Highlands of a new governing institution, a kind of sacred chiefship, suited for dealing with growing populations. Again this was a

FIG. 36 Obsidian blade, Eastern Rift Valley

Tools of this kind were typical of the Elmenteitan archeological culture and continued to be favored by Southern Nilotic peoples from around the eighth century BCE to the early centuries CE, even after they had already learned of ironworking. This particular example, from Gamble's Cave, Kenya, dates to the initial period of Southern Nilotic settlement in the highlands on the west side of the Kenya Rift Valley, between 1000 and 500 BCE.

development that affected both Omotic and Highland East Cushitic areas. The earliest we can be sure this institution existed is the first millennium CE, but it seems equally clear that there must have been many centuries of prior evolution of this kind of institution. Its roots lie in the old Omotic version of the Afroasiatic clan chief. In the old Omotic henotheism, the hereditary clan head was a priestly figure, responsible for making the annual livestock sacrifices to the society's or clan's deity, and at the same time an especially sacred person because of these duties. As early as 1000 BCE, it would appear, this kind of priestly role among the Omotic peoples of the central regions of the southwestern highlands had evolved into a chiefship able to make political as well as spiritual claims to the community's allegiance. This new ideology soon spread to several of the nearby Highland East Cushitic communities, becoming well established possibly even before the end of the first millennium BCE.

Around the drier southeastern fringes of the highlands, a different history took place between 1000 BCE and 300 CE. The major defining developments in this region were several population expansions of Lowland East Cushites, especially into the lower-lying country to the south and east.

The earliest of these population movements involved the Baz people, a southerly offshoot of the Konsoromo people. Between about 1000 and 800 BCE, the Baz extended their settlement across a wide stretch of country centered on the region where the modern-day borders of Sudan, Uganda, and Kenya come together. They had an especially powerful impact on the culture history of the Southern Nilotes and a lesser impact on one Eastern Nilotic people, the ancestral Ateker, each of which inhabited different parts of that region at 1000 BCE (see map 11 in chapter 4). From the Baz, the early Southern Nilotes adopted circumcision as the mark of male initiation into adulthood and clitoridectomy as the female right of passage, as well as a cycling age-set system. They also added a great many Baz words into their language. In about the ninth century BCE, as we have already learned, the Southern Nilotes moved away southward, out of the area of Baz influences and into western and central Kenya. There they intruded into a much different cultural environment, in which Southern Cushites were their most important neighbors. The ancestral Ateker eventually developed their own cycling age-set system under Baz influences but never took up such Cushitic customs as circumcision and clitoridectomy and were much less strongly influenced in their vocabulary by Baz words than were the Southern Nilotes.

A second major expansion of Lowland Eastern Cushites got under way during the second half of the first millennium BCE. The communities involved in these developments spoke a language we call Eastern Omo-Tana. One Eastern Omo-Tana group, the proto-Soomaali, moved south in the final few centuries before the onset of the common era into what is today northeastern Kenya. To survive in these very dry areas, they specialized in cattle raising, with little if any cultivation. Shortly after that, a closely related Eastern Omo-Tana people, the ancestral Jiiddu, traveled far eastward, settling near the lower Shebeelle River by about the first century CE. They combined the raising of the lowland African grain, sorghum, with extensive cattle keeping. At about the same time, the proto-Soomaali expanded again, this time directly eastward into the grazing lands between the Jubba and Shebeelle Rivers. There they became the neighbors of the ancestral Jiiddu (see map 16).

The arrival of the proto-Soomaali and the ancestral Jiiddu in the interriverine areas of modern-day southern Somalia in the first century CE initiated several hundred years of cross-cultural interactions. Already long resident in the region were the Dahaloan Southern Cushitic farmers and livestock raisers, as well as a large number of independent gatherer-hunter communities. The relationships of the original languages of the gatherer-hunters are unknown because they are all now extinct, but they may have been Khoisan. A complex patchwork of different soils—some highly fertile, some suitable only for grazing, and some too alkaline or too sandy for food production at all—had allowed a long-term stable coexistence of the two kinds of economy to persist since probably the third millennium BCE. The Jiiddu settlers competed for the same fertile soils that the Dahaloans had cultivated, while the proto-Soomaali probably moved into areas of mediocre soils, little utilized previously by food-producing people.

An entirely different population element, an offshoot of the Upland Bantu who had settled on the Kenya coast, then entered the region from the south by about the second or third century CE. Still another kind of environmental niche was available for their settlement—the woodlands all along the lower Shebeelle and Jubba Rivers. These areas had previously been avoided by the cattle-raising Dahaloans, Soomaali, and ancestral Jiiddu, because these lands harbored tsetse flies and thus cattle sleeping sickness.

By 300 CE, new patterns of cultural accommodation among the various inhabitants were taking shape. The Dahaloans rapidly began to be assimilated into the Jiiddu and, to a lesser extent, into the Soomaali communities and soon ceased to form a distinct population. The Upland Bantu communities gradually adopted the languages of nearby Soomaali or Jiiddu as their own but continued to form economically distinctive communities of cultivators along the rivers, maintaining many of the cultural features, notably in styles of music and dance, of their earlier Bantu ancestry. The gatherer-hunter groups in time all adopted dialects of the proto-Soomaali language while maintaining their distinct ways of getting food.

Still another expansion of Lowland Eastern Cushites took place along the Ethiopian Rift Valley, also around the close of the first millennium BCE. The instigators of these events were the Konsoromo, who entered into a period of population growth and spread. The reasons behind this development are not yet understood, but it had a variety of historical consequences.

In the southern parts of the rift valley, Konsoromo pressures on the Dullay Highlands led to the emergence of a new people, the Konso, during the first millennium CE. The Konso language derived from the earlier Konsoromo tongue, but a majority of the people in the new society had Dullay ancestries, and the economy of the area continued to depend on the intensive irrigation agriculture already long established among the Dullay people. Those Dullay communities who resisted the Konso expansion and remained culturally and linguistically distinct strongly maintained the old Cushitic institution of the ritual clan chiefship. In contrast, the Konso society replaced that feature of social and political culture with the Konsoromo social system of cycling age-sets and an age-grade-based system of government.

Farther north a second distinct Konsoromo society, the Oromo, took shape in the early first millennium CE. Still strongly tied to pastoral pursuits, the Oromo found room for expansion in the highland pastures of the Bali region, just east of the central parts of the Ethiopian Rift Valley (see map 16). The Oromo, like the Konso, organized their society and government around a system of cycling age-sets and elaborate age-grades. In later centuries, as we will learn in chapter 8, the Oromo and their *gada* (age-grade) institutions of government became a major factor in Ethiopian Highland history.

A further cultural impact, probably dating to the early first millennium CE, was the adoption of cycling age-sets by some of the Highland East Cushites, who lived along the central parts of the rift valley. By that time, however, the Omotic kind of sacred kingship had already taken hold among them. As a result, age-sets never became central elements in Highland East Cushitic governance, although they proved useful institutions for mobilizing young men in defense of their lands.

Nilotes and Central Sudanians in the Southern Middle Nile Basin

To the west, in the southern parts of the Middle Nile Basin, a different cultural accommodation took place in the final millennium before the common era. During the third and second millennia BCE, fishing people speaking languages of the Koman branch of the Nilo-Saharan language family inhabited much of the perennially flooded southern areas of the basin. Although the final stage of the Holocene wet phase came to an end in the third millennium BCE, only gradually did those southern areas dry out. After all, rainfall every year partially replenished what had evaporated away the previous year. Even today, seasonal flooding can cover great parts of the land on both sides of the Nile in that region.

But by the late second millennium BCE, more and more of the countryside must have become dry for a good part of the year. As that change overtook the land, it became more and more attractive for cattle raising. As a result, in the late second millennium and early first millennium BCE, a major new population of cattle-keeping, grain-cultivating Western Nilotes pushed into the region from the north. We call these people the Jii. Their modern-day cultural heirs are the Jyang (Dinka), the Naath (Nuer), and the various Luo peoples.

The process of accommodation between the Jii and the Koman peoples who had preceded them in the region lasted probably through much of the first millennium BCE. The Jii languages gradually displaced the Koman languages, although a great many Koman words passed into common use in the Jii tongues, especially in the ancestral Luo language. Sudanic religion, with its belief in Divinity, was part of the Jii cultural heritage, and it became the prevailing belief system throughout the region. In the economy, a strong blending of old and new emerged, in which cattle held first place in the male value system, but in which fish, in fact, provided the majority of the protein in the diet, and grains such as sorghum provided the majority of the calories overall (see map 16).

In the far southwest of the Middle Nile Basin, another major population spread, of Central Sudanians, was also under way during the first millennium BCE. The particular people involved in this expansion were the ancestral Bongo-Bagirmi. Starting in the middle of the millennium, their expansion carried by stages westward as far as Lake Chad by the early first millennium CE. What impelled their relatively rapid spread and what allowed it to take place is not yet known. Some scholars have proposed that they brought with them a new variety of sorghum, *Caudatum,* better suited to the dry savanna and steppe climatic zones through which they expanded than the sorghum varieties previously grown in those areas. But that hypothesis remains to be tested. What is clear, on the other hand, is that the Bongo-Bagirmi were among the earliest users of iron, with their knowledge of that metal going back to perhaps 1000 BCE. Could their possession of that technology have had something to do with their rapid westward expansion in the first millennium BCE and early first millennium CE? That will be a question that historians in the future will need to study.

North Africa in the Carthaginian and Roman Eras

Ethnic Shift and Economic Change

To the west of Egypt, the late second millennium and early first millennium BCE appear to have been marked by a sweeping realignment of ethnic divisions among the Berber peoples of those regions. One particular grouping of Berber communities, known in the ancient Mediterranean world as the Libyans, spread at that period across the whole of North Africa, from Morocco to Egypt. In the late thirteenth century Libyans raided Egypt from the west, sometimes in concert with the attacks of the "Sea People," raiders of eastern Mediterranean background. Toward the end of the second millennium BCE, a number of Libyans took up service in the Egyptian military forces. At the height of this period of ethnic expansion, from the mid-tenth to the mid-eighth centuries BCE, the Egyptian kingship itself was taken over by two successive Libyan dynasties—in the Egyptian annals they are known as the Twenty-second and Twenty-third Dynasties.

Far to the west, two of the Berber societies whose historical roots go back to the first age of Berber migration in the third millennium BCE seem to have missed the full effects of the Libyan expansion. In the rugged mountains of northern Algeria, the ancestral Kabyle remained a distinct people. Farther south, along the far west of the Sahara, the ancestral Znaga persisted in lands perhaps too dry to be attractive to the Libyans.

The causative factors that explain this era of ethnic shift within Berber North Africa are as yet entirely unknown. The attacks on Egypt suggest that the Libyan expansion was an aggressive one and not something peacefully brought about by a newly acquired technological or economic advantage. Might we have here a history in which internal divisions and a competition for power or material position within the ancestral Libyan society led some groups to seek advantage by incorporating neighboring people into their power base? And as other groups adopted this strategy, might a long-term process of ethnic expansion have been set in motion? We just do not know. But certainly no single widespread polity was created by the Libyan expansion, and it seems probable that this spread of people took place over a period of centuries and involved many regional struggles.

By about the ninth and eighth centuries BCE, the Commercial Revolution began to impinge significantly on the Mediterranean coast of North Africa. As in the northern Ethiopian Highlands, merchant colonies were the agents of change. The most important settlement in the western areas was the Phoenician city of Carthage, its founding traditionally dated to the late ninth century. On the Cyrenaican coast of modern-day western Libya, the major trading port was Cyrene, established by Greeks in the eighth century (see map 14).

In the early second half of the first millennium BCE, the cultural and economic impact of the Commercial Revolution began to be felt well into the North African interior. In the oases of the Fezzan region, the Garamantes federation arose, its power and influence centered around its ability to supply precious stones and other products to the Mediterranean coastal ports. One of the interesting questions to be resolved is whether the language of the Garamantes was a Berber tongue or an early form of Tibu, a Saharo-Sahelian language spoken then as now in the adjacent Tibesti Mountains just south of the Fezzan. In the immediate hinterland of Carthage, another consequence of this period was the development of a written form of the Libyan trade language of those times.

How far south did the impact of the Commercial Revolution extend? Herodotus in the fifth century CE learned of the Nasmonians, a people of the desert fringe, living near Cyrene and presumably Berber in language, who may have raided and possibly traded across the Sahara. Their relations with people farther south, however, seem from Herodotus's account to have been sporadic and incidental and without lasting effect.

Farther west, we have indirect evidence of the existence of occasional trans-Saharan connections, centered specifically around the acquisition of horses. Horses first appeared in Africa, as far as we know, during the era of Hyksos rule in Egypt in the eighteenth century BCE. The animal probably then spread more widely westward among the Berber peoples during the next several hundred years. Finally, during the first millennium BCE, as two kinds of evidence show, someone took the horse across the western Sahara desert. One bit of evidence consists of the numerous rock drawings of horses and even chariots in the Hoggar Mountains; these date broadly to the first millennium BCE. The second indication comes from the words for "horse" used in later times south of the Sahara, in the languages of the western Sudan region. All through the basin of the upper Niger River and into the Senegal Basin, words such as *seso* (Mossi language) and *so* (Malinke language) mean "horse." These words can be derived from the Carthaginian word, transliterated as *ssw* and probably pronounced something like *sisu*. This information shows us that knowledge of the horse first crossed the desert during the period of Carthaginian hegemony over North African trade, probably between the fifth and second centuries BCE.

An important political response to the growing commercial ties of North Africa to the Commercial Revolution was the emergence of fairly large territorial states among the Berber populations of what is today Tunisia, Algeria, and Morocco. In Tunisia and eastern Algeria, the Numidian kingdom was allied with Rome in its wars with the Carthaginians in the third and second centuries BCE. It remained a significant factor in the central North African interior down to the first century BCE.

A second major Berber kingdom, Mauretania, located to the west of Numidia in what is today Morocco, was in existence from at least the second century BCE. By that time both kingdoms had been drawn strongly into the orbit of Roman cultural as well as political influence.

Juba I, who was the king of Numidia in the 50s and early 40s BCE, made the mistake of allying with Pompey in his struggles for power with Julius Caesar. After being defeated by Caesar's forces in 46, Juba committed suicide, and the separate history of Numidia came to an end. Juba I's son was taken by the Romans back to Rome to be raised there. In 25 BCE Augustus Caesar placed this son, who took the name Juba II, on the throne of Mauretania, where he ruled until his death in 23 CE. Juba II was a remarkable man in a number of ways—a traveler and a scholar, who wrote in Latin on a variety of topics, as well as a king.

It now appears fairly certain that Juba II himself was responsible for the first human settlement of the Canary Islands, when he exiled a small group of rebellious subjects to those islands late in the first century BCE. This group became the basis for the Berber-speaking Guanche population of the Canaries, rediscovered by Europeans in the fourteenth century.

The ideological basis of state building in the western half of North Africa remains unclear. Did the ancestral Berber society maintain the sort of clan chiefs we can trace back to ancient Afrasan civilization, and did chiefship of this kind become the basis of the kingdoms known in Roman times? These are issues historians need eventually to address.

Up until around 40 CE, Juba's Romanized successors ruled over a subordinate territory within the empire. The Romans then turned the whole of Mauretania into directly ruled provinces, a situation lasting up to the fifth century. Under Roman influence, the North Africans adopted a variety of new agricultural practices and constructed aqueducts. Plants previously cultivated, such as the olive tree, took on an enhanced commercial importance for farmers. The northern areas near the Mediterranean coasts, especially in what is today Tunisia, became major suppliers of wheat for the empire, above all for the city of Rome. A number of cities, such as Volubilis far to the west in modern-day Morocco, grew into new centers of Romanized Berber culture (see map 16).

FIG. 37 House column, Volubilis, Roman Mauretania

Volubilis was the westernmost of the major cities and towns of Roman North Africa.

FIG. 38 Scene from wall of a Meroitic temple

The "lion-god" Apedemak is flanked on the left by Queen Amentarit and on the right by her consort Netekamen.

Egypt under Roman Rule

The last age of Egyptian independence came definitively to an end with the death of Cleopatra, the last of the Ptolemaic rulers, in 23 BCE. The Ptolemaic period had brought a Hellenistic overlay to a cultural world that still harked back in many ways to the ancient Egyptian ideas. In the Roman period, Greek influences remained strong, and Greek, more than Latin, was the language of commerce and cultural relations with other parts of the eastern Mediterranean regions. Nevertheless the indigenous population of the lower Nile Valley continued to speak a much changed version of the ancient Egyptian language, which is called Coptic, throughout the period of Roman rule. Coptic as well as Greek were the written languages of the country.

The Romans successfully established a long-running peace with the Meroitic empire to the south. They launched one early military campaign southward, attacking the Meroitic positions along the Nubian stretches of the river in 23 BCE. But the purpose of this invasion appears to have been to preempt any possibility of Meroe contemplating attacks on Roman Egypt, for in 21 or 20 BCE the Romans and Meroites by treaty set their mutual frontier at the southern edge of Egypt, with the Romans garrisoning Philae (near Aswan) and the Merotic state holding the fortress of Ibrim (modern-day Qasr Ibrim) not far south of there. In effect, Meroe held on to all of its territories, and the Romans settled for control of the portion of Egypt ruled by the Ptolemies (see map 16).

Camels and the Emergence of Pastoral Nomadism in Africa

There remains to be considered one other extremely important combination of developments that took shape between 1000 BCE and 300 CE in North Africa. It had immense repercussions for history not only in North Africa but for areas much farther south. It was not initially connected in any close fashion to the Commercial Revolution, but by the fourth century CE, as we shall see in the next chapter, its consequences became closely tied with those of expanding commerce. This combination of developments was the adoption of the camel as a productive domestic animal in North Africa and the associated rise of a new kind of economy, true pastoral nomadism.

Camels, despite their long use as a domestic animal in the Arabian deserts, were not known in Africa until the last thousand years before the beginning of the common era. Late in the millennium, the keeping of camels spread up the Nile to the Nubian-speaking people, who were then settling under Meroitic auspices along the areas between the first and fourth cataracts. From them, the animal passed to the nearby Beja of the Red Sea hills. At about the same time, camels were becoming known to the Berber populations farther west in North Africa.

For farming populations such as the Nubians of the Nile River, the camel was not a particularly useful or valued animal. Similarly for the Berbers of North Africa who successfully grew wheat and barley and raised cattle, camels were of no great interest. But for the marginalized Berbers of the desert fringes of North Africa and for the Beja of the Red Sea hills, who previously could raise only a few hardy goats and sheep in their arid lands, the adoption of the camel almost immediately had revolutionary effects. For the first time they possessed a large animal, a source of much meat and much milk, truly adapted to their arid climates—an animal, in fact, able to be taken deep into the desert, into areas where even goats could not well survive.

To pursue an economy that required travel to distant areas to seek out pasture engendered another kind of transformation. It brought about the first development in Africa of true pastoral nomadism. We have already learned about the ancientness of pastoral pursuits in Africa. Early pastoralists were often transhumant; that is, some members of the community would have to camp out far from the homestead to find pasture for the animals during certain seasons of the year, but nevertheless they maintained permanent homes to which they returned. In true nomadism, herding peoples live in impermanent structures, such as tents or mat houses that can be folded up and moved throughout the year, whenever new pastures are needed. During the first three centuries CE, both the Beja and the Berbers of the western desert, most notably the ancestral Tuareg, passed through this dual transition to camel raising and to a fully nomadic pastoral livelihood. What these developments meant for African history as a whole we shall learn in chapter 6.

An African Development of Commerce: West Africa, 1000 BCE to 300 CE

Early Commerce in the Western Sudan Region

South of the Sahara, in the drier savannas and steppes of the West African Sudan, the characteristic historical trend between 1000 BCE and 300 CE was the emergence and growth of long-distance trading links. The roots of these developments, as far as we can see now, lay in sub-Saharan Africa and not in the contemporary Commercial Revolution of the Mediterranean and Middle East. By no later than the third century BCE, trading towns and regular commercial relations had come into being in the basin of the middle Niger River and possibly in the Chad Basin as well.

The key element in this indigenous development of commerce was most likely the widening adoption of and reliance on metals across the whole Sudan region. As we have seen, African artisans, independent of the Middle East, brought into being a copper-smelting industry in the Aïr Range of the far southern Sahara over the course of the second millennium BCE. By 1000–500 BCE all across the Sudan, people were also beginning to smelt and forge iron.

Now metal ores, particularly those of copper, are quite unevenly distributed around the globe. To obtain copper, people in most of West Africa had to avail themselves of truly long-distance networks of trade. Iron ores, in contrast, were present in many more parts of West Africa, and so the production of iron accomplished for local and intra-regional exchange relations what copper trade did on a wider scale for the Sudan belt as a whole. Each required the transport of a product, increasingly in demand as the first millennium BCE wore on, over greater or lesser distances. They thus required specialist traders and effective means of transport to move the product to distant prospective buyers. Donkeys, known in West Africa probably since the arrival of Chadic-speaking peoples in the Chad Basin several thousand years earlier, rapidly became, we suspect, the important beasts of burden in the newly emerging commerce of the Sudan belt. Along the middle Niger River, an equally important alternative form of transport, by boat, soon began to shape the directions and impact of the trade there.

Another kind of manufactured good that rose early to importance in the Sudan commerce was cotton cloth. In the first millennium CE cotton textiles may already have been key commodities in the towns of the Bend of the Niger, and considering that we can trace the domestication and spinning of cotton back to 5000 BCE in the eastern Sudan, it is probable that weaving spread to the western Sudan even before the first millennium BCE.

Social and Political Change in West Africa's First Commercial Age

Over the course of the last millennium before the onset of the common era, the new economic relations had striking social consequences for the peoples living in the Inland Delta and the regions immediately west of the delta. As we already learned in chapter 4, the first age of productive specialization in the region, dating to the third and second millennia BCE, had been characterized by the rise of ethnically based production for the market. The Bozo, for instance, became fishing specialists in the delta, while the Marka turned to intensive rice cultivation. In the new era of economic specialization of the first millennium BCE, occupational and manufacturing specialization now became the preeminent means of participation in a greatly expanded trading system, and the new specializations were not ethnically linked but tended to spread across cultures and across regions. Not ethnic, but social differentiation was the correlate of the new kind of economic relations.

A new residential pattern, of village clusters founded by skilled artisans, accompanied the rise of commerce. By the later centuries of the first millennium BCE, such clusters often formed a set of satellite settlements around a larger, central town. The example best studied and best known so far of this kind of urbanization is Jenne, a city founded around the third century BCE and located among the eastern bayous of the Inland Delta of the Niger. But towns of this kind existed in other parts of the Sudan west of the delta and also east of there, along the Niger.

The cluster pattern in urban development lasted right down to recent centuries. When we look at the social and economic characteristics of the village clusters of later, better-known eras, we discover that each village tended to be the site of a different kind of manufacturing activity. One would be the village of the smelters and smiths, another the residence of leather workers, another the place of cotton weaving, and still another the potters' abode. Each village, in other words, had its own occupational specialization. The products of each occupation were then taken to the central market in the larger town near which the artisans' villages clustered. There they were bought by local consumers and also by traders, who might carry the items to more distant markets in other localities.

Out of this residential pattern there emerged a social system of occupational castes. A variety of evidence from many areas, both oral traditional and ritual in nature, suggests that the instigators of the new social relations were the ironworkers. When the practices of iron metallurgy took hold in the early first millennium BCE, the ironworkers surrounded their activities with taboos and the need for special rituals to ensure the success of their productive efforts. Whether by conscious intention or not, the ironworkers in this fashion secured their monopoly over the production of the important new material. As time passed, other specialist producers, in particular the leather workers, weavers, and potters, imitated the example of the ironworkers and began to claim the same kinds of status for themselves and their activities. Their jobs and their skills came to be passed down from father to son or mother to daughter. At first perhaps no more exclusive than guilds, in time these occupational groupings came to marry only among themselves and so became castes.

The final step in molding a wider-ranging system of mixed class and caste relations in the western Sudan came with the rise of militarized groups of men, under the leadership of erstwhile Niger-Congo clan chiefs and, in some areas, of Sudanic sacral chiefs. Seizing power over larger areas than had previously been combined in a single polity, and in effect establishing the first real states of the region, the new class of kings and their followers came to view themselves as a hereditary ruling stratum, born to rule just as much as the members of the ironworking caste were born to be smelters and smiths. Among the Mande and some of the West Atlantic peoples of Senegambia, an additional occupational caste of bards arose under the patronage of this new noble class. The great majority of the population, who continued to be rural cultivators of the soil and raisers of livestock, by default came to form a residual grouping of freeborn people, uncasted but not noble either. In addition, a lower stratum, of slaves,

FIG. 39 Megaliths of Sine-Saloum

Megalithic monuments, dating to as early as the fifth or fourth millennium BCE and as recent as the first millennium CE, occur in a large number of areas across the southern Sahara and the Sudan belt of Africa. In many cases such monuments appear to have marked the burial grounds of early kings. The particular megaliths shown here reflect developments connected with the period of early state building in the western Sudan, extending from the first millennium BCE into the middle of the first millennium CE.

soon came to be part of the social system, originating as captives taken in the wars of the noble class. The resulting social formations thus had a mixed structure, differentiating freeborn people into ruling and peasant strata while also recognizing the existence of several separate occupational castes of skilled artisans as well as a subordinated slave segment of society.

Exactly when the full range of intertwined class and caste relations emerged remains an uncertain matter. By the close of first millennium BCE, we suspect, the system was fully in place among the Mande of the areas in and south of the Inland Delta of the Niger and may soon after have spread to the West Atlantic peoples of the lower and middle Senegal River areas. This development tells us something else of importance. It shows us that, by the beginning of the common era, those who became the noble class must have already begun the conquest and foundation of the early territorial states across many of the regions from the Bend of the Niger to the lower Senegal River. We know nothing as yet of any of the particular states of that period. From the patterns of rule evident in the first millennium CE and after, it seems probable that Sudanic sacral ideas underpinned the formation of the early kingdoms in the areas inhabited by Songay people living east of the Inland Delta and were adopted, too, by some of the Mande groups living just west and northwest of that region, along the southern fringe of the Sahara. Farther west and south, the kings and the noble class probably initially evolved out of clan chief roles of an older Niger-Congo type. As late as the middle centuries of the second millennium CE in the kingdoms of the western and southern areas of this region, the old Niger-Congo matrilineal basis of society, and thus of chiefly and kingly power, still often prevailed.

Jenne: An Early Urban Center of the Western Sudan

The city of Jenne is the example best known at present of an early western Sudan commercial town. Founded around the third century BCE, Jenne would by no means have been the only such commercial center of its era—many probable sites of other equally early towns in the Sudan belt remain to be studied by archeologists. But its history provides apt insights into how the West African development of commerce took shape in the later centuries of the first millennium BCE. What made Jenne especially important in those developments was that it was a *transshipment* point. That is, it controlled a location at which goods were transferred from one kind of transport to another, in this case from boat to donkey or from donkey to boat (see map 16). (We will encounter the salience of the idea of transshipment points again in chapters 6 and 7.)

Located amid several channels of the Niger, Jenne was protected by nature from easy attack, while at the same time it could control the movement of products carried along the river. Copper, for instance, would have reached Jenne from the east via the Niger. By the first few centuries CE, gold was being transported to the city from the opposite direction, passing downstream by boat from mining areas in the Bambuk and Bure regions 600–800 kilometers to the southwest. From Jenne, merchants could then trade these materials to peoples who lived east and west of the Niger. Because the city was situated at the eastern edge of the Inland Delta, it was also close to overland routes, traveled by donkey, from a major iron-producing area less than 100 kilometers to the east. Anther long-important region of iron production, Mema, lay west of the Inland Delta. At Jenne, iron was unloaded from donkeys and from there could be sent long distances, upstream or down, by boat.

Finally, Jenne lay at a sharp environmental juncture. Extensive fishing and rice growing was possible in the waterways and moist soils of the Inland Delta of the Niger, while all around lay dry savanna country suited to the growing of sorghum, pearl millet, and other crops of the Sudanic agriculture. As a result, Jenne's inhabitants were middlemen in the exchange of greatly differing foodstuffs between nearby localities, just as much as they were dealers in the commodities of distant lands.

Jenne was surrounded by peoples of distinct historical roots—to the north and eastward along the Niger, Sudanic in their civilization, and to the south and west, of Niger-Congo background. The people of Jenne themselves spoke a Mande language, belonging to the Niger-Congo family, and their cultural norms, we suspect, fit mostly within that tradition. Politically, Jenne most likely remained an independent city-state through the first millennium CE. Of the actual structure of its government in these centuries, however, we know nothing.

Did trans-Saharan connections have any role in these events of the first millennium BCE? From the evidence available to us so far, it appears that we must say no. The commerce of the West African Sudan, as it had evolved by the beginning of the first millennium CE, seems fundamentally rooted in the emergence of a long-distance demand for processed goods produced within Saharan or sub-Saharan Africa, principally copper, then iron, and, latest of all, gold. Almost nothing of North African or Mediterranean provenance can yet be shown to have crossed the desert in these centuries, and nothing at all, as far as we can tell, crossed in trade in the other direction. The trans-Saharan commerce in African gold, it now seems clear, did not begin until around 300 CE. The horse did make it south across the Sahara in the first millennium BCE and became a relatively rare kind of prestige good, its possession monopolized, whenever possible, by the ruling segment of society. But however it may have reached the ancestral Soninke and Songay peoples, it was surely not a regular item of trade exchanged for any northward traveling product of the Sudan.

As we learned earlier in this chapter, currency in the form of coins appeared as part of the Commercial Revolution of the eastern Mediterranean. The presence of currency is in fact one of the diagnostic features of the appearance of the kind of trade that can be called commerce. In the northern Horn of Africa, the spread of the Mediterranean commercial connections after 500 BCE led to the use of coin currency there also. But the great majority of sub-Saharan Africans created a variety of quite different currencies over the past 2,000 years, as we will discover in the next several chapters. We do not yet know what kind of currency may have been used, if any, in the early stages of the indigenous West Africa invention of commerce during the first millennium BCE. In the first millennium CE, however, both gold dust and small, curved copper ingots served this function in the western Sudan.

Society and Economy in the West African Woodlands and Forest

If our knowledge of developments in the Sudan belt seems scant, our understanding of the course of change in the woodland savanna and rainforest areas of West Africa, 1000 BCE to 300 CE, is scantier still. In technology, ironworking had probably spread to every region by the beginning of the first millennium CE, but the course of its spread remains to be studied. The basic ideas of culture and the social customs among all the many, many small societies of the region were rooted in the older customs and beliefs of Niger-Congo civilization. For example, a distant Creator God continued to be recognized all across the woodland savanna and rainforest zones among Niger-Congo-speaking societies, while ancestors were the central focus of religious observances. Nearly everywhere in these regions, people still lived in villages and recognized the ritual, but not necessarily the political, authority of clan priest-chiefs.

The West African yam-based planting agriculture continued to predominate in most of these areas. Sorghum had already become an additional staple, however, in many woodland savanna locales. In western portions of the rainforest belt, in what is today Liberia, Sierra Leone, and Guinea, African rice increasingly displaced the yam as the staple food. In part, the cultivation of rice may have spread along with several Mande peoples into the areas inland from the coast. Nearer the coast, however, rice cultivation took hold among the already anciently established West Atlantic and Kru peoples of those regions.

Among the peoples living right on the coast, the invention of a sophisticated technology of rice production accompanied this changeover of diet. The new technology centered on clearing fields along the estuaries of rivers and the building of extensive dikes and specially constructed drains. The drains allowed the farmer to channel tidal flow of seawater onto a field, to leave the saltwater for a time in the field, thus killing the seeds of potential weeds, and finally to drain the seawater away again. The farmer could then direct river water onto the field, in order to leach out the salt left behind by the tidal water and also to deposit a new layer of fertile silt on the land. Much later, in the seventeenth and eighteenth centuries, captive Africans who were taken to the Carolinas of North America brought this technology with them from the Guinea coast of West Africa. Slave owners made use of the Africans' expertise—and tried to claim the credit for it as well—to turn the coastal areas of colonial South Carolina into a major rice-producing region.

At least one notable artistic development among Niger-Congo peoples of West Africa belongs to the first millennium BCE. In parts of what is today Nigeria, artists transferred the ancient Niger-Congo tradition of wood sculpture to a new medium, terra-cotta. The finest early terra-cotta figures come from the archeological sites of a people who lived in the Nok area of northern Nigeria in the first millennium BCE, and that area seems also to have been home to important iron production before 500 BCE. Perhaps the two developments are interconnected. A possible but—let the reader be warned—quite speculative proposal would be that the proceeds of extensive iron production created the material basis for an early kingdom to arise near Nok. The kings of this state would then have had the wealth to be able to give patronage to artists, who in turn created the new kind of sculpture (see map 16).

During the first millennium BCE, trade tended to be carried on mostly at the local level through the more southerly regions of West Africa. One interregional trading system, as we learned in chapter 4, may be quite old, however, predating the first millennium BCE. This system revolved around the exchange of fish and sea salt, produced by the Ijo people of the water-logged coastal Delta of the Niger River, for the yams and other crops of rainforest peoples living inland from them, on firmer ground.

But by the first few centuries of the first millennium CE, the commercial developments of the Sudan belt increasingly began to impinge on the woodland savannas and forests of West Africa. We have noted already how gold, mined in the erstwhile woodland savannas of the upper Niger and Senegal Rivers, was traded north to the Sahel by the first three centuries CE. To the east, around the lower Niger River, the southward penetration of Sudanic commerce may also have begun to be more widely felt by that time. Ironworking technology had taken hold far south in Nigeria by the close of the first millennium BCE, and it also seems probable that the raising of cotton and the weaving of cotton cloth spread south by this time from the Sudan to at least the woodland savannas at the north edges of the West African rainforest belt, both in Nigeria and in the Volta River regions to the west. The full impact of these influences belongs to the periods after 300 CE, however, as we shall discover in chapter 7.

NOTES FOR READERS AND TEACHERS

Issues, Themes, and Questions

One way to cope with the greater complexity of our knowledge of African history since 1000 BCE—evident in this chapter and in chapters 6–9 coming up—is for the class, from this point onward, to be divided into study groups. Each group can be responsible for knowing in more detail the history of a particular macro-region of the continent. When it is time to read a new chapter, each group then reports back to the class on the significant developments in its macro-region covered in the chapter. The organization of the book makes it possible to identify a number of macro-regions for most eras after 1000 BCE. In most chapters, the following are the usual divisions:

- Southern Africa
- East Africa
- West-central Africa (including the equatorial rainforest and the savannas immediately north and south of it)
- West Africa
- Egypt, North Africa, and the Sahara
- Middle Nile Basin
- Horn of Africa (including the Ethiopian Highlands)

On the other hand, the events in each of the regions are not isolated from developments in other regions, so there are other ways of dividing up the continent.

Making each group report relevant to the class as a whole is, of course, another important matter. One of the ways in which this goal can be met is for students to view their assignments thematically, with each group looking at the history in its region in the light of the same set of themes. Using the thematic areas described in chapter 1, readers might pay attention, for instance, to new developments in:

- food production
- social structure and institutions
- political ideas and institutions
- trade and commerce
- towns and cities
- technology

- religion and its cultural, social, and political dimensions
- art and music
- the diffusion of new ideas and things from society to society

But these are hardly the only possibilities, and each class might determine other, equally fruitful ways of directing the reading and reports.

Two developments of broad world historical significance also affected Africa in the period between 1000 BCE and 300 CE:

- the rise of long-distance, merchant-carried commerce
- the wide establishment of ironworking technology

Many scholars continue to disagree that more than one invention of iron metallurgy took place. But the reasons presented here for a separate sub-Saharan African invention seem compelling to this writer. Sample questions on these topics of global significance that readers might wish to consider include the following:

- What parts of Africa did the Commercial Revolution actually affect during the period 1000 BCE to 300 CE, and what kinds of consequences, social and political as well as economic, did it have in those regions?
- One part of Africa developed its own long-distance commerce in the last millennium before the onset of the common era. Where did this development take place? What kinds of commodities were involved? What kinds of socioeconomic changes accompanied the emergence of these commercial relations?
- Where did African ironworking first take hold as a new technology?
- Why do we think that ironworking was separately invented in sub-Saharan Africa?
- Did the spread of ironworking have significant political or social consequences?
- What did the making of copper and iron goods have to do with the growth of commerce in sub-Saharan Africa?
- What new set of crops reached Africa during the period 1000 BCE to 300 CE, and how did these crops get to the continent? Did any other features of culture arrive in the same way?
- What is a city-state? How does it differ from a territorial state?
- What constitutes an empire as opposed to a more everyday territorial state?

Further Reading
Several recent works have greatly broadened our understanding of the long-term historical processes in different parts of the African continent between 1000 BCE and 300 CE. For West African savanna history the reader will find many stimulating ideas and much to learn from:

McIntosh, Roderick J. *The Peoples of the Middle Niger.* Oxford: Blackwell Publishers, 1998.

A current book on the history of Meroe is:

Welsby, Derek. *The Kingdom of Kush.* London: British Museum Press, 1996.

A history of developments in eastern and southern Africa over the period from 1000 BCE to 400 CE appears in:

Ehret, C. *An African Classical Age.* Charlottesville: University Press of Virginia, 1998.

For the Congo Basin and the equatorial forest regions, the work of Jan Vansina provides one view on early Bantu cultural traditions. The richest part of his story, however, concerns the history of those areas in the periods since the middle of the first millennium CE, to be dealt with in chapters 6, 8, and 9:

Vansina, Jan. *Paths in the Rainforests.* Madison: University of Wisconsin Press, 1990.

Kairn Klieman's recent book *"The Pygmies Were Our Compass,"* cited at the end of chapter 4, is a major resource for this era of history in the equatorial rainforest. It complements Vansina's work in several areas. It also constructs an alternative overview and proposes correctives to some of Vansina's interpretations of early social developments in Bantu-speaking communities. Klieman's book, in particular, foregrounds the transformative impact of the combined changes in rainforest technology, agriculture, and trade that took place during the last millennium BCE and early first millennium CE. From her book we gain, for the first time, an appreciation of the roles BaTwa peoples played in these developments.

6

Southern, Central, and Eastern Africa: The Middle Centuries, 300–1450

Africa and the World: Issues and Themes of the Age

Two recurring themes of the more than eleven centuries of African history that stretch between 300 and 1450 CE are the growth of political scale and the emergence of new forms of social stratification. In a variety of regions—from the western Sahel to the Chad Basin and from the West African rainforest to the Upemba Depression of Central Africa and to Zimbabwe in southeastern Africa—states newly appeared as the agricultural population grew and the trade in high-value commodities expanded. In the Ethiopian Highlands, in contrast, a new basis for the state, feudal in character, emerged when Red Sea commerce declined in the seventh and eighth centuries CE, and then persisted despite a resurgence of commercial activity in later centuries. At the same time, many African societies stood apart from these trends, maintaining or refashioning in new ways the smaller-scale world of their forebears. Nevertheless, new kinds of social and political formations often took shape among them, and in several regions major agricultural innovations were instituted.

From the aspect of world history, the most important new factor in the Eastern Hemisphere was Islam, a religion linked, like Christianity, to the Judaic-Samaritan tradition of the Middle East. Preached by Muhammad in Arabia in Mecca and Medina in the 620s and early 630s CE, Islam was then spread by military conquest across North Africa between 639 and 711. In later centuries commercial contacts carried Islam across the Sahara and into the western and central Sudan, as well as eastward to the Indian subcontinent and eventually from there into the Malay peninsula and Indonesia. Here we see again, as in the case of the spread of Christianity to Aksum in the fourth century and to the Nubian kingdoms in the sixth century, the ongoing importance of the Commercial Revolution and its wide-ranging networks of commercial exchange for the spread of new ideas.

The centuries between 300 and 1450 also were characterized in the wider world historical context by three major shifts in the trade patterns previously established by the Commercial Revolution.

First, a new frontier of Mediterranean commercial activities opened up just before 300 and grew to great importance after the seventh century. This new sphere of commerce was the trans-Saharan trade, linking the indigenous African commercial world of the western and central Sudan with the Mediterranean region, Europe, and the Middle East. The key enabling event was the adoption of the camel by pastoralist North African cultures in about the first century CE. As the use of the camel spread to the Berbers of the central and northwestern Sahara, the previously sporadic, rare contacts between the Sudan and the Mediterranean were quickly replaced by a growing variety of commercial dealings that traversed the Sahara. The most striking demonstration of the power of the new trade relations was the arrival of African gold at the Roman mint at Carthage, probably near the end of the third century. A scattered adoption of Christianity by some of the Berbers of the Sahara after 300 CE provides still another case of the effects of commerce in the spreading of religious ideas.

Then, less than three and a half centuries later, political events of the middle seventh century created a major realignment of world trade routes. With the establishment of the first Islamic empire, the Umayyad Caliphate, the focus of the key routes shifted to Damascus, the capital of the caliphate. The main routes of sea trade began to pass through the Persian Gulf, and the Red Sea became a commercial backwater. The formation of the caliphate brought into being a large and dispersed new ruling stratum, enriched by the spoils of victory and well able to pay for the products of distant lands. Over the next century and a half, commerce passing overland through central Asia received a great boost from these developments, as did the seagoing Indian Ocean trade. Aksum, previously dependent on commerce for its most important revenues, transformed its political and social basis in the wake of the collapse of the Red Sea trade. The features of this transformation were remarkably parallel to those taking place in the same period in Western Europe, which, just like Aksum, experienced the collapse of commerce and of a money economy.

Finally, from the later eighth to the tenth centuries, a growing political diversity within the Muslim world led to the rise of economically competing Muslim states in Egypt and North Africa. These developments stimulated new growth in the volume of the trans-Saharan trade, revived the commerce of the Red Sea, and brought a new scale of commercial activity to the eastern African coast. The changes in commercial relations in turn had significant repercussions among the sub-Saharan African societies directly involved in the long-distance trade. The emergence of the new, commercially oriented Swahili city-states along the east coast of the continent in the ninth and tenth centuries is an especially notable example of African responses to the new opportunities. The effects of Swahili commercial activities also reached inland from the coast, as is clear from the close links of Indian Ocean trade to the thirteenth-century rise of the Zimbabwe kingdom of southeastern Africa.

Nevertheless, most of sub-Saharan Africa continued to build on its own variegated historical past throughout the period 300–1450. New developments in trade could, as in the western and central Sudan regions, provide additional sources of revenue or of prestige goods that enhanced a ruler's outward appearance of inward grace. In the Horn of Africa and in the Sudan, the trading connections led to the gradual adoption of Islam by one particular segment of society, the merchants and, in a few cases, by ruling African elites. But the institutions of nearly every African state still grew from earlier African roots. And over large parts of the continent, state institutions remained, as late as the fifteenth century, either unknown or something suitable perhaps for one's neighbors but not for oneself.

Two broadly differing geographical spheres of historical change characterize the African continent of those centuries. The Africans of the central, eastern, and southern regions of the continent, although not entirely sealed off from the effects of events outside Africa, nevertheless were most powerfully affected by factors internal to the continent. The peoples of the western, northern, and northeastern regions, in contrast, participated more often in economic and cultural developments with salient links to the wider course of history outside Africa. In this chapter we turn our attention to the southern half of the continent and the new developments of those regions from 300 to 1450. In chapter 7, we will shift our focus to the history of the more northerly regions of Africa over the same time period.

Subsistence and Society in Southern Africa, 300–1450

Trade and Subsistence Farming, 300–900

The economic history of southern Africa in the first millennium CE, and even as late as the seventeenth century, has often been treated as if a sharp dichotomy of interests and behaviors separated gatherer-hunter Khoisan peoples from cultivating Bantu-speaking societies. We now know that areas with purely gatherer-hunter occupations formed a minority portion of the historical landscape of southern Africa as early as the fourth century CE. A variety of Khwe communities, who mixed livestock raising with hunting and gathering, occupied lands far and wide across the northern areas of what is today Botswana and Namibia. A similar mix of activities characterized the numerous Khoekhoe communities, who by that time could be found through eastern Botswana and parts of the Transvaal and all through the coastal lands of the modern-day Cape region of South Africa. Across the eastern side of southern Africa, numerous scattered Bantu-speaking village communities carried on sedentary agriculture.

A variety of economic relations and social interactions took shape among these peoples. In the eastern areas, the Bantu communities became the focal points for economic exchange. The villagers manufactured a variety of items—among them iron goods, pots, and probably wooden goods and basketry—of kinds not previously found among the gatherer-hunter bands. The Khoisan gatherer-hunters who came to the villages to trade for such items could offer in return the products of their foraging activities—animal hides, ostrich eggshell for bead making, and so forth. In the Limpopo River areas and in the Transvaal, Khoekhoe herders were probably the more important trading partners of the nearby Bantu communities, able to exchange livestock for the products of the villages. To the west, in the eastern and northern Kalahari regions, Namibia, and the southern Cape, the Kwadi and Khoekhoe herding bands probably held a similarly central position in the exchange of commodities with the surrounding gather-hunter bands.

The consequences of these developments differed greatly in the different parts of southern Africa. In southeastern areas, a long process of assimilation of the Khoisan gatherer-hunters and of Khoekhoe herding people into the ancestral Southeast-Bantu and Sala-Shona societies began, a process that was to continue off and on for centuries. In the Transvaal between 300 and 800, the incorporation of erstwhile Khoekhoe into the Sala-Shona and Southeast-

Bantu communities of the region helped to consolidate a slowly emerging economic transformation of these Bantu communities from an emphasis on crop cultivation to a fully mixed economy of grain cultivation and cattle raising (see map 17).

The Khoekhoe were incorporated in especially significant numbers into two of the Southeast-Bantu societies of this era, the ancestral Sotho and ancestral Nguni, both of which resided in parts of the eastern Transvaal. The ancestral Nguni even adopted many of the click consonants of the Khoekhoe into their language during this era of social amalgamation. They also began to build a new kind of house, dome-shaped like the older Khoisan style, but considerably larger.

FIG. 40 Lydenburg head

This is one of several such terra-cotta sculptures known from sites of an early Bantu-speaking people in the Transvaal region of South Africa, dating to about the fifth to eighth centuries CE. The decorative motifs around the neck and head of this figure utilize many of the same design elements found on other cultural objects in the society, such as ceramic ware.

This economic changeover had both social and political consequences of lasting significance for southern African history. In the areas of the Transvaal in which the new economy first emerged, gendered access to production became more sharply defined, with cultivation still the women's sphere, but with men taking full command of cattle as their productive resource. The ownership of livestock, as it was among the Khoekhoe, now became the route to social influence and power.

We strongly suspect that the shift from matrilineal to patrilineal reckoning of descent, so general in southern Africa in recent centuries, proceeded in tandem with this development. The old Bantu matriclan system had been brought into southeastern Africa by the Kusi communities at the close of the first millennium BCE. Over the course of the first millennium CE, it dropped from use in those areas. The coexisting patrilineage system continued to function, however, and gave rise in time to a fully patrilineal organization of the kinship across most of the region. Especially among the ancestral Sotho and ancestral Nguni, the ongoing incorporation of Khoekhoe groups into the Bantu-speaking communities may have greatly shaped the cultural expressions of this shift in descent reckoning. The Khoekhoe emphasis on seniority ranking among kin groups appears, for instance, to have been adopted by many of the Nguni and Sotho.

The influence of Khoekhoe and other Khoisan peoples may have been felt in other ways as well. In music, stringed instruments of Khoisan origin have been widely adopted by the Bantu societies of southern African, while in many areas the drums of Niger-Congo ancestry became less important instruments. The ancient tradition of sculpture in Niger-Congo civilization is another element of culture that faced a mixed fate in southern Africa. Among the Sala-Shona peoples of the fourth and fifth centuries CE in the Transvaal region, the Niger-Congo sculpting tradition was still vibrant, with local artists adopting a new medium, terra-cotta, to fashion expressive stylized sculptures of human heads, called by archeologists "Lydenburg heads." But among the Nguni and Sotho, that tradition of sculpture appears to have gradually lost its importance.

Cattle Keepers and Kings, 900–1300

The economic shift in the central and eastern Transvaal to greater emphasis on cattle raising led to a political development of equally lasting importance. As we learned in chapter 5, the kin-group chiefship of early Mashariki Bantu times was reconstituted at the local level by the Kusi settlers of southeastern Africa in

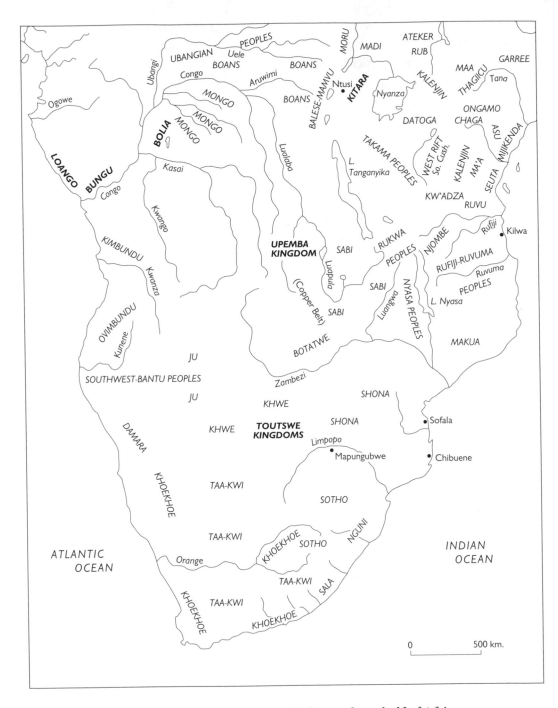

MAP 17 Peoples, states, and cities in the southern half of Africa, ca. 1200–1250

the first to third centuries CE. Among the institutional elements apparently maintained south of the Limpopo River were the roles of chiefs as the essential initiators of the rites of the harvest, as the intermediaries in relations with neighboring communities, and as the articulators of the outcomes of court cases within the community. If, for instance, villagers captured goods in fighting with a neighboring people, these items passed first into the hands of the chief, who was expected to keep some and redistribute the rest to the community in ways that respected the recognized relations of seniority among the men. Similarly in court judgments, the compensation to be paid by the losing party was pronounced by the chief and passed through his or her hands to be awarded to the aggrieved party.

In the early centuries of the first millennium CE, when goods of potentially high value, such as iron and copper, were still rare, the institution of clan chiefship maintained the social order well. But the acquisition of growing numbers of cattle between 300 and 900 gradually upset this balance. Some chiefs, taking advantage of their positions as adjudicators in the community's acquisition and disposal of property, were able to greatly build up their own personal herds. Possessing large numbers of animals, the chiefs began to be able to attract and hold new followers and clients by redistributing cattle to them. Because cattle were men's property, chiefship at the same time became increasingly the prerogative of men.

As some chiefs expanded their rule beyond their original small kin territories and established it over other kin groups, chiefship itself changed its original kin basis. Distinct chiefly and royal clans began to be recognized separately from the commoner clans who now made up the majority of society. As this new kind of chiefly legitimization gained currency, it became possible for the first time for large chiefdoms and even small kingdoms, consisting of many clans or lineage groupings, to arise. In this fashion, the old chiefly prerogatives, formerly of limited practical effect, were transformed into the basis of rule, all because those prerogatives gave chiefs a much greater access to a newly important kind of property.

The process did not necessarily end at that point. Chiefs commenced cementing their power and influence by contracting marriage alliances with many families from different parts of the chiefdom. By marrying their daughters to such a chief, these families not only now had a stake in preserving the chief's power but, at the same time, increased their own political and social influence within the society. Many wives also meant that there would be many chief's sons, only one of whom would succeed his father. Ambitious sons who were unsuccessful candidates for the chiefship after their father's death might then migrate with their supporters into new areas, setting up new chiefdoms or kingdoms over the peoples already living in those areas.

By the tenth century, this new ideology of chiefship was fully in place among at least one Sala-Shona people living in the Transvaal, as well as among the ancestral Nguni and some of the ancestral Sotho. We know this, because in the tenth century the ideology began to be exported to several other parts of southern Africa.

From the northern Transvaal, one set of people moved north across the Limpopo and onto the southern portions of the Zimbabwe Plateau. Of Sala-Shona ancestry, these people spoke the ancestral Shona language, and they brought a new style of pottery and, for the first time, extensive cattle raising into southern Zimbabwe. There they rapidly incorporated the earlier Bantu people of the region into their society. By probably 1000 this new Shona cultural complex was expanding its territories eastward into Mozambique. Then, between 1100 and 1300, it spread northward through the heart of the Zimbabwe Plateau almost as far as the Zambezi River (see map 17).

To the south of the Limpopo, in the eastern High Veld, a similar spreading out of the ancestral Nguni people can be dated to the centuries between 800 and 1000. Then, in about the eleventh century, some of the Nguni crossed the Great Escarpment, moving down off the High Veld and into Natal. Bearers of the new kind of political economy, the Nguni progressively incorporated the previous Sala communities into their society all through Natal. The Nguni settlement generated the emergence of a large number of chiefdoms of the new type. By the fourteenth century, the farthest south of these chiefdoms, the Xhosa and Mpondo, had begun to establish their authority in the eastern lands of the Cape Khoekhoe, between the Mzimvubu and the Kei Rivers (see map 17).

The impact of this history of Nguni settlement below the Great Escarpment in Natal is visible across the whole range of culture. The village-style settlements of the Sala period gave way to the smaller hamlets with the dome houses typical of the Nguni. New pottery replaced the older Lydenburg style of ceramics. Agricultural settlement with extensive cattle raising now spread all across Natal, including the many areas of poorer soil and drier climate that had not been favored by the Sala peoples.

On the High Veld, the early stages of expansion of the ancestral Sotho also belong to this period. We know much less as yet about this history than we do about the history of the Shona and Nguni. We begin to know more by about the fourteenth century, when the southwestern and west-central Transvaal seems to have been a key innovative area in political change. In the southwest of the Transvaal in the 1300s lay the country of the small Rolong kingdom, one of probably several iron-producing centers between the Vaal and Limpopo Rivers in those centuries. Iron smelted by Rolong smiths appears to have been traded as far south as the Khoekhoe of the southern Cape and possibly to other societies as far west as southern Namibia.

To the northwest of the Rolong country, in what is today northeastern Botswana, lay another area that participated in these political and economic shifts. There the Toutswe culture arose with the settlement of a Bantu-speaking people, probably of the Sala-Shona group, among Khwe herding and gathering communities. Initially, between 800 and 1100, the Toutswe people adopted a scattered homestead style of residence, better suited than villages to the sparser resources of their country. Gradually the sizes of their cattle herds grew, and the ownership of large herds came to be concentrated in the hands of fewer people (see map 17).

By the period 1100–1300, three small kingdoms had emerged in the Toutswe society. Three social strata are sharply visible in the archeology of all three. The great majority of the people lived in small homesteads of around 1,000 square meters, with only small livestock pens if they had one at all. Several much larger homesteads, of around 7,000 square meters, with livestock pens that would have held many cattle, existed in each kingdom. These, we believe, were the residences of the local chiefs. Finally, in each kingdom there existed a single enormous homestead, located in each case on a hill and having a pen capable of housing many hundreds of cattle at night. These clearly were the royal residences.

Sometime in the fourteenth century, the Toutswe society came to an end. Its homesteads were all abandoned, and its people moved elsewhere. What brought about this abrupt decline is unclear. One distinct possibility is that the great number of cattle possessed by the wealthier members of society may eventually have overtaxed the environment of the region. But they may well have faced other problems that we have yet to discover.

Indian Ocean Trade: The Swahili Factor, 700–1100

By the ninth and tenth centuries, a new factor began to impinge on the events of southeastern Africa, namely, seaborne international trade. To understand how this factor affected developments in southeastern Africa, we first have to look back northward to events along the eastern African coast. The old sea route from Arabia to the Tanzania coast at Rhapta lapsed sometime between the fourth and seventh centuries, and the town of Rhapta disappeared from the historical record. The new growth of the Indian Ocean trade that was brought about by the rise of the Umayyad Caliphate in the seventh century did not have immediate effects in East Africa, perhaps because the Middle Eastern links of this trade at first passed farther north, through the Persian Gulf rather than the Red Sea. By the second half of the eighth century, however, commercial activity began to revive along the eastern African seaboard.

The inception of the new commercial era in East Africa came about in a different fashion than had the earlier trade to Rhapta. Instead of foreign merchants introducing and controlling commerce, local East Africans quickly became the prime movers in the emerging new trading system of the eighth and ninth centuries. We call these people the ancestral Swahili.

The cultural roots of the ancestral Swahili society trace back to the early Northeast-Coastal Bantu people. These people, as we learned in chapter 5, settled just inland from the central Tanzanian coast in about the second or third century CE, as part of the great expansion of the Mashariki Bantu. In the fifth to seventh centuries, the Sabaki branch of the Northeast-Coastal society spread northward along the hinterland of the Kenya coast, displacing and absorbing the Upland Bantu people, who had lived in that region since the second century CE. In the eighth century, a new social identity began to emerge among one particular grouping of Sabaki villages located right along the northern Kenya coast and also on several islands just offshore. These particular communities practiced a mixed fishing and farming economy, including especially the raising of rice and the tending of coconut palms. They became the society we call the ancestral Swahili.

They evolved into a distinct people for one specific reason: they began rapidly in the eighth century to adopt a commercially oriented way of life, far different in its activities and in its worldview from the rest of the Sabaki communities. Their villages grew at first into small towns, entrepots for coastal trade. Between 800 and 1000, at least two of these towns, Shanga and Manda, became major cities, with populations of 15,000–18,000. Their populations were comparable in size to those of other important commercial cities of their time in history and far larger, in fact, than any contemporary town in Europe north of the Pyrenees (see map 17).

Both Shanga and Manda were located on islands of the Lamu Archipelago. Their wealth and influence probably had a dual basis. They occupied a crucial area past which all the goods going from eastern Africa to India and Arabia had to travel. But even more important, the ninth and tenth centuries were marked by a sharp growth in the demand for the products these two cities themselves could supply. Egypt, by this time an independent Muslim-ruled state, replayed the historical role filled by Ptolemaic Egypt ten centuries earlier, seeking its own outlet to the Indian Ocean via the Red Sea. The reviving of the Red Sea trade in the ninth century meant that ivory from East Africa could now go directly and more profitably to new markets in the Mediterranean. In addition, during the middle of the tenth century, a major new product from the African interior, rock crystal (transparent quartz), became a profitable item of export for Shanga and Manda. The stone was mined, it now appears, about 150–200 kilometers inland from the coast, in areas today comprising Kenya's Tsavo National Park. Local producers carried the stone overland to the coast at Shanga and Manda, and the Swahili merchants then shipped it to such distant places as Venice, where for several decades in the tenth century quartz items were all the rage.

A society with marked class differences emerged out of these economic developments. Merchants became the newly wealthy and influential leaders of the community. The leading merchant families formed the upper class. In most of the Swahili cities and larger towns, the older Mashariki office of clan chief evolved into a hereditary town kingship, but a kingship greatly circumscribed by the power of the merchants. In at least one city, Lamu, founded around the thirteenth century, the merchant oligarchy itself formed the governing body, and there was no position of king. At the other end of the social scale were the servants, both free and servile, who worked in the households of the merchant families.

A variety of skilled tradespeople, including masons, fishermen, and boat builders among others, carried on their callings in the coastal towns and cities of the Swahili, forming an economic class of intermediate status between the merchants and their servants. Masons made their mark early in this society by devising a new style of architecture in the tenth and eleventh centuries and built multistory houses of coral for wealthy merchant families. A specialized group of skilled workers cut blocks of coral from the reefs along the coast. The blocks turned hard when exposed to air, allowing the masons to use them like bricks to form the walls of the houses. The masons bound the coral blocks together with mortar made from broken-up coral. From the many stands of mangrove growing in nearby tidal flats and inlets, lumbermen cut the mangrove poles used as rafters in the ceilings and flat roofs of the houses. For the seagoing trade of the merchants, the boat builders constructed the sewn-plank boat, the *mtepe,* already made centuries earlier at Rhapta (described in chapter 5). Smaller boats, often with outriggers, served the needs of the local fishermen.

Armed with new sources of wealth and the new knowledge of distant places that came with far-flung commercial contacts, Swahili merchants explored far

FIG. 41 Swahili carved wooden doorway

Large, finely carved wooden doors and lintels have been a characteristic feature of Swahili urban architecture for many centuries. This example comes from the city of Mombasa on the Kenya coast.

south along the eastern coast of Africa, seeking out new supplies of the products of the trade. Already in the late eighth century, some merchants were sailing as far south as the southern half of modern-day Mozambique, where they set up the seasonal trading entrepot of Chibuene (see map 17).

Although the merchants had surely first sailed south seeking ivory, at Chibuene they found that another commodity, gold, was readily available. Gold mining by the Gokomere Bantu communities on the Zimbabwe Plateau began during the second half of the first millennium CE. Trade from one local community to another eventually spread the knowledge of this metal as far as the Mozambique coast, where the Swahili merchants in turn learned about its availability from the local inhabitants. The commercial connections of the Swahili merchants made them fully cognizant of the value of gold in the Middle East and India, and by the tenth century this metal had joined ivory as one of the lasting, most valued commodities of Swahili commerce.

Great Zimbabwe and the Indian Ocean Trade, 1100–1450

Through the trade in gold, the Indian Ocean commerce finally had an effect on the political history of the southeastern African interior. This effect was not strongly felt, however, until almost two centuries after the Swahili began to trade in gold, and it was felt then only because of the developments that had taken place independently within the interior. The crucial change that made it possible for gold trade to become a major factor in interior history was something we have already learned about, namely, the creation of a new kind of chiefship in the Transvaal before 900 and the spread of this ruling ideology into the southern areas of the Zimbabwe Plateau between 900 and 1100.

How did the effects of these developments converge? They converged around the political idea of the centrality of the chief or king in the social networks of wealth redistribution. In the tenth century, cattle were the chief form of wealth that a king had a special access to and a special ability to redistribute. Local trade would sporadically have provided small amounts of other kinds of wealth for redistribution. In such instances, ancient custom apparently dictated that one-half of the product to be traded belonged to the king. For example, one tusk of every elephant killed was presented to the ruler, while the other tusk remained the possession of those who had killed the elephant. The demand for both ivory and gold at the coast thus had the potential to shift the balance between trade and cattle raising as the material basis of a king's power.

If a king could control not only cattle redistribution but the redistribution of the proceeds of a lucrative trade, how much more powerful he could become.

In any event, many decades passed before the full impact of the new possibilities was felt in the interior. When it was felt, it was not the ruler of a gold-producing area who took advantage of the opportunities presented, but the ruler of ivory-rich land that lay along a key route to the coast. In the valley of the middle Limpopo River, the first state we know of in southern Africa took shape in the twelfth century. Its capital, located at the archeological site of Mapungubwe, was also southern Africa's earliest large town yet known. This town lay at what originally would have been a key juncture in the internal trade routes of Southern Africa, a place at which ivory from the Limpopo Valley and copper from the mountains of the northern Transvaal to the south would have been exchanged for gold from the Zimbabwe Plateau to the north. The rulers at Mapungubwe built their power in the twelfth century on their ability to channel the gold and ivory to the coast, to the Swahili merchants at Chibuene.

But Mapungubwe's preeminence did not last much more than a century. By the middle of the 1200s, a set of interconnected shifts in economic geography were underway. Among the Swahili city-states, a new balance of power took hold. Manda and Shanga declined greatly in importance after 1100, both eventually being abandoned. Two other city-states, Muqdisho on the Somali coast and Kilwa, located on an island along the southern Tanzania coast, gradually became the new leading city-states. Kilwa, in particular, seems to have become preeminent in the gold trade by the middle of the thirteenth century and to have centered its efforts around a new trade outlet at Sofala. This town, located on the Mozambique coast about 300 kilometers north of Chibuene, had a shorter and more direct access to the Zimbabwe Plateau via the valley of the Sabi River. At about the same time, in the middle 1200s, Mapungubwe was abandoned, and a new city, Great Zimbabwe, was founded on the Zimbabwe Plateau itself, not in an actual gold-producing area but in the upper watershed of the Sabi River, between the mining areas and the coast at Sofala (see map 17).

The relationship between Mapungubwe and Great Zimbabwe is disputed by historians. A relatively undeveloped technology of building in stone was present at Mapungubwe. This technology was then transferred to Great Zimbabwe, and many of the patterns of laying out the royal areas of the town were replicated in Great Zimbabwe. Does this mean that the royal family of Mapungubwe moved to Great Zimbabwe? Or did an entirely new kingdom arise at

Great Zimbabwe, but one that imported its stone masons from Mapungubwe? We do not yet know the answer.

But Great Zimbabwe was a significantly larger and more complex urban center than Mapungubwe. It was a true pre-industrial city, the first in southern Africa. With 15,000–18,000 inhabitants in its heyday in the fourteenth century, it was the capital of southern Africa's first large territorial state, the Zimbabwe empire. What do we mean by the word "empire"? We mean a kingdom that incorporates other smaller, formerly independent kingdoms and chiefdoms within its domain. The Zimbabwe empire, as we call this state today, ruled over a large number of other smaller Shona-speaking statelets (see map 18).

The capital city of Great Zimbabwe must have been an astonishing sight for the subordinate chiefs and kings who would have come there to seek favors at

FIG. 42 Wall of the Great Enclosure, Great Zimbabwe

This picture shows both the massive walls and the fine mortarless stonework of the largest structure in the capital city of the Zimbabwe empire. The human figure standing in the right foreground of the picture gives us some idea of the immensity of this building. The Great Enclosure was the central place of political authority, where royal audiences and other special activities of the king and court would have taken place.

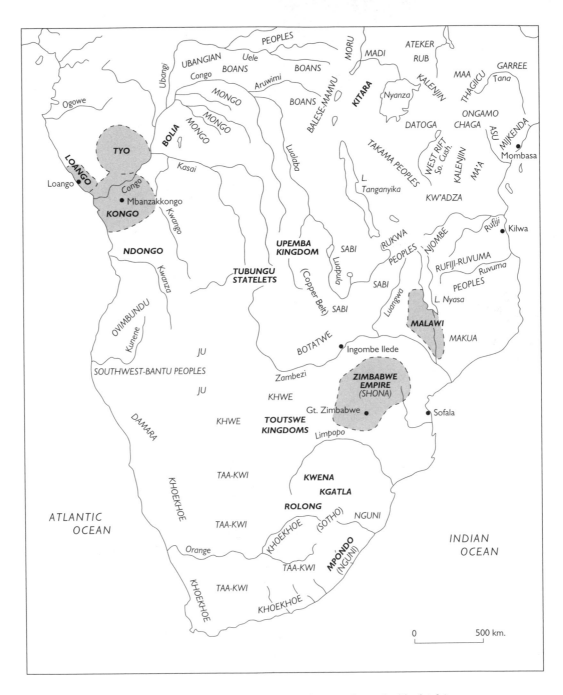

MAP 18 Peoples, states, and cities in the southern half of Africa, ca. 1400

court. Southern Africa's first truly monumental architecture was created at Great Zimbabwe. Large structures began to be built there in the mid-1200s and continued to be built through the 1300s, all constructed with drywall masonry. A progressive growth in the skill and artistry of the builders is evident. So marvelously well fit together without mortar were the later structures that many of them still stand despite the depredations of European colonial treasure seekers and 600 years of the ravages of nature. So impressive was Great Zimbabwe that subordinate chiefs and kings soon began to build their own smaller "zimbabwes" all through the areas tributary to the Zimbabwe state, both on the plateau and to the east, at the edge of the Mozambique lowlands.

Great Zimbabwe included a mixture of two architectural styles, one for the great buildings and another for the houses in which people lived. Around the great stone structures associated with the court and with state ritual lay many hundreds of round houses, made of wood and clay and crowded closely together. Here the bulk of the population of the city resided. One can easily imagine the noise and smells of daily life in Great Zimbabwe. It was a city closely integrated with its surrounding countryside. Narrow pathways, dusty in the dry season and muddy in the wet, would have led in intricate ways among the crowded houses. Wandering dogs nobody much cared for, chickens scavenging in the winding walkways between the houses, and goats tethered at doorways would have been among the sights and background noisemakers of city life. In the later afternoon, hundreds of cooking fires would have added to the melange of strong smells that filled the air and, if the air was still, would have created something much like smog.

In 1420s and 1430s, the Zimbabwe empire broke up, and by the 1450s the city of Great Zimbabwe itself was largely abandoned. In place of the Zimbabwe state, two smaller empires, Torwa in the south and Mutapa in the north, took shape from about 1440 onward, each with its own new capital city.

What happened? Some historians suspect that the crush of people and animals in and around the city may finally have overtaxed the environment. On the other hand, for almost two centuries the people had successfully dealt with this kind of problem. We know, for instance, that the rulers of several successor states of the Zimbabwe empire required the payment of grain as tribute from their rural subjects, and we suspect that this policy originated among the kings at Great Zimbabwe, providing them with a means of feeding at least the elite segment of the population of their capital city. Another old royal policy, originating even before the rise of the Zimbabwe state, was for southeastern African kings to loan out cattle from their enormous herds to their chiefs and clients in the provinces. In this way, the local elite became beholden to the central power for a significant part of their own prosperity, while at the same time the king's cattle, instead of overgrazing his pasturelands, were scattered about in many different locales.

In any case, there is strong, although indirect, evidence that the key factors in weakening the power of the Zimbabwe state were commercial in nature. In particular, the fifteenth century was marked by a major shift in the geography of trade relations in the region. Along the Zambezi River to the north of the Zimbabwe Plateau, a major competing route of access to the products of the interior came into prominence in the late fourteenth and early fifteenth centuries. Its interior terminus was a town at a site today called Ingombe Ilede, close to the confluence of the Luangwa and Zambezi Rivers, almost 700 kilometers from the Indian Ocean. To Ingombe Ilede came especially ivory from the Luangwa Valley to the north and the middle Zambezi Valley to the west and copper from mines in the northwestern parts of the Zimbabwe Plateau. These goods were then transported eastward down the Zambezi to the coast, probably along with gold, which would have entered the route at a point farther downstream. In this way the rulers at Great Zimbabwe lost their position as the sole intermediaries in the gold trade to the coast and so also, very possibly, a significant element in the material basis of their rule.

Mapungubwe and Great Zimbabwe were not the only towns or cities in southern Africa between 1100 and 1450. Still farther south, in the southwestern Transvaal, the Sotho-speaking Rolong and some of their neighbors began in the fourteenth or fifteenth century to live in towns of a few thousand inhabitants. Whether this development owes to economic factors or was a defensive response to increasing insecurity is not yet surely known. During the late fourteenth and early fifteenth centuries, however, the princes of two Sotho ruling families, the Kwena and Kgatla, first began to spread out to new areas with their followers, establishing by force of arms a number of new, small kingdoms. So security from attack might have indeed have been one of the reasons for the emergence of towns among the Rolong and their neighbors by the early 1400s (see map 18).

Long-Term Trends in Southwestern Africa, 300–1450

Farther west, in the Kalahari regions and in the lands that make up modern-day Namibia, a slower pace of historical change characterized developments during the centuries between 300 and 1450. Livestock-raising societies became gradually more widely established, interspersed in many areas with persistent gatherer-hunter communities of Khoisan language and culture. Various coastal imports, including glass beads, certainly reached all the way from the east coast to parts of the Kalahari before 1000, but they arrived only indirectly, after first passing through the hands of other communities residing between there and the Indian Ocean. Some routes of this trade led into the Kalahari region; others passed northwestward into the savannas across the Zambezi (see map 17).

In northern and north-central Namibia and in the areas along the lower Kunene River, the Kwadi and related Khoisan-speaking peoples carried on much the same mixed sheep-raising and food-collecting life as had been brought into the region by their ancestors in the first century or two CE (see chapter 5). But by the second half of the first millennium, they began to face increasing competition from other food-producing peoples, who spoke Bantu languages. All across the long east-west stretch of steppe and drier savanna, extending from the southern Benguela Highlands of present-day Angola to southern Zambia, a multifaceted encounter of Khoisan and Bantu peoples took hold from the fourth century onward. Out of this history of cross-cultural exchange came the emergence and spread of a new economic adaptation based on the raising of large numbers of cattle and the cultivation of such grains as sorghum and pearl millet. The bearers of this new mixed tradition spoke Bantu languages, although their debt to their Kwadi predecessors is clear.

Two groupings of Bantu societies played a role in these economic and cultural shifts. The Southwest-Bantu, whose present-day descendants include the Ovambo and Herero of northern Namibia, spread the new mix of cattle keeping and grain cultivation westward from the interior floodplain of the Zambezi in the middle of the first millennium CE. First settled in the region of the lower Kunene River in the first four centuries CE (as we learned in chapter 5), the Southwest-Bantu incorporated many former Kwadi into their communities.

The keeping of cattle then spread from the Southwest-Bantu to a second important set of Bantu people, the early Ovimbundu of the Benguela Highlands, who, like the Southwest societies, trace their linguistic and many of their cultural roots back to the original Western-Savanna societies (see chapter 5). The greater rainfall of the Benguela Highlands allowed a more diverse mixture of crops to be grown by the Ovimbundu than by any of their Southwest-Bantu neighbors. They built up an agricultural tradition in the higher areas that included finger millet, which had reached them from the woodland savannas to the east (see chapter 5), along with sorghum and pearl millet. In the northern parts of their lands, even the yams and oil palms of the old West African planting agricultural tradition could be grown.

The centuries of cultural interchange among the Southwest-Bantu and the early Ovimbundu gradually built up a pattern of widely shared features of culture common to both. The most notable such feature was a system of full double descent. The pattern in early Savanna-Bantu history had been for a society to have matriclans comprised of numerous matrilineages, but only shallow patrilineages without the higher level of patriclans. By the fifteenth century, a full-fledged system of patrilineal clans had developed among the peoples in both the Benguela Highlands and the drier lands south of the highlands, and patrilineal and matrilineal clans had come to be recognized as equally important descent groups. Each person had two primary kin allegiances, belonging to the clan of his or her mother as well as to the clan of his or her father (see map 18). In this system people commonly inherited possessions through

FIG. 43 The Dying Eland

This well-known South African rock painting is representative of one of the later styles of Khoisan rock art, dating to the past three or four millennia in the southern High Veld region.

their maternal connections but often succeeded to political position patrilineally.

Despite the spread of farming into more and more areas, gathering and hunting remained a powerful component in the regional economy of southwestern Africa for many centuries. Along the lower Orange River and through much of the central interior of today's Cape region of South Africa, numerous small societies, whose languages belonged to the Taa-Kwi branch of the Khoisan family, continued to follow a purely gathering and hunting existence between 300 and 1450. Their shamans carried on the ancient Khoisan rock art tradition, and many of the best preserved paintings known today in the mountainous areas of southern Africa probably date to these centuries.

Between the Benguela Highlands and the Zambezi River lay another region in which Khoisan gatherer-hunters—speaking languages of the Ju branch of Khoisan—long remained important inhabitants. But their economic and cultural experiences were quite different from those of the Taa-Kwi. Between 500 and 1450, the Lwena group of Western-Savanna Bantu gradually scattered out across the region, establishing themselves principally in a restricted set of environments. The Lwena found it difficult in most areas to raise cattle, because the climate, unlike the cooler Benguela Highlands or the drier areas settled by the Southwest-Bantu, was both hot enough and just barely wet enough to harbor the tsetse fly. On the other hand, the annual rainfall was only enough to support the cultivation of grains, gourds, black-eyed peas, and the like, and most of the soils were sandy and low in nutrients. In consequence, the Lwena communities tended to concentrate along the major streams of the region, where they planted their gardens and fields in the heavier, wetter soils along the rivers and supplemented their diet with a great deal of fishing. In this situation the Ju were long able to continue exploiting the hunting and gathering resources in areas away from the streams, although even there they faced competition for game resources from the Lwena communities (see map 17).

Interestingly, the existence of a few words for cultivation adopted long ago into the Ju languages suggest that an informal kind of farming, still practiced by some of the recent, more northerly Ju communities, first came into being during this period. In this set of practices, people clear small fields and scatter seed on them, but then leave the fields untended to pursue their usual gathering and hunting activities, returning only later in the year to harvest whatever portion of the crop might have survived the weeds and animal predators.

Cultural and Ethnic Shifts in East-Central Africa, 300–1450

For most of the period between 300 and 1450, the areas that make up today's Zambia and Malawi followed a different historical trajectory from the areas south of the Zambezi. Sweeping shifts in ethnicity, often taking place over a period of centuries, form the central, recurrent theme in the history of that region. This history of ethnic shift has two main strands: the Botatwe peoples and the Sabi societies.

In about the sixth century, the ancestral Botatwe, a Savanna-Bantu people who had previously resided along the upper reaches of the Lualaba River, moved south into the northern parts of the Batoka Plateau in what is today west-central Zambia. There they gradually increased their territories by absorbing the Muteteshi and Salumano peoples, who were the descendants of the Mashariki Bantu who had settled in central and southern Zambia in the late centuries of the first millennium BCE (see chapter 5). Ethnic shift in these areas was a long, slow process. As late as the fifteenth century, a few of the Salumano communities still maintained their separate cultural identity.

The new Botatwe society that arose out of these cultural interactions, as we will soon discover, mixed cultural ideas brought in by the expanding Botatwe with those already followed by the Muteteshi and Salumano. Early in these interactions, the Botatwe people adopted from their predecessors the keeping of large numbers of cattle. At the same time, there emerged a kind of cultivation that emphasized grain crops, as had the earlier Salumano and Muteteshi agriculture, but also included the yams grown by the ancestral Botatwe society (see map 17).

The local Botatwe communities maintained several of the important older Eastern-Savanna Bantu features of society. Their political units were based around matriclans and maintained the kind of clan chiefship designated by the word *mw-ami*. The old, relatively unimportant institution of patrilineages took on a new role among the now cattle-keeping Botatwe: they became the social basis for cooperation among related men in owning and protecting their herds of cattle.

The ancestral Sabi society, the other new strand in this history of ethnic shift, took shape far north in the early first millennium CE, in the areas in and to the southeast of the Upemba Depression in today's Katanga Province of Congo. The expansion of Sabi peoples out of that home region took place in two stages. First, in about the fifth and sixth centuries, some Sabi communities spread eastward to the southeastern shores of Lake Tanganyika. Then, from the eleventh to the fifteenth centuries, a much wider spread of Sabi communities took place across most of the central and eastern parts of modern-day Zambia. We call the archeology of this expansion the Luangwa Tradition. The cultural impact of the second Sabi expansion reached even wider, into Malawi and into parts of modern-day western Zambia. The Bantu languages already found in those regions continued to be spoken, but many cultural features of Sabi origin, including new styles of pottery making, gained wide currency in both areas between 1000 and 1400 (see map 18).

The Botatwe expansion and, most of all, the Sabi expansion each appear to have powerfully reinforced the existing matrilineal philosophies of social organization of the Bantu peoples of the region. Women's initiation ceremonies everywhere became defining societal observances. As we learned in chapter 5, in both the Botatwe and the Sabi cultures, female initiation had two steps, one coming at puberty and the other at the birth of the woman's first child. We suspect that male circumcision ceremonies had been important before the sixth century in the Muteteshi and Salumano societies, but the Botatwe and Sabi cultures that superseded them lacked this custom entirely. Only among the Botatwe was even a relatively unimportant, no-longer-communal male initiation ceremony maintained.

Wherever the Botatwe and Sabi influences spread, a new concept of the Creator God of Niger-Congo civilization as *Leeza*, the Nurturer, took hold. Among the Botatwe, though, an interesting religious syncretism accompanied the adoption of this idea. This concept of God as a nurturing force was coupled with the metaphors of the sky, rain, and lightning, which had characterized the earlier Muteteshi and Salumano beliefs about the Creator God. The Muteteshi and Salumano peoples themselves may in turn have adopted these Sudanic religious metaphors for the supreme being from the particular Eastern Sahelian communities who are thought to have brought cattle and sheep into these regions in the last few centuries of the first millennium BCE.

Political scale remained small throughout the thousand years between 300 and the 1440s. The Botatwe continued to maintain the old clan chiefship of the Bantu heritage until the twentieth century. The Sabi expansions across central and eastern Zambia, in contrast, brought in a new kind of chiefship, in which a chiefly kin group, call the *Bumba*, exerted a loose authority over people of other clans or lineages than their own. But the Bumba chiefdoms continued to be small, local units, composed of no more, we suspect, than a few nearby villages.

If later historical example is any guide, women not uncommonly became chiefs, even if they did so less often than men, in these tiny, strongly matrilineal, and, in their ritual concerns, strongly matrifocal chiefdoms.

An intriguing problem in culture history that may be associated with this era of ethnic shift is the disappearance of male circumcision all across east-central Africa. In part this development surely owes to the spread of Botatwe and Sabi cultural norms, in which circumcision had no role, across large areas of modern-day Zambia, Malawi, and far southeastern Congo. But the regions in which circumcision was dropped form part of a much larger contiguous run of territories, extending across Zimbabwe, northern Mozambique, and the western and southern parts of Tanzania. Did the influence of Sabi ideas spread even east and north of Lake Nyasa, or were separate factors responsible in those areas for the disappearance of this custom, old in the history of Bantu-speaking societies? These are questions historians cannot yet answer.

Growth of Political Scale: The Southern Woodland Savannas and Equatorial Rainforest, 600–1450

Farther north and west, in the savanna woodlands of the southern Congo Basin, a different direction of historical change can be discerned in at least two widely separated regions. Both in the country of the upper Lualaba River and in the areas around the lower Congo River, larger and more complex scales of political organization took shape in the centuries before 1100, giving rise after 1100 to the first states of south-central Africa. Still farther north, in most parts of the rainforest zone, true states did not develop, although another kind of growth of political scale, the creation of extensive village alliances, did take place in the heart of the Congo Basin.

Political and Economic Growth in the Upemba Depression, 600–1100

In the lands surrounding the upper Lualaba, an emerging interregional trade in a variety of different products, including fish, copper, salt, and iron, undergirded the changing political culture of this region. The early center of the new directions in economy and politics appears to have lain in the Upemba Depression, an area of lakes and bayous along the upper Lualaba River. The defining development of the new era was the spread across this region of a new archeological tradition, which we call Early Kisalian. The Early Kisalian period began around 600 and lasted until the eleventh century. The makers of this tradition, the early Luba people, spread into the Upemba Depression from the northwest, incorporating the formerly Sabi-speaking communities of the region into their expanding society. We suspect that matrilineal descent still determined the inheritance of wealth and position over the next several centuries. On the other hand, male circumcision was newly established in the region by the Luba, and the balance of gendered access to position and influence probably shifted more strongly in favor of males than had been the case in the previous era of Sabi-speaking communities, before 600 (see map 17).

A multidirectional trade in natural resources took shape already in the Early Kisalian era. Salt and iron deposits could be found in several areas close to the Upemba Depression. The striking new trade commodity of the era all across the upper Lualaba region was copper. Found 300 kilometers to the south of the Upemba Depression, in the region today known as the Copper Belt, cop-

FIG. 44 Copper cross currency

Currency in the form of copper crosses came into use among the peoples of the upper Congo Basin and the Congo-Zambezi watershed region in the late first millennium CE and continued to be a common means of exchange down to the beginning of the colonial period. Its use shows us that more varied trade in valued commodities as well as payments of tribute had already become part of the social and political life in those areas by the tenth century. Shown here is a late example of this kind of currency, dating to the eighteenth or nineteenth century.

per ore was being mined and smelted there by the fourth century CE. Copper soon became a key marker of wealth, in much the fashion of gold in other parts of the world. Before the Early Kisalian period was over, copper fashioned into small crosses began to be used as the regular and common currency of trade in the region.

Another important aspect of economic exchange in the upper Lualaba regions involved the exploitation of the aquatic resources found in the lakes and bayous of the heart of the Upemba Depression. At an early period—we are uncertain just how early—regular public works began to undertaken by the communities living along those waterways. They built up levees, on which they situated their villages, and they periodically cleared floating vegetation from the different stream channels. In this way they controlled and maintained the mix of open stream and riverbank environments essential to the balance of aquatic resources on which they depended. Because of their relative inaccessibility amid the various channels of the Lualaba River, the riverine villages long retained a great deal of economic autonomy. Their more than ample supplies of fish and also of reeds, valued as material for thatching, basketry, and mat making, attracted people from many other nearby areas, who in return for payment in goods or copper currency were allowed by the river villagers to come and use those resources.

The Upemba Kingdom and Its Neighbors, 1100–1450

A new era, the Classical Kisalian, began in the twelfth century. What principally differentiated the Classical Kisalian age from the preceding Early Kisalian era was a leap upward in the scale of political organization and in the concentration of wealth. The indirect testimony of the archeology tells us that in Classical Kisalian times the first large state in this part of Africa emerged among the Luba of the Upemba Depression. It is perhaps not inappropriate to call it the First Luba Empire, but we will settle for a less ambitious name, the Upemba Kingdom (see map 17).

Royal burials at Sanga in the Upemba Depression, characterized by rich arrays of copper and other grave goods, confirm our impression that central control over the trading of copper, iron, and salt across the region laid the material basis for this new scale of political authority in the Upemba state. The existence of the word *musonko,* meaning "tribute paid by subordinate chiefs," in the Luba language of this period shows us that tributary relationships must already have been a crucial political tool for exerting this kind of control. The location of the central sites of this kingdom in the Upemba Depression itself suggests that access to the aquatic resources of the bayous also in some way must have been essential to the state. Did the Upemba kings perhaps seek legitimization by claiming a role as the protectors of the riverine resources and as patrons of the public works that kept the various courses of the Lualaba clear and flowing? We simply do not as yet know the answer to that question, but it does raise intriguing possibilities for future investigation.

The Upemba state may have been the largest political formation of its time in the southern savanna regions, but the Luba were not the only people of the woodland savanna zone among whom the institutions of state-building were taking shape. Three hundred kilometers to the west, the Lunda, a Western-Savanna Bantu people residing in the Nkalaany Valley of the upper Kasai River region, created several mini-states under the authority of competing royal lines, known as the Tubungu kings. Here a different old word for tribute, -lambula, came into use in the Lunda language, indicating that more complex relations between differing levels of political authority were a characteristic of the early Tubungu kingships, just as they were in the Kisalian society.

By late in the Classical Kisalian period, other small kingdoms probably existed in the areas between the Upemba Kingdom and the mini-states of the Nkalaany Valley. Studies of the vocabularies of politics and political institutions used in later kingdoms in this span of the southern savanna belt reveal a multifaceted flow of ideas during the years from 1100 to 1450. Luba ideas spread to the Lunda cultural area; Lunda ideas spread the opposite direction as well. The Kanyok, who in later centuries built up their own separate kingdom in the intervening area, seem often to have been key intermediaries in the transmission of such ideas from the one region to the other (see map 18).

The farthest reach of Classical Kisalian influences extended into Malawi. In about the fourteenth century, a new ruling group, the Phiri, took power among the Nyanja-Chewa peoples of areas to the immediate west and southwest of Lake Nyasa. Founders of a loosely confederated Malawi Empire by or before the early fifteenth century, the Phiri rulers traced their origins back to the land of the Luba. The senior ruler of the empire bore the title *Karonga*. Lesser kings of Phiri descent, with the titles *Undi* and *Lundu*, governed different portions of the wider Malawian domains.

The claim of the Malawi rulers to Luba background was an authentic one. Among the notable features of governance put into effect in the early Malawi Empire was the collection of tribute from subordinate chiefs. We know that a

Luba idea was directly involved here because the Malawian word for tribute, *musonko,* was borrowed from the Luba language. Descent and inheritance among the common folk in Malawi society, as well as succession to office among the chiefly families, continued to be governed by matrilineal principles. Kings in this kind of system inherited their positions from their mothers' brothers and not from their fathers.

The formation of the Malawi state in the fourteenth or early fifteenth century coincided closely in time with the development of a major new trade route along the Zambezi River, immediately south of Malawi, and these commercial relations are likely to have been an important material factor in the rise of the empire. A major Malawian resource in high demand along the Zambezi would have been ivory. The local manufacture of cotton textiles was already established in the region and provided another kind of item valued both for commerce and as tribute (see map 18).

Just how early the weaving of cotton textiles began in these areas is not yet known, but this kind of manufacturing is attested in the archeology of Zimbabwe by as early as the thirteenth century. The loom technology in the region itself shows connections back to West Africa. The most probable explanation of that link in the present state of our knowledge is that the technology diffused originally with the spread of raffia cloth weaving, possibly as long as 2,000 years ago, and was readapted in Malawi and Zimbabwe to cotton textile production sometime between then and the thirteenth century.

Farming, Trade, and Politics: Western Equatorial Africa, 300–1450

Two other regions marked by political developments of major historical significance lay in the areas surrounding the Malebo Pool on the lower Congo River and in the middle parts of the Congo Basin. To understand these developments, we need first to consider the long-term trends of change across western equatorial African as a whole. As we have already learned, ironworking had become an important manufacturing activity well before 300. Because iron ores were unevenly distributed, the demand for iron in areas lacking ores became a major stimulus to trade. The emergence of specialized fishing societies along the major rivers added another dimension, a trade in differing kinds of foodstuffs, to the overall mix of commercial relations that were beginning to take shape by the middle of the first millennium CE.

In this evolving pattern of communal economic specialization, the BaTwa gatherer-hunters carved out an important niche for themselves by providing

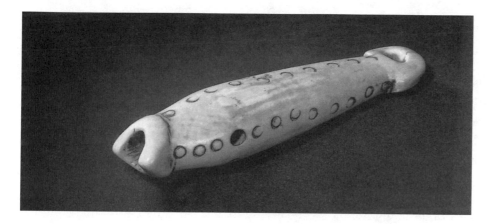

FIG. 45 Ivory whistle

Whistles made of wood and bone were ancient musical instruments of the BaTwa peoples. As Bantu communities expanded through the equatorial rainforest after 3000 BCE, they often adopted the making of whistles from their BaTwa predecessors. The example shown here comes from the Lega, a Bantu people of the eastern side of the rainforest. Its fashioning from ivory, a more expensive material, reflects the fact that this particular instrument was used by people of power and position in Lega culture in socially important rituals.

skins, honey, ivory, and other products of their food-collecting activities. As they began to spend more time producing goods for commerce, many BaTwa turned increasingly to trade to obtain some of their food from the cultivating Bantu groups around them, rather than supplying themselves entirely by their own activities. Different social consequences eventuated for the BaTwa. Some gatherer-hunter communities entered into periods of especially close relations with nearby agricultural communities characterized by the loss of their former languages and their adoption of those spoken by their Bantu neighbors. Other BaTwa communities, in contrast, were able build on their new commercial importance to take a more independent stance in their relations with their more numerous farming neighbors.

Still another factor in the growth of commerce may have been the widespread adoption of the raising of bananas among the rainforest cultivators. This crop appears to have added greatly to the agricultural productivity of the rainforest environment. Beginning in the period 300–1000, we suspect, the cultivation of the banana revolutionized life for many of the forest Bantu, providing a large and more secure base of food and leaving them more time for manufacturing activities, among which was the making of raffia cloth and barkcloth.

Bolstered by this enrichment of agriculture productivity, Bantu-speaking farmers continued to spread cultivation into more parts of the rainforest. One notable expansion involved the Mongo. Their early ancestors were one of the societies that emerged during the Sangha-Nzadi period of Bantu expansion, dating to the second half of the third millennium BCE. Originally inhabiting lands somewhere to the south of the confluence of the Congo and Ubangi Rivers, the Mongo as early as 300 CE began to spread their settlements successively farther up the various rivers that flowed west to the Congo out of the heart of the Congo Basin. By the period 1000–1450, different Mongo communities had established themselves all across the middle of the basin. BaTwa people continued to reside in these areas, but increasingly they had to accommodate to a new cultural and economic environment.

Another region of expanding Bantu cultivating peoples lay in the hilly areas of rainforest immediately north of the middle Congo River and south of the Uele and Ubangi Rivers. Here the Boan societies continued to play a central role in a long-term set of cultural and ethnic shifts. During the middle of the first millennium, some Boan groups resettled northward among the Ubangian societies of the upper Uele and Bomu River regions, while others spread west, through and around the lands of the Medje-Lombi Central Sudanians. By the fifteenth century, the westernmost Boans had come to reside almost as far west as the confluence of the Ubangi and Congo Rivers. Settling principally in areas with highly lateritic soils, the Boan women farmers relied on the old Bantu practice of planting by slicing into the soil and placing their yam cuttings in those slices. There was one major difference, however, in how they did this: as befitted peoples who had adopted iron technology by around 500 BCE, they used large machete-like knives, forged by the Boan blacksmiths, to slice into the ground.

The First Kingdoms of Western Equatorial Africa, 1000–1450

True states evolved after 1000 in the southwestern part of western equatorial Africa. One center of state formation lay just east of the Congo River, around Lake Mai Ndombe, in a region of rainforest intersected by an intervening patch of savanna. The other straddled the lower Congo River, and though it comprised mostly savanna lands, it also included areas of rainforest to the northwest and east (see map 17).

The states of Lake Mai Ndombe remained very small kingdoms through-out their long history. The earliest among them, Bolia, appears to have been founded in the twelfth or perhaps even the eleventh century. Several equally tiny sister kingdoms emerged as its neighbors between the fourteenth and six-teenth centuries. A common core of political and religious ideas legitimized and sustained these mini-states, with the most fundamental idea being a con-cept of the king as the ritual mediator between the people and both the ances-tors and the local territorial spirits.

The second region of state formation lay close by, in the areas around the Malebo Pool on the lower Congo River. A wide turbulent cascade marked the downstream outlet of this 20–25 kilometer-wide pool, forcing those traveling along the Congo to take a long portage around this point. For this reason, the Malebo Pool formed a key transshipment point for goods moving either up or down the river.

There a number of small kingdoms took shape between 1000 and 1300. The key component in the ruling ideology was encapsulated in the word for "king" or "lord," *-kani, used all across the region. This term derived from the proto-Bantu verb *-gan-, which had originally meant "to tell stories," including both folktales and oral histories. In this region the word took on an additional mean-ing, "to pronounce judgment." The power and legitimacy of kings came from their being understood as the final arbiters of intercommunity disputes, able to wield the knowledge of historical precedent (hence, "to tell stories") to estab-lish and maintain peace and order among groupings of formerly independent clan polities.

Trading activities along the Congo in the later first millennium and early second millennium CE formed the other key element in the building up of po-litical scale across the region. Some of the areas just north of the lower stretches of the river possessed fine deposits of copper ore, which local metalworkers be-gan to exploit and trade widely sometime probably before 1000. Several parts of the region also produced other manufactures, including raffia cloth, bark-cloth, and iron goods. Valued shells, known as *nzimbu*, were brought from the shores of the Atlantic, while from far upstream came products of the rainfor-est, such as ivory.

The ability of chiefs and kings to control and draw tribute from the move-ment of the goods across their territories created the material means for building political power and prestige. Seen in this light, the fact that the first two really large kingdoms of the region, Tyo and Kongo, arose on opposite sides of the Malebo Pool, the key juncture in the regional trade, is hardly surprising.

The Tyo kingdom, which formed in an area of originally woodland savanna just north of the pool, may have been the earlier of the two, but we remain uncertain of its founding date. The importance of the Teke peoples of the kingdom came from their roles as intermediaries in trade coming both from the forest to the north and from the coast and forest belt to their west. The authority of the kings was built around their control of the national shrine. How that shrine gained popular recognition in the first place as the most important religious site of the region, and how the Tyo kings took control of it, is a history about which we have no reliable information. The characteristics of the shrine suggest, however, that it may have originally have been the sacred site of a Niger-Congo territorial spirit. The territories of the Tyo kingdom comprised a number of formerly independent small kingdoms, each still with its own *-kani who had become a vassal of the Tyo king.

In later times, in the late eighteenth and the nineteenth centuries, the Tyo kings maintained a more nominal than real political authority over a loose, decentralized collection of such principalities. But in the earlier centuries of Tyo history, it seems clear that the direct power of the kings was considerably greater, and that their kingdom was a far more cohesive territory, able, for instance, to wage war in the sixteenth century on an equal footing with its powerful neighbor, the kingdom of Kongo, on the other side of the Malebo Pool.

Kongo, the second large state of the region, was founded in the fourteenth century. Previously several small kingdoms, located along the north bank of the lower Congo River, had prospered from the production of copper from locally available copper ores. In the second half of the century, one of these kingdoms, Bungu, sent a member of its royal family, Lukeni Nimi, across the river to better manage the copper trade with the Kongo people living in that region. But Lukemi soon allied with a group of powerful local clan chiefs, called the Mwisikongo. With the support of the Mwisikongo and their people, he successfully claimed the title of *Manikongo*, or ruler of Kongo. On these foundations, he and his immediate successors built up a large territorial state (see map 18).

The Kongo capital, Mbanzakongo, lay at the hub of a vigorous network of commercial relations. The Nkisi Valley, to the east of the capital, was a major raffia cloth manufacturing area. The kings of Kongo soon extended their eastern boundaries well beyond the Nkisi Valley, to the Malebo Pool, so as to gain access to goods coming downstream along the Congo River.

FIG. 46 Nkisi figure

The nkisi were powerful ritual objects, possessed by chiefs and kings of the lower Congo River region and considered to be essential instruments of their power. This kind of artifact was a probable innovation of the era of the earliest founding of larger-scale polities in the region, between around 500 and 1200 CE.

A second important area of Kongo political and trade expansion lay between Mbanzakongo and the coast. Particularly important to the kingdom during the first 150 years of existence was the island of Luanda, located on the Atlantic coast, at the far southwestern edge of the kingdom. From that island came *nzimbu* shells, the basic currency of fifteenth- and early-sixteenth-century trade in the regions all around the lower Congo River. By controlling access to the currency, the Kongo kingdom consolidated its preeminent position in a web of trade relations that led far inland up the river and extended far beyond its own territories.

By the later fifteenth century, the prestige and wealth of the Kongo kings had allowed them to impose tributary status on the neighboring small Ndembu kingdoms and the somewhat larger Mbwila state, both located to the south, and to bring the small kingdoms on the north, just across the Congo River, such as Bungu, Kakongo, and Loango, under their hegemony. The Matamba kingdom south of Mbwila and its western neighbor Ndongo, located to the south of the Ndembu region, also fell into Kongo's sphere of political and economic influence (see map 22). Ndongo, ruled by a king whose title, *Ngola a Kiluanje,* gives us the name of the modern country of Angola, was a kingdom of whose early history we know almost nothing. Its early institutions possibly drew some influences from the common legacy of ideas that developed in the states of the lower Congo River in the period before 1400.

Despite the strength of their state, the fifteenth-century kings of Kongo seemed to have lacked a powerful legitimizing ideology that was truly their own. Their legitimacy depended above all on their mutually beneficial ties, as we have seen, with the clan chiefs of the central areas of the kingdom, the Mwisikongo. These chiefs, of course, drew their own legitimacy from the older kin-based ideas of Bantu chiefship, which included the metaphor of the chiefs as the "owners" of their kin group. All through Kongo history, its kings sought to balance off the influence of the Mwisikongo by frequently contracting marriage with the daughters of the especially powerful and wealthy clan chiefs of the Nkisi Valley to the east of Mbanzakongo. The kings needed backing as well from the *kitomi* priests, who presided over the particularly Kongo version of the old territorial spirit beliefs of Niger-Congo civilization. The religious map of the country, in contrast to the clan map, divided Kongo up into the separate watersheds of important streams, each such drainage area forming the territory of a particular spirit and the religious domain of a different *kitomi.* The leading *kitomi,* of the areas right around the capital Mbanzakongo, was normally a leading member of the king's council.

The "Spoils of the Leopard": Politics and Society in the Central Congo Basin, to 1450

North of the woodland savannas, in the equatorial rainforest zone, the centuries immediately before 1450 were not yet a time of state building. But polities very much resembling states did take shape across the middle of the Congo Basin. There the Mongo and their neighbors developed a system of hierarchical village alliances, reflective of both their settlement history and the evolving patterns of riverine trade.

The beginnings of this system, it can be argued, go back to the early centuries of the Mongo expansion into the heart of the Congo Basin. Settlers would advance deeper into the basin by leaving their former village and founding a new village farther upstream. There they would reconstitute the social and governing system they had followed in their former village, by centering their social loyalties around their lineage relations and by giving their allegiance to a village chief whose historical roots lay in the older Bantu institution of the *-kumu* (see chapter 4). From the beginning of this particular history, trade in iron must have been important because of the sparsity of good iron resources in the inner Congo Basin.

Around the thirteenth century a powerful new factor rapidly intruded into this history. Communities living at the northeastern edges of this zone, along the lower Aruwimi River, reorganized their societies around ideas of patrilineal descent, along with new battle tactics involving disciplined fighting and larger forces than had ever existed before in this region. They built huge war canoes from massive rainforest trees, and their smiths forged new kinds of weaponry, including stabbing spears and long curved swords, with the blade bent back at the middle, allowing the wielder of such a sword to kill his enemy by thrusting the curved end around behind the edge of the enemy's shield.

By the fifteenth century the bearers of this new kind of social organization and military power had reshaped the political world of regions all along the north side of the middle Congo River and widely in the interior basin south of the middle Congo. New hierarchical alliances of villages arose, with sometimes thousands of citizens tied together by a chain of successively greater political seniority, in which the chief of each successive village along a river, although independent in the day-to-day affairs of the community, was junior to the next chief farther downstream. At the apex of each alliance was a high chief, the most senior and the central figure in the ideology that bound the alliance together (see map 18).

The central symbols of this system were certain noble animals, the leopard above all, but also the eagle and the pangolin, which were emblematic of chiefship. When a leopard was killed in the territory of a particular village, it had to be passed up the hierarchy of political relations until it reached the high chief of the village alliance. There the leopard was skinned and cut up and "spoils of the leopard" apportioned by seniority among the village chiefs.

The distribution of the "spoils of the leopard" along the chain of seniority from village to village was fundamentally important because it legitimized the whole system of political and social relations. But the lasting vitality of the system may have been crucially reinforced by the centrality of river routes in the trade relations of the region. Goods such as raffia textiles, iron ore, raw iron, and iron tools manufactured in the villages, along with wild products collected in the forest by the BaTwa neighbors of the Mongo, were traded along the rivers that connected the villages, in this way accentuating the power of the customs that defined and structured the relations among the villages.

Not surprisingly, for both historical and economic reasons, the domains of the great chiefs often lay at the junctures of important rivers. Early in history, the spread of settlers up each tributary river would have brought into being a different conjoining chain of villages, with each chain forming a junior offshoot of the same senior village, located at the confluence. In later centuries the seniority of the village at the confluence, and of the high chief of that village, would have been continually revitalized by its position as the juncture point in the riverine trade networks, as well as by the transmission of the "spoils of the leopard" to the great chief. By the middle of the second millennium CE, because of the growth of trade, the villages of the great chiefs, we suspect, frequently reached the size of towns. (In the still more aggressively commercial era of the later eighteenth and nineteenth centuries, some of these chiefly towns in the inner Congo Basin grew, in fact, into small cities of as many as 10,000–15,000 inhabitants.)

The development of this system of village alliances in the inner Congo Basin had important consequences for gender relations. Patrilineal descent became the widely recognized norm in the inheritance of wealth and position among nearly all the Mongo peoples. Only here and there in peripheral areas did matrilineal ideas remain strong. The increasing wealth in trade and the hierarchization of political authority also appears to have been accompanied by enhanced male authority in political as well as social matters. In addition, this period was surely characterized by an increased reliance among the leading men on polygynous marriages as the way to build up their wealth and social connections and enhance their standing and influence in society.

A notable feature of the history we have just been considering—of the southern savanna belt and the equatorial rainforest—is how there were few connections with developments taking place outside the continent. Nevertheless, it was a time when agricultural populations expanded, trade in both raw materials and manufactured goods grew in importance, and, along the lower Congo River at least, states emerged.

Eastern Africa, 300–1450

Broad Themes of Change in Eastern Africa

Trends of historical change both similar to and strikingly different from those of western equatorial Africa took place in the eastern African interior between 300 and 1450. The long-term themes of that history similarly included the gradual increase of Bantu-speaking agricultural populations in many areas, and in the African Great Lakes region, new political institutions and the first large state took shape between 1000 and 1400. On the other hand, new expansions of Nilotic peoples dominated events across the grasslands and dry savannas of the middle parts of East Africa, and a varied and complex diffusion of ideas among societies often characterized the relations among the peoples of those regions. In several areas distinctively new agricultural systems were brought into being.

The social history of this era played out in different ways in different regions. In the vast drainage basins of the Rufiji and Ruvuma Rivers (today's southeastern Tanzania), Kaskazi Bantu societies slowly and gradually spread into areas with less rainfall than their forebears had been accustomed to. As yet we know only of the broad trends of this history. The communities involved in these developments would have had to place a much greater reliance on grain cultivation, and throughout the period they continued to live in small-scale, village-based societies and in hundreds of tiny, localized chiefdoms. We suspect that Khoisan gatherer-hunter people may have been the previous inhabitants of the region, but we know nothing of their relations with the Rufiji and Ruvuma Bantu societies and what became of them.

In western East Africa, other Kaskazi Bantu communities also expanded into drier areas previously occupied just by Khoisan gatherer-hunters. The notable example in this region was the ancestral Wembere people, who moved into areas along the Sibiti River late in the first millennium CE. They dealt with the problem of lower rainfall, less than 700 millimeters per year, partly by using the wet soils of the river bottomlands for their fields and partly by raising more grain crops, such as sorghum and pearl millet. The older Mashariki style of clan chiefship, with responsibilities in community rituals and in distributing land for cultivation, continued to prevail in the Wembere society (see map 18).

Kalenjin and Maa-Ongamo Peoples along the Eastern Rift, 300–1000

In the heart of East Africa, societies with strikingly different institutions based on age-sets came to predominate. In the western Kenya Highlands, the early Kalenjin, a Southern Nilotic people of the period 300 to 1000, developed a new version of the cycling age-set system. The Southern Nilotic system of the first millennium BCE had consisted of a cycle of eight age-set names, divided into two generational groupings of four age-sets each. The son's age-set had to belong to the opposite generational group of sets from that of his father. By late in the first millennium CE, most of the Kalenjin communities had dropped the generational component entirely and had expanded the periods between the initiation of their young men into new age-sets from around ten years to about fifteen years. It now took about 120 years to use up the eight age-set names and then begin the cycle anew.

The more important historical consequences may have come, however, from what happened to the age-grade component of this system. Once the generational component of the older Southern Nilotic system had been dropped, the Kalenjin as a whole came to recognize just two adult life stages for males, the *muren*, or young man age-grade, and the *payyan*, or elder grade, to which men belonged for the remainder of their lives. Because it now took around fifteen years until the initiation of the next age-set into the *muren* state of life, the young men remained together for a decade and a half in the *muren* grade, the responsibilities of which, among others, were to defend the community and raid other communities for cattle. This longer period of membership in the "warrior" age-grade, we suspect, increased the ability of the Kalenjin to exert military pressure on their neighbors and strengthened their capacities for defending themselves in case of attack. Apparently bolstered by these changes in their basic distribution of social and political responsibilities, the Kalenjin between about 800 and 1000 expanded far and wide across the plains and mountain grasslands of central East Africa. Some Kalenjin communities moved into the high moorlands around Mount Kenya; others spread far south along the Eastern Rift Valley into what we call today the Maasai Steppe of north-central Tanzania (see map 17).

Why the Kalenjin expansion took place just when it did is not clearly understood. The eighth and ninth centuries were, however, a period of considerable social and economic rearrangement in the areas all around the Eastern Rift Valley. At around 700, a major new population element, the ancestral Maa-Ongamo people, an Eastern Nilotic group, moved south from the Lake Turkana Basin into the plateaus along the east side of the rift, just north of Mount Kenya. The histories of the Kalenjin and Maa-Ongamo closely entwined from then on. A further divergence of the Maa-Ongamo into separate Maa and Ongamo societies took place after the eighth century, with the ancestral Ongamo moving off to the south, to settle in the grazing lands surrounding Mount Kilimanjaro, while the ancestral Maa remained in the plateaus just north of Mount Kenya (see map 17).

Like the Kalenjin, the Maa-Ongamo peoples relied on a combined age-set and age-grade system to organize themselves politically and militarily. Their

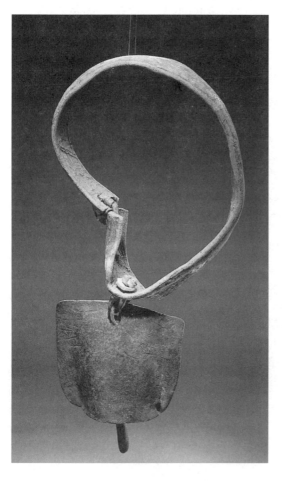

FIG. 47 Maasai forged iron cowbell

Cowbells were originally made by Lowland Eastern Cushitic peoples, such as the Konsoromo, in the Ethiopian Highlands during the last 3,000 years BCE (see also fig. 34). Before the iron age, and sometimes in recent centuries as well, people fashioned them from hard wood or, in some cases, tortoiseshell. The Maa-Ongamo ancestors of the Maasai introduced the iron variety seen here into the Kenya Rift Valley and surrounding regions in the later first millennium CE.

system was linear rather than cycling, but as in the Kalenjin system, young men remained in the "warrior" stage of life for many years. The Maa-Ongamo, in fact, even while retaining their older linear age-sets, rapidly adopted the Kalenjin ideas of age-grades, even taking over from the Kalenjin the terms *murran* (from *muren*) and *payyan* (giving the words their own slightly different pronunciations) for the respective grades of young man and elder.

Most interestingly, a new kind of economic relationship, involving all the peoples of the central parts of the Eastern Rift Valley region, began exactly in this period. The descendants of the Eburran gatherer-hunters, called Okiek by the Kalenjin, added to their gatherer-hunter pursuits the occupational specialization of pottery manufacturing, and both the Maa-Ongamo and those Kalenjin peoples who lived immediately adjacent to the rift began to acquire their pots, of a type called Lanet ware, from the Okiek. These close economic ties had a linguistic consequence, too: almost all the Okiek during this period took up the Kalenjin language as their own, in place of whatever languages they had previously spoken.

The eighth and ninth centuries were also the period in which the full establishment of specialist ironworking took place throughout the rift valley regions of Kenya. Even though we are certain that iron had been known there for centuries, the Kalenjin still had a tendency as late as the sixth or seventh century to prefer obsidian in toolmaking. The disappearance of that preference dates to about the eighth century.

Markets, Agricultural Innovation, and Ethnic Shift in Kilimanjaro, 1000–1450

There is evidence as well that the period around 1000 saw the first development of regular market locations, where peoples living in the different environmental zones of the Eastern Rift regions came to trade their different products. By the eleventh and twelfth centuries, markets of this kind were located especially along the southern sides of both Mount Kenya and Mount Kilimanjaro, in environmental transition zones. These zones lay between the Bantu-speaking Thagiicu and Chaga cultivators of the forested slopes, of whom we will have more to say in a moment, and the Eastern-Sahelian-speaking Maa-Ongamo and Kalenjin of the surrounding grasslands and open savannas. Early market relations revolved around the exchange of herders' products, such as leather and leather clothing, and gatherer-hunter products, such as skins and honey, for the cultivated foods and wooden goods, such as stools, of the cultivators. In subsequent centuries, as manufactures, in particular, iron tools and pottery, took on increasing importance in the overall mix of goods traded, regular periodic markets were established in such locations, operating on four-day weeks.

Two factors greatly facilitated this development of regular markets. One factor was the growth of accentuated differences in productive strategies in the distinctive environments, thus making for sharp productive variations in adjacent lands. The dissimilarities meant that each environmental zone had specialties of its own to offer in the intra-regional trade. The second factor was the uneven distribution, especially around Mount Kilimanjaro and the nearby Pare Mountains, of two essential natural resources, iron ore and suitable clays for potting. Particularly on Kilimanjaro, there was a lack of adequate resources of both kinds, whereas the Pare Mountains, especially the North Pare Range, had each in abundance (see map 17).

Accompanying these developments in market relations was the invention of a truly new agricultural synthesis among the Bantu-speaking communities who lived in the highland areas east of the rift. The beginnings of this new, highland planting agriculture, as we can call it, took place in the Pare Mountains to the south of Mount Kilimanjaro between about 700 and 1000. Banana growing had spread inland from the coast to this region sometime before 700, becoming an established crop among the Asu people of the South Pare Mountains and among the ancestral Chaga of the North Pare Range. By 1000 these farming communities had already developed a large number of distinctive banana varieties. Increasingly they came to rely on bananas as the staple of their diet. They continued to grow a variety of yams in their high rainfall environment, but they grew almost no grains at all except finger millet, from which they obtained the malt for brewing a new kind of alcoholic beverage, banana beer.

What is more important, they put into effect a number of technological changes in their cultivating practice, highly reminiscent of those earlier developed in the Ethiopian Rift Valley region. These included irrigation, the use of cattle manure, and sometimes terracing of fields. The Chaga in particular followed a practice we know also from the Konso peoples of Ethiopia: they kept cattle in stalls and fed them there, to make it easier to collect the manure for their fields. One of the interesting issues for future historical study will be to determine if separate invention took place here, or whether ancient Cushitic influences, preserved in East Africa by Southern Cushitic peoples or perhaps brought south by the Southern Nilotes, might be involved.

In the North Pare Mountains, where the ancestral Chaga lived, the growth of population by about the eleventh or twelfth century led a number of people to begin looking for a new land on which to live. They found it on the nearby and, in those days, still heavily forested southern and eastern slopes of Mount Kilimanjaro. The movement of the early Chaga banana farmers to Kilimanjaro set off a period of rapid and extensive cultural amalgamation, in which large numbers of both the Ongamo people and the Rift Southern Cushites were assimilated into the newly expanding Chaga communities.

A striking blending of features of ancient Afrasan and Niger-Congo civilizations, with some features of Sudanic civilization contributed by the Ongamo, emerged out of this period of cross-cultural encounter. The dominance of the new highland planting agriculture ensured that the new communities came to speak the Chaga language of the makers of that agriculture. Initially these communities took the form of villages built along highland ridges. This custom apparently preserved an old practice coming from the Kaskazi and Upland Bantu side of their ancestry. The Chaga also circumcised boys and initiated them into age-sets of the typical old Bantu type, but at the same time they adopted from the Southern Cushitic side of their ancestry the practice of female clitoridectomy. In a variety of other respects, Cushitic or Nilotic ideas prevailed in Chaga culture, a notable case being music, in which drumming anciently typical of Niger-Congo civilization was entirely lost. The drawing of blood from cattle was a specifically Southern Cushitic addition to the sources of food. And like the Ongamo and the Southern Cushites, the emerging Chaga society was entirely patrilineal. In religion a thoroughgoing syncretism took place. The importance of the ancestors, a Niger-Congo feature, was strongly maintained by the Chaga, but they merged the idea of Divinity, metaphorically identified with the sun as in the Rift Southern Cushitic version of the Sudanic religion, with the Creator God concept of early Niger-Congo belief.

Still other features of their society appear to have been specifically Chaga in origin. Chiefship was such an institution. In the nearby South Pare Mountains, the old clan chiefship of the Mashariki Bantu world continued to be the ritual center of local life among the early Asu and remained so, in fact, down through the nineteenth century. Even today, the Asu word for "chief," *mfumua,* comes from the old verb root *-kum-* (proto-Bantu *k* changes an *f* before the vowel *u* in the Asu language), which encodes the old Niger-Congo conception of the chief as "honored person." But among the ancestral Chaga of North Pare and among their descendants who settled around Mount Kilimanjaro, a new kind of chiefship, *mangi,* probably originally meaning "the arranger, planner," came into being probably not much before 1000.

The terrain of Kilimanjaro encouraged the founding of a great many small, independent chiefdoms on the eastern and southern sides of the mountain. The newly emerging Chaga communities took up residence on the numerous parallel ridges and valleys that stretched down the slopes, and each ridge became home to one or more chiefdoms (see maps 17 and 18).

In a change from the old Mashariki clan chiefs, the Chaga rulers were not tied to an individual clan but instead ruled over a small territory. The typical *mangi* would have acted as the adjudicator of disputes and thus would have been able to preside effectively over the melding of different peoples into the expanding Chaga communities of the early second millennium around Kilimanjaro. He (a chief appears nearly always to have been male in this region) had the right to use the age-sets as communal labor in building and maintaining irrigation works, and so he was the "arranger" or "planner" of public works. From these responsibilities, it seems, came the origin of the word for "chief."

Under the authority of the *mangi* were the *njili,* the local elders of the several clan groups that made up each chiefdom. Interestingly, the word *njili* appears to be a borrowing into Chaga of one of the Southern Cushitic terms for the Cushitic type of clan headman, a synonym for **wap'er.* Apparently the earlier Rift Southern Cushite communities may have often been incorporated as coherent groups into the expanding Chaga society. The clan headmen retained their leadership over their kin group but were co-opted along with their people into the new society through their taking up of a new role as members of the chief's council.

The coming together of two factors, the trade in iron and the new type of political ideology embodied in the term *mangi,* led to the emergence of the first known state in the region between about 1100 and 1400. Called Ugweno in later centuries, this small kingdom was founded in the North Pare Mountains by rulers of the WaShana clan. The name of this ruling clan means literally "blacksmiths." Both this name and the sketchy traditions that have come down to us from this period make it clear that control of the major sources of iron in the region is what allowed the early Ugweno kings to turn their original role of local *mangi* into the kingship of a small but economically important territorial state (see map 18).

Agricultural Expansion in the Mount Kenya Region, 1000–1450

Banana cultivation spread north also before 1000 to the Thagiicu, who like the Chaga were an Upland Bantu people. The Thagiicu inhabited the southern slopes of Mount Kenya in those centuries. The banana became an important crop among them, but they developed a different version of the highland planting agriculture. In the Thagiicu's version, yam cultivation remained as important as the growing of the banana and was further enriched by the addition of Southeast Asian yams, arrowroot, and eventually taro and sugarcane to the crop repertory. In addition, the raising of sorghum and pearl millet continued to be important in the dryer, lower parts of the Thagiicu land. This variety of crops encouraged trade in foodstuffs between lower and higher farming zones on Mount Kenya, to go along with the trade of cultivated crops for the animal products of people living in the plains areas away from the mountain.

The Thagiicu, like the Chaga, were a society of mixed cultural background. On the mountain, Southern Cushitic communities, some farming and others probably emphasizing hunting and the gathering of forest resources, were still numerous as late as the period 1000–1200. Known by the Thagiicu as the Gumba, these Southern Cushites also included among their numbers most of the iron smelters and blacksmiths of the region. Like the Chaga, the Thagiicu also added the practice of female clitoridectomy under Southern Cushitic influence. To the south of the Thagiicu in the forests of the Nyandarua Range, another people, the Okiek gatherer-hunters, remained important trading partners until 1500 and later.

The Gumba had a notable impact on the history of political culture on Mount Kenya. Among the Thagiicu, the earlier type of Bantu chiefship disappeared entirely. In its place, they recognized clan headmen of a distinctly Southern Cushitic type, lacking a political role but with ritual responsibilities for the community, as encoded in the Thagiicu word *mulamati*, literally "guardian." The transition among the early Thagiicu from matrilineal to patrilineal reckoning of descent probably belongs to the period in which this Cushitic kind of clan headmanship was adopted. Dim historical memories of this transition lingered on in the form of mythologized stories, still told by the early-twentieth-century descendants of the Thagiicu, who sought to explain why the legendary founders of their patrilineal clans had been women.

An additional population group, made up of Kalenjin-speaking pastoralists, became prominent during the era of the great Kalenjin expansion, 800–

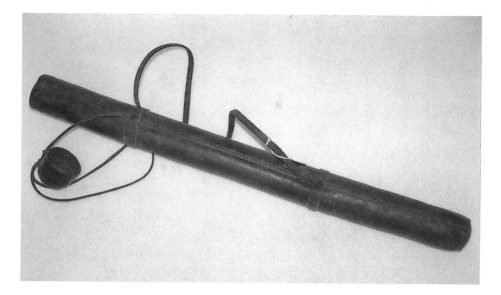

FIG. 48 Okiek leather quiver

This quiver may preserve a style the Okiek people inherited from their earlier Eburran gatherer-hunter forebears of the Kenya highlands. A different kind of quiver, made from alpine bamboo (*Arundinaria alpina*), appears to have been an ancient feature of Cushitic material culture, especially among the Southern Cushitic peoples of East Africa.

1000. They moved into the plains to the south of Mount Kenya and also into the higher grassy moorlands on the mountain above the forest. From these neighbors, the Thagiicu adopted a prohibition against eating fish, which the forebears of the Southern Nilotes themselves had still earlier adopted from Cushitic peoples. The Kalenjin communities were also important trading partners of the Thagiicu at the marketplaces around the mountain (see map 17).

   Even more notably, several Thagiicu communities adopted a feature of declining importance by that period in the Kalenjin age-set system, the generational component, and combined it with the Bantu type of simple linear age-sets. In the resulting Thagiicu system, a new age-set, with a distinctive name of its own, would be initiated every few years. Seven or eight such age-sets in succession were combined into a generation set, which had the responsibility both for protecting the society and for deliberating and resolving political and juridical issues in open public assemblies. About every forty years a new generation set would be opened up and would eventually take over the conduct of public affairs from the previous generation set. The effect of this system was to create an assertively democratic, non-chiefly society, a sharply different outcome from the kind of government that developed in the same era in Kilimanjaro and, most notably, in the Ugweno state of North Pare.

Environment, Economy, and Political Change among the Great Lakes, to 1450

In the areas between the Western Rift and Lake Nyanza, the Lakes Bantu societies continued to grow in population, a fact amply attested in the progressive deforestation of land all across the heart of the African Great Lakes region between 300 and 1200. By 1200, most of what is today western Uganda had been turned into grassland or open savanna as people cut down trees to clear areas for planting and to obtain firewood, timber for building, and wood to be made into charcoal for smelting and forging iron. But forest clearance had the unintended effect of making more and more of the land well suited for livestock raising. The communities that had specialized in cattle raising ever since the later centuries of the first millennium BCE now found new scope for expanding with their herds into ever more areas in the western Great Lakes regions. These cattle specialists came to be called the BaTutsi in southern parts of these regions and BaHima in the northern and central areas.

The growth of specialized herding activities would not have been unwelcome to the majority of people who depended on crop cultivation. Allowing cattle raisers to graze their stock on fallow fields meant that cattle manure would be left behind, refertilizing those fields and allowing a much shorter fallow period between crops. In this way more crops could be grown to feed the growing population. The gradual growth in importance of specialized cattle raising also had long-term consequences for political history after 1450, a topic we will consider in chapters 8 and 9.

In concert with the long-term trend of population growth, a variety of new political institutions and roles emerged in the region between 300 and 1100. This is an intricate history in its own right, and one we cannot cover in detail here. But the upshot was that a great many tiny kingdoms had come into being by the twelfth and thirteenth centuries, scattered irregularly all across the areas from western Lake Nyanza to the great Western Rift. They were kingdoms not in their territorial size or population—they typically may have included a few thousand people at most—but in the nature of their institutions. They had developed an ideology of political authority that had transformed hereditary ritual clan chiefs into rulers, and they had widely adopted an aurally compelling insignia of kingship, a set of special royal drums.

Between about the twelfth and the fourteenth centuries—we do not yet know exactly when—certain of these petty kings, living in what is today western Uganda, brought these elements of economy and ideology together in a new political synthesis. In so doing they built up at least one large state, the kingdom of Kitara, and possibly several such states. Oral traditions remember this era as the age of the Bachwezi (see maps 17 and 18).

We can deduce that something like the following probably took place: Building on the established royal ideology of petty kingship, the rulers of the first large kingdom or group of such kingdoms allied with the BaHima pastoral specialists of the western savannas of the Great Lakes region. In the process, the kings increased the size of their own herds to such an extent that they could begin to loan out cattle to selected followers and to redistribute cattle captured in war to those who had fought for them. Because the ability to pay a dowry in cattle to the bride's family was by this time becoming essential for the man who wanted to make a socially advantageous marriage, the kings now could use cattle redistribution to create a network of clients beholden to them and to their authority. With this kind of support, the kings would have been able to impose their hegemony across wide expanses of western Uganda.

By the fifteenth century, such kings ruled from capitals, consisting of numerous scattered-out homesteads, set amidst various extensive earthen embankments. The embankments seem not to have been built as defensive works but may have been meant instead, by their sheer extent and size, to express the kings' ability to mobilize labor and thus to invoke indelible images of royal power. An early important capital site of the thirteenth century was Ntusi; an important similar site of the fifteenth century was Bigo. Control over iron production and over the salt deposits of certain lakes near the Western Rift probably contributed additional wealth with which the Bachwezi kings could sustain and expand their power.

Southern, Central, and Eastern Africa: Taking the Long View

The complexity of economic, political, and social change across the southern, central, and eastern parts of Africa between 300 and 1450 dispels any lingering notion that those regions might somehow have lacked a significant history. Transformative shifts in food and tool production came into being in several areas, and both the local and the long-distance transmission of raw materials and goods helped to create commercial networks, market systems, and the material basis for social stratification and job specialization. Major episodes of early state building took place in widely separated regions, and a great variety of new social relations emerged—among them the stratified urban cultures of the Swahili towns, Great Zimbabwe, and the lower Congo region; the double descent systems of a number of southwestern African societies; and the adoption of patrilineal descent, in place of earlier matriliny, by Bantu-speaking peoples in the far southeastern sections of the continent, in the Great Lakes region, in some parts of the Congo Basin, and in the areas around Mounts Kenya and Kilimanjaro.

The most powerful causative factors driving these histories tended to be local or regional in source. Still, the spread of new crops of non-African origin, especially bananas, clearly played significant roles in enabling certain kinds of change to take place in several separate areas. Along the eastern edges of the continent, a limited but much more direct encounter with the trends of world history reached into the East African coastal hinterland, the Zimbabwe Plateau, and the lower Zambezi region, mediated by the long-distance, seagoing commerce of the Swahili merchants.

NOTES FOR READERS AND TEACHERS

Issues and Questions

Among the striking features of history in the southern half of Africa in the period 300–1450 CE were the emergence in many areas of new kinds of trade relations and the first development of large states in several regions. The areas around the lower Congo River constituted one such region; the upper Lualaba areas of the southeastern Congo Basin formed another. Two other regions of early large states were Zimbabwe and the western Great Lakes areas. Along the eastern African coast the older commercial connections of Indian Ocean seagoing trade revived in about the ninth century, and the Swahili city-states then expanded these relations more widely southward. In the areas surrounding Mount Kilimanjaro, the regional exchange of the commodities of adjacent environmental zones stimulated the founding there of a system of local markets during the centuries after 1000. Just as important in many cases, new developments in agriculture and in agricultural technology changed daily life in several parts of the continent. East and southern Africa between 300 and 1450 were home as well to notable instances of the long-term blending of customs and cultural practices from different African civilizations.

The following questions focus attention on these issues:

- In which regions did important networks of trade and commerce emerge in this period?
- Did different or similar categories of goods predominate in the various commercial networks?
- What new commodities became prominent in the period 300–1450 in the Indian Ocean trade of East Africa? In the trade of the Congo Basin? In the trading networks of southern Africa?
- What might trade in valued commodities have had to do with the growth of political scale in different regions?
- What prior courses of change in culture, politics, or economy lay behind the rise of kingdoms in southeastern Africa? In the lower Congo regions? In the Upemba Depression? In the African Great Lakes region?
- In several distantly separated regions in southwestern Africa, southeastern Africa, and the Great Lakes region, royal ownership of great herds of cattle seems to have independently become a primary element in the material basis of kingship. What were some of the notable kingdoms characterized by this feature? In what ways did kings in these particular states use this kind of cattle ownership to bolster their authority and power?
- What kinds of longer-term historical effects did the adoption of banana cultivation have for people around Kilimanjaro? In the Congo Basin? In the African Great Lakes region?
- What roles did Khoisan peoples play in the cultural, economic, or political history of southern Africa in this period?

Cross-cultural interactions in the areas that lie between the Great Lakes and the East African coast brought into being a variety of new societies that blended features of earlier Southern Cushitic (Afrasan), Southern Nilotic (Sudanic), and Kaskazi Bantu (Niger-Congo) cultures.

- What were some of these societies, and what were some of the particular ways in which they combined the different cultural backgrounds?
- What factors of culture, society, or environment might have encouraged the prevalence of non-state political formations in the areas between the Great Lakes and the eastern African coast?

Further Reading

Several scholars deserve special mention for having broken new ground in their explorations of the regional histories of the southern half of Africa in the period covered in chapter 6.

The history of the equatorial forest regions receives both broad and deep coverage in a book already briefly cited in the "Notes for Readers and Teachers" for chapter 5:

Vansina, Jan. *Paths in the Rainforests.* Madison: University of Wisconsin Press, 1990.

It is possible to disagree with a number of specific interpretations in this innovative work. In particular, the claim that certain Bantu peoples created matrilineal descent and spread it more widely in parts of the rainforest regions since 1,500 years ago might seem a reasonable proposition if one does not take into account evidence from outside that zone. But when one looks at the wider Niger-Congo historical frame, matrilineality emerges as a truly ancient feature of the Niger-Congo ancestry of the Bantu. Matrilineage or matriclan bases for society appear in a scattered, remnant distribution in regions as far apart as the present-day extremes of the Niger-Congo Tradition, in Senegambia in the west and on the Tanzania coast in the east, and in many regions in between. In addition, in still other Niger-Congo-speaking areas, residual matrilineal features persist in societies that have otherwise become patrilineal. But overall, Vansina's work richly evokes the immense variety of social, cultural, political, and economic change in the equatorial rainforest in the centuries since 300 and introduces us to many histories little known before.

A similarly evocative work deals both broadly and deeply with social, cultural, and political history in the Great Lakes region up to 1500:

Schoenbrun, David. *A Green Place, A Good Place.* Portsmouth, NH: Heinemann, 1998.

Schoenbrun plots out the changing cultural and social milieus of the African Great Lakes region, from the small-scale societies of 500 BCE up to the first emergence of large states in the first half of the second millennium CE. He presents in impressive detail the different historical paths by which new, more encompassing expressions of power and authority came into being during the first millennium CE, along with new ruling and ritual institutions and new kinds of political and social relations.

Two especially useful books on the history of particular states in the southern savanna zones are:

Hilton, Anne. *The Kingdom of Kongo.* Oxford: Clarendon Press, 1985.
Reefe, Thomas Q. *The Rainbow and the Kings.* Berkeley: University of California Press, 1981.

The body of Reefe's book actually deals with the Luba empire of the eighteenth and nineteenth centuries. Its relevance for this chapter lies in its careful depiction of economic, social, and political developments in the upper Lualaba River region between 600 and 1500, presented as background for Luba history since that time.

Two important works survey from different perspectives the cultural and political world of the Zimbabwe kingdom:

Beach, David. *The Shona and Zimbabwe, 900–1800.* New York: Holmes and Meier, 1980.

Garlake, Peter. *Great Zimbabwe.* London: Thames and Hudson, 1973.

A seventh book provides a finely crafted view of the long-term development of the eastern African coast, capturing both the African essence and the wider global connections of Swahili society:

Pouwells, Randall. *Horn and Crescent: Cultural Change and Traditional Islam on the East African Coast, 800–1900.* Cambridge: Cambridge University Press, 1987.

7

Northeastern, West, and North Africa: The Middle Centuries, 300–1450

Themes of Change

In the history of West Africa, North Africa, the Sahara, and the Horn between 300 and 1450 CE, we can discern the same broad themes, such as growth in political scale and in social stratification, as operated during those centuries in central, southern, and eastern Africa. But events in the northern half of the continent encompassed as well developments unknown to the more southerly regions. These included the spread of the so-called world religions, Islam and Christianity, to several areas, where they became in time a basic part of the indigenous cultural milieu.

And to a much greater extent than central, eastern, and southern Africa, the western, northern, and northeastern parts of the continent became integrally linked to the course of events outside Africa. After 300 the prosperity of the old indigenous commercial networks of the Sudan belt of Africa began to be tied more and more to the emerging and then expanding trans-Saharan trade. Between 500 and 1000 the tendrils of these trade connections reached still farther south into the West African rainforest zone, with consequences for both urban life and the distributions of peoples and cultures across that wide region. In North Africa and the Horn, where long-distance commercial relations went back to the Commercial Revolution of the first millennium BCE, new kinds of trade relations and new social and cultural patterns took hold.

Northeastern Africa, 300–1450

The Ethiopian Highlands: Feudalism and Christianity in the North, 300–1270

In northeastern Africa, as we have seen, two large and important states had already long existed at 300 CE—Meroe along the Nile, and Aksum in the northern Ethiopian Highlands. Meroe seems to have gone into an advanced state of decline before the fourth century, with its commercial connections blocked by Aksumite control over the Red Sea outlets of trade. Aksum, on the other hand, remained a powerful and centralized state up until the seventh century.

Aksumite intellectual history in the fourth to sixth centuries illustrates a recurrent influence of trade on world history: trade routes are not only the conduits of goods from one part of the world to another, but also the conduits of ideas. In particular, the Levantine merchants who plied their commerce at Aksum's port city of Adulis included a number of Christians in the fourth century, and through these contacts Christianity was adopted by the fourth-century Aksumite king, Ezana. At first a religion of limited outreach beyond the towns, Christianity in the late fifth and early sixth centuries began to be widely proselytized about the countryside by a number of Syrian monks. During this period, called in Ethiopian tradition "the Era of the Nine Saints," large numbers of Agaw became Christian, and in many rural areas different dialects of Ge'ez, the written language of government and the towns, gradually became the first language of country folk, too.

Meanwhile, the kings of Aksum continued to pursue many of the policies of earlier times. King Caleb mounted military campaigns in South Arabia in the sixth century that included the use of African elephants. His successors continued these struggles later in the century. The most well-known campaign, under the command of the Aksumite general Abraha in 570/571, carried as far north as the gates of Mecca before it was turned back. That year, traditionally the year of Muhammad's birth in Mecca, is known in Muslim lore as the Year of the Elephant, because Abraha's forces included African war elephants. Victories by invading Sassanid Persian forces in the 570s and 580s ended any Aksumite claims to hegemony in South Arabia and gave the Sassanid rulers a preeminence there that they were able to hold on to from the 570s to the 620s.

But it was another development, the rise of the First Islamic Empire after the death of Muhammad in 632, that once and for all transformed Aksum into a state no longer able to intervene across the Red Sea. This impact came about not through direct military action but indirectly through the shift in the central axis of world trade. The establishment of the capital of the caliphate at Damascus in the 640s redirected the main lines of commerce away from the Red Sea. Deprived of this trade, the kings of Aksum rapidly lost their ability to maintain their state through taxation. Before the mid-seventh century, they had ceased to mint coins, and the great buildings at Aksum city and its sister towns thereafter began to fall into ruin. From that point our knowledge of events in the kingdom becomes almost non-existent; only the broad trends are clear.

Here the parallels with contemporary western European developments are remarkable. Similarly faced with the loss of monetary revenue, the Aksumite kings, like their counterparts in Europe, began quite independently, and with no knowledge of Western Europe's travails, to build a feudal system. The major architect of these developments may have been the ninth-century king who is known to us only by his nickname, Digna-Jan. Digna-Jan sent military colonies southward to bring new areas under his rule, rewarding his soldiers by endowing them with fiefs known to later history as *gwult*. In this way, a military class was created, its support coming from a yearly payment of a portion of the crops grown by the peasant families of the *gwult*.

But a telling difference distinguished European from Ethiopian feudalism. In Europe, feudalism was built on the ruins of the late Roman system, in which great magnates owned the land, and the land was worked by both tenants and servile workers. The European fief thus came to comprise land granted to the fief-holder, and its population came to include a large number of serfs bound to the land. The feudal dues were owed the lord because it was his land.

In classical Aksum, however, land had belonged to the peasantry who worked it. Aksum's rule had been imposed on top of the older land tenure systems of the Agaw without greatly changing them. In the emerging feudal world of late Aksum in the ninth century, the bestowal of a *gwult* gave the local lord, called the *bala-gwult*, the right to a proportion of the production of the peasants living on that land and also the right to be the ruler and magistrate over the people of the *gwult*. But the ownership of land continued to be vested in the families living on it. In a typical *gwult*, a few families were relieved of duties to the *bala-gwult* because they had the responsibility of providing food for the parish church, its priest and deacons, and their families. But the rest owed a

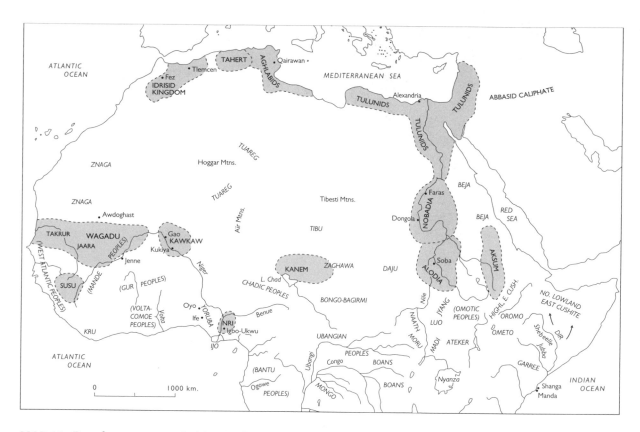

MAP 19 Peoples, states, and cities in the northern half of Africa, ca. 850–875

portion of their harvest, usually around 20 percent, to the *bala-gwult.* Because there was scope for negotiation in the relations of the lords who possessed the fief with the peasants who owned the actual plots of land within the fief, the farmers in some areas owed less and in other areas more.

There are parallels to European religious history as well. The spread of Christianity in the Era of the Nine Saints was carried out by monks, and to help this process along the Aksumite kings bequeathed land for monasteries. When the feudal system evolved, monasteries were granted *gwult* rights, too, and used the produce of their fiefs to support their activities. As the old economic and political world of Aksum collapsed, the monasteries, like those of contemporary Europe, became the sole repositories of learning, among whose responsibilities were the preserving, copying, and illuminating of manuscripts.

FIG. 49 Rock church of St. George at Lalibela

The greatest architectural accomplishments of the Ethiopian middle age, splendid churches like this one were commissioned in the twelfth and thirteenth centuries by the Zagwe rulers of the Ethiopian Christian kingdom. Ethiopian artisans sculpted the whole church, inside and out, straight from the solid bedrock. The upper picture shows the church from above, formed in the shape of a cross and surrounded by the rock out of which it was hewn. The lower picture gives a close-up view of the same church.

As a consequence of the transformed economic circumstances of Aksum, the state expanded in an entirely new direction, far southward into the heart of the Ethiopian Highlands. By the period of the tenth and eleventh centuries, it is clear, the farthest south that the feudal system, and with it Christianity, had reached was into the upper Awash River watershed. In this region, a different South Ethiopic language, Amharic, closely related to Ge'ez, became the spoken language of feudal society. Ge'ez remained, though, as Latin did in Europe, the language of religion. Amharic is actually a descendant of the South Arabian dialect brought to the Awash region in the third century BCE by settlers who themselves came from the northern Ethiopian Highlands (see chapter 5). Two daughter languages of Ge'ez, called today Tigre and Tigrinya, continued to be spoken in the old heartlands of the Aksum kingdom.

The city of Aksum shrank to a small town, much as did the former Roman cities of western Europe during the same period and for similar reasons. It continued to be revered for its history and was the seat of an important bishop, and royal enthronement often still required a visit of the new king to Aksum. But no longer was it the capital city. A new capital, Kubar, was founded somewhere to the south, in the direction of the feudal expansion of the state, but just where it was located still remains to be discovered.

The spread of the feudal system southward was not unopposed. In the second half of the tenth century, we hear of the first powerful resistance to the new social order. Led by a Queen Gudit, Agaw forces registered several severe defeats on the armies of Kubar. Of developments in the eleventh century we know nothing. But in the twelfth century, a new dynasty, the Zagwe, of Agaw origin, took power over the feudal kingdom. By now, however, the feudal system and Christianity were strongly entrenched in the countryside. The Zagwe kings sought legitimacy for their rule not in the older Agaw social order, with its *wambers,* or ritual clan chiefs, but by supporting the feudal system and by making themselves patrons of Christianity.

Their most famous accomplishment was to build the great rock churches of the Lasta region of Ethiopia, notably those at Lalibela, a town named after King Lalibela, the most noted of the Zagwe rulers. The immensity of the technical and artistic achievement involved in hewing these churches out of the solid bedrock is difficult to fully grasp. Here, too, the Agaw cultural heritage of the Zagwe is apparent. We have already encountered (in chapter 4) the importance of rock shrines in the early Agaw observance of the Sudanic religion, with its sky Divinity. The rock churches preserved this tradition, but in a Christian guise.

The Ethiopian Highlands: Political Relations and Commerce in the Eastern Areas, 300–1270

The late Aksumite feudal kingdom, ruled from Kubar, and its Zagwe-rule successor state were by no means the only significant kingdoms of their period in northeastern Africa. To do justice to the wider context of northeastern African history, we need to consider the course of trade and political change on other parts of the Horn of Africa over the same period.

In the later ninth century and in the tenth century, commerce again began to be a major factor in the region. The Red Sea trade once more became a primary route of trade, and the overall scale of commerce, if anything, grew as new Ethiopian products, in addition to the old, began to be desired in the markets of the Middle East.

In the Aksumite kingdom of the later ninth century, however, the feudal system was irrevocably established, and the older class system of Aksum was only a distant historical memory, lost for 150 years and not experienced by anyone living. In the eyes of feudal Aksum's population, the proper avenues to position and influence came through the feudal order. Merchants were now an exotic category of people, no longer possessing an indigenous place in the social system. As a result, the newly growing commerce became the sphere of foreigners, of Muslims from across the Red Sea or of African Muslims from the northeastern fringes of the Ethiopian Highlands. Small trading towns arose within the feudal world, along with one city, the capital, Kubar.

In the eastern and southeastern areas of the Ethiopian Highlands, the reemergence of regular commerce had rather different effects. In the ninth century the foundation of the small kingdom of Showa, which became a Muslim sultanate in around the eleventh century, was one of those consequences. Along the Ethiopian Rift Valley farther to the south, and to the east of the rift, in southwestern Ethiopia, a variety of small independent polities seem to have linked themselves up with trade.

In the thirteenth century, the historical picture finally becomes clearer and more detailed. By that time along the rift valley, several kingdoms of Highland Eastern Cushitic peoples, notably Dawaro and Hadiya, were ruled by monarchs of the Omotic sacred type. One large, powerful state of this kind, Damot, occupied areas immediately to the west of Showa. East of the rift valley, alternative kinds of governance existed. Among the ancestral Oromo society, the institutions of the *gada,* or age-grade, republic served to hold together many thousands of people in a single political unit. Farther east, in the lowlands and mountains of the eastern Horn of Africa, a myriad of clan-based communities of the old Afrasan style, owing social and religious respect to a hereditary clan head, persisted among the Soomaali and other Lowland East Cushites as the usual form of political organization.

The Founding of the Solomonic Dynasty

The thirteenth century was a period of immense political and religious ferment and crucial reordering of relations of power. The whole region around the upper drainage basin of Awash became in that century the focus of intense struggle for political power and access to commerce. Competing actors in this drama were the feudal lords of the southeastern marches of the Zagwe kingdom, the Muslim merchants of the Awash Valley and their allies, and the several kingdoms of the south, especially Damot, which lay astride some of the key routes of access to producing areas still farther south. The sultanate of Showa was no longer a key player, but another Muslim-ruled kingdom, Ifat, had taken over the preeminent role by the mid-thirteenth century in the upper Awash Valley. The world of the mid-thirteenth century in which Yekunno-Amlak, the future founder of the Solomonic Dynasty, grew up was a turbulent zone of cross-cutting economic, political, and religious currents.

In these developments, the Zagwe kingdom faced a double-edged challenge. On the one hand, a period of religious revival had begun within the kingdom. An important revitalization of the monastic movement got underway in the mid-thirteenth century, in which differing schools of thought competed for adherents. The important figures in these movements were the monk-scholars Takla Haymanot and Ewostatewos. At the same time discontent with Zagwe rule grew strong among the Amharic-speaking feudal lords of the southern marches, one of whom was the ambitious Yekunno-Amlak.

All these factors came together in the late 1260s, when Yekunno-Amlak, a southern lord imprisoned for a time by the Zagwe rulers, took the lead in campaigns against them. In 1270 he succeeded in bringing about the abdication of the last Zagwe king and in replacing the Zagwe line with his own dynasty. Yekunno-Amlak's success was ensured when the monk Takla Haymanot helped to rally religious support behind him.

Yekunno-Amlak and his successors sought legitimacy in two distinct ways.

The most obvious and well known was the claim of descent from Solomon, the tenth-century BCE king of Israel, and the queen of Saba' (Sheba), a South Arabian kingdom of the early first millennium BCE. In this way, the sanction of the Bible and the Ethiopian Christian church could be attached to the kingship. In addition, the genealogical claims of the kings traced their ancestry back to Solomon by way of the pre-Zagwe kings of Aksum, thus linking their legitimacy to that of the early Aksumite rulers.

What is often not recognized, however, is the extent to which the kings of the new "Solomonic" dynasty sought legitimacy in the symbols and ideas of the Omotic and Highland Eastern Cushitic kind of sacred kingship. They relied on Aksumite rituals in their enthronement ceremonies, but the important symbols of their kingship were more often patterned after those of the smaller kingdoms to the south.

A characteristic feature of the Solomonic state all the way up until 1636 was what we can call the "wandering capital." Very much like the twelfth-century England of Henry II, the Solomonic state lacked a fixed capital. Instead, for the first three and a half centuries of its history, it had a movable capital town of pavilions and tents, inhabited by courtiers, court officials, aspiring young noblemen who fought for the king, artisans, churchmen, and camp followers. All of these people, after some months or occasionally a year or two in one locale, would pack up and move to some other, perhaps distant, location. In this way, the immense burden of supplying the court and its vast entourage with food and supplies was spread around, with each host area able to recover economically and ecologically after the court had left for another area. At the same time, the fact that the capital and army moved about the country helped remind the higher lords in the feudal system to remain loyal and supportive of the state.

A few decades of shifting fortunes intervened for Yekunno-Amlak's immediate successors, but under Amda-Sion (1314–1344) the power and influence of the Solomonic kingdom was fully established. Amda-Sion consolidated the dynasty's rule over the older Christian and feudal areas of the north. In the south he conquered new areas never previously under control of the Christian Ethiopian kings and sought to incorporate these areas politically by awarding new *gwults* there to those who had fought under him. He and his successors encouraged the expansion of Ethiopian monasticism into the new areas, in order to preach Christianity and to try in this way to bring people into the same cultural world as the core areas of the state.

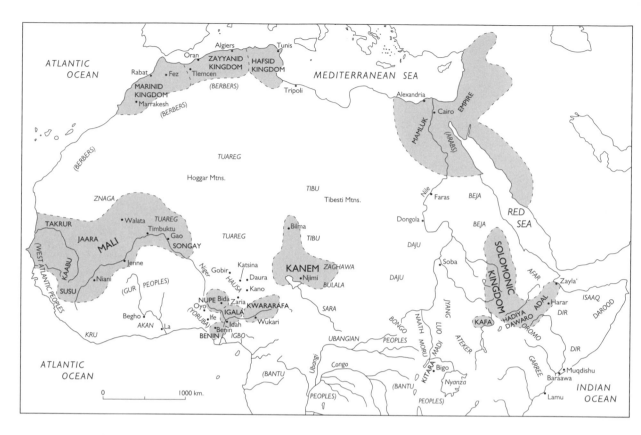

MAP 20 Peoples, states, and cities in the northern half of Africa, ca. 1340s

The conquests of Amda-Sion reshaped the balance of power in the eastern and central Ethiopian Highlands for the next 190 years. For one thing, they brought about the final destruction of Damot. The feudal system slowly took hold in the most northerly parts of Damot's former territories, and Christianity and the Amharic language spread along with feudalism. Over the next century, the state that Amda-Sion built engaged in recurrent warfare, especially on its southeastern frontiers, but overall the Solomonic Dynasty maintained its suzerainty, or indirect overlordship, over those peripheral areas up to the late 1520s (see chapter 8).

Religion in the Political Relations of the Solomonic Era

Amda-Sion's dealings with Muslim populations set a number of long-lasting precedents. The crucial military event for Amda-Sion in this respect was his defeat of Ifat. Seeking to establish an indirect, tributary rule over the areas in and to the immediate east of the upper Awash River region, he recognized the Walasma Dynasty of Ifat as the rulers over all the Muslims in his territories. The Walasma family in the meantime had relocated their rule to Adal, a territory east of the rift valley in the highlands of the modern-day Hararge province of Ethiopia.

The Solomonic kings after Amda-Sion treated the rift valley kingdoms of Dawaro and Hadiya to the south of Adal as similarly tributary, self-governing areas, on which they did not try to impose feudalism. Muslim merchants remained the primary carriers of commerce throughout these regions. The rulers of Dawaro and Hadiya, for their part, continued to follow the old customs and religion of their Omotic sacred kingship, while claiming a nominal allegiance to Islam in their dealings with the merchants.

The indirect, tributary political relationship of the southeastern regions to the Solomonic state was open to repeated episodes of rebellion and unrest. Not until the campaigns of King Dawit in 1415 did a period of long-term peace finally set in. Thereafter a precarious accommodation to the distant overrule of the Solomonic kingdom seems to have held for the next 100 years.

Religion was a recurrent element in the considerations of state policy and could at times become the central calculation. Because Islam and Christianity were associated with opposing interest groups—Islam with the merchants and their commercial enterprises, and Christianity with the feudal system and Solomonic overrule—the religious opposition between the two tended to be accentuated by the developments of the period from 1270 through the fifteenth century. We will see just how central a motivating factor this religious conflict could become for political and economic change when we look in the next chapter at sixteenth-century developments in the Horn of Africa.

A further religious factor, Judaism, came into play not on the southeastern frontiers of the Solomonic kingdom, but instead farther north in areas long part of the Ethiopian Christian kingdom. Agaw peoples remained an important element in those regions, often still not fully reconciled to the dominant culture; and among them an indigenous kind of Judaism, long cut off from the developments in Jewish thought elsewhere and dependent on the Ge'ez Old Testament of the Ethiopian Christians for its scriptures, gained a goodly number of new adherents, called the Falasha, in the thirteenth to fifteenth centuries. The Judaism of the Falasha became an important alternative source of religious legitimacy to people at odds with the feudal state. In the fifteenth century, especially in the reign of the pious Christian king Zar'a Ya'iqob, military suppression of Falasha rebellions combined with religious persecution of the Falasha.

Developments of the Solomonic Era in Southern Ethiopia

Commerce tapped deep into the interior of southern and southwestern Ethiopia during these centuries. As early as the ninth century a variety of new products were being exploited for profit in this era of revitalized commerce. The three most notable new commodities were coffee, civet extract, and slaves.

Coffee was a crop anciently grown in the old Omotic agriculture. Originally the coffee beans were chewed as a stimulant. Only as the beans began to be exported for the first time out of the Ethiopian Highlands after the ninth or tenth century did the idea of grinding the beans and making a coffee drink take hold. The Arabs living across the Red Sea were the first to make the new drink. Through the commercial contacts of the Muslim world, coffee making then gradually spread wider and wider across the Eastern Hemisphere.

Civet extract was secreted by a gland of the civet cat, a native African wild animal. It became an important base for perfumes in the Middle East during these centuries. To more easily extract this valued substance and market it, many people in the southwestern highlands began to keep civet cats in cages.

One new major state, Kafa, arose in the fourteenth century farther to the southwest of the Solomonic kingdom, beyond the lands that had formerly been the kingdom of Damot. Omotic in language, the Kafa kingdom is the best-known example of how Omotic and Highland Eastern Cushitic sacred kingships operated. Under the sacred king of Kafa were a large number of officials, each responsible for different areas of government or of court life and ritual. Each such office was customarily expected to be filled by a person from a particular clan or part of the country, in this way ensuring that the important areas of the kingdom each had a high-ranking representative at court.

The Kafa kingdom clearly had important relations with the Solomonic state, of which as yet we know very little. Its territories and those of several neighboring, much smaller Omotic kingdoms were apparently the important early sources of coffee beans and may have contributed slaves to the Muslim merchants plying the routes between southern Ethiopia and the Red Sea. Christian proselytizing in Kafa between the 1330s and early 1600s appears to have made some headway but never convinced the bulk of the population to change religion.

On the other hand, the Cushitic belief in Divinity had begun even earlier to make inroads into the religious culture of the southwestern Ethiopian Highlands. We do not yet know how early this belief first began to be taken up by Omotic societies nor the reasons for its adoption. The most probable scenario is that it spread initially from Eastern Cushites to the Ometo group of peoples during the period of intense cross-cultural interactions in the Ethiopian Rift Valley region in the second and first millennia BCE. By no later than the fourteenth century CE, this belief seems largely to have supplanted the older henotheistic belief in ethnic deities within the heartland areas of the newly emergent Kafa kingdom. Beyond the western marches of Kafa, however, the old Afrasan henotheism continued to prevail for centuries longer among the Omotic societies, such as the Bench and Nao, of the southwestern mountain forests.

Camels and the Development of True Pastoral Nomadism, 300–1000

Over the long term of northeastern African history, one key new economic factor first became prominent early in the period between 300 and 1450, and that factor was camel nomadism. Camel-raising nomadic pastoralists soon became a significant historical force not just in northeastern Africa but, in fact, all across North Africa and the Sahara. The adoption of camels revolutionized the economic potential of vast areas previously marginal to human settlement. These regions included the Red Sea hills, the northern littoral, or coastal regions, of the Horn of Africa, large areas in the interior of northern Somalia, and most of the Sahara desert. As we learned in the introduction to chapter 6, the coming of the camel to the Saharan regions made truly regular and voluminous trans-Saharan trade possible for the first time, from the early fourth century onward.

In northeastern Africa, camel keeping reached the Beja via the Nubians of the Nile River by early in the first millennium CE. Within a short time, it spread farther south to the Afar people of the Danakil Depression and from them to the region of the middle Shebeelle River, where a number of early Soomaali communities, previously transhumant cattle pastoralists, began to shift over to fully nomadic camel raising between about 500 and 700.

The cultural and demographic repercussions of this changeover spread still wider in the three centuries between 700 and 1000. Soomaalis belonging to the Dir family of clans expanded gradually across the whole of the northeastern Horn. In the drier areas, they implanted nomadic camel raising; in the high-

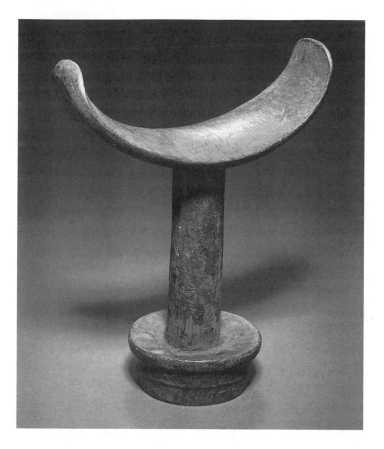

FIG. 50 Soomaali neckrest

This kind of artifact would have been among the usual possessions of males in the eastern Horn of Africa in the period 300–1450 CE. The use of neckrests had spread probably much earlier from the Middle Nile Basin to the Cushitic peoples of the Horn (see figs. 23 and 30 for more on the history of this item of culture).

land areas of higher rainfall in the far north, the pressure of their settlements gradually led to the adoption of Soomaali language and cultural identity by the local population, who themselves had previously spoken a North Lowland Eastern Cushitic language. In those areas, the older settled agriculture, which combined grain crops and the raising of cattle, continued to be the norm, despite the ethnic shift. Far to the south, at around 1000, another Soomaali people, the Garree, spread a nomadic economy that mixed cattle and camel raising all across the areas between the Jubba and Tana Rivers.

Religion, Commerce, and Social Reorganization in the Eastern Horn, 300–1450

We have seen that religion had become a major independent motivating factor by the fifteenth century in the rift valley region of the Ethiopian Highlands. The history of northeastern Africa between 300 and 1450 provides other telling examples of the ways religious belief can intersect in history with economic and political factors.

Events in the eastern Horn of Africa among the Soomaali-speaking peoples provide a notable case study. Islam, as we have learned, was at first a religion of merchants in northeastern Africa. Not until the adoption of Islam in the sultanate of Showa in the eleventh century did it begin to be taken up by populations farther from the centers of commerce. Later, in the thirteenth and fourteenth centuries, the adoption of Islam among people of the Dir clan family coincided with, and probably helped to set off, a major reformulating of kingroup relations. In the very dry northeast corner of the Horn, two new clan families, Isaaq and Darood, emerged in those centuries, claiming maternal ancestry from the Dir group but paternal descent from immigrant Arab Muslim saints who had settled in their lands. The adoption of a new religion, it appears, led to the adoption of a new set of kin identities among many of the Dir. As adherence to the new religion spread, the new clan-family identities, Isaaq and Darood, were then progressively adopted during the next several centuries by former Dir groups all across the northern and north-central parts of Somalia.

The Soomaali case offers us an example, too, of how the old Afrasan cultural traditions might co-opt Islam. The newly Muslim Soomaalis of the thirteenth century maintained the old clan principles and the idiom of patrilineal descent as the basis of clan allegiance, but they identified new patrilineal forebears. Now Muslim, their suitable forebears were therefore the particular Arabs who had been important in first preaching Islam among them. The new Isaaq and Darood clan families also maintained the older clan religious role of the hereditary clan head, but now these clan heads were linked to Islam. Nevertheless, several of the words for the clan head used in various Soomaali areas, such as *waab* or *waber* (each is a version of the original Cushitic term **wap'er*) and *rooble* (literally "rain-possessor," i.e., bringer of rain), still encoded the old Afrasan perceptions of the clan chief. At the same time, the Soomaali continued widely to use the older Cushitic word for God, *Waak'a* (spelled *Waaq* in Soomaali), especially in poetry and folk sayings.

The Nubian Kingdoms, 300–1450: Commerce, Political Change, and Religion

A different kind of long-term historical interplay between religion and political and economic history can be seen in the Nubian kingdoms of the fifth to fifteenth centuries. With the eclipse of Meroe in the third and fourth centuries CE, a number of small Nubian statelets at first filled the political vacuum left by Meroe's demise. By the sixth century, two larger Nubian states had emerged. The northern state, Nobadia, consisted of two provinces, Makuria, located along the extensive farmlands of the Dongola Reach of the Nile, and Nobadia proper, comprised of a string of arable stretches along the Nile between the Dongola Reach and Egypt. The southern kingdom, Alodia, ruled the lands south of the Dongola Reach, previously the heartlands of the Meroitic kingdom. Both Nubian states began as distinctly Sudanic sacral kingships, and in many respects they continued to be so as long as they lasted as independent kingdoms.

Nobadia had two capitals, Faras in the northern parts of its territory and Dongola as the overall capital where the king and court resided, situated in the middle of the Dongola Reach. An interesting cultural and economic distinction characterized the two parts of the kingdom. Although farming was important in the northern areas, this region had a more commercially oriented economy, with a merchant class, church authorities, parish priests, and a bureaucracy, along with its majority class of peasant farmers. Makuria, in contrast, was a strongly subordinated region. Society appears to have had two sharply different social strata, one consisting of government and court figures and church authorities, and the other of a large, enserfed farming majority.

Alodia, with its capital at Soba near the confluence of the Nile and Abbai Rivers, was a multi-ethnic state, with probably a number of culturally as well as ethnically different provinces. Nubian was the language of government, but a large number of other languages would have been spoken within its domains, most of them Eastern Sahelian tongues related to Nubian. We know next to nothing about Alodia's history between the sixth and the fourteenth century, by which time it had already broken up into a number of smaller states. From travelers' descriptions we know its capital, Soba, was a city of many fine buildings and its kings were rich in gold, obtained no doubt from the gold-mining areas that lay to the southeast up the Abbai River. These mines had earlier been exploited in the Meroitic era.

FIG. 51 Burial stone, medieval Nubia

This burial stone, of Yesu, a bishop of Sai Island, is of uncertain date in the eighth to tenth centuries. The writing is in Coptic, the late version of the ancient Egyptian language. Nubian scribes also wrote in Greek as well as in their own tongue, which we call Old Nubian.

Christianity first came to the two Nubian states in the 540s. In both kingdoms, many of the population fairly rapidly and sincerely adopted Christianity. We can say "sincerely" because one immediate effect of Christian conversion is apparent in the archeology of this era: namely, the complete and abrupt disappearance of one ancient practice of Sudanic sacral kingship, the burying of servants to serve the king in the afterlife. Clearly this custom did not comport with the requirements of Christian belief.

Christianity had a variety of other cultural effects. The building of churches and monasteries added new kinds of architecture. A tradition of church painting and portraiture grew, influenced by Byzantine examples from the eastern Mediterranean but distinctively Nubian in many respects. By about the ninth century, the educated clerical class in Nobadia, trained at first in Coptic and Greek, began to write extensively in their own language, which we call Old Nubian.

The Nobadians on several occasions took on special roles in their relations with other Christians in their part of Africa. They became important intermediaries between Ethiopia and the Coptic patriarch in Alexandria, Egypt, passing diplomatic messages in the tenth century, for instance, from the Christian kings at Kubar in feudal Ethiopia to the patriarch. In the 960s, under King Georgis II, Nobadia occupied a goodly part of Upper Egypt, where support for the Egyptian Coptic Christians may have been part of the motivation for invasion. Most Egyptians had become Christian during the late period of the Roman Empire, and a majority probably continued to follow the Coptic (Monophysite) variety of Christianity for centuries. Possibly until as late as the proselytizing drives and persecutions of the twelfth century, the majority of the Egyptian population may still have been Christian.

The Daju: Pastoral Power in the Middle Nile Basin

The economic and political decline of the Nubian states set in between 1100 and 1300, when fortifications, not before needed, began to be built along the Dongola Reach. The placement of these fortifications, facing southward, indicates that a new era of attacks coming from the south had begun. The attacking peoples most probably formed the northerly outliers of the much larger ethnic expansion of the Daju people across the desert steppe and dry savanna regions to the south of the Dongola Reach, a development taking place between 1000 and 1300.

We have only the sparsest information as yet on the Daju. Between 500 and 1000, they were one of a set of closely related Eastern Sahelian peoples living in the northwestern parts of the Nuba Mountains region, west of the middle Nile. Why they embarked around 1000 on a rapid ethnic spread, which by 1200 or 1300 had scattered them all across the regions from the Nuba Mountains to the western side of the Marra Mountains, 600 kilometers to the west, is wholly unknown. One strong possibility is that the Daju adopted a more mobile and more fully pastoral economy, but that idea has not yet been fully investigated by historians. Around the Marra Mountains, this time is remembered as a period of Daju overrule. Whether a single Daju empire accounts for these historical memories, or whether the Daju might have belonged to several loosely held-together regional Sudanic sacral kingdoms, is unclear. From the cultural evidence of more recent Daju societies in the Marra Mountains region, the latter alternative seems more probable.

New Ethnic and Commercial Changes in the Middle Nile Basin, 1300–1450

By the fourteenth century, the age of Daju preeminence was over. The coming together of several new factors then changed the situation drastically for the Nubian kingdoms. A new Tunjur kingdom conquered most of the areas around the Marra Range itself. To the east, in far northern parts of the Middle Nile Basin, a new pastoralist population, of Bedouin Arab origin, began to replace the Daju in the dry areas at the southern edge of the Sahara. Although Arab merchants had moved across the Red Sea and settled among the Beja of the Red Sea hills as early as the ninth century, it was the arrival, in the fourteenth and fifteenth centuries, of Arab camel-raising nomads, coming south from Egypt, and their establishment across the southern desert fringes that most shifted the religious and political balance across the region.

An additional factor in the changing political and cultural makeup of the northern Middle Nile Basin were the Beja themselves. Already strengthened by their own adoption of nomadic camel raising in the first millennium CE, the Beja in the tenth century were organized into a number of alliances, headed by chiefs of some kind. The chiefs of the southern Beja in that century seemed to have recognized the distant indirect authority of the feudal, late Aksumite kings of the northern Ethiopian Highlands, and outside observers viewed them as at least nominally Christian. Commerce passed through their lands between the Nile and the Red Sea but seems nevertheless to have been controlled by the Nubians as late as the tenth century. Between the tenth and twelfth centuries, however, the Beja established growing links of their own to the Red Sea trade by incorporating a number of Arab immigrants into their communities. By probably as early as the twelfth century, they were becoming Muslim in religion, and by the thirteenth and fourteenth centuries, several Beja groups were able to use their growing social connections across the Red Sea to gain a new degree of control over the movement of goods between the Red Sea and the Nile and to profit from that control.

So the Nubian kingdoms in the twelfth and thirteenth centuries faced from several sides a growing challenge to their once unrivaled position in the northern Middle Nile Basin. The beginning of the end for Nubian preeminence came in the 1320s when a Muslim Nubian king took power in Dongola. The consequences of the preceding 800 years of Nobadian cultural and economic domination over Makuria is strongly evident in these events. As a long subordinated area, where Christianity was a religion associated with an oppressive ruling class, the Dongola Reach rapidly took to Islam. To the north the political cohesion of the Nobadian stretches of the Nile broke down after the loss of control over the important Dongola Reach, but Christianity continued to be practiced there for some time. Farther south, Alodia seems to have broken up by the fourteenth and fifteenth centuries into a number of smaller Nubian kingdoms, still nominally Christian, but surrounded by other peoples among whom either Islam was beginning to take hold or the old Sudanic religion still held its appeal.

West Africa, 300–1450

The Early Age of Empire in the Western Sudan

Far to the west, in the western and central parts of the Sudan climatic belt of Africa, major new historical trends characterized developments after 300 CE. Large and powerful states arose for the first time in several regions, and a new scale and diversity of commercial relations took shape.

The earliest empire of which we have knowledge was Wagadu. The regnal title of its ruler was the "Ghana," and so historians have often called this state the Ghana empire. At the height of its power from the ninth to the eleventh centuries, Wagadu dominated the whole western Sahel zone from the lower Senegal River in the west to the Bend of the Niger in the east. The core population of the kingdom spoke Soninke, a language of the Mande branch of the Niger-Congo family. The tributary states of Wagadu included most notably the kingdom of Takrur, whose lands lay to the west, along the middle and lower Senegal River.

A tenth- or eleventh-century tradition, of uncertain reliability, places the foundation of Wagadu in about the third or fourth century CE. This dating fits well with what we know about the commercial basis of the state, and so we have good reason to think that this tradition may not be far off the mark. In particular, the power of the Wagadu state came from its long-maintained control of the crucial transshipment points of the trans-Saharan gold trade, and that trade, as we have already learned, first came into being just around 300. The early sources of gold lay several hundred kilometers to the south of the territories of Wagadu, in Bambuk and Bure. Carried north to Wagadu by donkey, the gold had to be transferred there to camels in order to be taken successfully across the Sahara to North Africa. From Wagadu two major early routes led northward across the desert, one passing northeastward via the Hoggar Mountains toward Tunisia and the other passing through the far western side of the desert to Morocco. Up to the eleventh century, the empire of the Ghana monopolized the access of the rest of the world to the gold of West Africa.

FIG. 52 Tuareg wooden camel milk bowl

Camels were the essential carriers of the trans-Saharan commerce from Wagadu and Gao as well as farther east in the Chad Basin. For the Tuareg, who controlled the central Saharan routes in the later first millennium CE, camels were even more essential as sources of meat and, as this item attests, milk.

Interestingly, even though the language of this state was Soninke, a Niger-Congo tongue, and dance and art in Wagadu owed much to the Niger-Congo civilization, the state ideology derived instead from the Sudanic sacral tradition. The most strikingly Sudanic feature in the royal practices of Wagadu was the burying of servants along with the king, so that they could continue to serve him in the afterlife.

At least two other early centers of important state building in the centuries between 300 and 1100 lay to the east of Wagadu. A few hundred kilometers downstream from the Inland Delta of the Niger, the once small city-state of Gao grew between about the eighth and tenth centuries into a kingdom of lesser power than Wagadu, but one with similar commercial importance as a trans-shipment center. Salt brought to Gao by camel from mines in the Sahara desert was transferred there to boats that plied the river in both directions. Copper smelted in the Aïr Mountains to the northeast of Gao probably constituted another important item in the riverine trade of that city.

Gao was as well a major manufacturing center. Besides dealing in locally produced cotton cloth, the merchants of Gao imported carnelian stone from the Sahara. From as early as the third century CE, skilled craftspeople in Gao fashioned the carnelian into finely wrought beads, highly valued in the commerce of the Sudan and as far south as the West African rainforest.

The people of Gao spoke Songay, a language of the Saharo-Sahelian branch of the Nilo-Saharan family. As we learned in chapter 3, the ancient ancestral form of this language was brought into the region around the great Bend of the Niger as early as the sixth millennium BCE. The kings of Gao belonged to the Sudanic sacral tradition, and it was probably from the early Songay people that the ideas of Sudanic sacral kingship spread farther west by the early first millennium CE to the Soninke people, among whom these beliefs provided the ideological basis of the Wagadu empire.

States and Commerce in the Central Sudan

In the Chad Basin, 1,000 kilometers still farther east, lay the lands of another early empire of the Sudan belt of Africa, Kanem. The formative era of Kanem lay in the eighth to tenth centuries, during which time it appears that a long series of military struggles between several different societies took place, each society seeking preeminence in an emerging new arena of trans-Saharan trade. Again a key region of transshipment was involved, where goods had to be transferred from donkey to camel transport. One major route led north from the Chad Basin to Tripolitania on the Mediterranean shore, and other lesser routes connected with the Aïr region to the northwest and the Tibesti Mountains to the northeast. Kanem finally emerged as the dominant power in the late tenth and early eleventh centuries. The ruling ideology, like that of Gao and Wagadu far to the west, drew strongly on the Sudanic sacral chiefly tradition. A single ruling dynasty, established by the beginning of the eleventh century, continued to hold power throughout the history of Kanem and the history of its successor state, Borno, up to the early nineteenth century.

To secure their preeminence in the commerce of the Chad Basin, the kings of Kanem directed their efforts toward exacting tribute from the peoples all around their state. Under Dunama II in the thirteenth century, Kanem extended its rule as far north as Bilma in the south-central Sahara, 500 kilometers north of Lake Chad. Bilma had a special importance because it was a major salt-producing area, and salt was an especially highly valued commodity of the trade. Unlike Wagadu, Kanem from the beginning appears to have been a major supplier of slaves, much in demand across the Sahara in the by-then Muslim lands of North Africa. Perhaps the repeated taking of war captives during the off-and-on warfare of the ninth and tenth centuries, out of which Kanem arose, helped shape this emphasis in their trade.

The region immediately west of Kanem, in what is today northern Nigeria and far southern Niger, followed a strikingly different course of political his-

FIG. 53 Cowry shells

Cowry shells became an important currency by around the thirteenth century in West Africa and remained important into the nineteenth century. Here we see cowry shells sewn in large numbers as decorations on a leather headdress from the Mossi people of the upper Volta River areas.

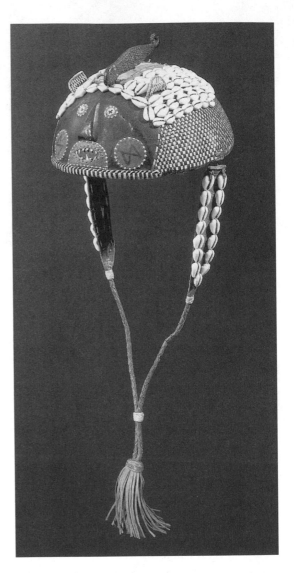

tory. From the eleventh century onward, it became the center of a great flowering of commerce and urban life, associated with the establishment of the language and culture of the Hausa people all across the region. The political consequence of this economic and ethnic realignment was not the building up of an empire or a large territorial kingdom, as was true in nearby Kanem, but rather the founding of a large number of independent city-states, each ruled by its own king.

The origins of Hausa kingship are unclear. Elements in the oral traditions suggest that the Hausa city-states displaced an earlier political order characterized by small Sudanic sacral kingdoms. On the other hand, the Hausa language itself is an Afrasan tongue belonging to the Chadic branch of that language family, and the origins of the Hausa kings may actually trace directly back to the old clan-chief institution of early Afrasan civilization, although with an admixture of ideas adopted from Sudanic sacral kingship.

The Hausa city-states in part prospered as middlemen in the transport of goods from other regions, bringing, for instance, kola nuts from the forest regions to the south and passing them northward into the trans-Saharan trade, or obtaining copper from the Aïr region. But they also engaged in manufacturing activities, most notably the weaving of cotton textiles. It was probably this variety of commercial activities that favored their city-state type of governance. Like the early city-states of the Mediterranean, the Hausa townspeople were carriers and primary producers of goods for the market, competing with each other on relatively equal terms. Unlike the empires of the Sudan, such as Kanem or Wagadu, they did not control the key points of transshipment of singularly high-value items, such as gold or salt, that might have allowed empire building.

One notable consequence of the growing importance of the trans-Saharan trade in the Hausa and Kanem regions was the appearance of a new kind of currency, as early as the eleventh or twelfth century. The new currency was the cowry shell, imported from the Indian Ocean by Arab merchants and transported across the Sahara. The word *wuli* or *wuri*, widely used for the cowry in the central Sudan, appears to have originated in the Old Kanuri language of the Kanem kingdom, indicating that the new means of exchange first arrived by way of the central Saharan trade route between Tripoli and Kanem. By the fourteenth century, cowry shells had become widely known in the Sudan belt, and their use soon spread farther south toward the rainforest zones of West Africa.

Commerce and Islam in the Western and Central Sudan, 300–1100

Commercial relations, as we have already seen, have often been the means of both spreading new ideas and diffusing new kinds of commodities. The commercial dealings of the Sudan belt of Africa in the centuries before 1450 were no exception. Islam took hold relatively quickly in the later seventh and the eighth centuries among the North African and Berber merchants who operated the trans-Saharan links of the trade. As a result of their close ties with these carriers of the trade, the merchants of the older West African indigenous interregional commerce began in time to adopt Islam.

Islam long remained a class-bound religion in the Sudan belt of Africa. By the eleventh century, it had become increasingly characteristic for the members of the merchant class to be Muslim but for the people of the countryside, the vast majority of the populace in all regions, to still hold strongly to either Niger-Congo or Sudanic religion, depending on the cultural heritage of their particular society.

The ruling stratum of society faced a difficult problem in this respect. They needed, on the one hand, to adhere strongly to the historically grounded ideologies of kingship if they were fulfill the religious and cultural expectations of their subjects and be able to hold their allegiance. On the other hand, many of the major material resources for maintaining the state came from commerce, which was largely in the hands of Muslims. A few kings chose to convert to Islam by as early as the eleventh century, notably the rulers of Takrur and Kanem.

Most kings did not take this step. In Wagadu in the tenth and eleventh centuries, for instance, the capital city was actually two towns, one at which the king and court resided and "traditional" customs were observed, and a second several kilometers away where the merchants and other Muslims resided. In subsequent centuries, many rulers, such as those of Gao, walked a sort of ideological tightrope. They carried out the rituals essential in the eyes of their rural subjects, even ones at variance with Islamic proscriptions, while at the same time claiming to be Muslims. One particular Sudanic custom, however, seems to have been given up nearly everywhere across the Sudan belt by the early twelfth century, even where Islam had only a peripheral influence, and that was the burying of servants with the dead king.

States and Urban Life in the Eastern Rainforest and Woodland Savanna of West Africa, 300–1450

South of the Sudan belt, the rise of urban life and states seems in most areas to have developed later. The roots of urban development in the rainforest belt of West Africa belong to the period between 300 and 1000. In what is today Nigeria, a growing long-distance trade, exchanging forest products, such as kola nuts, for products of the Sahara and Sudan, including copper from the Aïr Range and other areas, surely played a role in this development. To the west of

Nigeria in present-day Ghana (not to be confused with the ancient empire of the Ghana), new gold fields began to be exploited. Some historians think that by as early as 900–1000, these new sources of the precious metal may have begun to contribute to the trans-Saharan trade. But historians suspect also that other factors of intra-regional significance as yet little studied had even more important roles in the first emergence of towns in the rainforests of West Africa. These factors include growing population densities and the establishment of regular markets for local products, such as cotton textiles.

The early era of scattered towns gave way around about 800–1000 to a major burst of urban development in what is today southern and central Nigeria and to the emergence of the first large states. The focal region of state development lay around the confluence of the Niger and Benue Rivers and the stretch of the Niger River immediately south of the confluence. The rise of urban life encompassed a wider set of areas all around that region, notably to the west of the lower Niger River among the Yoruba peoples.

The earliest large kingdom we know of was the Nri state. In existence by the eighth and ninth centuries, it was located to the immediate east of the middle parts of the lower Niger River, in and along the northern fringe of the rainforest belt. Its core population was apparently Igbo, a people whose deeper historical roots lay in the Benue-Kwa branch of Niger-Congo civilization. We believe that the capital of the Nri state was located at the archeological site of Igbo-Ukwu. Igbo-Ukwu and its rulers had abundant wealth, as revealed by the rich goods and fine brass sculptures found in the site. But the legitimacy of the Nri state rested very much on the ruler's ritual functions as the intermediary between the society and the territorial and ancestral spirits, and not on secular power and military force. The Nri was a king, in other words, whose legitimacy was rooted in the kind of authority exerted by the old ritual clan chiefs of Niger-Congo civilization and in a mastery of the realm of the territorial spirits as well.

In about the thirteenth century, a major shift in the architecture of political authority began to take place across the region. The institution of the Nri lost its political dimension, although maintaining its ritual importance, and a new form of kingly rule appeared, in which the ability to bring large armed forces into the field mattered as much as claims to ritual authority. A powerful new kingdom, that of the Igala, arose in the woodland savannas around the confluence itself of the Niger and Benue Rivers, with its capital city at Idah located just south of the confluence. The continuing power of history is nevertheless evident in the legitimization of Igala kingship: the kings of the Igala claimed descent from the Nri of Igbo-Ukwu, and they continued to be enthroned by Nri ritual experts right down to the early twentieth century.

To the northwest of the Igala kingdom, a second powerful savanna state, Nupe, came into being by the fourteenth century. The extent to which its origins were connected to those of the Igala remain unclear, but its institutions and ideas of kingship appear to have drawn both on the kinds of ideas associated with the Nri state and on ideas that may have come from the Sudanic sacral kinship.

A third major kingdom, Benin, emerged also in about the fourteenth century, in the rainforest region between the Igala kingdom and the Niger Delta. Benin traditions of the past few centuries claim Yoruba origins for their ruling family, but it appears from archeological evidence and sixteenth-century written documentation that the actual impetus for the establishment of the kingdom came from the north, most probably from the Igala.

West of the Igala, still another strong kingdom, Kwararafa, dominated the middle stretches of the Benue River in the thirteenth to eighteenth centuries. It repeatedly blocked the ambitions of the rulers of Kanem and later of Borno to expand their territories southward, and in fact Kwararafa seems often to have been the stronger power. Of its origins, however, we are uncertain. The kings of Kwararafa ruled over peoples mostly of the Niger-Congo cultural heritage, but with a governing ideology that included features strongly reminiscent of Sudanic sacral kingship. Their northern conquests included people of Chadic background, and their armies raided as far north sometimes as the Hausa city-states of Kano and Katsina.

The common material basis of the rise of these several large kingdoms surely rested on their involvement in increasingly important and complex commercial relations. Products such as cotton cloth, camwood for dye, and iron goods crisscrossed the region, coming from a variety of producing areas, while kola and food products from the rainforest were exchanged for the crops, animals, and manufactures of the savanna. The importance of trade from as far north as the southern Sahara and as far west as the Bend of the Niger was already great in the ninth and tenth centuries, as we can see from the abundance of copper at the Nri capital, Igbo-Ukwu, as well as the presence there of carnelian beads, imported from Gao, more than 1,000 kilometers away. The rise of the Igala kingdom around the confluence of the Niger and the Benue reflects the continuing importance in the thirteenth century of the two rivers as key routes of transport. Kwararafa's position along the middle Benue probably similarly took advantage of the movement of goods east and west along that river and between the rainforest to the south and the Chad Basin to the north. By the fifteenth century the commodities of commerce in these regions included large numbers of horses, brought overland from the drier savanna and steppe to the north. The possession of horses allowed the kings of both Nupe and Igala to use cavalry forces to exert their power over long distances.

Rainforest City-States: Yoruba History, 300–1450

To the immediate west of Igala and Benin, in what is today southwestern Nigeria, a different sort of political and demographic geography took shape during the same span of centuries. Among the Yoruba of that region, the political manifestation of the new scale of trade was the city-state, not an empire or a large kingdom. At the cultural heart of these developments lay the Yoruba city-state of Ife, founded already before 1000. In the twelfth and thirteenth centuries, various Yoruba groups established a large number of other city-states in the rainforest zone during a time of vibrant cultural expansion and commercial growth. But Ife remained the wealthiest and most powerful city down to the fifteenth century, and the Yoruba continued even after that to esteem Ife for its role as the founding place of Yoruba culture.

Each major Yoruba city was the capital of a small city-state ruled by a king or *oba*. The role of king in these cities appears to have developed out of the earlier Niger-Congo role of clan priest-chief. The royal role was as much religious as political. The kings presided over the community rituals and were intermediaries between the community and the ancestors, and they gained a high degree of personal sacredness from fulfilling these duties. The genealogies of ruling families show us that, although a majority of the rulers were men, women *obas* were quite common in many of the Yoruba city-states up until the nineteenth century.

The religion of the early Yoruba recognized an additional level of spirit not found in the ancient Niger-Congo belief system, a category of gods intermediate between the Creator God and the ancestor spirits. Just how anciently the Yoruba developed this kind of polytheism is unclear, but it was already well established by the early second millennium CE. The stories told about such gods indicate that many of them originated as the ancestor spirits of kings or as legendary heroes, rather than ordinary people. Other gods may once have been territorial spirits, subsequently elevated to this intermediate status.

New Developments in Art and Social Relations in the Lower Niger Region

A striking innovation of this era, not only in Benin and at Igbo-Ukwu, but also in the Yoruba city-states, was a new kind of artistry and its associated technology. In all the urban areas in the Nigerian rainforest between 800 and 1400, a magnificent tradition of sculpture in brass, which made use of the lost-wax technique, became the characteristic art form patronized by the kings and the emerging ruling classes. The old sculpting tradition of Niger-Congo civilization in this case adapted to a new medium. Here, indirectly, we see how valuable the trade in copper, of which brass is an alloy, must have become by 800. The lost-wax technique used in this sculpture was known earlier in the Classical Mediterranean; we lack evidence of this technology in the connecting areas between the Mediterranean and southern West Africa, and so independent technological invention may well account for its presence among the early Yoruba, Benin, and Igbo peoples.

One notable social feature also became an integral element of culture all through the lower Niger regions before the fifteenth century. In Igala, Nupe, and Benin and among the Igbo people as well as the Yoruba, patrilineal descent appears to have been well entrenched. How much farther back in time the development of this pattern of social relations goes is not known. A number of small societies of the surrounding regions, to the east beyond the Cross River and also north of the Benue River, still maintained elements of matrilineal structure down to more recent centuries. But in all the areas influenced by the early Nri state, patrilineal institutions have a long history. Did the formation of states, beginning with Nri in the eighth or ninth century, have something to do with the prevalence of patrilineal ideas? Or did the changeover from matrilineal descent begin at some earlier, as yet unidentified, period in this region?

Whenever the shift to patriliny might have taken place, its presence in the regions on all sides of the lower Niger did not necessarily mean the exclusion of women from political office or economic activities. In Benin the rulers do seem generally to have been male. On the other hand, women rulers were not at all uncommon in the Yoruba city-states, and in most parts of the region women in past centuries appear to have participated in trade on an equal basis with men. Marriage did not make women wards of their husbands either, as it did in Europe right up to the twentieth century. Instead, women, as they did in most areas of Niger-Congo civilization, carried on their own economic activities and

FIG. 54 Sculpted brass head, Benin

This figure from the kingdom of Benin is a fine example of the tradition of sculpting in brass, using the lost-wax method, which was known at least as early as the ninth century in the regions on both sides of the lower Niger River. Other exquisite works in this genre were fashioned at Igbo-Ukwu and in Ife and other Yoruba towns. In the lost-wax method, the figure is first sculpted in wax; next clay is molded over the wax form; and then molten metal is poured into the clay mold, melting and replacing the wax. After the metal cools, the clay mold is broken up, revealing a metal sculpture inside with the same shape as the wax figure it replaced.

maintained their own wealth and possessions, separate from those of their spouses.

Economic and Political Change in the Western Rainforest and Savanna, 300–1450

Urban life also made its appearance farther west between 800 and 1450, in the areas around the lower Volta River. Here towns emerged in connection with three overlapping new developments. One was the spread of the Akan peoples between approximately the eighth and fifteenth centuries all through the rainforest areas immediately west of the lower Volta. A second was the bringing into production of a new gold-mining region, which because of its association with the Akan we call the "Akan goldfields." The third was the growth of interregional trade along the lower Volta.

In the middle of the first millennium CE, the proto-Akan inhabited woodland savanna at the northern edge of the rainforest, south of the Black Volta River. They began as just one of the various Volta-Comoe peoples who had inhabited much of the region between the Black Volta and the Atlantic coast since the early first millennium BCE. (The Volta-Comoe were an offshoot of the Benue-Kwa, who earlier spread the West African planting agriculture into the forest zone in about the fifth and fourth millennia BCE.) The movements of Akan communities south into the rainforest apparently displaced and assimilated other Volta-Comoe societies already resident in those areas. Whether the initial motivations of this expansion had anything to do with the emerging northward gold trade of the period 800–1500 is not known. But, in any case, in the wake of the Akan expansions many of these lands became prosperous producing areas for the Sudan and trans-Saharan commerce.

An especially notable early Akan city-state was Begho. Founded around 1000 and located in the older Akan areas in the woodland savanna near the Black Volta, this city became a primary outlet through which Akan gold production of the rainforest zone entered the commercial networks of the Sudan and the Sahara. The forest Akan communities began as well to market kola nuts, for which a strong demand developed farther north in the Sudan. The political outcome of this commercial growth was the emergence of a multiplicity of small polities ruled by chiefs or kings—what we might call "town-states"—each centered on a small town or large village and supported by farming and hunting in the surrounding rainforest and on the production of trade commodities, most notably, but not only, kola nuts and gold.

FIG. 55 Pot from city of Begho

Pot making in Begho, an entrepot from around 1000 CE onward in the trade of gold from the Akan gold fields north to the Djouf Basin, illustrates in a different way how the rise of regular commerce encouraged the appearance of specialized craft occupations. In the Djouf Basin and Senegambia, the potting specialists, as we have seen, often evolved into an occupational caste in the late first millennium BCE and early first millennium CE. Farther south in Begho this specialization became ethnically based, with a particular small society known as the Mo acting as the potters for everyone else in their region.

The spread of the Akan language and ethnicity reinforced a strongly matrilineal basis for inheritance and succession to office. Men tended to hold the highest political offices, but this factor was balanced off by the evolution of formal political positions for women, such as those of queen mother and queen sister. These positions provided a considerable degree of female access to power and influence in the governing of the small Akan polities, at least for female members of the ruling elite.

From as early as the thirteenth century, other modest-sized towns evolved farther south, along the lower Volta River. The founders of these towns were Guang, Ga, and Dangme peoples, rather than Akan. Their towns, such as La, flourished as centers of the trade that passed along the river itself. Goods from the interior savannas, such as shea butter, were exchanged there for the products of the coastlands, such as salt and fish, and for the wares of the coastal hinterland and the rainforest, among which were farm products and different kinds of cotton cloth.

About the area still farther west, in the rainforests of the Guinea region, we know as yet almost nothing for the period up to 1450. The characteristic staple of the diet through most of these areas was African rice, rather than yams, a changeover in agricultural production that probably took place as long ago as the third or second millennium BCE. Iron production, which had been adopted in these areas in possibly the last few centuries before the beginning of the common era, already had great importance in certain areas where rich iron ores could be found, principally in eastern Guinea, in the lands that today make up Sierra Leone and Liberia.

A considerable variety of Niger-Congo peoples inhabited these regions. The oldest established population groups of Guinea and southern Senegambia, such as the Temne and Dyola, all spoke languages of the West Atlantic branch of the Niger-Congo family. Their ancestors had been present in many areas for possibly as long as 6,000–8,000 years. Along the present-day Liberian coast, the Kru peoples, whose languages belong to still another branch of the Niger-Congo family, probably had an equal antiquity of settlement. Mande societies, which occupied several inland areas, represented more recently intrusive populations into the rainforests of the Guinea Coast. As we learned in chapter 4, their forebears pressed south from the interior basin of the Niger River during the last two millennia BCE and are thought to have contributed to the spread of rice cultivation to the West Atlantic and Kru peoples of the coastal areas.

Commerce, Politics, and Social Change: The Western Sudan, 1000–1450

To the north of the West African rainforest, in the savanna, steppe, and desert of the Djouf Basin, the Wagadu empire came to an end sometime before 1200. Its decline has long been attributed to one of the major Muslim religious jihads, or holy wars, of history, the Almoravid movement of the 1070s. This jihad began among the most southerly Berber communities, who were camel-raising nomads living near the Senegal River. These Berber adherents then turned their attacks northward to Morocco and Spain. Historians have commonly assumed that the Almoravids also attacked and fatally weakened the empire of the Ghana. Recent work has cast doubt on this idea, and it now seems probable that the final decline of Wagadu did not take place until sometime in the middle or later twelfth century.

The Almoravid conquests reflect one kind of impact that true nomadic pastoral populations have had in world history on more sedentary populations. Nomadic pastoralists are difficult groups for states to deal with because they are hard to pin down in one place and therefore hard to control for purposes of taxation or military security. The Almoravid conquests in the eleventh century and Mongol expansions of the thirteenth and fourteenth centuries, extending from east Asia to eastern Europe, are perhaps the most startling examples of this kind of problem. Nomads are potentially dangerous not because they are rich and powerful but because, in fact, they are generally far poorer in material goods than the upper strata of town populations or the kings and chiefs of the settled countryside. They are therefore susceptible to calls to war against urban and other settled cultures in which rich booty might be found. They often have reason as well to take offense, having often been looked down upon by settled peoples because of their presumed turbulent and uncultured ways.

On the other hand, nomads tend to have a lasting impact only if they adapt to the cultures they attack, and become settled members of those societies themselves. The Nubians may have had such a role in ancient Meroe (as described in chapter 5). They began as transhumant rather than fully nomadic pastoralists, but they would have had much the same kind of relation to urban culture—poorer, economically marginal, and so drawn to the wealth and ease of life of the urban upper class. Serving the Meroitic state as settlers in the northern marches of the kingdom along the Nile would have been a way for them to become settled folk, able to gain some access to a less impoverished kind of life.

At around 1000, along the western fringe of the Sahara desert, in Takrur, a new kind of nomadic population, the Fula, began to develop in the late period of Wagadu. Their own cultural roots lay in Niger-Congo civilization, and their language belonged to the West Atlantic branch of the Niger-Congo language family. But they seem also to have been strongly influenced by their Znaga Berber neighbors of the western Sahara. Living in areas with around 150–200 millimeters of rainfall a year, the Fula were able to create a different kind of pastoral nomadism from that of the desert Berbers, centering their economy around the herding of cattle, rather than camels. They coexisted with the cultivating populations of Takrur, who lived along the Senegal River and also spoke the Fula language, by grazing their livestock both in areas away from the recession-irrigated farms of the river bottomlands and in fields already harvested or left fallow. In this latter respect, the Fula provided a service of sorts for the cultivators: the cattle manure left behind by their animals increased the crop yields and the frequency with which the farmers could replant their fields.

A second great kingdom, Susu, formed the most important southern neighbor of Wagadu in the eleventh century. How much farther back in time this state existed is not yet known. The heartland of the Susu kingdom lay in the upper Senegal and Niger River regions. Its power, in the last analysis, probably rested on its early control of the sources of the best gold, but in addition its territories included major iron-producing areas. The lands of the Susu kings encompassed rainforest areas in the south, the cooler mountain farmlands and pastures of the Jallon Mountains in the center, and the woodland savanna to the immediate north and east of that range. In the thirteenth and fourteenth centuries, the Susu merchants brought malagueta pepper and kola nuts from the Guinea rainforest to the south, as well as the cloth, gold, and iron of their own lands, to the networks of Sudan and Sahara trade. From later records, we know the Susu weavers to have been the producers of especially fine cotton cloth, widely prized and sought after in the western Sudan commerce. Interestingly, despite the importance of manufactured goods for their economic relations, the Susu never adopted the occupational caste system of the peoples living north of them.

With the decline of Wagadu in the twelfth century, the Susu rulers took advantage of their economic power to create an empire that at its widest extent appears to have surpassed Wagadu in size. It included the former territories of Wagadu as well as most of the upper Senegal and Niger River country. For as many as a hundred years, the great empire of the western Sudan was that of the Susu.

But in the third quarter of the thirteenth century, a new rising power, Mali, successfully challenged Susu hegemony. Under its king, Sunjata, whose mother may have been related to the ruling Konte clan of the Susu, the forces of Mali decisively defeated the Susu sometime around 1240. Between 1240 and the 1260s, Sunjata's forces built up a new empire that included in its territories not only the whole of the lands of the earlier Wagadu state but most of the areas south of Wagadu that were part of the Susu empire. The Susu kings lost an empire but retained the original territories of their kingdom as well as control over their internal government, although becoming tributary to Mali. Sunjata's followers carried the westward expansion of Mali's domains to the Atlantic Ocean, establishing other subordinate states, tributary to the *mansa* (king) of Mali, in

FIG. 56 Fula woolen cloth

Fula weavers for centuries have used wool in their weaving. The cloth seen here consists of strips sewn together, as was typical also of cotton cloth in much of West Africa. The idea of using wool in making cloth may have spread to the Fula from their Znaga neighbors of the later first millennium CE, since the weaving of woolen fabrics was an earlier feature among the Berber of North Africa and the Sahara (see chap. 4).

the lower Gambia and Senegal River areas. The core population group of Mali, to which Sunjata himself belonged, spoke a Mande language, related to but quite distinct from the Soninke language of Wagadu and from the language of the Susu empire. From Mali's language derive the widely spoken Malinke (Manding) and Bamana languages of the modern-day western Sudan belt.

The founding of the Mali empire had a number of lasting consequences. It finalized the shift of the centers of political power south from the edges of the desert that had already begun with the shorter-lived Susu empire. One has to argue, in fact, that the strength of the Mali empire rested, as had Susu power, more on the larger population it could draw on for its armies, and on its direct access to the most important trade commodity, gold, than on control of the transshipment points of the trans-Saharan trade.

Commerce in the Mali Empire

More important, the bringing of so much territory under the rule of a single power gave impetus to a vast new expansion of commercial activity. Mali extended across a range of environments, from the dry steppe of the Sahara fringe almost to the rainforest belt of West Africa, and these differing environments produced quite different products. The rule of the *mansa* of Mali created peace and security for merchants to travel freely from one end to the other of the Malian domains, carrying goods and seeking out new markets and new products to take back with them. As a result, merchants began to establish family firms, with different individuals settling in far-flung parts of the Mali empire to carry on trade there, while at the same time maintaining their familial and thus commercial ties with other merchants in many other locales. In the eastern and southern parts of the empire, these enterprising traders were called Juula; in the west, in the Senegambia region, the Jakhanke merchants carried out this kind of activity.

By the fourteenth century, some of the Juula had begun to move their places of business eastward and southeastward, outside of the areas directly under Malian political authority, establishing relations with the kings, chiefs, and towns of neighboring regions. The city of Begho, just north of the gold-producing, rainforested country of the Akan peoples, was among the localities than benefited from this development. Many new areas came into regular commercial relations with the peoples of the Sudan belt, and a great variety of new products began to enter into the trade. A complex and multifaceted exchange of the products of the land, such as kola nuts and shea butter, and of manufactures, such as textiles and metal goods, gradually began to take shape, linking up new and distant markets and producing areas through an intricate network of trade routes.

In the northern territories of Mali, near the fringes of the Sahara desert, merchants of Soninke background similarly expanded their operations far beyond Mali. There are some indications that the Soninke commercial diaspora may have begun even earlier, during the decline of Wagadu. While the Juula expanded and deepened commercial ties all across the upper Niger drainage basin and southward into the Volta River regions, and the Jakhanke spread their commercial activities westward into the Gambia and Senegal regions, the Soninke turned their attentions eastward across the Sahel zone. Hausa records date the appearance of such "Wangara" merchants in their city-states to around the thirteenth and fourteenth centuries.

Because the Juula, Jakhanke, and Soninke merchants of these centuries were all Muslims, their arrival in a region often brought new directions to religious history. The Hausa oral traditions, for example, credit the Wangara as the introducers of Islam, even though we know from other evidence that the Hausa actually first learned of the new religion as early as about the tenth or eleventh century through their relations with their eastern neighbor, the kingdom of Kanem. Most Hausa townspeople probably became only nominal followers of Islam, while rural citizens of the Hausa city-states often remained non-Muslim even as late as the end of the eighteenth century.

The ruling stratum of society gained an important part of their material basis from the wealth that came from controlling and supporting merchant activities. Already by the beginning of the fourteenth century, this connection had led to some acceptance of Islam at the court and within the ruling castes of the Mali society. The best known instance of ruling-class Muslim piety is, of course, that of the famous Mali king, Musa ("Mansa Musa"), who in 1324 went on the pilgrimage to Mecca. While in Cairo on his way to Mecca, so the story goes, Musa was so generous in presenting gifts of gold that for several years the price of gold was depressed in Egypt and other nearby parts of the Middle East.

Not all merchants, it should be noted, became Muslims. In particular, the Susu traders, the main carriers of commerce between the Atlantic coast and the upper Senegal and Niger Basins, continued to hold to the version of the older Niger-Congo religion practiced in their country right on down to the eighteenth century. Within the Sudan belt itself, the religious connection to Islam provided a key basis for wide cooperation. But in the woodland savannas and rainforest to the south, and in the internal commerce of those regions, the development of merchant classes proved compatible nearly everywhere with the older cultural practices and worldviews of the Niger-Congo civilization.

Economic Diversification in the Sudan Belt, 1200–1450

There was one other far-reaching consequence of the deepening and broadening of commercial activity during the period from the thirteenth to the fifteenth century that we need to consider now. As new regions and new products began to be tapped by Juula, Jakhanke, and Soninke enterprise, a multiplicity of new areas experienced real economic growth. Local productivity created new economic foundations on which could be built the material basis for larger political units. Increasingly, the control of access to one particular, exceedingly valuable commodity could no longer, by itself, provide a sufficient material basis for a powerful state. By the fifteenth century, no longer was the control of a single, narrow point of transshipment a broad enough basis on which to build an empire. Instead, the expansion and diversification of commerce tended to allow a new kind of kingdom, intermediate in size, to sustain itself in many regions. It allowed city-states to persist and, in the instance of the Hausa, evolve into small territorial states ruled from their walled, commercial, capital cities. The age of empire was nearly over in the western and central Sudan. One other great empire, Songay, grew up in the second half of the fifteenth century, but that is a topic for chapter 8.

As early as the 1360s, in the aftermath of a struggle over the succession to the kingship in Mali, one major section of the Mali empire broke away. In the regions between the lower Senegal and Gambia Rivers, the Wolof-speaking provinces of Waalo, Baol, and Kajoor were united in a newly formed Jolof empire under the rule of its first king, Njajaan Njaay. The rulers of the Jolof state, interestingly, were elected in a manner not unlike the titular emperors of the contemporary Holy Roman Empire of northern Europe. A council of electors, themselves members of the noble class, chose the next Jolof king from one of three royal matrilineages. The Jolof domains, like the Holy Roman Empire, were a confederation of states, although the Jolof kings appear to have had a greater ability to dictate policy in their subordinate states than the Holy Roman emperors of the fifteenth century usually had in the constituent states of their "empire."

The Susu kingdom may have ceased to be tributary to Mali almost as early, but areas to the south and inland from the Jolof kingdom, notably Mali's strong subordinate state of Kaabu along the middle Gambia River, continued to hold their allegiance to the Mali rulers well into the fifteenth century. By the second half of that century, however, the ability of the central authorities of the empire

FIG. 57 Mosque at Jenne

This mosque, although it has been repaired many times and probably rebuilt several times, provides us with a good idea of what large buildings, built of clay, looked like in the empires of the western Sudan 700 or 800 years ago.

to mount large military campaigns and exert direct power over wide areas was becoming a thing of the past.

The cultural heritage of Mali nevertheless was a powerful, deep, and lasting one. In its successor states, including not just the various Manding kingdoms of later times but also the Jolof kingdom, the mixed system of classes and castes continued to be the accepted order of society. The Juula and Jakhanke laid down merchant colonies in the towns and cities of the western Sudan and established a lasting pattern of commercial relations that persisted even after the political unity of empire had been replaced by numerous medium and small kingdoms. Mali's cultural tradition and its literature continue to be vibrant elements of cultural life down to the present day.

North Africa and the Sahara, 300–1450: Competing Legitimacies, Competing Hegemonies

North Africa and the Sahara from the fourth to fifteenth centuries were lands deeply interlinked by common economic developments but divided by competing claims to cultural correctness and political power. The growth of the trans-Saharan trade and the re-energizing of the Mediterranean Sea trade after the spread of Islam tied together the economic fates but not necessarily the political allegiances of North Africans. At several points during the period, polities of great geographical spread arose in rapid fashion but almost as rapidly lost cohesion and departed the historical stage. The "world" religions, first Christianity and then Islam, became widely adopted, but often in dissenting or "heretical" varieties, and the religious choices of the subjects of rule not uncommonly differed from those of the ruling elites.

The Later Roman Empire in Northern Africa, 300–640

Historians, when viewing northern African developments of the fourth to early seventh centuries, tend to focus on a limited range of political changes. The invasion of the Vandals, a people of Germanic background who entered western North Africa by way of Spain in the early fifth century and supplanted Roman rule in the farther northern parts of today's Algeria and Tunisia, form one major topic in this kind of history. The re-establishment in the second quarter of the sixth century of the authority of the Eastern Roman or Byzantine Empire, under Justinian, as far west as Tunisia marks the second major period. Byzantine control then lasted after a fashion down to nearly the middle of the seventh century.

What this approach to northern African history tends commonly to neglect are two key themes. First, the interior parts of western North Africa, in the Atlas Mountains and south of them in the northernmost parts of the Sahara, became a world of numerous, now independent, Berber communities. These regions fell outside the reach of either Vandal or Byzantine rule, which remained restricted for the most part to the coastlands. Even more important, these regions, and not the North African coasts, were the centers of the most significant developments of the time for the longer term of African history: namely, pastoral nomadism based on camel raising and, associated with it, the rise of the trans-Saharan trade. We learned about the significance of this development already at the beginning of chapter 6. The people who brought about this transformation in economy and society were the Berber peoples of the Atlas regions and the northern fringes of the Sahara.

Religious developments in both Egypt and western North Africa between the fourth and seventh centuries illustrate another recurrent theme of northern Africa—the adoption of dissenting religious views. In Egypt, Christianity became widely adopted by both urban and rural populations by the fourth and fifth centuries, most often in its Monophysite variety. Monophysite Christians accepted the orthodox view that God was manifested in the three "persons" of the Trinity but held that the three "persons" were of *one* "*nature*" (*monophysis*), in contrast to the orthodox view that God combined *two natures* in the three "persons." To many of us today, it hardly seems an issue worth arguing about one way or the other, but to the people of the time it did matter (as it still does to many modern-day Monophysite Christians). In the time of Justinian's rule in the sixth century, and already in the previous century, the holding of Monophysite views became a major element in the cultural self-identification of the indigenous, Coptic-speaking Egyptians.

Far to the west, in the areas that make up Tunisia today, another dissident Christian sect, the Donatists, similarly became the predominant strain of indigenous Christian belief in the fourth and fifth centuries. Christianity established its presence in the towns all across western North Africa and drew adherents in several parts of the rural hinterlands as well.

Political Change: The Muslim Conquest and After, 640–1450

The Arab Muslim conquest, first of Egypt between 639 and 642 and then slowly, piece by piece, of the rest of North Africa between 642 and the end of the century, for a time brought again a single rule, as there had been during the heyday of the Roman Empire, to the whole of the regions from Sinai to the Strait of Gibraltar. But it was a tenuous and short-lived unity. In the African territories of western North Africa, rebellion among Berber subjects, who allied with adherents of the Kharijite sect of Islam, created turmoil already in the 740s.

By 750 the Umayyad rulers of the early Islamic empire had been displaced by the Abbasids. Before the end of the next century, the political subordination of the North African territories to Abbasid caliphs, based in Baghdad in western Asia, had everywhere come to an end. North Africa then entered a long period of shifting political hegemonies. History books dealing with these centuries typically organize the periods of this history in political ways. In Egypt, for example, this kind of history begins with the era of the Tulunid rulers from the 860s to 905, which was followed by a period of reassertion of Abbasid rule, then by the Fatimid period from 969 up to the mid-twelfth century, and finally by the Mamluk period, which lasted until 1517.

FIG. 58 Hammered brass bowl

This bowl is from Mamluke Egypt.

In the Maghrib (western North Africa) a far more complicated history of political change can be charted. In the areas that today make up Tunisia and Algeria, one Abbasid governor and his descendants contrived around the beginning of the ninth century to make themselves into independent rulers, called the Aghlabids after their founder ibn-Aghlab. In 909 they were replaced by new rulers, the Fatimids, who shifted the center of their rule to Egypt sixty years later. Within a few years of moving to Egypt, the Fatimids lost their western territories, which then broke up into a number of independent states. Between 1056 and the 1090s, motivated by both religious fervor and commercial travails, the Lamtuna, a Znaga Berber confederation of the southwestern Sahara, launched an invasion that created the al-Murabitun (Almoravid) Empire and brought the whole of the western Sahara, much of western North Africa, and a large part of the Spanish peninsula under one rule. Lasting hardly two generations, their empire came to an end between 1130 and 1150, when a new religiously based Berber regime, the Almohads, seized possession of all of North Africa west of Egypt, along with portions of Iberia. Within another eighty years, this empire, too, was in decline.

With the weakening of Almohad power in the early thirteenth century, three different regimes took control of different parts of the Maghrib. In the east the Hafsids ruled from Tunis, their capital city, from the later 1220s up to the second half of the sixteenth century. In the center, in the areas today making up northern Algeria, Zayyanids ruled from the city of Tlemcen, although they often came under the overrule of the Hafsids. To the west in Morocco the Marinids, originally Berbers from the Saharan side of the Atlas Mountains, gained power in the middle of the 1200s and maintained their rule down until the later 1400s. The strength of these states lay in the urban areas and the countryside around the towns and cities. Although the Berbers of the Atlas Mountains, as well as the nomads of other areas of the Maghrib, often nominally accepted the authority of these rulers, they were usually, in effect, independent peoples.

Society and Economy in Northern Africa

North African history up to 1450, seen in this light, appears disjointed and difficult to follow. But if we turn our attention instead to the social and economic long term, we discover both recurrent tendencies and important themes of lasting historical impact. The early centuries of the period saw the establishment all across the west-central and western Sahara of those Berber peoples who had fully adapted to a nomadic, camel-raising way of life. The Tuareg expanded all through the Hoggar Mountains and southward to the Aïr Range probably before the ninth and tenth centuries. In each of these regions, they would have displaced or absorbed Saharo-Sahelian peoples, whose ancestors may have inhabited those areas as long ago as the eighth or seventh millennium BCE. In the eleventh to thirteenth centuries, some of the Tuareg groups took over steppe grazing lands still farther south, on both sides of the Bend of the Niger. The famous city of Timbuktu was founded during this time by Tuaregs. Farther west in the first several centuries CE, the Znaga, who inhabited the desert steppe inland from the Atlantic coast and the southwestern Sahara, restructured their previously goat- and sheep-raising economies around camel raising.

All through these centuries the Tuareg and the more westerly Berbers of the Sahara controlled the major routes of the emerging trans-Saharan trade. Along these routes both Berber and Arab merchants from North Africa passed southward, bringing the products of Mediterranean and Middle Eastern commerce southward and taking the products of West Africa back north when they returned. In the ninth and tenth centuries, the northern part of the Maghrib developed into a region of many flourishing commercial towns and cities, prospering from their trans-Saharan and Mediterranean trade connections. Commerce and cities persisted despite recurrent turmoil in the eleventh and twelfth centuries. After the twelfth century, as a longer-lasting political stability took hold, the major cities, especially those that were centers of administration as well as commerce, entered into a new period of growth and prosperity. In the mid-fourteenth century, the Marinid capital, Fez, reached around 100,000 in population. Tunis was of a similar size, and Tlemcen had perhaps 40,000 inhabitants.

In western and central North Africa another kind of long-term process, a gradual Arabization of the indigenous populations, took place from the mid-seventh century onward. With the Muslim conquests of the late seventh and early eighth centuries, Arabic quickly became the language of government, religion, and often commerce, replacing Latin and Punic. In the urban centers of the Maghrib it soon became the first language of city folk. But outside the cities the various Berber languages continued for centuries longer to be spoken nearly everywhere. The Almoravid and Almohad regimes, as Berber-derived movements, in fact relied on Berber dialects in their armies and in their own governing deliberations.

The significant change in this situation came in the mid-eleventh century, when the Fatimid rulers of Egypt expelled a large group of troublesome Bedouin Arabs, the Hillali, from their domains. The Hillali moved westward to Tunisia, where they clashed with the local people and where, according to contemporary observers, their large herds of camels, goats, and sheep disrupted cultivation and overgrazed the pasturelands. In the next couple of centuries the descendants of the Hillali, along with other nomadic Arab groups, scattered farther west, filtering into Berber areas, intermarrying, giving rise to new Arab clan families, and hastening the adoption of the Arabic language and ethnic identity in a number of areas.

Although the Marinids, who established their rule over a goodly portion of Morocco in the twelfth century, were of Berber background, their policies hastened this process. They chose to bolster their initially precarious position by giving a significant military role to the Hillali nomads and allowing them move into the Atlantic plains of western Morocco. Their regime established more strongly than before the use of Arabic in all the dealings of people with government and in the day-to-day affairs of the country. Nevertheless, the Berber lan-

FIG. 59 Chellah Gate, Rabat, Morocco

This fourteenth-century gate was built during the Marinid period of rule.

guages continued to be spoken by probably still a majority of the peoples of the Maghrib and the western Sahara until after 1500.

Several important centers of Muslim higher education developed in Africa between 1000 and 1450, in which not only Islamic law and theology but also the classical fields of knowledge among the Greeks and Romans—rhetoric, grammar, logic, astronomy and astrology, history, and geography—formed the courses of study. The most famous of these institutions was Al-Azhar, founded in Cairo in the late tenth century, originally as a school for training Muslim missionaries. Already in the eleventh century Al-Azhar had become an early form of what we could today call a university, to which famed scholars of the age came to teach and debate. Another such university, Jamiʻ al-Qarawiyyin, rose to prominence in the city of Fez in Morocco during the Marinid period of rule. South of the Sahara the city of Timbuktu was already known in the fifteenth century for its scholars, although the apogee of its reputation as a center for higher education came somewhat later, in the sixteenth and seventeenth centuries.

In the overall intellectual history of both North Africa and the Sahara, the tendency toward dissenting belief that we already encountered in the late Roman period long continued to be a strong current. Even today pre-Islamic ideas continue to strongly flavor the practice of Islam among Berber peoples. Early in the period of Muslim rule, various Berbers were attracted to more purist Muslim sects, such as the Kharijites and Ibadis, and Islamic religious fervor of not exactly orthodox kinds provided a strong part of the basis for recruitment into the military forces of both the Almurabitun and the Almohad movements.

North Africa also became a major center of Sufism, a more mystical trend of thought within Islam. A number of important Sufi brotherhoods originated between 1000 and 1500 in the Maghrib. Through the medium of the trans-Saharan trade several of the Sufi orders took strong hold among the Muslims of the Sudan belt, south of the Sahara, and the members of those orders often played a major role in later centuries in the proselytizing of Islam among the peoples of those regions.

In western North Africa Christians remained a significant element for some time after the Muslim conquest, at least among the urban populations. But by the ninth and tenth centuries Christianity was well on the way to dying out in those areas. In contrast, a resilient small Jewish minority continued to exist in most urban areas all across North Africa right down to recent centuries.

In Egypt much of the rural population and many in the towns and cities appear to have held to Monophysite Christianity as late possibly as the eleventh or twelfth century and to have continued to speak the Coptic language at home, despite the dominant position of Arabic and Islam among the governing and land-holding elite. By the thirteenth or fourteenth century things had changed radically, with the countryside shifting to Arabic language and to Muslim belief, and with Christianity persisting as the religion of a literate minority living mostly in towns and cities. The use of the Coptic language thereafter gradually died out, too, bringing to an end the long existence of ancient Egyptian as a living language. An intriguing problem for future historical study will be to identify what it was that so changed the historical milieu in Egypt at this particular period that a sea change in cultural history took place. Why did the everyday people of the country give up their long-held emblems of cultural self-identification as indigenous Egyptians and adopt a new religion and new ethnic identity as Arabs?

Agriculture, Technology, and Culture: A Continental Overview, 300–1450

We began our consideration of African history, 300–1450, with an overview in chapter 6 of the broad outlines of social and political change across the continent. To round out our understanding of that period in Africa, we now return again, here in chapter 7, to a continental perspective. This time we find our integrative themes in the history of culture and livelihood. On a continental scale, the centuries between 300 and 1450 in Africa were characterized by the wide diffusion of important new elements of technology and domestic economy. Additions to agricultural practice had direct repercussions for population growth and the expansion of political scale and complexity in a number of regions. Developments in metallurgical knowledge and practice fed directly into the expansion of commercial relations and in more indirect fashion shaped the course of political change in many areas. Amidst the spread of new elements of material life came also the diffusion of new developments in art and music.

Developments in African Agricultural Productivity

One new crop, the banana and its cousin the plantain, and one new domestic animal, the chicken, became established across large parts of the continent after the third century CE.

The distributions of different words for bananas and plantains in Africa reveal that this new kind of crop spread initially by several routes inland from the Indian Ocean coast of East Africa. One line of transmission passed along the mountain ranges of northeastern Tanzania, first to the Kilimanjaro region before 700 and from there to the peoples of Mount Kenya. The second important area of introduction, as early as the first four centuries CE, probably lay along the Indian Ocean seaboard east of Lake Nyasa (Lake Malawi). From there bananas and plantains spread rapidly north along the Western Rift into the African Great Lakes region and northwestward across the Congo Basin.

In each of these large regions, Africans soon developed a large number of new banana varieties. In the mountainous parts of today's northeastern Tanzania and east-central Kenya, as we learned in chapter 6, bananas were turned by the Chaga and their neighbors into the staple of a new, highly productive planting agricultural system especially adapted to tropical highland climates. The resulting growth of farming productivity played a key part in the development of regular markets in the region and also provided the material basis for the spread of the Chaga society, with its system of many small independent chiefdoms.

In the equatorial rainforest between 500 and 1000, the local development of new varieties of bananas greatly enriched agricultural productivity, as did the westward spread of other new varieties from the Western Rift region. Also, between 500 and 1500, new forms of political cooperation emerged. These included the first small kingdoms in several parts of the Congo Basin and large confederacies of chiefdoms in the heart of the basin. It is hard to avoid concluding that their emergence rested in large part on the ability conveyed by banana cultivation to support larger concentrations of population and to allow greater time for people to engage in more specialized kinds of production for trade.

After 1000, the knowledge of the banana spread farther west across the better-watered parts of West Africa. There, however, the banana tended to remain a crop of secondary importance.

The adoption of the chicken certainly also had no great impact on political and economic relations. But the raising of this animal did spread rapidly and widely across nearly the whole of the continent during the period. The chicken had the virtue of being able to thrive in dry as well as wet climates. It added a further source of protein to the diet, and although many people certainly continued to raise the guineafowl right down to the present, in most areas the chicken supplanted it as the most important domestic bird.

The Political Economy of Iron, Copper, and Gold in Africa

The spread of ironworking took place in most regions of Africa before 300 CE and, in many areas, even centuries earlier. The period between 300 and 1450 was one, however, in which iron gained increasing importance in commercial relations. Iron also gained new political significance, particularly in the central parts of the continent, as a material used in various kinds of chiefly and kingly insignia.

The best studied of such new insignia were the clapperless single and double bells. The double bells spread through many parts of the Congo Basin and into the middle Zambezi regions during the period between about 800 and 1200. They reached the lower Congo region in the west by 1000 and diffused equally fast into the southeastern Congo Basin and then as far as Zimbabwe by the early centuries of the second millennium. Everywhere they were adopted as strictly chiefly or royal implements, and their spread confirms the indications

FIG. 60 Flange-welded double bell

The double bell in all instances was an item of the regalia of rulers, and its presence in an archeological site demonstrates the existence there of hereditary chiefship or kingship. Invented in perhaps the Cameroon region between 500 and 900 CE, this royal instrument spread to an emerging class of chiefs and kings all across the Congo Basin, as far west as the lower Congo River and as far south as the Copper Belt by around 1000 CE, and it diffused still farther south to the Zimbabwe Plateau soon after 1000. Wherever double bells spread, they marked the spread also of a new kind of technology, flange welding. Each bell consisted of two sheets of iron, forged by the smith into long rounded shapes with flanges, or flattened edges, along both sides. The smith then welded the two sheets into a bell by hammering the flanges together in the hot fire of his forge. The particular example shown here is from Cameroon.

of other kinds of evidence that this period saw the emergence in many areas of a new scale of political authority, unparalleled earlier in the history of central Africa.

The bells have a double historical significance, because their manufacture depended on a new technological development, flange welding. Invented apparently by smiths in West Africa in the middle of the first millennium CE, this type of welding involved forging sheets of iron into desired shapes and then hammering separate sheets together at their edges under conditions of high temperature. Welding allowed much more complex iron implements to be forged, among them the single and double bells.

Another new kind of welded implement that probably first began to be manufactured during this period was the throwing knife, a weapon with multiple blades. The place in which the first relatively simple varieties of this implement were invented is not known with certainty, but it appears to have been located somewhere in the central Sudan, somewhere broadly between Lake Chad and the Marra Mountains. Over the first half of the second millennium

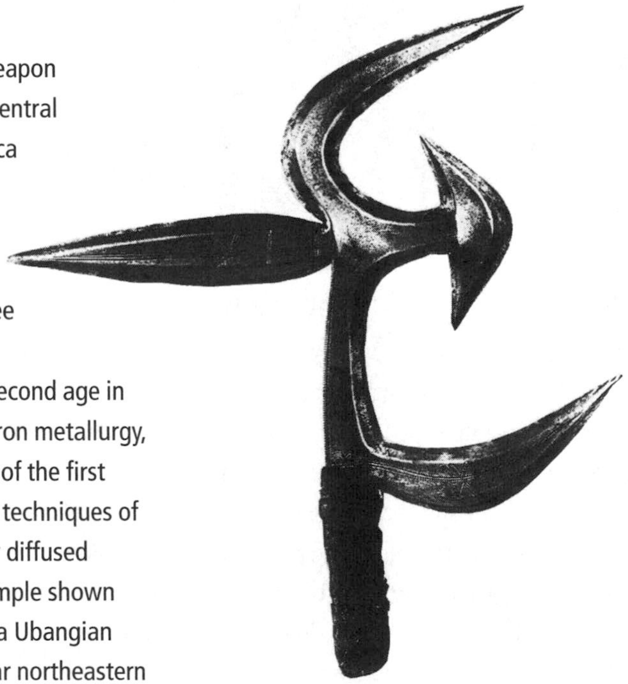

FIG. 61 Throwing knife

The making of this kind of weapon originated in the eastern or central part of the Sudan belt of Africa and then diffused southward through the equatorial rainforest well before 1450. Like the double bell (see fig. 60), the throwing knives reflected the inception of a second age in the development of African iron metallurgy, beginning in the second half of the first millennium CE, in which new techniques of forging took hold and widely diffused among blacksmiths. The example shown here comes from the Zande, a Ubangian Niger-Congo people of the far northeastern Congo Basin.

CE, the practice of making throwing knives spread south to the Ubangian peoples and then to the Bantu of the equatorial rainforest. As the technology diffused southward, the local blacksmiths invented more and more elaborate styles of throwing knives. So horrendous a weapon did it seem to the later, seventeenth-century rulers of the Kuba kingdom, located in the far southern parts of the rainforest, that they outlawed its use.

Copper mining and smelting do not seem to have only one origin in Africa. As we already learned in chapter 4, the earliest use of copper in Africa dates to before 3000 BCE in Egypt, but another separate discovery of copper and development of copper working took place in the Aïr Mountains of the south-central Sahara between the early third millennium and 1500 BCE. While the knowledge of copper in North Africa surely derives from the Egyptian and Middle Eastern practices, the practice of copper working in most of West Africa probably spread originally from the Aïr region.

Even more surprising to the usual expectations Westerners bring to history, it appears that farther south in Africa, opposite to the historical sequence in the rest of the world, iron was well established before copper came into use. In those regions a third area of apparently independent development of copper working by Africans lay along the divide between the Congo and Zambezi basins, in an area we call today the Copper Belt. Iron working arrived in the region on the heels of the arrival of Savanna-Bantu and Mashariki peoples, sometime between the fourth century BCE and first century CE. Copper working, in contrast, is known from only about the fourth century CE. But within a short time, the copper of the Copper Belt began to be traded over a region hundreds of kilometers wide, extending east and west across the southern savanna belt, northward into the rainforest, and southward to the Zambezi River. In the first half of the second millennium CE, as the use of copper spread wider and wider, other copper deposits began to be exploited—to the south, in the northern Transvaal and in northern Zimbabwe, and far to the west, near the lower Congo River.

The production and trade in copper in central Africa had further-reaching social and political effects than had the earlier adoption of iron. People gave copper a greater intrinsic value than iron because of its color, malleability, and greater resistance to corrosion and because it was much rarer and harder to obtain than iron. It became the preeminent material for making valuable jewelry, and in the regions all around the Copper Belt, as we learned in chapter 6, a kind of currency in the shape of small crosses had begun to be made from it before 1000.

In West Africa, too, as we have seen, copper gained new political and social importance between 300 and 1450. The most notable examples were the royally patronized work of sculptors in brass, a copper alloy, in Ife and other Yoruba city-states, in Benin, and at Igbo-Ukwu. This politically tied art form had its greatest flowering between 800 and 1600.

The most powerful political consequences of the possession of metals emerged, however, in regions able to benefit from the exploiting of African gold resources. Gold, which began to be mined in sub-Saharan Africa in the early first millennium CE, rapidly attracted a strong demand from the other side of the Sahara, and that made all the difference. Because of that external demand, and because of the extraordinarily high value people gave to gold, empires could be built by those who controlled this commodity. In West Africa, the goldfields of Bambuk and Bure in the upper Niger country supplied the first regular trans-Saharan trade from the early fourth century CE onward. With the added revenues that the gold trade provided, the empire of Wagadu became a powerful state as early perhaps as the fourth century. The later empire of Mali founded its power on the control of the gold production and its commercial distribution. Later, merchants of the Sudan traveled south to tap into the resources of the Akan goldfields. Far away to the south and east, between the Limpopo and Zambezi Rivers, the kings of Zimbabwe used the proceeds of the gold and ivory production of their people to create, in the thirteenth and fourteenth centuries, the first large state of southern Africa.

Sub-Saharan Africa's Introduction to Slave Trade

Another, not nearly so positive, feature of history marks this period in Africa. For the first time, from the eighth century onward, slave trade emerged as a major factor in the relations of Africa with the rest of world. Despite common assumptions to the contrary, few sub-Saharan Africans had ever been enslaved before the rise of the first Islamic empire. We need briefly to consider the overall history of slavery in the western parts of the Eastern Hemisphere if we are to understand why.

The institution of slavery arose first in the ancient Middle East and in Egypt and was already in existence there by the fourth and third millennia BCE. Slaves and slave owning became a characteristic social feature of the early commercial towns of the Mediterranean, such as "democratic" Athens, and slaveholding continued to be a major feature of society in the Roman empire. Where did the slaves of ancient history come from? The principal supplying areas of the earliest eras of slave trade lay in Europe and in and to the north of the Caucasus Mountains. A certain number of the slaves of ancient Egypt came from the south, from the Middle Nile Basin, but they formed only a tiny minority of the overall slave population of Mediterranean and Middle Eastern worlds in ancient times.

The rise of the first Islamic empire changed this situation in basic respects. The Islamic conquests encompassed a great many of the regions that had long kept slaves. In much of Europe, in contrast, the shift to feudal economies and the lack of access to new sources of slaves meant that slavery gradually withered away, to be replaced by serfdom. But in the Islamic world, the newly rich ruling classes acquired slaves in greatly increased numbers. Commercial prosperity led as well to a heightened demand for slaves by the expanding merchant class.

The majority of the slaves in the early Islamic period continued to come from areas located around the western, eastern, and northern sides of the Middle East. Still, the Muslim conquests greatly stimulated trans-Saharan trade and, in so doing, opened up major new trading connections to the south, from which slaves soon began to be transported. The principal early sub-Saharan sources of slaves were the kingdoms of the western Sudan. The initial routes of this trade in people passed from the lands around the Bend of the Niger River north and northeastward across the desert.

The most striking indicator of the new importance of sub-Saharan Africa as a source of slaves in North Africa and the Middle East was the great "Zanj" revolt from 866 to 883 in southern Iraq, in which thousands of enslaved Africans for a while were able to throw off their servitude. By about the ninth or tenth century, sub-Saharan slaves in North Africa and the Middle East had begun to include some who had originated in the Chad Basin, captured in the wars that created the kingdom of Kanem. In subsequent centuries a certain number of slaves from the southern Ethiopian Highlands also passed to the Middle Eastern countries. But overall, the western and central Sudan regions remained the major suppliers of sub-Saharan Africans to this market down to recent centuries. Interestingly, before the eighteenth century few if any slaves in the Muslim world, it appears, came from the east coasts of Africa.

New Elements in African Art and Music

What is often not taken account of in the writing of African history in the era 300–1450 are the developments in art and music. We have already seen some of the major new forms in which the ancient sculpturing tradition of Niger-Congo peoples was carried on. These include the terra-cotta sculptures of the Nok people of Nigeria in the first millennium BCE (chapter 5) and those of the Lydenburg peoples of fifth-century South Africa (chapter 6), as well as the sophisticated and beautiful brass casting of Ife, Benin, and Igbo-Ukwu in the early and middle second millennium.

Those were by no means the only vibrant artistic centers. In Ethiopia, both in the Zagwe and early Solomonic periods, the painting of religious and historical events and the painstaking copying and illuminating of manuscripts were prominent forms of artistic expression. In the Nubian Christian kingdoms of the Nile, the high centuries of prosperity between 800 and 1100 were similarly a time of a flourishing of painting, especially of religious subjects and figures. Along the Ethiopian Rift Valley, the Dullay and their neighbors began in a genre of wood sculpture unique to them, probably in the second or first millennium BCE, about which we as yet know next to nothing. Far to the south, in the mountains of South Africa, the ancient Khoisan rock painting tradition remained strong between 300 and 1450, although often a new theme—the encounter with the expanding herding and cultivating peoples of the region—can be glimpsed dimly in the representations of those centuries. In the Congo Basin, a variety of new motifs and representational idioms gradually appeared in the wood sculpture and masks of the different Bantu and Ubangian peoples of the region. Wood does not withstand the ravages of mold and termites, and so we know about these changes only indirectly—through our knowledge of the rich and immensely varied forms of sculpture created by their descendants of the past century and a half (see, for instance, figure 79 in chapter 9).

In broad respects the underlying musical principles of the Niger-Congo and the other major early African civilizations tended to be carried on wherever peoples of those civilizations could be found. For example, polyrhythmic music and dance involving multiple body movement persisted among most Niger-Congo peoples of the period. But if we were to study Eastern African cultural history more closely, we would soon discover, for instance, that a combining of elements from different civilizations took place between 300 and 1450 in the music of Bantu-speaking peoples of the African Great Lakes. Drums, the old Niger-Congo instrument, continued to be important among those societies, even giving rise, as states emerged, to the idea of special sets of royal drums as the insignia of legitimate kingship. But increasingly drum music was supplemented by the playing of flutes, adopted from the Eastern Sahelian or perhaps BaTwa cultures, and of lyres, probably in this instance adopted from Southern Cushites. Similar histories of change in musical expression will be discovered in many other areas of Africa, once scholars begin to study these issues.

Two instruments spread particularly widely across Africa between 300 and 1450. One was the mbira, a thumb piano with iron prongs. Originating apparently in the lower Zambezi region before 300, as we learned in chapter 5, it came in later centuries to be used throughout most of East Africa, all across the Congo Basin, and eventually as far west as Sierra Leone in West Africa. The other instrument was the xylophone, introduced from Indonesia, apparently by the ancestors of the Malagasy of Madagascar. The xylophone spread almost as widely as the mbira, but in a more scattered distribution, from the lower Zambezi through the Congo Basin to West Africa. Xylophones especially seem

FIG. 62 Zither, East Africa

One of the notable developments in music in the period 300–1450 CE in Africa was the development and wide diffusion of new kinds of stringed instruments into regions, especially of Niger-Congo civilization, where such instruments had previously been rare. For instance, several kinds of trough zither, of which this instrument from the modern-day country of Burundi is one example, spread among Bantu peoples of western East Africa and parts of the Congo Basin, apparently during these centuries. Musicians played the zither shown here especially to accompany singing.

to have often become court instruments, played for kings and chiefs, while the mbira remained more the instrument of common folk. Both instruments reached the Great Lakes region of Africa, probably between 1000 and 1450, where they soon became two further elements in the elaboration of musical performance among the Lakes Bantu societies. After the fifteenth century, kings in this region sometimes established royal orchestras, with musicians who played both of these instruments, as well as lyres, zithers, flutes, and different kinds of drums.

Another instrument that came into vogue over wide areas before the fifteenth century, both in West Africa and in the equatorial rainforest, was the side-blown trumpet. Usually associated with the court music of chiefs and kings, this instrument took on a variety of forms among the different peoples who made and played it. Carved wooden versions became common in West Africa, and artisans in both West Africa and the western equatorial regions produced finely carved ivory trumpets, made from elephant tusks. Some West African artisans also made copper side-blown trumpets for their royal clients.

All in all, the period from 300 to 1450 was a time of immense and varied change across the African continent. It encompassed the rise of states and towns in many new areas, the expansion of existing commercial networks and the establishment of many new economic ties, the elaboration of technology and agricultural production, and a slowly and irregularly growing impingement of the course of developments outside Africa on the course of history deep within the continent. At the same time, the older cultural traditions of Africa built on the new directions of change—reshaping religious beliefs, creating new forms of art, applying older sculptural forms in newer mediums, and enriching forms of artistic and musical expression.

NOTES FOR READERS AND TEACHERS

Issues and Questions

The themes and issues that characterize history in the northern half of Africa between 300 and 1450 are sometimes similar and sometimes different from those of the southern half of the continent (covered in chapter 6). Some of the many questions that we might ask about these developments include:

- Why did the trans-Saharan trade begin when it did?
- What was the significance of transshipment points in commercial and political history in the western Sudan?
- What varied kinds of historical consequences did the development and spread of camel nomadism have in the northern half of Africa?
- How did Ethiopian feudalism differ from the European variety?
- In what ways did religion and the interests of kings affect each other in the Nubian Christian kingdoms? In the Ethiopian Christian kingdoms?
- How did religion shape political history at various periods in North Africa?
- What kinds of effects did the spread of Islam to different parts of the Sudan belt of Africa have on political history? On commerce?
- What sorts of changes in culture and society did the adoption of Islam bring to the Soomaali peoples of the eastern Horn of Africa?
- What might explain the fact that several large states (Nri, Igala, and Benin) arose between 800 and 1300 in the areas around and to the south of the confluence of the Benue and Niger Rivers?
- What new commodities became prominent in the period 300–1450 in West African commerce? In the commerce of the Horn of Africa?
- In what ways were artistic and musical traditions enriched in different parts of Africa during the period 300–1450?
- What new developments in the technologies of metal working did African smiths put into use during that period in sub-Saharan Africa?
- What were the principal means of the transport of goods in, respectively, the rainforests, the savanna zones, and the Sahara desert areas of West Africa?
- What kind of tactical fighting force grew into the most important segment in the armies of the states of the Sudan belt of Africa over the period from the thirteenth to the sixteenth centuries? (For more on this, see chap. 8.)

Further Reading

The histories of the Maghrib and Egypt in the centuries from 300 to 1450 CE have an extensive historical literature. For the Sudan regions and West Africa, in contrast, the number of books both available and written in easily accessible style is small, although growing. With the exception of Thurstan Shaw's book on the archeology and art of Igbo-Ukwu, the several books and one article chosen for mention here present us with histories of the long term in North Africa, the Horn of Africa, the Middle Nile Basin, and the western Sudan. The stories their authors tell often extend into periods after 1450 and sometimes take us back before 300 as well:

Bühnen, Stephan. "In Quest of Susu." *History in Africa* 21 (1994): 1–47.

Laroui, Abdallah ('Abd Allah al-'Arawi). *The History of the Maghrib: An Interpretive Essay.* Princeton: Princeton University Press, 1977.

Law, Robin. *The Horse in West African History.* New York: Oxford University Press, 1980.

Levtzion, Nehemiah. *Ancient Ghana and Mali.* New York: African Publishing, 1980.

Shaw, Thurstan. *Igbo-Ukwu.* 2 vols. Evanston: Northwestern University Press, 1970.

Shinnie, P. L. *Ancient Nubia.* New York: Kegan Paul International, 1996.

Tamrat, Taddesse. *Church and State in Ethiopia, 1270–1527.* Oxford: Clarendon Press, 1972.

8

The Early Atlantic Age, 1450–1640

Africa and the World Enter a New Historical Era

Defining the Atlantic Age

To call the years from 1450 to 1640 the "Early Atlantic Age" risks overemphasizing one aspect of African history at the expense of other equally important themes. It puts us in danger of reading later history back into the past and assuming that Europeans sailing the Atlantic Ocean in the fifteenth and sixteenth centuries already were as technologically and economically dominant as they became in the nineteenth century. They were not. Their scientific revolution in thought had only barely begun by 1640, and the first Industrial Revolution, out of which came all of Europe's later material advantages, lay another century and a half in the future.

On the other hand, "Atlantic Age" is an appellation that directs our attention to an emerging new factor in the wider history of the world. It tells us that the chain of developments by which the Europeans gradually shifted from being peripheral actors on the world stage to chief protagonists began in this period. During this time, Europeans spread the Commercial Revolution along the western side of Africa and across the Atlantic Ocean, and they opened up new sea trade routes of global reach between the Atlantic and the rest of the oceans of the world. They became a gradually growing commercial presence along the coasts of Africa, but in only a few areas was their impact felt before the 1640s by peoples of the interior (see map 20).

Africa and the World, 1450–1640

In the centuries between 300 and 1450, the key linkages of world commerce bundled together in the Middle East. Through those regions were funneled all the commodities that came from the distant ends of the Eastern Hemisphere. Both in West Africa between 700 and 1450 and in Europe from about 1000 onward, a gradual expansion and diversification in commerce and in the production of manufactured goods took place, and distinct merchant classes emerged as a result in both these parts of the world. Both these macro-regions held the same kind of relation to the Middle East—they lay at the far western ends of the commercial networks of the Eastern Hemisphere, while the Middle East lay at the hubs of those networks. Middle Easterners thus held the commanding positions in world trade. They dictated the prices of commodities coming through those hubs and took the middleman's cut, which together with the costs of transport raised immensely the prices that Europeans and Africans had to pay for goods from the East.

Europeans, however, because of their sharp religious differences with the Middle East, viewed this economic disadvantage in a consciously adversarial manner that the merchants and kings of the western Sudan would not have understood. In the Iberian Peninsula, the ongoing "reconquest" of the land by Christian rulers from Muslim rulers made this view particularly acute. And there, in the country of Portugal in the first half of the fifteenth century, this competitive and adversarial stance conjoined with a variety of new factors to set off the first age of European expansion. Several elements made up the first small steps in what was eventually to become a sea change in the directions of world history:

1. a growing European demand for the products, especially the spices, of the Indian Ocean trade
2. an expectation, derived from the writings of the Greek historian Herodotus, that Africa could be circumnavigated, allowing one to circumvent the Middle Easterners' control of access to the Indian Ocean and its products
3. new developments in tacking, for the first time allowing ships to successfully sail south down the far western African coasts against the prevailing winds, which always blew northward
4. a developing experience of deep-sea travel by Iberians sailing out to the Canary Islands and the Madeiras and Azores in the nearby parts of the Atlantic
5. bringing all these elements together, a patron, Prince Henry of Portugal,

who was more interested in defeating Muslims than in commerce, but who provided the social and economic means to support the Portuguese trade expansion as a way of pursuing his own more religiously oriented goals

The establishment of Portuguese commercial activities around the coasts of Africa took place over an eighty-year period. In the 1440s Portuguese ships first arrived at the mouth of the Senegal River, made contacts with the coastal territories of the Jolof empire, and began to tap into the existing gold and slave trades of the western Sudan. By the 1470s, they had carried their travels south and east along the West African coast as far as a land that soon came to be called the Gold Coast, because of the availability there of the gold from the Akan area. In the 1480s the Portuguese reached the lower Congo River, there dealing with the Kongo kingdom; a few years later, in 1488, Bartolomeu Dias sailed around the southern tip of the African continent. Finally, in 1497, a Portuguese expedition under the command of Vasco da Gama traveled not only around the Cape of Good Hope but also up the East African coast to the Swahili city-states and then across the Indian Ocean to Goa in India. Subsequent Portuguese voyages extended these commercial links to the East Indies. The goal of circumventing the Middle Eastern middlemen of world trade had been accomplished.

Between the 1460s and the 1490s, first the kingdom of Castile alone and then the unified kingdom of Spain under Ferdinand and Isabella joined in the trade to the West African coast. Christopher Columbus gained his early experience in long-distance sea travel in the 1480s as a participant in the Castilian commerce of West Africa, and that experience served him well in obtaining royal backing for his expedition that "discovered" the New World in 1492. Columbus's American adventure led directly to the signing of the Treaty of Tordesillas and to the supporting papal proclamation in 1494, by which the pope set aside Africa as the sphere of Portuguese activity and reserved most of the New World for the Spanish.

The fact that the pope in 1494 could feel able to proclaim a division of the world into the spheres of influence of two southern European kingdoms tells us a lot about the arrogance, presumption, and sheer lack of knowledge with which the Europeans of those days approached the rest of the world. (It also tells us something about the Catholic Church and the papacy's disregard for northern Europe in those times, a disregard that was itself a significant factor in setting off the Protestant Reformation fewer than twenty-five years later.)

The truth of the matter was that, in Africa at least, what a pope or treaty makers in Europe might do was inconsequential. For the first 200 years of the Atlantic Age, Europeans remained peripheral historical actors in African history, in most cases able to strongly influence the course of events only in those regions where their activities were allowed and encouraged by Africans. But over most of the continent they were not involved at all in what took place. Often the Portuguese—and from the 1560s to the 1640s, the French, Dutch, and English as well—acted as carriers of trade goods from one part of coastal Africa to another and as buyers of African manufactured goods as well as raw materials. Not until the second era of the Atlantic Age, from about 1640 to the 1800s, did the European demand for African raw materials and slaves and the availability of manufactured goods carried from Europe, India, and the East Indies begin to penetrate successively deeper into the continent, to the detriment nearly everywhere of African productivity and, increasingly, to the detriment of African economic independence.

There is also a basic mistake that modern-day readers and writers of history books commonly make when they look at European activities in the non-Western world in earlier centuries, and this mistake brings us to a new version of a lesson we have already learned. We should not read back into past times the technological advantages of the nineteenth-century Europeans. The Portuguese and other Europeans before the nineteenth century generally operated in Africa at the sufferance of Africans. If they traded, it was because they paid the necessary duties or taxes. If they defeated Africans in battle, it was because they allied with other Africans. (The same point holds for the Americas in the early sixteenth century. Consider Cortez's conquest of Mexico: he won not because of European technological advantage but because of the support of the great majority of the indigenous people, who wanted to throw off the yoke of the Aztec empire.)

Because Westerners assume the long-term technological advantage of Europe, they are ready to embrace the idea that tropical diseases kept Europeans from overrunning Africa earlier. Indeed, Europeans did initially die at a much higher rate in Africa from disease than the acclimated local populations of the continent. But, in fact, many Portuguese and other Europeans of the fifteenth to the eighteenth centuries lived for years along the West African and East African coasts, married locally, and established families and livelihoods there. Europeans conquered Africa in the late nineteenth century not because they then had quinine to fight malaria, but because of two elements of military ordnance invented only in the second half of the nineteenth century, the repeating rifle and the Gatling gun, a precursor of the machine gun.

Guns, including cannons, in the fifteenth to the eighteenth centuries gave a narrow kind of advantage in limited circumstances, mainly when fired from already well-fortified positions. A musket could create the fear of death at long distance, but its aim was incredibly poor, and it took so long to reload that, in the open field, one's enemy could easily rush up and spear, stab, or bludgeon one to death in the meantime. We have only to look at European warfare as recent as the late seventeenth century to see that pikes and swords were still the most important weapons of the individual European soldier. Between then and the twentieth century, bayonets were an essential weapon, important even after the adoption of repeating rifles.

All this is not to say that Europeans did not have a lasting impact on the areas with which they did directly trade. They brought new kinds of manufactured goods, ranging as widely in kind as metal basins and distilled alcohol, to the coasts of Africa. New kinds of currency, including a type of copper ring called a "manila" and, later on, different kinds of iron bars, all manufactured in Europe, took hold in the coastal West African milieu of the early European trading era. The Portuguese and later the Dutch probably over the long haul helped bring about a slow devaluation of the older West African cowry shell currency by shipping immense numbers of cowries directly by sea from the Indian Ocean to West Africa. The total number of these shells brought by the Eu-

FIG. 63 Manila

People in many parts of West Africa continued to value and use this kind of copper currency until the nineteenth century.

ropeans over four centuries' time eventually amounted to many billions. Of course, the largest scale of importation of cowries did not belong to the early Atlantic Age but rather to the middle Atlantic period, which we consider in the next chapter. Nevertheless, the availability of the new source of the currency surely did nothing to enhance its value.

The trade relations of the Atlantic Age also had a long-term and widespread impact on African agriculture through the introduction of American crops to the continent. Among these crops, domesticated thousands of years earlier by Native Americans in the New World, were tobacco, peanuts, maize ("corn"), cassava, and new kinds of beans.

Tobacco spread widely in Africa after its introduction. Portuguese traders brought the plant to West Africa as well as to the East African coast and to Zimbabwe and the Zambezi regions in the sixteenth century. Probably because of its addictive qualities, the smoking of tobacco advanced rapidly eastward from Senegambia along the trade routes of the Sudan belt in the sixteenth century, reaching all the way to the Middle Nile Basin and the northern parts of the African Great Lakes region by sometime in the seventeenth century. (We can track this diffusion through the spread of a single word, *taba*, for tobacco all the way across Africa, from the western Sudan to the eastern shores of Lake Nyanza.)

The history of peanuts in one part of Africa throws a special light on the continent's trans-Atlantic connections with the Americas. A crop of South American origin, peanuts arrived in the lower Congo River region apparently in the sixteenth century, and there the inhabitants gave this new crop a new name, *nguba*. In the seventeenth century, captive Africans transported to the Caribbean carried their knowledge of peanuts as well as the name *nguba* along with them. When peanuts were introduced from the Caribbean into the North American colonies of the British, this word then passed into southern American dialects of English as the first element of the term "goober pea," as peanuts came to be called in those areas.

Two other crops of major importance in modern-day Africa, maize and cassava, generally became significant crops only from the eighteenth century onward. Maize, unlike any of the indigenous African grains, could adapt to rainforest conditions and so had the potential to further enrich the agricultural productivity of rainforest farmers. Cassava, a tuber crop, gained importance later on because of its ability to survive drought times in the savannas of Africa.

But it was not only American crops that spread because of the new commercial links of the Atlantic Age. The Portuguese introduced Asian rice, for instance, to the Congo Basin, and after the seventeenth century this crop spread far eastward up the Congo and its tributaries. The African species of rice had previously been widely raised in West Africa, as we have already learned, but had never spread to the equatorial parts of the continent. In addition, the Portuguese most probably were the first introducers of sugarcane, another Southeast Asian crop, to western equatorial Africa and West Africa. Sugarcane, as we discovered in chapter 5, probably came first to the eastern coasts of Africa in the early first millennium CE, and in later centuries it diffused inland to several parts of East Africa. But that spread apparently never reached the western side of the continent.

With the wider landscape of Africa and its world historical connections depicted, we can now turn our attention to what was going on in different parts of the continent of Africa between 1450 and 1640. What new directions of change appeared? With what factors, new or old, did the varied African cultural worlds that had taken shape by the early fifteenth century now have to deal? And what consequences did the opening up of new outlets of commerce along the Atlantic shores of the continent have, anyway?

Western Africa, 1450–1640

The End of the Age of Empire in the Western Sudan

In the western Sudan belt of Africa between 1450 and 1640, the age of empire came to an end, but not before one more great empire, Songay, flourished. Songay grew out of the kingdom and former city-state of Gao, with its Sudanic sacral king. By the fifteenth century, the city of Gao had long been nominally Muslim. Kings are usually called by Muslim names in the records available to us, and there is no evidence that servants were buried along with them when they died. But it is also clear that the attachment of the general rural populace to the kingship rested on the continued observance of older royal rites and practices.

Sunni Ali, who ruled from the 1460s to the early 1490s, was the chief architect of the early Songay empire. His wars expanded Songay rule all through the regions around the great Bend of the Niger River and westward into the northern territories of the already much shrunken Mali empire. To control these areas, Sunni Ali had to walk a sort of ideological tightrope. He had to maintain his cultural and religious roots in the general population while at the same time

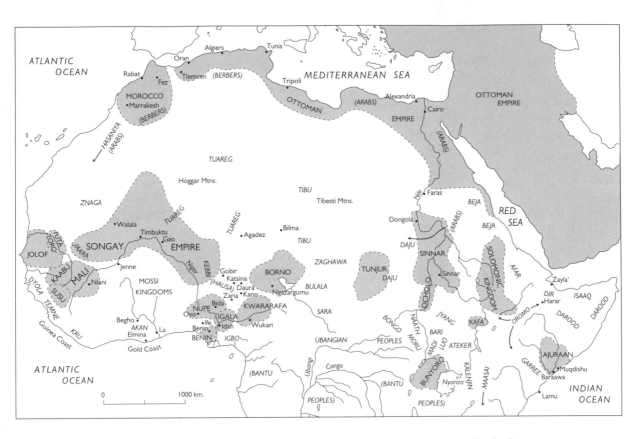

MAP 21 Peoples, states, and cities in the northern half of Africa, ca. 1550

getting along with the economically important Muslim merchant class of the cities newly conquered along the Bend of the Niger, most of all Timbuktu. Continuing opposition in those cities led him eventually to take military action to bring the urban communities into line. In this he was successful in his lifetime, but he paid a historical price. Timbuktu by that period had emerged as a center of Muslim higher learning, and the later scholarly historians of seventeenth-century Timbuktu who wrote the histories of Sunni Ali's time were not at all kind to him.

After Sunni Ali's death in 1492, his son ruled just two years before being overthrown by a former general of his father's time, Muhammad Ture. Muhammad, who took the title Askiya and so is often called in the history books Askiya Muhammad, was a pious Muslim, and he seized power with the backing of the disaffected urban dwellers of the Niger Bend. As have many usurpers in history, Muhammad embarked almost immediately on a series of new wars. His conquests spread Songay power hundreds of kilometers north into the Sahara desert, seizing control there of important salt mines. He also led his forces far to the east, defeating a number of the Hausa city-states and turning them briefly into tributary states of the empire. To the west he completed the subjugation of the northern territories of the former Mali empire.

A key new element in Askiya Muhammad's wars was the use of cavalry on a large scale. Horses, as we have learned, first were introduced to the western Sudan region in the first millennium BCE. Around that same time horses were also introduced across the Red Sea, and during the first millennium CE horses spread widely in the Middle Nile Basin and from there westward to the Chad Basin. So, by the beginning of the second millennium BCE, horses had long been kept by peoples living all across the Sahel zone south of the Sahara. Horses were valued prestige animals, associated with chiefs and kings, and important commodities in trade between the Sahara fringe areas, where they were bred, and the savanna areas of higher rainfall immediately to the south. Gradually horses came to be used in battle by war leaders in several parts of the Sudan belt, and the formation of effective cavalry forces began to change the nature of warfare by the fourteenth and fifteenth centuries. The rapid success of Songay campaigns in Hausa country may have been important in encouraging the subsequent development of cavalry forces in the Hausa country and farther east in the Chad Basin. In battle, horses were outfitted, as were their riders, with a thick armor of quilted cloth, serving to blunt the sword swipes of the enemy, much in the way that Kevlar vests slow up the impact of bullets today.

The Songay empire came to an end in the 1590s, less than three-quarters of a century after Askiya Muhammad's death. In 1591 Ahmad al-Mansur, ruler of Morocco, sent an invading army of 5,000 men south across the desert in search of more direct access to the gold trade and particularly to the trade in slaves, from whom he wished to create a slave army. These marauders did bring with them muskets and a few cannons, but to attribute their victory to their weaponry, as most historians have done, is to misunderstand the historical context. Askiya Muhammad and his successors had chosen an allegiance, to Islam and to the city elites, that in the short run gave them the profits of the trade and the revenues with which to run the state. But their choice of allies ultimately cost them the support of the countryside, whose ties were still to the older Sudanic ways of kingship. The pious Muslim kings of the late period of the Songay empire could not tap into the same wellsprings of awe as the earlier kings. The Moroccan invaders lacked even the semblance of legitimacy in the eyes of rural populations. Feeling little allegiance to the far-off sultan of Morocco, the invading forces soon divided the areas along the Bend of the Niger into several tiny principalities, bringing the age of empire truly to an end in the western Sudan.

An Age of Kingdoms in the Western Sudan

Many historians have viewed the era after the fall of Songay as a long period of decline. But to equate the end of empire with decline is to apply uncritically an old class-based assumption, held not just by Europeans but by people in other societies as well, that empires are something great, that bigger is automatically greater. We have already seen that there is good reason to eschew such a viewpoint. The growth in diversity and complexity of production and exchange that had taken place all across the western Sudan during the time of the Mali empire (see chapter 7) meant that in most areas it was a time of real economic expansion. As a consequence, many possible centers for the accumulation of economic and political power could now emerge in place of the few empires of the previous centuries. The replacement of an age of empire by an age of kingdoms was a sign of a fuller and wider participation of the people of the western Sudan in a thriving exchange economy, and not a sign of decline.

By the early seventeenth century, medium and small kingdoms became the characteristic form of political authority in the lands south of the Niger bend and upstream along the river. Two Manding kingdoms, Segu and Kaarta, ruled different parts of the old heartlands of the Mali empire. Both kingdoms built their power on a new institution, a standing army composed of slaves. In the Sahel to the north of Segu and Kaarta, the Soninke-speaking Jaara kingdom formed another of the independent states of this zone. Tributary to the Susu in the twelfth century, to the Mali empire in the thirteenth to fifteenth centuries, and to Songay in the sixteenth century, Jaara was a longtime important iron-producing area. Through all these countries, the old western Sudan mixture of class and caste institutions still laid down the lines of access to authority in these states.

To the east, in the areas south of the Bend of the Niger and north of the rainforest, the several Mossi kingdoms took shape in the sixteenth and seventeenth centuries. These states were not of the Sudanic sacral kind, nor did they include an occupational caste system. Their rulers used cavalry-based armies to impose their rule over the older Niger-Congo kind of local clan-based village cultures of the region. Juula merchants came to live in the Mossi capital towns and helped tie the material strength of the Mossi states strongly to the commercial networks of the Sudan. The power of the kings of these states appears to have rested less on ritual relations than on the rulers' ability to keep trade flowing and to overawe recalcitrant subjects with the prowess of their cavalry. The historical records relating to the Mali and Songay empires suggest there was an earlier era of states in the region, dating to as early as the fourteenth century, so the idea of kingship was not entirely new to the many small societies of the region in the seventeenth century. But nothing is known as yet of the history of that earlier era.

Senegambia: Commercial Growth and Political Realignment

Farther west along and between the Gambia and Senegal Rivers, and also to the south of the Gambia, lay the lands that we call the Senegambia region. Early on the Portuguese became an important element in this region's economic history. Between the 1440s and the early 1600s, their presence at the coast provided an alternative outlet for two important commodities, gold and slaves, which already passed through the hands of the merchants of Senegambia northward across the Sahara to the Muslim states of North Africa and to the far southern Iberian Peninsula. The resulting competition between trans-Saharan caravaners and the Portuguese enhanced the profitability of trade for the Senegambian merchants and increased the wealth available to the Jolof state and, farther south, to the kingdom of Kaabu. A former province of the Mali empire, Kaabu controlled the most direct access from the coast to the Bure and Bambuk goldfields (see map 21).

Here we again face the danger of reading the developments of later times back into the past. The early consequences of the trade with the Portuguese were not the overtly destructive ones that often accompanied the high era of the slave trade after 1640. All along the Atlantic coasts in the later fifteenth and the early sixteenth centuries, the arrival of European ships put peoples formerly at the far margins of the thriving economic networks of the Sudan region at the hubs of a new network for the exchange of goods. Cloth manufactured in Benin, for instance, gained a newly important market to the west, in the Gold Coast region. The Portuguese and later, in the early seventeenth century, the Dutch bought cloth from Benin, shipped it to the Gold Coast, and exchanged it there for gold. Similarly, Portuguese shippers purchased African iron in Sierra Leone along the Guinea Coast and carried it by boat to Senegambia to buy gold and also to acquire slaves from societies with a significant population of servile laborers, some of whom were already being sold to the merchants of the trans-Saharan trade. Hides were also a longtime important export of Senegambia; many a boot of "Spanish" leather, then as well as in later centuries, must actually have been a boot of Senegambian leather.

A more subtle consequence of trade with Europeans along the coast may have been the creation of new areas of competition and tension among the African polities of Senegambia. It has been argued that the Waalo, Baol, and Kajoor kingdoms successfully asserted their independence from the Jolof empire in the mid-1500s because of their own more direct access to the coastal outlets of seagoing trade. But the collapse of the Jolof empire cannot be blamed solely on outside factors. For over a century, after all, Jolof dealt quite successfully with the combined Portuguese and Spanish presence along the coast before 1494 and with the Portuguese alone after that date.

A more abruptly disruptive challenge to Jolof power came in 1495 from Fula pastoral nomads. The distinctive economy of this people, as we learned in chapter 7, came into being early in the second millennium CE. By the beginning of the 1400s, the nomads of the middle Senegal River and their cattle herds had grown so large in number that many of these Fula began to seek new grazing lands for their animals. Some communities moved farther east across the northern territories of the Mali empire, of which they were at that time nominal subjects. In the 1450s another large body of Fula trekked in a different direction, moving 400 kilometers south to the part of the Susu kingdom that lay in the Jallon Mountains. This region, reaching above 1,500 meters in elevation, was high enough to have relatively few tsetse flies; and with its formerly woodland savanna areas cleared by several thousand years of Niger-Congo agricultural activity and by centuries of cutting wood to make charcoal for iron production, it provided good grass for the intruders' cattle.

Although some of the Fula adapted to living under the rule of the Susu kingdom, others may have clashed with that authority. Possibly for that reason, in 1490 the Fula leader Tengela and his son Koli led a reverse migration of many of the Fula back from the Jallon region, marauding with a large army first north through Kaabu and then through the Jolof territories before finally settling their followers along the middle Senegal River. There, in the lands from which his Fula forebears had come forty years earlier, Tengela established the new kingdom of Futa Toro under his own Denyanke dynasty. To consolidate their power, Tengela and Koli set about creating a new aristocratic social order by distributing land among their faithful followers. In the regions of flood recession agriculture along the Senegal, where the bulk of the population of the new kingdom resided, this new social and political dispensation created a quiltwork of large landholdings of the new aristocracy, side by side with the many small family holdings of the peasantry.

In the aftermath of the Fula invasion, the kingdom of Kaabu along the Gambia River asserted its independence from the Mali empire. The Jolof empire at first seemingly weathered this sudden storm. Still, the fierce political and economic disruptions of this short period, as some scholars suggest, may well have helped to weaken the ties of the constituent states of Jolof to the central kingship and thus contributed at least indirectly to the final breakup of the state a little over a half century later. When the breakup took place in the mid-sixteenth century, it did not come about peacefully or easily. Kajoor split off first, followed some years later by the secession of Waalo and Baol, but not before a series of violent battles with the armies of the Jolof rulers.

Atlantic Commerce and the Coastal Hinterlands of Africa

Benin and Its Encounter with Atlantic Trade

The history of several other major African kingdoms, already well-established powers before the European arrival, reveal in different ways how the new commercial relations intertwined with old in widely separated parts of the continent.

In the rainforest inland from the Niger Delta, the reign of Ewuare the Great in the mid-1400s brought the Benin kingdom to the high point of its power. Already by that period, a number of the key features of Benin society were in existence, notably artisan guilds, among which were the guilds responsible for making the state-patronized art of the kingdom. Some of the greatest masterpieces of Benin brass-casting sculpture belong, it appears, to Ewuare's century. Benin city, as described by European visitors, was a large and impressive urban center with wide straight streets. Extensive earthworks surrounded the city and many of its outlying villages.

The Benin kingdom included numerous small territories tied in differing degrees to the central government. In the capital and nearby towns, there prevailed a patrilineal stratified society centered around the court and the leading chiefly families and an economy focused on the production especially of elite goods by occupational guilds. In villages far from the center, matrilineal rules of descent and succession to local chiefly and ritual positions still could be found. Women in those areas, until at least the seventeenth century, had a much greater say in day-to-day affairs and much more often held positions of authority than was possible at the center of the state.

Benin entered into the Atlantic trade very much on its own terms. The Portuguese were able to buy slaves from time to time in Benin, but state policy continued throughout Benin's history to resist allowing the trade in human beings to dominate its relations with others. In the sixteenth and early seventeenth centuries, cotton cloth was the key export of both Benin and its tributary kingdom, the Yoruba city-state of Ijebu. European merchants bought the cloth and then transported it by sea to other areas, such as the Gold Coast, where they exchanged it for African gold or other products. Trade in this case enhanced African manufacturing capacities and brought real economic growth. A still more fascinating aspect of this trade was that the cloth producers were women engaged in individual, small-scale operations, often in the outlying village areas of the kingdom. Thus women especially benefited from the cloth trade, and the relatively high status of women in some parts of the Benin kingdom may have owed a great deal to this fact (see map 20).

FIG. 64 Brass plaque, kingdom of Benin

Brass plaques such as these often depicted historical scenes.

The Kingdom of Kongo and Its Neighbors

The Kongo kingdom had a more mixed experience with the Atlantic trade between 1483, when the Portuguese first appeared on its shores, and 1640. In the second half of the fifteenth and the early years of the sixteenth centuries, its kings apparently exerted a loose hegemony over a number of Kimbundu-speaking kingdoms to the south of it. The several small Ndembu statelets were indirectly tied through their owing of tribute to the government of Mbamba, the southwestern province of Kongo, while the larger Mbwila kingdom apparently paid its tribute directly to the court at Mbanzakongo. To the south of Ndembu and Mbwila, the Ndongo kingdom, whose ruler was titled the Ngola a Kiluanje, was the most distant state claimed as a tributary by the kings of Kongo.

Initially, the Atlantic trade reinforced these hegemonic relationships. In fact, in the early fifteenth century, the ruler of another Kimbundu state, Matamba, located in the interior, offered tribute to Kongo in order to gain access to the imported goods that the new trade brought to the region. The Matamba state is especially interesting because its primary ruler was a woman, whose title was *muhongo.* The official male consort of the *muhongo,* called the *kambole,* had the responsibility for waging war, however.

After the 1560s, if not already by the 1550s, Kongo's power over the Kimbundu regions began to wane, in large part because Ndongo was able to develop its own direct commercial links with the Portuguese at the coast. As this new outlet developed, the *muhongos* of Matamba increasingly shifted their commercial ties to Ndongo and before the end of the sixteenth century had ceased to pay tribute to Kongo. The Mbwila kingdom and the small Ndembu kingdoms continued to feel Kongo power, however, for several decades longer, and Kongo's economic position remained strong in the Atlantic trade and in the trading system of the lower Congo region. The Kimbundu states to the south added a new arena of commercial relations, but up to the 1640s their activities did not directly threaten the old sources of Kongo's commercial power.

The aspect of dealing with the Portuguese that most arrested the attention of the Kongo ruling class in the two decades after 1483 was religion. The kings of Kongo, as we saw in chapter 6, lacked a solid ideological basis of their own in the religious beliefs of their country. Catholic Christianity, with its emphasis on saints, appeared to offer a new category of spirits who could be appropriated as royalty's religious domain. This religious connection was all the more

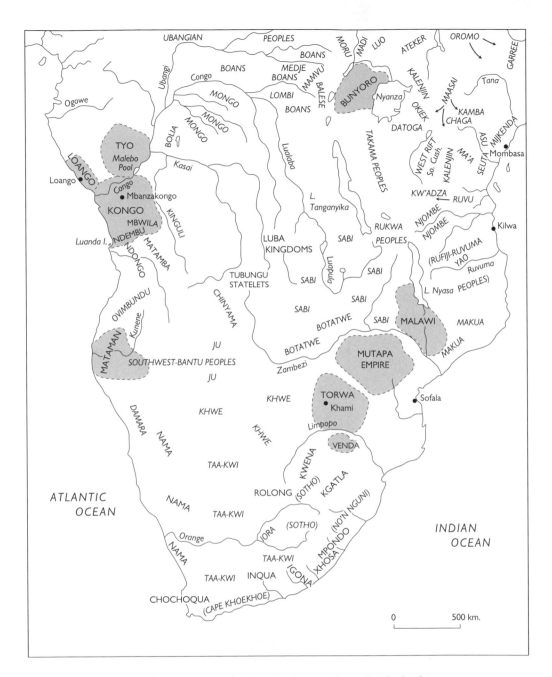

MAP 22 Peoples, states, and cities in the southern half of Africa, ca. 1550

appealing because the Iberian version of Christianity back in Europe legitimized the kind of rule that the kings of the decentralized Kongo state aspired to, a centralized monarchical rule over a hierarchy of subordinated nobility. The king who most tried to indigenize this vision to the Kongo was the early sixteenth-century ruler Afonso I, who took power in 1506 and ruled until the 1540s.

How did Christianity fit in with the existing religious beliefs of the region? In Kongo in the fifteenth century, the two important categories of spirit were the ancestors and the territorial spirits, one the sphere of the clans and their chiefs and the other the domain of the *kitomi* priests. Christianity evoked a third category of Kongo belief that did not properly belong to any particular social grouping, the spirits of the sky and sea. The Christian Portuguese came from the sea, and the Catholic saints and the Christian imagery of heaven fit the Kongo notion of a sky-connected spiritual dimension.

Rather than supplanting the older religion of Kongo, Catholicism became a further element in that religion. In the sixteenth and seventeenth centuries, the leading *kitomi*, whose religious territory included the capital Mbanzakongo, continued to be a key participant in the central councils of the state alongside the Mwisikongo and the leading churchmen. Here we have evidence from the center of society for the extent to which Christianity and Niger-Congo religion coexisted in the kingdom of Kongo.

The degree to which the drive to centralize Kongo succeeded can be debated. Nevertheless, the rulers took a number of practical measures in the sixteenth century that did indeed strengthen royal authority. Because of the Christian connection, the kingdom began to rely on written, and no longer simply oral, documentation of the affairs of state. Early in Afonso's reign, the kingdom established its own diplomatic relations with the Vatican, so as not to have to depend on an inconstant ally, Portugal, for its connections with Europe. A local body of scribes was trained, able eventually to communicate in written Latin, Portuguese, and KiKongo. A messenger system was put into effect in the later sixteenth century and first half of the seventeenth century. Runners stationed at different posts along the main routes of communication between the capital and the provinces and between the capital and coast quickly carried government correspondence and proclamations by relay right across the country.

In the midst of these developments, in 1569, disaster struck Kongo in the form of an invasion by a people called the Jaga. The leaders of this invasion may previously have lived well to the east, in the upper Kasai River regions, although their military following was probably drawn from the local communities along the Kwango River, just east of Kongo. These people were probably deeply involved in the already growing trade in slaves. How their leaders may have come to the Kwango region is an issue we will explore later in this chapter. What is important here is that the Jaga incursions brought about a sudden and unprecedented disruption of the Kongo political and social order, in the wake of which famine and a six-year period of economic breakdown ensued. Marshaling all their forces, and with the help of a Portuguese contingent of 600 men, Kongo was finally able in 1575 to expel the Jaga and restore internal peace.

Elements of the Jaga then retired to the southeast, settling down in the areas around the upper Kwango River. Between 1575 and the early seventeenth century, they may have contributed to the rise of the Imbangala kingdom under a new line of kings, who adopted a new title, Kasanje. In the early seventeenth century the Imbangala emerged as a powerful society in the interior of Angola.

Historians have often viewed the Jaga episode as the beginning of the end for the power and independence of Kongo, but this view cannot be sustained. The Kongo kingdom gradually emerged from the crisis of the early 1570s as strong as ever. Nevertheless, the Jaga invasion did mark a significant watershed in Kongo history. To understand why, we need to look more closely at the checkered history of Kongo's commercial ties to the Atlantic trade.

When the Portuguese first arrived, the chief commodity they sought from Kongo was slaves. Because of its frontier wars and its trade links at the Malebo Pool, the Kongo kingdom was usually able to supply this still relatively small demand. Interestingly, these early human cargoes sometimes stayed in continental Africa, being shipped to the Gold Coast to be exchanged there for gold. Within the regional economic context of the lower Congo Basin, the Kongo aristocracy continued to prosper from their control of access to such local products as copper and raffia cloth transported from one part of the region to another, and their control over Luanda Island, the source of the *nzimbu* shells, the major currency of the whole lower Congo country.

In the 1570s, this situation changed in several key ways, partly because of the disruptiveness of the Jaga invasion and partly because the Portuguese crown in 1575 took advantage of Kongo's troubles and seized Luanda Island just off the coast of the Ndongo kingdom, south of Kongo. The Portuguese followed this up in 1576 by establishing a small colony they called Angola on the mainland opposite the island. The founding of the colony ended Kongo's control over the *nzimbu* shells. In time, the Portuguese overproduced the shells, weakening the value of that currency. The markets of the Kongo and its neighboring areas responded by shifting to raffia cloth as the new major currency. And because the Nkisi Valley in Kongo was the main producer of the best raffia cloth, the Kongo kingdom emerged by the end of the sixteenth century in, if anything, a stronger position monetarily than when it had depended on the *nzimbu* shells.

A second consequence of the Luanda colony was that between 1575 and 1610 Portuguese officials concentrated on building up their economic and political ties with kingdoms to the south of Kongo, particularly Ndongo and Matamba, to the detriment of Kongo's Atlantic trade. But the potentially debilitating effects of this Portuguese policy shift for the Kongo economy were offset by another development, connected directly to the Jaga episode. Many of the Portuguese column of 600 men who assisted in defeating the Jaga chose to stay on in Kongo after the fighting. Marrying locally, they established themselves as something Kongo had not previously had, a merchant class. In later decades, the loyalties and, perhaps more important, the economic self-interests of this small ethnically Portuguese and Afro-Portuguese population strongly tied them to their adopted home, Kongo. Their activities in pursuit of trade goods helped revive commerce in Kongo, all the more effectively because, from the 1570s onward, a new competition for African commodities emerged, as merchants of other European nations—France, Netherlands, and Britain—began to visit the coasts of western equatorial Africa.

The Kongo kingdom thus entered the seventeenth century with its institutions intact and with elements of infrastructure, such as its messenger system, that strengthened the reach of those institutions. Warfare in the areas of Portuguese commercial penetration to the south created several periods of insecurity on Kongo's southern borders in the first forty years of the seventeenth century. But on the whole it was a time of continuing independence and prosperity for at least the chiefly and royal classes of Kongo.

Political Change and Commerce to the South of Kongo

South of the Kongo kingdom, however, in what is today western Angola, political and social developments took a quite different turn. There the Portuguese, despite having only a slight advantage in armament over Africans, were able to have a deep and often direct impact on the course of historical change as early as the 1580s and 1590s. Two factors help account for this difference. To begin with, the colony at Luanda gave the Portuguese a base from which they were able to meddle more directly in the affairs of the interior kingdoms. For another, in these areas the Portuguese concentrated on the slave trade. Western Angola in the late sixteenth and early seventeenth centuries gives us an unhappy preview of the sad effects that the high slave trade era of the late seventeenth and eighteenth centuries would only too often set in motion elsewhere on the western side of the continent.

From the 1570s to the 1620s, the Portuguese at Luanda gradually and unevenly extended their influence into the lands of the Ndongo and Matamba kingdoms. The relations of these two kingdoms with the Portuguese were often contentious ones in the 1580s and 1590s, but gradually the Portuguese expanded and strengthened their territorial foothold at the coast and built up their political influence, particularly at the court of the *ngola* of Ndongo. From about 1611, they increasingly began to follow a new tack, and that was to ally with the Imbangala kingdom of the Kasanje, located inland along the upper Kwango River to the east of Matamba and Ndongo. Kasanje, because it was organized around the pursuit of war to an extent that no previous African state in the region had been, proved to be a reliable source of slaves for the Portuguese. Over the next twenty years, the Ndongo kingdom collapsed in the face of this new configuration of forces (see map 21).

The most interesting outcome of this often sordid history of intrigue and brutality was the emergence of one of the most striking figures of African history, Queen Nzinga. Born a royal princess of Ndongo, Nzinga laid claim to the Ndongo kingship in 1618 and over the next six years sought to sustain her claim by playing up to the Portuguese and playing off the various factions within the kingdom. In the mid-1620s, as her position became precarious in Ndongo, she took advantage of a vulnerable period in the neighboring state of Matamba, caused by the succession of a new *muhongo* (the female ruler of Matamba) and the death of the current *kambole* (the muhongo's consort). Abandoning her base in Ndongo, Nzinga sent her forces into Matamba, successfully conquering that state and turning it into her new domain. Perhaps because Matamba had long been ruled by queens, Nzinga built a lasting base for her ambitions there. Hers was a long and complex career, and as the ruler of Matamba she more than held her own against the military forces of the Kasanje and fended off Portuguese intervention right up until her death in 1663.

Even farther south a still different course of historical change eventuated.

In the lands all about the lower Kunene River, the new Atlantic trade relations had no strong effects on political or economic developments until probably after 1700. One large state, the Mataman empire, founded before 1500 and possibly well before then, ruled over a mix of Southwest-Bantu and Khoisan peoples. The heartland of the Mataman state lay in the floodplain of the Kunene, an area of good soils, dependable water supplies, and relatively dense farming population. The sphere of Mataman influence extended north from there into the Benguela Highlands, and the ruling line of at least one of the Ovimbundu kingdoms of that region, Bie, was apparently established by a tributary lord from Mataman.

The power of the kings of Mataman, we believe, rested, like that of later, lesser kings in this region, on their rights over the distributing of land and their ability to mobilize labor to clear river channels and to maintain reservoirs of water for the dry season. They would have been able to conscript labor for the royal fields as well. The surrounding dry savanna and steppes away from the Kunene floodplain provided pasture for great numbers of cattle, sheep, and goats, and the Mataman rulers undoubtedly consolidated their authority, as later kings in the region did, through the loaning out of cattle from their own huge herds to chiefs and lesser kings.

To the south of Mataman lay the large, but sparsely populated, lands of central and southern Namibia, ruled by the kings of the clan-based kingdom of the Nama Khoekhoe. The Nama moved north from the lower Orange River region sometime probably after 1000. Their kingdom, as it existed by the seventeenth century, comprised four autonomous clan chiefdoms, each owing allegiance to the Nama king. Together they controlled a large expanse of the better grassland of the central uplands of modern-day Namibia and held a dominant position over the Khoisan gatherer-hunters and the Damara herding peoples of the surrounding regions. The Damara, probably the descendants of the Kwadi who had originally brought livestock to the region 1,500 years earlier, all spoke the Nama language by the nineteenth century, when we begin to know more about them. A newly expanding presence on the north borders of the Nama lands in the seventeenth century were the Herero, a group of Bantu cattle-raising communities with close cultural links to the peoples of the Mataman state. In the eighteenth century the Herero spread into more of the northern territories of the Nama kingdom and began to constitute a growing challenge to Nama hegemony in the region (see map 21).

After the late sixteenth century, a trade in goods from the Atlantic coast reached indirectly into Mataman and Namibia from a recently established Portuguese post at Benguela, farther north along the Atlantic seaboard. For instance, European glass beads were traded from community to community southward to the peoples of the Nama kingdom and from them eventually as far south as the chiefdoms and tiny kingdoms of the Khoekhoe along the southern African coasts. But the political economy of Mataman rule continued primarily to depend not on trade but on royal and chiefly control over labor and access to land and over the redistribution of key resources.

Zimbabwe: The Mutapa and Torwa Kingdoms

On the other side of the continent, in Zimbabwe and parts of southern Mozambique, lay another area of major kingdoms for which the establishment of a European connection did not at first greatly change anything. This region went through a period of major historical transition in about the second quarter of the fifteenth century. As we learned in chapter 6, a newly important trade route appears to have been pioneered in the late fourteenth century along the Zambezi River. Six hundred kilometers upstream, near the confluence of the Zambezi with the Luangwa River, a key crossroads of this trade developed at Ingombe Ilede. Archeological excavations there show that copper from the northwestern parts of Zimbabwe and ivory from the Luangwa Valley were among the high-value commodities traded along this new route (see map 21).

Although gold from the Zimbabwe Plateau still passed down the Sabi River Valley to the coast at the Swahili entrepot of Sofala, the city of Great Zimbabwe lost its unique position as the single major outlet of the inland trade. For that reason, and possibly also because of environmental degradation, the city was largely abandoned between the 1420s and 1440s. The kingdom of Zimbabwe itself came to an end, and in its place, as we learned in chapter 6, two new kingdoms arose during the middle decades of the century, one in the north of modern-day Zimbabwe and the other in the southwest.

The southerly kingdom, Torwa, constructed a new capital city, Khami, built on the plan of the city of Great Zimbabwe. Gold continued to be mined and exported from its territories, but its material basis probably rested to a greater extent on the kings' control and redistributive powers over immense royal herds of cattle.

The northern kingdom, Mutapa, was built up through a series of military campaigns, waged between the 1440s and 1480s by its first two rulers, Mutota and Matope, and clearly directed at establishing their hegemony over the lands

FIG. 65 Ruins of Khami

The rulers of Torwa, the successor state of the Zimbabwe Empire located in southwestern Zimbabwe from the mid-fifteenth century to the 1680s, built their capital city Khami according to much the same plan as the earlier city of Great Zimbabwe. The Torwa kings seem to have been less wealthy from trade and so built less impressive royal structures that have not withstood nature and vandals as well as Great Zimbabwe has. Shown here are the steps leading into the central areas of Khami.

that led down to the Zambezi River route of commerce. The Mutapa kingdom controlled a few significant gold-producing areas and claimed sovereignty over the copper-mining areas of the northwestern Zimbabwe Plateau as well as ivory-producing areas on the southern side of the Zambezi Valley.

The Portuguese seized Sofala in 1505, hoping to grow rich on the proceeds of the gold trade. When that hope faded, they established several settlements successively farther up the Zambezi River between 1531 and the 1550s, in order to gain better access to the interior products, especially ivory, and to supplant the Swahili merchants in the trade. The Mutapa state firmly resisted being drawn into either the Portuguese religious or economic orbit right up to the 1590s.

This policy broke down during the reign of Gatse Rusere (1592–1626). Facing revolts in certain areas of his kingdom, this ruler recruited certain Portuguese adventurers living in the Zambezi Valley, who by that time commanded small contingents of their own African soldiers and slaves, to help him put down the rebellious forces. His new policy initiated a period during which Dominican missionaries were allowed into the country, and a number of Portuguese individuals, including at times the Dominicans, became involved in the internal politics of the country. At the death of Gatse Rusere in 1626, open conflict broke out between political factions supporting a candidate for the kingship who was averse to the increasing Portuguese presence and factions backed by the Portuguese. The immediate outcome was the enthroning in 1627 of a king, Mavura, beholden to his Portuguese supporters. Mavura tried to follow an independent path thereafter, but in the eyes of many of the subjects of the kingdom, his accession to power must have seriously compromised the legitimacy of the Mutapa kingship.

East-Central Africa: The Malawi Empire and Its Kingdoms

It is surely no coincidence that the rise of another large state, the Malawi empire, to the north of the Zambezi River also occurred during the fourteenth and fifteenth centuries. Malawi's territories, lying north of the river in parts of the modern-day countries of Malawi, Zambia, and Mozambique, were major ivory-producing areas for the Zambezi River route of trade, which developed in the fourteenth and fifteenth centuries. The ruling Phiri clan of the Malawi empire and of its successor states traced its own origins, as we learned in chapter 6, back to the Luba cultural and political world of the Classic Kisalian Era in Katanga. The Phiri arrived in Malawi in about the fourteenth century, but the unification of the Malawi empire under the over-rule of a single Phiri king, who bore the title Karonga, may not have fully taken place until sometime in the 1400s.

The Malawi empire was a loosely tied-together polity, with a number of titled Phiri acting as subordinate kings in different parts of the empire. In the 1570s and 1580s, one of these kings, bearing the title of Lundu, launched a series of campaigns aimed at gaining control over the lands between his domains, located around the lower Shire River, and the Indian Ocean coastlands north of the Zambezi River. Competition over trade resources, caused by the increased Portuguese presence in the lower Zambezi Valley in the second half of the sixteenth century, played an as yet uncertain role in this upsetting of the balance of power in the region. The Lundu's armies, remembered in the oral traditions and the written sources as the Zimba, rapidly conquered the Makua peoples of the areas between the Shire and the coast. Whether this short-lived empire lasted much beyond the death of the particular Lundu who sent the Zimba out to war is not clear. The leaders of the Zimba forces, however, established lasting chiefdoms and tiny kingdoms in the areas they conquered, and their descendants continued to rule those polities down to the colonial era.

The Early Atlantic Age and Its Effects on Smaller Coastal Polities

The larger kingdoms with direct access to the new coastal commerce tended to remain stoutly independent during the period up to the 1640s, and trade relations perhaps as often as not served to strengthen the hand of the central authority. Only where individual Portuguese adventurers inveigled their way into internal politics, as in the Mutapa kingdom, or where the Portuguese officials were effectively able to ally with one African state against others, as in Angola, did outsiders seriously disrupt the independence of the large states. In the many African coastal areas where much smaller-scale polities predominated, however, a more mixed picture of the effects of early Atlantic trade appears. Strongly contrasting examples of the relation of trade to politics are provided by the Guinea and Gold Coasts of West Africa and by the East African seaboard.

In West Africa along the Gold Coast, the Portuguese began close relations with several tiny states in the 1470s. They initiated one policy in particular that continued to characterize European-Africa relations in that region right down to the nineteenth century: the African governments allowed them to build trading posts in the form of large stone forts ("castles") located next to the seashore in coastal villages, in return for yearly payments of duties and rent. The key point here is that the African states of the coast and its immediate hinterland, tiny as they were, set the terms of this relationship and often continued to do so down to the end of the eighteenth century.

The early important Portuguese "castle" was Elmina. There the African merchants of the late 1400s brought gold from the nearby Akan gold-producing region to trade to the Portuguese. As other Europeans began coming to the West African coast from the 1550s and 1560s onward, new forts were established by the Dutch and English and eventually also by Danes and Germans. Elmina itself eventually fell to the Dutch. In the late fifteenth and early sixteenth centuries, the imports of the coastal towns of the Gold Coast at times included slaves carried by the Portuguese from Kongo, some of whom were apparently put to work mining gold in the interior. In the sixteenth and seventeenth cen-

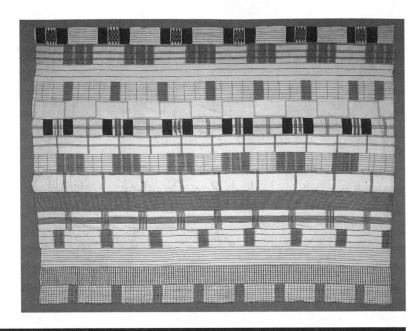

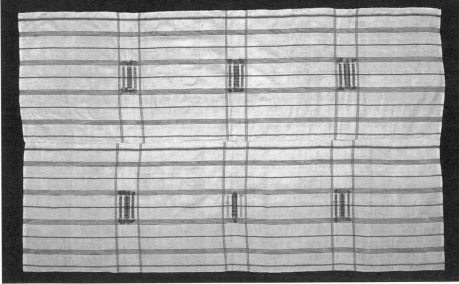

FIG. 66 Cotton cloth

In the period from 1450 to 1640, the long-distance trade of African cotton textiles continued to grow in importance both in West Africa and in the areas all around the lower and middle Zambezi River. The two examples shown here are from, respectively, the Akan people of the West African rainforest zones and the Hausa of the Chad Basin.

turies, cloth manufactured in Benin, as we have already discovered, figured prominently among the imports of the Gold Coast, while slaves became an increasingly important export from the region.

On the Guinea Coast between Senegambia and the Gold Coast, the Portuguese, and other Europeans after them, usually did not establish such permanent bases for trade. More often, they relied instead on sailing their ships to regular anchorages located up the estuaries of the coastal rivers and there engaging in trade with nearby towns and chiefdoms. From the local producers in different parts of this region came variously malagueta pepper, iron, ivory, and tropical woods, such as mahogany, highly valued for making items of furniture in Europe, and cam, which was used to make red dyes. Malagueta pepper, interestingly, had previously become known to southern Europeans as early as the fourteenth century, when it had been traded first by the Susu merchants to the Juula and Jakhanke, who in turn had passed this product across the Sahara to North Africa. From there it was traded across the Mediterranean Sea to the Iberian Peninsula and Italy.

For a long time, the European impact in the internal affairs of the Guinea Coast peoples remained weak, in part because often the lines of trade leading back inland to the Sudan belt still remained more important to the local African communities. An illustration of the continuing importance of this inland orientation is provided by the Gola people, who in the sixteenth century moved to the coast of what is today Liberia, specifically to exploit the salt-making potential of the seaside areas. Salt making was a commercial enterprise whose chief markets lay in the salt-poor Sudan regions of the interior and not at all with the Portuguese or other European visitors to the coast.

The Impact of Seagoing Commerce in Southern Africa

Along the far southern coasts of Africa, no regular trading ports developed before the seventeenth century. Portuguese ships did sometimes stop at one location between Ndongo kingdom and Sofala during years from 1497 to 1510, and that was at Table Bay, at the present site of the city of Cape Town. There they bought meat and water from the pastoral Khoekhoe inhabitants. But a misunderstanding in March of 1510 between the Portuguese and Khoekhoe, neither of whom knew the others' language, brought an end to even this small contact. Thinking themselves cheated, about 150 crewmen from Portuguese ships anchored offshore marched inland to attack a Khoekhoe settlement. A Khoekhoe force estimated at about 170 men showered the Portuguese with arrows and stampeded cattle into their ranks, driving them back to their ships with the loss of 65 Portuguese lives.

The renewal of coastal trade on the far southern shores of Africa did not take place until the 1580s and 1590s, when Dutch, French, and English ships began to stop by at Table Bay, seeking fresh meat and water to replenish their supplies. The long nine-month journey to the East Indies and India from Europe, and the lack of an intermediate stopping place, such as the Portuguese had established for themselves by this time in Mozambique, made this rest stop essential for the crews of the other European nations (see map 21).

Table Bay soon grew into a regular stopover spot for passing European ships, and with that development the economic relationship of the Khoekhoe around the Cape of Good Hope to older trading links with the interior began to change. Previously, the Chochoqua and other Khoekhoe chiefdoms of the southwestern Cape region lay at the farthest end of inland networks. In the early sixteenth century, iron reached them, for instance, from the interior only by being first traded from the Rolong or other Sotho peoples southward to the Khoekhoe of the Orange and Vaal River confluence region; then retraded farther south to Khoekhoe living in the basin of the Sundays River; and finally retraded still again via several other Khoekhoe chiefdoms westward to the Cape. The development of regular commercial relations with Europeans from the early 1580s onward gave the Chochoqua and their neighbors direct access to new commodities, such as copper and glass beads. Able to pass these items inland, they became key suppliers of the interior trade network and no longer marginal and unimportant consumers.

Historians have a clearer idea how this network of inland trade operated in southeastern Africa in the mid-seventeenth century than they do for the sixteenth century. The major, central route of the seventeenth century connected the northern Transvaal with areas along the southern coast of the continent. In the Sundays River region it joined another route that passed between the Cape in the west and the lands of the Nguni peoples in the east. A further north-south route linked the Nama Khoekhoe kingdom in central Namibia with the Khoekhoe of the Cape region to the south and with Angola to the north. Still another route, following the Orange River, connected the central north-south route with the Namibian north-south route.

A variety of goods passed along these trade connections. Copper entered the routes at the north, coming from mines in the northern Transvaal, and also at the south, coming from trade with Europeans at the Cape. Iron was produced in several areas in the southwestern and eastern Transvaal and in a few areas in Natal. Beads, acquired from Portuguese traders in Angola, passed south along the Namibian route and then eastward along the Orange River route into the central parts of the southern African trade network. Marijuana, grown initially in Nguni areas, was carried west along the southern coastal route and northward following the central route. (Just when marijuana reached the continent is unclear, but it probably arrived first in East Africa via the Indian Ocean trade between 800 and 1400.)

This southern African trading system involved no merchant class and only the medium-distance carrying of goods by any single party of people. The commodities of the trade moved from local community to local community through a series of transactions, passing through many hands before reaching the far ends of the network. In some cases, we know that the producers traveled seasonally in small bands as far as 150–200 kilometers away to sell their goods, but that was as far probably as any traders ever took their products themselves.

Even without the development of an actual commercial class of merchants, this trade had important political accompaniments. Because Inqua, a chiefdom of the upper Sundays River region, lay at the juncture of the main central and south coastal trade routes, it grew into the strongest of the Khoekhoe polities of the early seventeenth century, able to send small armies several hundred kilometers away to enforce its commercial interests. Another especially significant Khoekhoe chiefdom, Gqona, lay near the Fish River, at a key crossroads of the movement of cattle traded from the west, iron from the north, and marijuana from the east. (*Gq* in *Gqona* represents a click, an unusual kind of consonant found in Khoisan languages.) The Rolong kingdom, located in the middle areas along the central route, was already important in the fourteenth century, as we saw in chapter 6. It was a significant, but by no means the only, producing area of an important material, iron, the ores of which were not available in many of the Khoekhoe and Nguni areas to the south.

The Impact of the New Seagoing Trade on the Swahili

The experience of the Swahili city-states of the east coast with the commerce of the early Atlantic Age was sharply different from that of the other areas we have been considering. The Swahili towns had already entered into an extended period of economic recession from about the 1420s onward. Considering that the effects were especially visible at Kilwa, which had been the key intermediate entrepot in the shipping of Zimbabwe gold northward, it is hard to avoid concluding that the collapse of the Zimbabwe state in the 1420s or 1430s and the accompanying decline of gold exports via the cities of Great Zimbabwe and Sofala were central factors in bringing about this recession.

When the Portuguese arrived on the Swahili coast at the end of the fifteenth century, they soon took measures aimed at redirecting the trade through their own hands. Already during the first years of the Portuguese presence in the Indian Ocean, from 1497 to the 1520s, this policy led to Portuguese attacks on several city-states. Portugal's particular advantage in these battles was the possession of shipboard cannons, able to bombard a coastal town from a distance, causing death and destruction in the town while minimizing casualties to its own forces. The Swahili towns' disadvantage was that, unlike the towns of the Gold Coast, they were not part and parcel of a larger polity that extended inland, on whom they could draw for military reinforcements, but tended to consist of little more than the town and its immediate environs.

FIG. 67 Swahili chair

This lovely example of Swahili carpentry replicates the style of chair to be found in the houses of the well-to-do merchant upper class of a Swahili city in the seventeenth and eighteenth centuries.

As well, the Swahili townspeople were cut off from strong ties to mainland communities in many cases by their town's location on an island just offshore and also by their own view of themselves as culturally superior to the "barbarians" of those rural societies. The Swahili, who called themselves Waungwana and the rural folk Washenzi ("uncouth people"), have by no means been the only ones in world history to think this way. Townspeople often have held such views, the ancient Greeks and twentieth-century American urban dwellers among them.

In the middle and late sixteenth century, the Portuguese became especially closely involved in the affairs of certain northern Swahili towns, notably Mombasa and Malindi, both located along today's southern Kenyan coast. In the seventeenth century, Mombasa became the home of a Portuguese military fortress bearing, ironically, the name of the "Prince of Peace," Fort Jesus. But although the Portuguese were able to hold Mombasa and exert an intermittent power in several other towns, such as Malindi to the north and Kilwa to the south, most of the numerous Swahili towns remained effectively independent of Portugal. What the Portuguese presence did create for nearly everybody, however, was a long period of commercial and economic uncertainty that did not come to an end until after the fall of Fort Jesus in 1697 (see map 21).

Commerce, Religion, and Political Struggle in Northeastern Africa

Religious Wars and Ethnic Expansion in the Ethiopian Highlands

A third kind of historical experience characterized the portions of the African continent that stretch from the Horn to the Maghrib. Great-power politics in a particularly fifteenth- and sixteenth-century form impinged there from time to time in a variety of ways. The new great power in world history of the fourteenth century was the Ottoman Empire. Under Suleyman the Magnificent and his successors, the Ottoman state extended its rule from Turkey into the Balkans, the Levant, Iraq, Arabia, Egypt, and western North Africa. The expansion of its sea power westward in the Mediterranean was finally halted by the Battle of Lepanto in 1571, but the strength of its land empire remained unassailed right through the seventeenth century.

In the Horn of Africa, the main historical developments between the 1450s and 1640s had deep historical roots in the region. Nevertheless, the rise of Ottoman power to the north, and the establishment of a competing Portuguese sea presence in the Indian Ocean from 1497 onward, had significant implications for the trends of change, as we shall shortly learn. Commercial relations ensured a lively interchange of ideas between the mostly Muslim Middle East of those times and the Muslims of the Horn. In the first half of the fifteenth century, the Christian Church in the Solomonic kingdom of the Ethiopian Highlands had begun to build its own links to Western Christianity, notably by sending observers to the later sessions of the Council of Florence at the beginning of the 1440s. So the courses of events in the Middle East and, to a lesser extent, in southern Europe were not entirely unknown to the better-informed inhabitants of the northern and central parts of the Horn of Africa.

Through the second half of the 1400s, the preeminent position of the Solomonic kingdom in the central and northern Ethiopian Highlands remained mostly unchallenged. One of the more intriguing characters of the period was the Solomonic king, Zar'a Ya'iqob, who ruled from the 1440s to the 1460s and whose career illustrates something of the intellectual as well as the political currents of his time. A pious Christian, Zar'a Ya'iqob himself wrote a number of religious treatises, waged wars against neighboring peoples, and at times followed a policy of forced religious conversions, a practice not unknown but uncommon in the region before that time.

During the first quarter of the sixteenth century, however, new and fundamental challenges to the Solomonic kingdom were taking shape. The most immediate threat came from a new configuration of forces, centered around the tributary state of Adal. The Muslim merchants of Adal, who plied the land routes between the southern interior and the Red Sea coast and who abhorred the duties and more informal exactions laid on their activities by the Solomonic state and its officials, formed one key element. A second element ready to make common cause against Solomonic dominance was the military class within Adal (see map 20).

Two additional elements, a charismatic leader and a source of manpower, then turned a growing sentiment in Adal for change into practical action. In the early and mid-1520s, a young man of charismatic personality known to history as Ahmed Grañ or Ahmed Gurey (the nickname Grañ or Gurey means "left-handed") seized the role of leader in this movement. Beginning as a fervent proselytizer of the cause, he consolidated his position by marrying a daughter of the emir of the Adal army in 1525 and then, in 1527, by proclaiming a jihad against the Solomonic state. Directing his appeal outside Adal's own territories, Ahmed attracted the bulk of his military forces from the camel-raising, Eastern

Cushitic–speaking Afar living to the west of Adal in the Danakil Depression and from the Soomaali of the northeastern areas of Adal itself. In each of these regions, as we learned earlier, Islam had gradually established itself as the religion of the countryside during the previous several centuries. Much more ready for war, as nomads often have been in history, than the peasant farmers who made up the bulk of the population of central Adal, the Afar and Soomaali contingents were combined under Ahmed's leadership into a formidable force. A shared adherence to Islam provided the basis for cooperation among the various groups.

Ahmed sent his army first southward into areas where the Solomonic kingdom's authority was most tenuous—between 1527 and 1529 defeating the Solomonic garrisons of occupation in the territory of Bali and gaining the allegiance of the kingdoms of Dawaro and Hadiya, which had been tributaries of the Solomonic kingdom. In 1529, Ahmed and his forces turned northward and over the next six years marauded stage by stage through the feudal heartlands of the Solomonic state, living off the land and repeatedly destroying monasteries and churches and engaging in the forced conversion of people to Islam. Libna Dingil, the Solomonic king who opposed him, retreated successively farther northward in the face of Ahmed Gurey's advance.

The rise of the Ottoman empire in the fifteenth and early sixteenth centuries clearly had at least an indirect role in helping to inspire the renewed Muslim opposition in Adal to Solomonic over-rule in the early sixteenth century. By around 1540, when the struggle seemed to be reaching a sort of stalemate in the northern Ethiopian Highlands, the Ottomans responded to the appeals of their co-religionist Ahmed Gurey in a more practical way, by sending a contingent of musketeers to help him. The Portuguese, by this point also involved in the region because of their Indian Ocean trade interests, reacted by sending a similar body of musketeers in 1542 to help out the beleaguered Solomonic armies.

What then happened had little to do with guns, but a lot to do with a shift in morale and leadership. The arrival of the Portuguese soldiers, we suspect, gave the Solomonic forces a sense that they were not alone in their battles and that fellow Christians supported them. At the same time, an energetic son of Libna Dingil, Galawdewos, took over the effective command of the kingdom. In early 1543, his forces soundly defeated Ahmed Gurey's army, in the process killing Ahmed himself. Almost immediately the jihad, after sixteen years of successful warfare, collapsed, and over the next decade Galawdewos reestablished

Solomonic rule over most of its old territories, except those in the far southeast. The Adal state appears to have so overextended itself in the wars that it ceased to be a major factor any longer and declined over the next century into a small and unimportant kingdom.

The psychological and physical toll of a decade and a half of repeated unpredictable military disruptions of peasant livelihood in the central and northern Ethiopian Highlands and of forced, if only temporary, conversion was surely very great. In some areas, the credibility and legitimacy of Solomonic rule in the eyes of the populace must have been fatally weakened. The Portuguese became a further potential element of discord. Taking advantage of the favor with which they were now viewed by many in the Ethiopian Christian ruling class, they launched a period of Catholic missionary activity, aimed at converting Ethiopians to what the Portuguese considered the right kind of Christianity.

But a much greater potential danger to the state and to the feudal system came from a rising new factor in the south, the Oromo. Cattle-raising pastoralists who had lived in Bali on the edges of the Solomonic empire in the fifteenth century, they took advantage of the disruptions of the wars of Ahmed Gurey to begin expanding their pastures, first more widely in Bali in the 1530s and then, in the wake of the collapse of the Adal army, settling in among the peasant populations of Showa to the west of the Ethiopian Rift Valley. Over the course of the second half of the 1500s, many of the Oromo spread their sway over large areas of the south-central Ethiopian Highlands, while others began to filter north into the territories of Adal, contributing to the rapid decline of that kingdom, and also into the highland areas on the western slopes of the Danakil Depression.

In each of these regions, the local peoples soon began to adopt Oromo ethnicity as their own. The expansion of Oromo culture and ethnicity was especially rapid around the southern fringes of the old Solomonic state, where Solomonic rule had been weakest. Not only did the Oromo offer an alternative worldview to replace the seemingly failed feudal, Christian vision, but their worldview encapsulated a more democratic view of politics, in which at least all the males had the possibility of participating, through the *gada* (age-grade) system, in the governance of their society. They were no longer mere subjects owing feudal duties to a ruling lord. In the Oromo economy, a family's household production, once people had been fully assimilated into the Oromo society, was entirely their own to dispose of as they wished and needed. As Oromo society expanded by absorbing the peasant majority already inhabiting the new lands into which they moved, the Oromo economy came less and less to rely on pastoralism and more and more to be founded on the cereal and plow agriculture anciently established among the forebears of the newly recruited members of their society (see map 20).

In the west this Oromo expansion pressed hard upon the lands of a number of small Omotic sacral kingdoms, some of which continued to maintain their existence as late as the nineteenth century despite being increasingly surrounded on almost all sides by Oromo people. One of the intriguing sidelights of this history is the extent to which some of these states, which had not been attacked during Ahmed Gurey's wars, continued to recognize the over-rule of the Solomonic state right into the early seventeenth century, even though separated from that kingdom by a wide band of Oromo-controlled land. Merchants, officials, and churchmen, accompanied by armed escorts, could and did continue to travel from the main Solomonic domains to these small states and as far south as the major Omotic kingdom of Kafa as late as the 1620s.

In the 1630s these relations came finally to an end. The southern territories began to be too difficult to hold militarily any longer. Already from the late sixteenth century onward, a new direction of expansion of the Christian feudal culture and of the Amharic language, into the formerly Agaw areas all around Lake Tana, had begun to predominate.

Within the established domains of the Solomonic kingdom, a long-brewing religious crisis, engendered by the Portuguese presence, also came to a head at the beginning of the 1630s, when it became evident that the king, Susenyos (1607–1632), had adopted Catholicism and wished to spread that version of Christianity in his country. In the resulting civil strife, Susenyos was forced to abdicate in 1632 in favor of his son, Fasiladas.

Fasiladas then expelled the Portuguese entirely from his domains and in 1636 took the step, momentous in retrospect, of bringing to an end the era of wandering capitals: he established a permanent capital city for the Solomonic state at Gondar on the north side of Lake Tana. Essentially, Fasiladas wrote off the old southern territories of the kingdom, and by establishing a fixed capital, he lost for future kings the ability to keep a tight rein on distant provinces. No longer could a king bring to bear the threat of moving the whole court and the army into such a region. Thus began an era, called by Ethiopian historians the

FIG. 68 Ethiopian silver cross

This fine example, ca. seventeenth or eighteenth century, is about 25 centimeters high. Crosses of this kind were often carried on staffs in ceremonies of the Ethiopian Christian Church.

Era of the Princes (Zamana Masafint), in which the great regional lords of the Solomonic kingdom became increasingly autonomous rulers, and feudal decentralization set in with a vengeance.

The Ajuraan State: Religion and Commerce in the Eastern Horn

To the east of the Ethiopian Highlands, the period from 1450 to 1640 seems to have been a time of the development of new and deeper ties between the city-states of the coast and the Soomaali-speaking interior. In the lands surrounding the middle and lower Shebeelle and Jubba Rivers, this development had a political dimension. There the first territorial state we know of in the eastern Horn, the Ajuraan imamate, prospered from the fifteenth century until the early seventeenth century, when it declined in power and then came to an end. The material basis of this state seems to have rested specifically on its control and support of interior commerce. The Ajuraan are remembered especially for having built large wells along the trade routes, and they established and maintained close cooperative ties with coastal city-states, mostly notably with Muqdisho (Mogadisho), through which the exports of the interior and the imports of the Indian Ocean had to pass.

The Ajuraan state was theocratic in conception. Its rulers sought legitimization not in the older Cushitic institutions of cultural life but in a growing adherence to Islam among the various Soomaali peoples of the region between the Shebeelle and Jubba Rivers. To that end, they claimed for themselves the Muslim religious role of *imam,* taking neither an indigenous Soomaali clan-chief title, such as *waab* or *waber,* nor a foreign royal title, such as *sultan.*

Northern Africa and the Sahara

In the fifteenth century the division of much of North Africa into a large number of separate polities continued, as had been true ever since the decline of the Almohads after the twelfth century. The Ottoman Empire in the early sixteenth century then radically changed that situation. First the Ottomans seized Egypt, bringing an end to the Mamluk regime by 1517. They then turned their attentions farther west, initially establishing their control over key port towns and cities as far west as present-day western Algeria. In the 1570s, as the Europeans began to be successful in turning back Ottoman naval dominance in the Mediterranean, the agents of Turkish rule expanded their influence into the inland areas of North Africa (see map 20).

To the west of Algeria, in Morocco, the pressure of the Ottomans from the east and recurrent Spanish and Portuguese attacks in the sixteenth century stimulated the rise of a coordinated opposition, headed by leaders of the Sa'idi clan, who claimed descent from the prophet Muhammad. Between 1515 and 1550 these leaders progressively expanded their power northward out of their own lands, located on the desert side of the Atlas Mountains, until they had established a loose authority over the whole of the Moroccan region. The major sixteenth-century figure in this new political configuration was Ahmad al-Mansur. He strengthened his power after coming to the throne in 1578 by hiring Turkish and European soldiers and recruiting slave soldiers from south of the Sahara. The event of his reign most momentous for wider African history was his sending of a mercenary army south across the desert to the Bend of the Niger in 1591. Here this army, as we learned earlier in the chapter, brought an end to a Songay empire probably already in terminal decline. After Mansur's death in 1603, the fragile unity he had presided over rapidly broke down.

South of Morocco, in the desert steppes of the far western Sahara, a major ethnic transition began in these centuries. There a collection of pastoral Arab clans and lineages, the Hasaniya, whose putative ancestors had come into the Moroccan regions around the time of the Hillalian Bedouin expansion in the eleventh century (see chapter 7), gradually spread out more widely to the south at the expense of their Znaga and other Berber neighbors. Over the longer term the pressures of this expansion, often strongly backed by claims of noble Arab ancestry and Muslim religious authority, led to the progressive Arabization, at least in language, of the local nomadic populations across most of the region. That process has continued down to the present day. In the central Sahara and around the Bend of the Niger, and in the Atlas Mountains of Morocco, however, a wide variety of Berber peoples continued strongly to maintain their languages and their distinct social and cultural identities (see map 20).

History in the Eastern and Central Sudan, 1450–1640

Commercial and Political Change in the Eastern Sudan Region

To the west of the Ethiopian Highlands, the northern half of the Middle Nile Basin began the fifteenth century as a land of small states, mostly of the Sudanic sacral variety, interspersed with peoples who recognized no higher unity than their local set of small communities. A variety of Eastern Sahelian languages were spoken among the kingdoms. Along the Nile itself the prevailing languages were Nubian, and many of the inhabitants were still Christian in religion. Among the communities that stood politically outside the small kingdoms was a newer ethnic element, Arab camel-raising nomads. Passing south from Egypt along the west side of the Red Sea hills, they found the sparsely inhabited, very dry steppes just south of the Sahara desert to be admirably suited to their camels. In the southern Red Sea hills, the Hadariba, a loose confederation of Beja groups, had established their authority over the movement of trade goods between the Nile and the Red Sea in the fourteenth century, after the breakup of Nobadia and Alodia, and they maintained their commercial preeminence well into the fifteenth century.

In the late fifteenth and early sixteenth centuries, however, a decisive change in the economic balance of power took place, shifting the power back to the peoples living along the Nile and culminating in 1504 in the founding of the kingdom of Sinnar. At Sinnar's height of power in the early and middle sixteenth century, its territories extended to the Dongola Reach on the north. On the south, its political hegemony stretched up the Abbai River to the edge of the Ethiopian Highlands and southward up the Nile River almost as far as the Sudd region. On the west, the Nuba Mountain region seems to have also been part of the areas subjugated by the Funj rulers. The capital city of Sinnar, from which we take the name of the kingdom, lay along the Abbai River, 300 kilometers upstream from the confluence of the Abbai and the Nile.

The establishment of the Sinnar kingdom consolidated a major cultural shift as well. Its founding king, Amara Dungas, seems most probably to have been of Nubian background, and there is evidence to suggest that he began life as a Christian. But the world with which he had to deal was one in which the major intrusive and potentially quite disruptive element, found here and there all across his northern domains, consisted of nomadic Muslim Arabs. It was also one in which foreign commerce, a major source of the kingdom's wealth, was in the hands of local Muslim merchants and passed through the country of the Beja, by then Muslim, too, in religion, to reach the Red Sea. From there other Muslim merchants carried the goods of the trade to and from the Ottoman Empire to the north and the Indian Ocean sea lanes to the east. The connections important for the future maintenance of Amara Dungas's conquests would be better served by his adopting Islam, and this he did. Christianity continued to be practiced by a declining minority of people along the Nile for another 200 years, but eventually died out there (see map 20).

In other respects, the society of the Sinnar kingdom preserved practices that reveal the Sudanic sacral roots of its political culture. The idea of burying servants with the dead king had, of course, been dropped in the region with the coming of Christianity to the early Nubian kingdoms in the sixth century. But the king in Sinnar still held court behind a screen, hidden from the view of his subjects. He was not supposed to be seen eating or drinking or performing other mere mortal activities. An elaborate hierarchy of officials, as was typical of other large Sudanic sacral states, mediated between the king and his subjects.

The most fascinating aspect of Sinnar politics was the system by which the kings sought to hold the loyalty of the provinces. The provincial rulers were required to marry women of the royal family, who could thus act as the eyes and ears of the central government in the provincial centers of authority. In addition, the sons of these wives, who were expected to inherit the provincial posts after their fathers' deaths, were sent to the court of the king to be brought up there.

A thousand kilometers to the west of Sinnar, around the Marra Mountains, lay another large sixteenth-century state, Tunjur. We suspect it to have been a Sudanic sacral polity like the Funj kingdom of Sinnar, but we know almost nothing about it, even its precise dates. It was founded probably around the fourteenth or fifteenth century, after the political power of the Daju had declined in those areas. In the seventeenth century, the Tunjur state was itself replaced by the Darfur kingdom of the Keira, about which we will learn more in chapter 9.

To the south of Sinnar, two major sets of changes, involving respectively the Ocholo and Jyang (Dinka) peoples of the Western Nilotic group of Eastern Sahelian peoples, characterized the period from the sixteenth century onward. In these regions none of the developments associated with the northern Middle Nile took place. Merchant-based commerce touched only the northern periphery of the Ocholo and Jyang countries. Arabic language and Islamic religion would have no roles to play until the nineteenth century. Instead, the old Sudanic religion remained a powerful influence on people's lives (and continued to do so right into the twentieth century, in fact), and many of the old ways of Sudanic civilization continued, often little changed.

Along the Nile between the southern boundaries of the Sinnar kingdom and the Nile's confluence with the Bahr-al-Ghazal, the Ocholo kings united a string of Luo-speaking communities settled in the region since around the fourteenth century. The power and influence of the kings in Ocholo society rested on their highly ritualized position as Sudanic sacral rulers. The Ocholo engaged at different times in both trading with Sinnar and raiding its southern marches. Fishing was a major occupation of the Ocholo villages and towns, because of their location right along the Nile, and cattle raising and the cultivation of grains and other crops provided for a varied diet.

A sharply different social historical picture is presented by the related Jyang (Dinka) people, who resided to the east of the Ocholo in the sixteenth century. Entirely without hereditary leaders, the Jyang, besides fishing and cultivating sorghum and other grains, raised large herds of cattle, an animal highly esteemed in their society. In the seventeenth century, they entered into a two-century-long period of successive expansions southward across the seasonally flooded plains of the southern Middle Nile Basin, or Sudd region as it is also

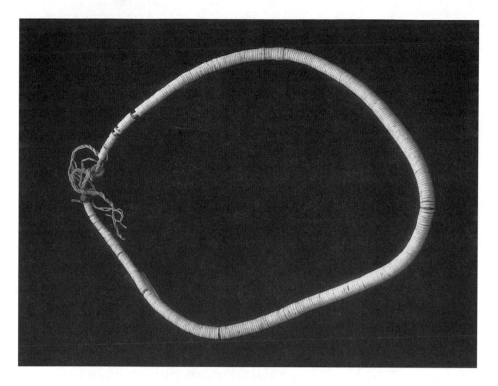

FIG. 69 Ocholo ostrich-eggshell bead necklace

The Ocholo people lived along the Nile south of the Sinnar kingdom in the sixteenth to eighteenth centuries and belonged to a kingdom often at odds with Sinnar and just as often involved in trade with that state. The use of ostrich eggs in the making of beads goes back many thousands of years in the steppes and drier savanna areas of Africa. Not only the very early peoples of Khoisan civilization but peoples of Sudanic civilization as well valued the hard, yet easily shaped, ivory-colored shell of this kind of egg.

called. Here their expansions incorporated into Jyang society the closely related Luo peoples previously inhabiting the region (see map 20).

Borno in the History of the Chad Basin

Far to the west of the Middle Nile Basin, in the central parts of the Sudan belt, the fifteenth century was a period of political fragmentation. The Kanem empire contracted to a small state under the attacks of pastoral societies on the fringe of the Sahara such as the Bulala and the Zaghawa. To the west of Lake Chad lay the lands of the numerous Hausa city-states. To the south of the lake, the Chadic peoples of that region had probably never been organized into states, although some had previously recognized the distant authority of the Kanem kings. Farther to the east of Lake Chad, in Wadai, small-scale Sudanic sacral kingships probably existed, but about them we have as yet no solid historical information at all.

In the sixteenth century, the ruling Sefawa dynasty of Kanem reasserted itself, but in a new region, Borno, located on the western and northwestern side of Lake Chad. By shifting the center of their authority to the west of the lake, these kings consolidated their rule away from the disruptive political struggles that still characterized the areas east of the lake. Initially, the Borno kingdom grew slowly through the gradual incorporation of Chadic peoples into its society. The kings used the same kinds of social and economic tools as their forebears in earlier Kanem to more fully incorporate new areas into the state: they granted land holdings to those who had fought with them in conquering new areas, and in this way they built up a class of landed nobility.

From one point of view, what the kings created in Borno was very much like a feudal system. The landed stratum formed a military class, the owners of horses and quilted armor, and owed military service as the price of their having been granted fiefs. But Borno was also very much a slaveholding society. More than perhaps any other sub-Saharan African state of its time, except perhaps Jolof, Borno prospered from trading human beings to North Africa. The kings of Borno, called *mai,* built up an army that included slave military forces, and they quite often assigned the governorship of the most insecure province, on the northwest bordering the Sahara desert, to a trusted royal slave.

The wars of the *mai* Idris Alauma, whose rule covered the last third of the sixteenth century, rebuilt Borno into a modestly large empire. His armies brought the salt mines of Bilma in the Sahara under his rule. To the west they battled with some of the Hausa city-states; on the east his forces attacked the Bulala and other areas and peoples beyond Lake Chad. Alauma also established strong diplomatic relations and commercial relations across the Sahara with Ottoman North Africa. The trans-Saharan trade in kola and slaves to the Ottoman Turkish rulers of Tripoli brought him in return muskets, which he then used in further conquests and in the capture of more slaves to be traded for more muskets. His wars, in fact, involved the first really extensive use of guns by a sub-Saharan African army.

Of newly growing importance in the time of Alauma was a new route for the Muslim pilgrimage to Mecca. African pilgrims no longer had to pass across the central Sahara, as "Mansa Musa" of Mali had in the fourteenth century, and follow the Mediterranean routes to Arabia. Now they began to travel eastward right across the Sudan belt all the way to Sinnar and the Red Sea, where they then boarded ships for the short crossing to Arabia. For the first time the kind of east-west routes of commerce and movement of people that had long been well developed in the western Sudan belt began to link the Chad and Middle Nile Basins. In a way that was not at all linked to Atlantic commerce, another part of the African continent came to be tied into the emerging interconnections of world economic and social history (see map 20).

History in the African Interior, 1450–1640

Thus far we have looked principally at the parts of the African continent where, from 1450 to 1640, commercial connections with the Europeans or with the Muslim world of the southern Mediterranean and the Middle East had a significant role in historical change. All across the heart of the continent, however, lay regions in which the course of history was little affected, if at all, by these links. Some regions were the scenes of new eras of state building. In other areas, small-scale institutions of governance continued to predominate. Nevertheless, two major spheres of historical interchange in this period can be discerned, tied together by the trans-regional flow of people and ideas. One such sphere stretched from the Western Nilotic peoples of the southern Middle Nile Basin to the Bantu peoples of the Great Lakes region in the south; the other, from the western side of Lake Tanganyika to Angola in the far west.

Cattle Keeping, Farming, and Political History in the Great Lakes

In the far southern Middle Nile Basin, a considerable rearrangement of three Western Nilotic peoples and their languages and cultures was underway in the fifteenth century. Across the flat, seasonally flooded, middle areas of the region, south and east of the confluence of the Nile River and the Bahr-al-Ghazal, the early stages of the expansion of the Jyang (Dinka) were taking place. At the same time, the numerous communities of the Luo society, who inhabited much of the southern half of this zone, were themselves moving out into new areas, especially farther south, to the land called Pabungu in Luo oral tradition, located in the far north of today's Uganda. There the Luo began a long period of interaction with the Madi, a Central Sudanic people of that area, and also with the Ateker, an Eastern Nilotic people. In the late 1400s and early 1500s, the Luo immigration spilled over farther southward, into the northwestern part of the Great Lakes region, with consequences to which we will shortly return.

In the western Great Lakes area, as we learned in chapter 6, one or more states, the most notable being Kitara, had emerged sometime before 1400. In the early fifteenth century, this state fell apart, for reasons not yet understood by historians. In the interregnum of perhaps two generations that followed Kitara's collapse, a large number of aspiring princes spread far south through the region establishing new dynasties, sometimes taking over previously existing tiny kingdoms and sometimes establishing new states. Through political maneuvering wholly unclear to us, because its story remains shrouded in legend and mythological idioms, the leader of an intrusive Luo clan from Pabungu, the Bito, successfully laid claim in the later fifteenth century to the kingship of the lapsed Kitara state and brought into being the successor state of Bunyoro. In the sixteenth century, the Bito kings of Bunyoro ruled over a territory that included all of western, central, and southeastern Uganda. They held direct sway over a large central territory, claimed tribute from a great number of smaller states located around the south and east of that territory, and on occasion launched great cattle raids as far south as Rwanda. The several leading provincial chiefs of the kingdom owed their positions to the king, who granted them estates and required them to maintain houses at the capital.

The central element in Bunyoro's material basis, as it had been for Kitara, was the royal possession of great herds of cattle and the king's role as the redistributor of cattle captured in war or paid as court fines for transgressions of the laws. But Bunyoro, like Kitara before it, also included important iron-producing areas and incorporated some of the key salt-producing sites of the Western Rift region in its territories. In the sixteenth and seventeenth centuries, a variety of regular markets had apparently developed in Bunyoro, through which passed the products of many parts of the Great Lakes region—to name a few, barkcloth and banana flour from the then tiny and tributary kingdom of Buganda along Lake Nyanza and from its neighbors, dried fish from several lakeside areas, sorghum and sesame from the southwestern grasslands of Bunyoro, and, of course, salt and iron goods. The traders at these emporiums were not full-time professional merchants, but rather people who marketed the commodities that they themselves or their friends and neighbors produced.

South of Bunyoro, a large number of small states occupied the lands that today constitute Rwanda, Burundi, and far northwestern Tanzania. There, as in Bunyoro, two economies coexisted, one practiced by the majority of the population and emphasizing the production of crops, and the other practiced by a minority of the population and centered around cattle raising. In Bunyoro, the ideological identification of the king as belonging to the cultivating majority, the BaIru, checked the tendencies of the cattle-raising specialists, the BaHima, to evolve into a distinct nobility. In contrast, to the south of Bunyoro, no such check on the conversion of pastoral wealth into political power existed (see map 21).

In consequence, from about the fifteenth century onward, the cattle specialists in Rwanda and Burundi, called in those regions the BaTutsi, engaged in wars that gradually built up several states ruled by BaTutsi kings. By the early seventeenth century, these included the then still relatively small kingdoms of Rwanda, Gisaka, and Burundi. In these particular states there evolved a social system that divided the population into a distinct noble class of BaTutsi, who in theory owned all the cattle and held the key chiefships and the kingship, and a class of BaHutu cultivators, who owned feudal duties and service to their BaTutsi overlords. In time, as these relations solidified and a supporting ideology was established, the class differences grew into distinctions of caste.

A third caste, very small in number, comprised the BaTwa, the descendants of the forest gatherer-hunters who had lived in the Western Rift region before the arrival of the Mashariki Bantu around 1000 BCE. In keeping with the productive distinctions assigned by custom and ideology to the BaTutsi (cattle owners) and BaHutu (cultivators), the BaTwa were relegated to non-food-producing activities, such as hunting and pot making.

East of the Great Lakes: Changing Livelihoods in Small-Scale Communities

Between the east side of Lake Nyanza and the East African coast lay a region in which social and political history followed quite different paths from those of the Great Lakes region. Instead, the societies that most influenced the directions of historical change followed belief systems and had institutions that generally resisted the creation of states. Age-grades and age-sets provided the social and political framework in many areas, and agricultural elaboration and the opening of new lands to cultivation or to livestock raising were important themes. It is a complex history to which we cannot do justice in a general civilization text, but we can at least cover a few examples to show how varied this historical experience was.

The characteristic development of the middle parts of East Africa was the expansion of the Maasai people into successively wider areas. As we discovered in chapter 6, the ancestors of the Maasai, the Maa (not to be confused with the Southern Cushitic Ma'a people), occupied the plateau grasslands just north of Mount Kenya in the first half of the second millennium. The initial spread of the Maasai into the Eastern Rift areas of central Kenya took place in the sixteenth century. By the later sixteenth century, several Maasai communities had expanded farther south, into the extensive grazing lands around Mount Kilimanjaro. In the early seventeenth century other Maasai were pressing into parts of the Mau Range and into the vast Mara Plains south of the Mau Range. In the heart of these areas, the earlier established Kalenjin communities gave way before the Maasai expansion, in most cases eventually adopting Maasai ethnicity and being absorbed into Maasai society.

One Kalenjin people, the Sirikwa, followed a historical path similar to that of the Maasai, spreading out as specialized cattle raisers across the Uasingishu Plain in the sixteenth century. In the rest of the Kalenjin-speaking regions of western Kenya, however, a gradual and slow expansion of farming took place between the middle of the fifteenth century and the middle of the sixteenth century, as new areas of forest were cleared back for fields. The most interesting problem for historians is posed by the Marakwet communities who lived along the western slopes of the Kerio River Valley. Well before 1500, they had already begun to build elaborate terraced field and irrigation works strongly reminiscent of the Highland Eastern Cushitic agriculture of the Ethiopian Rift Valley. Do these works go back to a much earlier period of Cushitic influences in Kenya, or did a separate invention of this kind of farming take place here? This is another of those questions that historians in the future will need to answer.

A hundred kilometers to the west of the Kerio Valley, the areas around Mount Elgon became the scene of a long-term encounter of peoples of strikingly different cultural backgrounds. A varied array of Luyia peoples, whose historical roots in part trace back to the Lakes Bantu of the late first millennium BCE, gradually became the predominant population to the west and south of Elgon. All along, however, erstwhile Kalenjin peoples continued to be assimilated into the Luyia communities, and this Kalenjin element provided another important portion of the Luyia ancestry.

FIG. 70 Maasai spear and shield

The Maasai, living in the sixteenth and seventeenth centuries along the Kenya Rift Valley, used age-grade systems to organize themselves for military action to an extent unparalleled previously in eastern Africa. They fashioned a particular style of large, oval-shaped leather shield (a style they had earlier adopted from their Southern Nilotic neighbors), and their blacksmiths, who belonged to an occupational caste separate from the rest of the society, forged finely balanced spears, with large steel blades and sharp steel spikes at the butt end.

Because of this history, a mix of cultural traditions arose among the Luyia. In clan governance, the office of *mwami*, the old Mashariki clan head, persisted. As the recognized head of a local collection of clans, and having a ritual role but little effective political authority, the Luyia *mwami* seems to have maintained much the sort of position that the *mwami* would have held in the early Mashariki society, 2,500 years earlier. Most Luyia communities continued to follow the old Mashariki customs of circumcising boys and initiating them into linear age-sets. But several of the Luyia peoples most deeply influenced by Kalenjin ideas added the custom of clitoridectomy for girls, and by the mid-seventeenth century, a few of these groups were starting to adopt in toto the Kalenjin cycling age-set system. Religious ideas spread both directions. Many of the Kalenjin added the concept of ancestor spirits to their Sudanic religion, while the Luyia religion took up a more Sudanic view of God, or Divinity, as a salient force in human life.

At the same period, a variety of agricultural changes seem to have been underway. The most significant of these—the development among the Luyia and Kalenjin who lived on the slopes of Mount Elgon of a banana-based highland agriculture—actually had already begun to take shape by the thirteenth century. This agriculture differed from that of the contemporary Chaga in its dependence on rainfall rather than irrigation and in its heavier reliance on a variety of subsidiary crops, such as grains, yams, and beans of several kinds. Intensive banana growing then spread west as early as perhaps the fourteenth century into the areas along the northern and northwestern shores of Lake Nyanza. There the creation of a heavily banana-based agriculture among the BaGanda people in the fifteenth and sixteenth centuries allowed a considerable growth of population densities to take place and laid the productive basis for the subsequent rise of the Buganda kingdom (of which we will learn more in chapter 9).

In the later sixteenth century, a new ethnic complication, the arrival of Luo immigrants from Pabungu, began to affect developments south of Mount Elgon along the northeastern shores of Lake Nyanza. Additional Luo settlers from Pabungu continued to filter into the region all through the seventeenth century, gradually assimilating various communities previously Luyia in language.

On the other side of the Eastern Rift, in the Eastern Highlands of Kenya, pressures on land seemed to have been an important factor among the various Thagiicu societies of the southern slopes of Mount Kenya. Intercropping and the extending of forest clearance higher up the mountain were two important responses to feeding the growing farming populations of that region. Inter-cropping is a technique of planting different crops interspersed with each other in the same fields. In this way nitrogen-fixing plants, such as beans, can grow next to grain crops or yams and replenish the soil fertility that the other crops tend to use up.

Another response to the land pressures in this region was for whole communities to move into new areas of settlement. The Gikuyu first emerged in the sixteenth century as a distinctive Thagiicu society because they spread south into the then still heavily forested eastern slopes of the Nyandarua Range, just southwest of Mount Kenya. These lands had previously been occupied only by the forest gatherer-hunter people, the Okiek (called Athi in the Gikuyu language). Other Thagiicu communities moved entirely away from Mount Kenya in the period of the fifteenth to seventeenth centuries, some to the Taita Hills and the Pare Mountains, and others as far away as the Usambara Mountains of modern-day far northeast Tanzania and the hinterland of the Kenya coast. One Thagiicu people, the Kamba, shifted to a more strongly pastoral economy and moved in the fifteenth century from the southern Mount Kenya areas to the grasslands on the lower slopes of Mount Kilimanjaro, 200 kilometers to the south.

On Kilimanjaro and in the Pare Mountains, the successful, slow expansion of the irrigated, banana-based highland planting agriculture of the Chaga and the Asu continued to take place at mid-millennium. In North Pare, the era of the WaShana kings came to a close around the early sixteenth century. Their replacement by a new line of kings ushered in a new period in the political history of the Ugweno kingdom. But even though the WaShana era was over, iron resources continued to be a key element in the material power of the Ugweno state.

One large area of eastern Africa, the region south of the Jubba River, underwent considerable turmoil in the sixteenth century. In the second half of the century, a southern offshoot of the Oromo people, who played so prominent a role in Ethiopian Highland history at this time, invaded the whole region between the Jubba and Tana Rivers, displacing or absorbing the previously dominant population, the Garree. In the same decades, Segeju immigrants from eastern Mount Kenya moved into the immediate hinterland of the coast south of the Tana, where they fought a series of wars with the established Mijikenda communities of that region. (You may have recognized that Segeju is a version of the old ethnic name of the Mount Kenya Bantu people, Thagiicu.) In the late sixteenth and early seventeenth centuries, the Oromo extended their settlements south of the Tana, moving into the dry interior behind the Kenya coast and from time to time raiding Mijikenda peoples nearer the coast.

The upshot of all this turmoil was that, by the first half of the seventeenth century, Oromo cattle and camel raisers controlled much of the lowland areas around and east of the Tana River. A rearrangement of Mijikenda society took place as refugees from north of the Tana were absorbed into their communities. Gradually, too, a peaceful assimilation of the once disruptive Segeju into the Mijikenda cultural world took place.

Farther south, all across central and western Tanzania, the period from the 1440s through the seventeenth century was a time of many small expansions of Bantu cultivating communities into drier lands. The Iringa Southern Cushites of the Southern Highlands of Tanzania and the Kw'adza Southern Cushites of the dry savannas to the north of the Southern Highlands both began to be assimilated into these expanding communities. In western Tanzania, the spread of the Takama Bantu peoples led to the clearing of lands still at that time occupied only by Khoisan gatherer-hunters. In several parts of western Tanzania, the farmers developed the technique of systematically burning back the brush in the dry season to remove the kind of environments that harbored tsetse flies. In this way, they created conditions that allowed them to begin raising cattle in significant numbers (see map 21).

In the Southern Highlands of Tanzania, just north of Lake Nyasa, the growth of overall population in this period stimulated new agricultural innovations. Among these were green manuring methods, by which plants that were known to be rich in nutrients needed by food crops were hoed into the soil before replanting the field with a new crop. Intensive banana cultivation, mixed in some areas with extensive cattle raising, also took hold before the end of this period in several of the wetter parts of the Southern Highlands.

An Era of Political Transition: The Southern Savannas, 1450–1580

A second sphere of far-flung political and cultural diffusion that owed little or nothing to outside influences stretched across the southern savannas to the west of southern Lake Tanganyika. In the east of this zone, the Luba peoples resided. Their ideas and institutions played a key creative role in the spread and development of new political and cultural institutions. In the west, it was the Lunda (Rund) who fulfilled this kind of role.

For the southern savanna belt, the fifteenth and sixteenth centuries were a transitional period, marked by wide-ranging movements and resettlements of aspiring chiefly families. In and around the Upemba Depression and the upper Lualaba River, the Kisalian era and the first large Luba state had come to an end probably before 1450. Between then and the early 1600s, it seems probable that a number of smaller Luba states and statelets occupied the region.

In the Nkalaany Valley, no large state yet existed in the fifteenth century as far as historians presently know. Instead, the small Tubungu kingdoms divided up the Lunda-speaking region. The mid- and late fifteenth century was a time of political conflict among these statelets. The evidence that has come down to us from that period tends to collapse together the events from the mid-fifteenth century to the end of the sixteenth century into one epic tale of queens and kings, so our reconstruction of the period remains highly problematic. Among the features of this history was the fifteenth- or sixteenth-century movement into the Nkalaany Valley of men of Luba chiefly ancestry, who may or may not have set off the disruptions in the first place. The upshot of these events was the emergence of the first large state of the region, the Rund kingdom, in the late sixteenth and early seventeenth centuries.

At least two kings, whose ruling titles were Kinguli (or Chinguli) and Chinyama, migrated away from the regions near the Inkalanyi Valley, perhaps sometime around the second half of the fifteenth century, taking their followers with them. The problem of whether or not these two royal titles may have been part of the Tubungu system has been a contentious issue for historians. In recent Rund (Lunda) kingdom traditions, the Kinguli and Chinyama both have been considered to be Tubungu kings who lost out in the struggles to form the Rund state. Their stories, however, do not form an original part of the Rund oral history but appear to have been grafted onto those traditions, probably in the eighteenth or early nineteenth century. Prior to that time, the Rund, Kinguli, and Chinyama traditions, it is now believed, had been separately preserved oral histories that did not directly mention each other (see map 21).

Nevertheless two salient bits of evidence suggest that Kinguli and Chinyama titles, like the Rund kingship, did at least originate in the same cultural world as the Tubungu kingdoms of the pre-Rund era. One indication that the Kinguli and Chinyama titles derived from the same earlier cultural milieu as the Rund kings is the diffusion of a common verb, "to pay tribute," *-lambula, throughout the regions ruled or culturally influenced by each. The second was their common sharing of the unique political idea of perpetual kinship. In the political ideology of perpetual kinship, the rulers' legitimacy came from their being able to successfully lay claim to particular political titles that were considered to be related, or kin, to each other. Kinguli and Chinyama were two early titles of this kind, held by several successive rulers whose individual names have been forgotten. A new title could be created and taken to new areas, but it attained legitimacy only if its holder could successfully claim that the founding titleholder was a brother or nephew or other kinsperson of some already established titleholder. The new titles then came themselves to be understood symbolically as the brothers or nephews or the like of other, older titles. By succeeding to a particular title, a king or chief was considered to take on the role of a brother or nephew or uncle to the holders of other titles. Generation after generation, this metaphorical relationship, once established, would continue to be recognized.

The Kinguli title, when it first comes into historical knowledge, applied to kings ruling in the upper Kwango River region, just east of the Matamba kingdom and more than 300 kilometers west of the Nkalaany Valley. The followers of the Kinguli may have been the Jaga invaders of the kingdom of Kongo in 1569. In the last quarter of the sixteenth century, a new title, Kasanje, replaced Kinguli, and the holders of the Kasanje title then built up the Imbangala kingdom along the upper Kwango. The role of this kingdom and its important relations with the Portuguese in the early seventeenth century have already been discussed previously in this chapter.

The first Chinyama, in contrast, moved south into the upper Zambezi region. His descendants did not set up a lasting powerful state. Nonetheless, the influence of the Chinyamas on the surrounding areas must have been great. The Chinyama title itself, we think, continued to be passed down from uncle to maternal nephew for about a century and a half, from approximately the late fifteenth century to the early seventeenth century. The prestige of the title was such that, right up to the twentieth century, most of the chiefs and kings of the upper and middle Zambezi had to claim a historical relationship to the Chinyama in order to legitimize their own positions.

An Era of Large Kingdoms Begins: The Southern Savannas, 1580–1640

The late sixteenth and early seventeenth centuries marked the beginning of a new era of larger states in the central parts of the southern savanna belt (see map 21). To the immediate west of the Upemba Depression, a new Luba kingdom emerged in the seventeenth century and laid the political foundations on which the Luba empire of the eighteenth and nineteenth centuries would be built (see chapter 9). One of the social changes that may belong to this period was a shift from matrilineal to patrilineal reckoning of descent in the central areas of the emerging Luba state. In the neighboring Kanyok state to the west, the same shift took place, perhaps at roughly the same period.

In the Nkalaany Valley, the Lunda (or Rund) empire was consolidated by the early seventeenth century. New Luba influences, some of them probably coming directly from the Luba-related Kanyok kingdom rather than from the Luba kingdom itself, helped shape the institutions of the newly developing Lunda empire of the seventeenth century, especially those relating to female royalty. Interestingly, the Lunda did not go over to a fully patrilineal system as the Luba had, but continued to recognize matrilineal as well as patrilineal connections in inheritance.

To the south of the new Luba state, the wider repercussions of its formation were already becoming evident in seventeenth-century Zambia. Among the Sabi-speaking peoples, such as the Bemba, Bisa, Lala, and Lamba, a number of new chiefly families moved in from the north in that century and established a large number of chiefdoms with matrilineal rules of succession to the chiefship. Some of the older, equally matrilineal Bumba chiefs (see chapter 6) of the region held on to their small polities, but in a majority of areas, the new ruling families gradually established their preeminence. In some cases, as with the Bena-Ng'andu, who provided the kings of the later Bemba kingdom, a Luba origin for the new ruling clan is clear.

The Luba connections of the new kind of chiefs in the seventeenth-century Sabi societies are also indirectly evident in some of the new political terminology dating to this period. One notable example is the word *musonko*, "tribute." A Luba loanword in the Sabi dialects, it connoted a political relationship new to the region, involving the payment of tribute from a lesser chief to a higher one. Clearly, in some instances, the new chiefly families had begun to create larger chiefdoms with more layers of chiefly authority than had existed before under the Bumba chiefs.

What caused the southward spread of these new chiefly families into the Sabi regions? The fact that they adhered to matrilineal rules, at a time when the governing stratum in the Luba regions from which they came probably was shifting to patrilineality, suggests that they were among the losers in the struggles that created the new Luba kingdom of the seventeenth century. As chiefly refugees from Luba country, they would have been bearers of the prestigious associations of their Luba cultural origins, associations that would have been part of the historical and cultural lore of east-central African peoples ever since the Kisalian era. Themselves matrilineal, the new chiefs held a worldview that allowed them to fit in with the existing strongly matrilineal orientations of the Sabi societies. With prestigious associations to Luba power and a worldview con-

FIG. 71 Luba royal bowstand

The rulers of the new Luba kingdom, which formed in the seventeenth century and grew into a large empire in the later eighteenth century, adopted a new overall set of royal insignia, distinguishing themselves from previous rulers of the region. Among these emblems were elaborate iron bowstands. The use of carved wooden bowstands as royal insignia actually began, it appears, in the previous period, possibly during the time of the Upemba kingdom of the twelfth to the fourteenth centuries. More ancient kinds of royal insignia, notably the flange-welded double bells of earlier kings (see fig. 60), in consequence became the emblems of lesser chiefs within the Luba state.

gruent with what people in the region already believed, they possessed the attributes necessary for building chiefly authority for themselves in the new areas.

Political and Social Change in the Northern Congo Basin, 1450–1640

At the north side of the Congo Basin, among the Ubangian-speaking peoples, an era of state building also ensued from the late sixteenth and early seventeenth centuries onward. The political changeover began in the regions where the Bomu and Uele Rivers flow together to form the Ubangi River. To the north of the Ubangi, the Nzakara kingdom took shape around 1600. At about the same time just to the west of the Bomu-Uele confluence, Ngbandi kings founded several smaller kingdoms based on the same ideas and military practices as the Nzakara. The crucial element in legitimizing a new, larger scale of political organization was the spread of the ideas associated with the "spoils of the leopard," earlier found among the Mongo and their neighbors in the central Congo Basin (see chapter 6), and the reshaping of those ideas into an ideology of actual kingship. Just as important, the builders of the new states adopted the innovations in military tactics and materiel that went along with the new political ideology, bringing the new scale and kind of military power into the Ubangi country (see map 21).

The economic underpinnings of these developments have been little investigated. A key factor, however, is likely to have been the existence of a long-established and thriving riverine commerce. This trading system not only extended along the Ubangi and Bomu Rivers but also included the Aruwimi River to the south, a major tributary of the Congo, and stretched across both woodland savanna and rainforest environments. For the nineteenth century a system of regular markets held every five or seven days provides clear evidence of an extensive and varied commerce. Unfortunately, we do not know yet how far back before the nineteenth century these markets were present, but the commercial relations themselves are likely to have been operating well before the seventeenth century. Bantu-speaking Boan peoples carried the trade in the southern areas, while various Ubangian peoples were the traders of the Ubangi, Uele, and Bomu River areas.

As in the western equatorial rainforest, commerce in the Ubangi-Aruwimi region was built upon local and regional economic specialization. By early in the second millennium CE, various specialized fishing populations inhabited the banks of the Uele and the middle Ubangi Rivers, trading fish for the products of their neighbors. By the seventeenth century, ironworking had been established for possibly 2,000 years in the region, and iron tools and implements, including throwing knives, were fashioned by smiths in several parts of the region. Copper entered the regional network of trade, coming into the region from the Marra Mountains far to the north. The local manufactures, raffia and barkcloth, both passed along the routes of trade in several directions. From the rainforests the specialized BaTwa hunters provided such products as monkey skins, leopard skins, ivory, and meat. Most intriguing of all, the Boan peoples produced and traded all across the regions to the north a plant poison used for the *benge* poison ordeals, which aimed at discovering who was telling the truth in court cases. The peoples of the Bomu and Uele River regions, most of them Niger-Congo in civilization, also employed the *benge* ordeal to identify supposed "witches," people who, according to old Niger-Congo religious ideas, were believed to use medicines to harm others.

The region of the Bomu and Uele Rivers, like the African Great Lakes region, lay still beyond the effects of the new historical directions taking shape around the coasts of Africa in the period 1450 to 1640. The most potent new influences for change, as we have seen, spread from neighboring areas of the Congo Basin to the south, in the form of a new political ideology that legitimized the first creation of states along the middle Ubangi River and its tributaries. There, as in many parts of the center of Africa, the indigenous development of productive specialization and the growth in the variety and complexity of commercial activities over the previous centuries laid the essential material basis for the emergence of a larger scale of political organization and the beginnings of social stratification.

NOTES FOR READERS AND TEACHERS

Issues and Questions

A number of new historical issues catch our attention when we consider the period from 1450 to 1640 in Africa. For one thing, a new set of regions, the Atlantic coasts of Africa, entered directly into long-distance international trade. They became primary suppliers, rather than distant and marginal participants at best, in world commerce. Around the northern sides of Africa, a powerful new political presence, the Ottoman Turkish Empire, made itself felt. At the same time, peoples in other large areas of the continent continued to be little affected by this set of developments and instead followed courses of change rooted in the deeper historical past of their part of Africa.

- In what different ways in the period from 1450 to 1640 did the activities of the Portuguese and then, later, the Dutch, English, French, and other Europeans along the coast of Africa change commercial relations in Senegambia? In the regions of West Africa between Senegambia and the Niger Delta? In the regions of Angola and the lower Congo? In southern Africa? In Zimbabwe and Malawi? In eastern Africa?
- How did overseas commerce in the Atlantic Age affect agriculture in Africa?
- What effects did Ottoman expansion have on northern Africa? On Borno and its neighbors in the Chad Basin?
- In what way did the struggles of the Ottoman Turkish Empire and the southern European states to control the Mediterranean in the sixteenth century spill over into the Horn of Africa?
- Why did an age of empire in the western Sudan give way to an age of kingdoms?
- What does it tell us about social and economic change in the northern Middle Nile Basin that the founding king of the Sinnar state chose to become Muslim?
- Nonstate forms of government based on age-grade institutions can form a strong counterforce to the power of neighboring states. How do events in the Ethiopian Highlands in the sixteenth and early seventeenth centuries illustrate this point?
- A recurrent issue in twentieth-century history writing was the argument over whether ideas or material circumstances are the more fundamental causative factors in historical change. Which do you think better explains the vast spread in western equatorial Africa in the fifteenth through eighteenth centuries of ruling ideologies based on rights of chiefs and kings to the "spoils of the leopard"?

Further Reading

For Africa from the fifteenth century onward, a far more abundant historical literature exists. The closer one approaches the present, the more the problem becomes one of selection from among many possibilities. I have taken the tack here and in the notes to chapter 9 of naming just a few works, but ones that seem to me to contribute, in one way or another, an especially challenging or thought-provoking perspective on events in one or more regions of the continent during the period covered by the chapter. Again, as we have seen in the notes to previous chapters, books such as these sometimes do, and sometimes do not, cover the same period as the chapter, and they may well have important things to say about the immediately preceding centuries as well as more recent times.

Boubacar, Barry. *Senegambia and the Atlantic Slave Trade.* Cambridge and New York: Cambridge University Press, 1998.

Cassanelli, Lee. *The Shaping of Somali Society.* Philadelphia: University of Pennsylvania Press, 1982.

de Corse, Christopher. *An Archaeology of Elmina: Africans and Europeans on the Gold Coast, 1400–1900.* Washington: Smithsonian Institution Press, 2001.

Thornton, John. *Africa and Africans in the Making of the Atlantic World, 1400–1680.* Cambridge and New York: Cambridge University Press, 1992.

Vansina, Jan. *The Children of Woot.* Madison: University of Wisconsin Press, 1978.

Wright, Donald R. *The World and a Very Small Place in Africa.* New York: Sharpe, 1997.

9

Africa in the Era of the Atlantic Slave Trade, 1640–1800

The Middle Era of the Atlantic Age: Themes and Issues

From the 1640s onward, the tenor of historical change began to shift across much of the African continent. A new era in African history and in the world history of which Africa was a part—a second period of the Atlantic Age—had begun. This new era brought new configurations of political power. In the complex commercial relations of the early Atlantic period, Europeans had often transported local products, including African manufactured goods, from one part of Africa to another. In the new era, the direct exchange of African commodities for products from outside the continent increasingly became the norm. The growing volume of imported manufactures slowly began to undermine the manufacturing capacities of many African economies.

The most powerful factor in the emerging new patterns of exchange, and often the key factor in the reconfiguration of political relations within the continent, was a leap upward in the magnitude of the trade in human beings out of sub-Saharan Africa, beginning in the 1640s and 1650s. The numbers of enslaved people transported out continued to surge upward right on through the eighteenth century. The initial sharp rise in the mid-seventeenth century was generated by the establishment of sugar-plantation economies, based on slave labor, in the West Indies by several European nations. The spread of European colonial settlement in other parts of the Americas in the later seventeenth and the eighteenth centuries further fueled the demand for human cargoes. And it was not only European demand that drove this "trade." As we shall learn when we look at the history of the Darfur kingdom in the eastern Sudan, a strong and persistent demand for slaves in North Africa and the Middle East stimulated an increased trans-Saharan shipment of human beings.

A new feature of history in this period in Africa south of the Sahara was the establishment of the first lasting European colonies on the African mainland. Most were very small, but they formed the bases from which the Europeans much later, in the 1880s and 1890s, were to create a colonial partition of the continent.

West Africa in the Era of the Slave Trade

Developments in West Africa between 1640 and 1800 illustrate the whole range of effects of the changing world historical environment. In the regions along the Atlantic coasts, the social and political changes were often great. In some areas, large and powerful new states were built up in response to the shifts in exchange relations. In other areas, the wider unities of the previous centuries broke down, and small polities, often at war with each other, came to predominate. In the Sudan belt, long-distance overland commerce continued to flourish and to take on new forms. The social and political relations that appeared in the late sixteenth and early seventeenth centuries were often reinforced in those regions, rather than greatly changed. Significant new intellectual currents coursed through these developments as well, as we will shortly discover.

Commerce, States, and Social Change in the Eastern Rainforests of West Africa

In the southern parts of West Africa, in the regions most powerfully affected by the growing slave trade, the consequences of the new trade relations varied immensely. In some areas, older patterns in political and economic relations were reinforced, but with a decline in the relative importance of African manufacturing beginning to take place and sometimes with greatly changed social relations emerging. Three newly important states, strongly tied in each case to the new central factor of the Atlantic trade, the trade in human beings, also first rose to historical prominence in the seventeenth century—Oyo, Asante (Ashanti), and Dahomey.

The old kingdom of Benin successfully resisted the direct impact of the growing trade in human beings, although it did participate in some degree in supplying that trade. Nevertheless the changing nature of the demand for

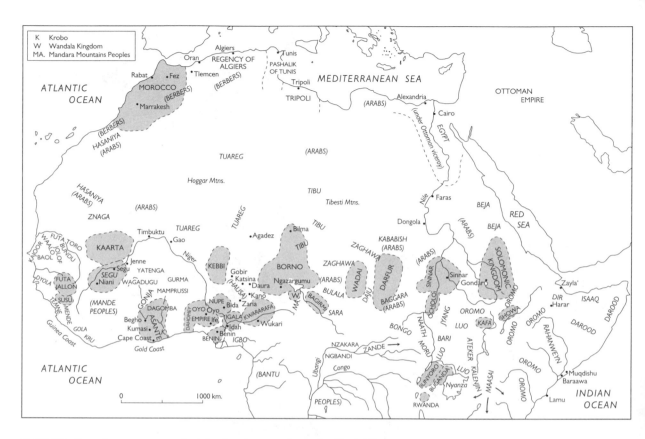

MAP 23 Peoples, states, and cities in the northern half of Africa, ca. 1750–1770

African products at the coast after the mid-seventeenth century had severe long-term consequences for Benin social and economic history, consequences well illustrated by the cloth trade. Cotton textiles from Benin continued to be in demand in the Gold Coast regions for several more decades after 1640, and as late as 1700 the Dutch still carried some cloth between the two regions. By the early eighteenth century that trade had come to an end. Benin cotton textile manufacturing declined greatly in volume, as its product began to go principally to local markets. The decline in the profitability of cotton cloth manufacture in turn greatly weakened the economic and social position of the women who up until then had been the chief producers and chief beneficiaries of that industry. Benin continued, however, to export raffia cloth to France and, via Dutch and Portuguese ships, to South America and to Angola until later in the century.

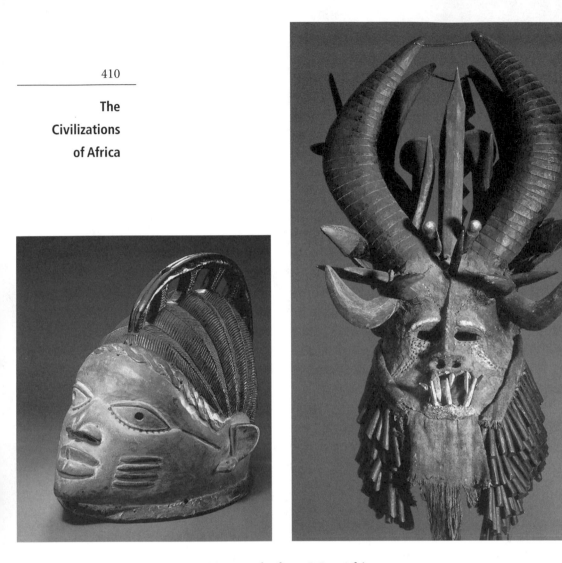

FIG. 72 Two masks from West Africa

Masquerades and masked dancing at public ceremonies and holidays remained a popular part of life among West African peoples in the seventeenth and eighteenth centuries and, indeed, right on into the twentieth century. As captive Africans began to be transported to the New World, they brought these customs with them and helped create the tradition of holding carnivals, such as Mardi Gras, in the Western Hemisphere. The first mask is a Yoruba mask of the Gelede festival, still celebrated in Nigeria and brought by captive Africans in modified form to the New World. The second mask is an example from the Igbo people, who live in what is today southeastern Nigeria.

To the east of Benin, the new trade situation at the coast had quite different social and political ramifications. The Igbo-speaking regions between the Niger and Cross Rivers, as well as the lands of many less numerous neighboring peoples, had long formed the hubs of an intricate interregional network of trade in a large variety of products. Among these products were copper from the Sudan to the north, iron goods from several areas in and around Igbo country, locally manufactured cotton cloth along with cloth imported from Benin and from the north, barkcloth and raffia cloth from areas to the west and east, and salt and fish from the Niger Delta in the south. In place of the kind of security a large state could provide, the great number of small town-states, characteristic of Igbo politics since before the sixteenth century, relied on different kinds of cooperative networks to enable trade to proceed.

In the eighteenth century, the most famous of these was the alliance of Igbo towns that owed religious allegiance to the Aro Chukwu, an oracle of God. The ability of the Aro priests to invoke divine sanctions, and of the Aro town-state to put a small military force into the field, was generally enough to maintain peace and the flow of commerce over a considerable part of the Igbo region. The Aro statelet, located along the Cross River, was founded at the end of the seventeenth and beginning of the eighteenth centuries. It arose out of a period of strife in the second half of the seventeenth century, set off by the movement of Igbo settlers into an area inhabited by Ibibio peoples. Under the leadership of a priest and doctor-diviner, Nachi, the Igbo made alliance with the Akpa people living just east of the Cross River. Together the allied forces defeated the local Ibibio, and the Akpa military leader Akuma established the Aro chiefdom. After Akuma's death, though, the rulership passed to the descendants of Nachi, who adopted and transformed the existing Ibibio oracular shrine in the area, probably dedicated originally to a local territorial spirit, into the Aro Chukwu oracle.

Over the course of the first half of the eighteenth century, the Aro set about creating a confederation of Igbo town-states, with their own town as the dominant member. From the time of their alliance with the Akpa, the Aro forces used firearms, brought upriver from trade with Europeans at the coast, to enhance the effectiveness of their efforts at spreading their economic hegemony. The importance of these weapons, mostly muskets, had probably more to do with their potential for threatening death at a distance than from their actual overall effectiveness against other weaponry.

The rise of the Aro power coincides in clear fashion with the period of transformation of the commerce of the Cross River and Niger Delta regions and was surely tied closely to that changeover. Throughout the sixteenth and seventeenth centuries the most important export of that region by far was ivory. In the early eighteenth century, the volume trade in enslaved human beings was still fewer than 5,000 people per decade. But thereafter the totals leaped upward, reaching 140,000 or more per decade in the second half of the century. The Aro state and its subordinate allies grew wealthy and powerful feeding that demand.

The growth in the trade in people after 1700 greatly strained the peace, even with the emergence of cooperative networks of towns like the one headed by the Aro, and serious fighting between different Igbo towns most certainly continued to take place. Unscrupulous Igbo merchants also were not above kidnapping children while passing through the lands of town-states other than their own, as we know from the autobiography of Olaudah Equiano, who was enslaved in such a manner in the eighteenth century.

In the rainforests west of the Niger River, many of the Yoruba city-states were incorporated as self-governing but tributary components of the Oyo empire. Before the mid-seventeenth century, Oyo was just another one of the numerous Yoruba city-states that had come into being during the first half of the second millennium CE. In the sixteenth century it seems to have been under the thumb of its more powerful northern neighbor, the Nupe kingdom. Then, in the early seventeenth century, Oyo's fortunes began to change. Unlike most of the Yoruba cities, it was located on the northern edges of the Yoruba cultural world, in the savanna fringe of the rainforest belt. Situated along the routes by which forest products were carried north to the Sudan belt and savanna products brought south to the forest, Oyo began to prosper from these connections.

At the same time, its military leaders adopted an innovation in tactics, the use of cavalry, that greatly strengthened Oyo vis-à-vis its neighbors. Because of the climatic restraints of a wet savanna environment, Oyo could not breed its own horses, but the establishment of firm and regular commercial connections with the Sudan allowed it to continually replenish its supply of horses for the cavalry. To secure its unhindered access to horses, as late as the eighteenth century the rulers of Oyo continued to pay a nominal tribute to Nupe, through whose territories the trade routes leading to the Sudan passed. In every other way, however, the Oyo state was by that time a powerful and independent empire in its own right. The city of Oyo at its height in the eighteenth century covered 5,000 hectares (50 square kilometers, or almost 20

FIG. 73 Dahomey copper side-blown trumpet

Trumpets like this one were used in royal funerals and other ceremonies in the kingdom of Dahomey.

square miles) and had around 100,000 inhabitants. The king's palace complex spread over more than a square kilometer.

When the Benin kingdom resisted the growing demand for slaves at the coast in the mid-seventeenth century, Oyo responded to it. With their fast-striking cavalry forces, the Oyo military leaders launched a series of wars that between 1600 and 1750 brought most of the Yoruba city-states under its sway. These wars produced slaves directly in the form of war captives. Oyo's conquests gained for it as well new wealth from the duties and tribute it could levy on its subordinate states and on their commercial activities, including the trade in human beings.

A second notable state, Dahomey, became even more intimately bound up with the slave trade than Oyo. Dahomey, founded in about the 1620s, started out as a small interior kingdom located in the region of woodland savanna that separates the eastern and western parts of the West African rainforest. Competition over the proceeds of the growing slave trade led its rulers to attack and finally defeat the equally small coastal states of Popo and Whydah in 1727. The Dahomey kings then appointed their own officials at Whydah, maintaining through those officials a direct royal control over the trade with Europeans at the coast and restricting the access of Europeans to the interior of the country. After an Oyo invasion in 1730, Dahomey became for the next eight decades a tributary state of the Oyo empire. The Dahomey kings paid tribute to Oyo throughout that period but otherwise continued to run their own internal affairs and to maintain their own foreign policies.

Women had a number of uniquely significant roles in the Dahomey polity. From perhaps the founding of the kingdom in the early seventeenth century, a women's guild of elephant hunters served directly under the king. In the second half of the eighteenth century a regular women's military corps fought in combat alongside male contingents in the Dahomey army. The origins of this corps probably go back the king's female contingent of bodyguards, in existence by the early eighteenth century. In the court establishment the king's numerous wives formed another influential element, particularly at times of the succession of a new king.

Commerce, States, and Social Change in the Gold Coast of West Africa

Farther west, in the Gold Coast, the process of building larger states began as early as the 1630s among the Akan peoples. Through the rest of the century, the main wars to control the growing trade in people involved Akan kingdoms located in the immediate hinterland of the coast. The Akwamu state held the pre-eminent position in these areas in the middle of the century; their major competitor was the Denkyira kingdom.

In the early eighteenth century, the balance of power shifted decisively inland with the rise of the new Asante kingdom. Asante was founded between the 1660s and 1680s as a confederation of tiny inland kingdoms located within the rainforest. Its capital was established at the town of Kumasi, and the key figure in building the power of the new state was Osei Tutu, who ruled from around 1680 until his death in 1718. From the indirect testimony available to us, Osei Tutu appears to have been both a compelling personality and a far-sighted head of state. On the foundations laid during his reign, his successor, Opuko Ware (1718–1748), launched a large number of successful military campaigns, which transformed Asante from a small confederation of mini-states into an empire ruling directly or indirectly over most of the territory of the modern-day country of Ghana and over parts of southern Burkina-Faso in the north.

The impetus for the formation of the Asante state seems to have been growing new pressures, commercial and political, coming from the north as well as the south. The kingdom produced gold and, perhaps equally important in those times, kola nuts. If one looked northward from Kumasi in the late seventeenth century, the recurrent problem for state policy was how to gain advantage from the emerging importance of Hausa merchants in the trade networks of the Sudan. The Hausa city-states, especially the great walled cities of Kano and Katsina, were prospering as never before. Their cloth manufactures were known far and wide. Their merchants were becoming the most important traders of the middle areas south of the Bend of the Niger as far as the expanding Asante empire, and they were the major middlemen in the supplying of kola nuts to the Sudan and trans-Saharan trades. If one instead looked southward from Kumasi, the essential issues had to do with how the people of the Kumasi region were to deal with the turmoil stirred up by the growing trade demands, above all for captive people, at the coast.

The consolidation of Asante under the leadership of Osei Tutu stabilized the local political arena and put in place a unified approach to commerce. The conquests of Opuko Ware and his successors produced war captives, who could then be sold at the coast. Asante thus became the leading producer of kola nuts for the northern markets, slaves for the coastal and, to a lesser extent, northern markets, and gold, more and more of which began to stay at home, to be used for the ornamentation and personal adornment of a now very wealthy ruling class. To keep the subversive potential of merchant capitalism at bay, the Asante kingdom maintained a policy of restricting most foreign commerce to state-controlled entrepots at the fringes of the state's directly ruled areas. By the later eighteenth century, the most important of these was the city of Salaga, 200 kilometers northwest of Kumasi, where the Hausa traders were required to stop and trade.

Despite all the changes in material and political life, Asante remained a strongly matrilineal society, true to its Niger-Congo roots in that respect. Men did hold most key political positions (and men found ways to speak slightingly of women, as is the case in many cultures), but powerful women remained a recurrent feature of Asante politics and society throughout its history.

Asante ruled over a mixture of different provinces and dependencies. The heart of the state consisted of the confederacy of tiny, once independent kingdoms, whose rulers formed the central governing councils under the king. These territories all lay closely grouped around Kumasi, the capital. To the north of Kumasi, the large Dagomba kingdom paid tribute to Asante and recognized Asante over-rule, although its kings continued to be responsible for governing their own territory. To the south, a large number of small, Akan-speaking kingdoms, lying between Kumasi and the coast, owed allegiance to the Asante state because of the conquests of Opuko Ware.

Within this coastal hinterland, there were also several small areas with anomalous relationships to the Asante state. The Krobo of the lower Volta River region provide an interesting example of the slipperiness of maintaining state sovereignty over noncentralized people. The areas most effectively held by the Asante empire were those where the rule could be asserted indirectly through already established local rulers. The Krobo lacked such an institution before the nineteenth century.

Krobo society took shape in the fourteenth or fifteenth century, with the joining together of a number of small communities of different ethnic backgrounds who all used the same steep-sided mountain as a refuge in time of war. Krobo government before the nineteenth century depended on a council of ritual clan priest-chiefs of the type found in early Niger-Congo civilization. In the late seventeenth and early eighteenth centuries, with warfare intensifying among the southern Akan states as they competed to supply the Atlantic trade,

FIG. 74 Asante stool

The craftsmen of the Asante kingdom made a kind of chair quite different from the three-legged stool carved widely in East Africa (see fig. 28). Shown here is an early twentieth-century example of this chair, which the artisan sculpted out of a single great block of wood.

hundreds of new refugees flocked to the Krobo mountain. A great many of these refugees were themselves of Akan background and came from cultures with war chiefs and kings. The Krobo gradually assimilated these people over the first half of the eighteenth century, but not without adopting from them the idea of having war chiefs as a means of organizing for defense in those turbulent times. In periods of peace in the eighteenth century, the Krobo farmed the plains below the mountain. When Asante armies passed through their lands, they retreated for protection to their steep-sided mountain, offered tribute if necessary, and for the most part avoided conflict.

A factor of growing significance to warfare all through the coastal hinterland of West Africa in the later seventeenth century and the eighteenth century was the use of guns. The Portuguese first imported muskets to West Africa in the sixteenth century, and other European powers added to this trade from the 1570s and 1580s onward. From the 1690s European flintlocks became the chief kind of gun available along the coast. Not surprisingly considering the state of firearm technology in those times, guns can hardly be said to have revolutionized warfare, and older kinds of weaponry long continued to be essential. Still, the nature of war gradually changed in several areas of West Africa. Asante and Dahomey both built disciplined fighting forces in the eighteenth century armed with muskets of various kinds. By the close of the century, Asante had an army of around 80,000 men, half of them armed with muskets, and Dahomey had 10,000–12,000 troops in the regular army, most with muskets. At the same time, the African smiths in these regions responded to the new military technology by developing tools and techniques for repairing old muskets and making new ones.

Commerce and Slaving in the Chad Basin

The prosperity of the Hausa city-states, whose merchants traveled as far away as the Asante empire in search of valued commodities, was just one reflection of the vitality of commercial activity all across the Chad Basin in the seventeenth and eighteenth centuries, although an important indicator. Although the fortunes of the trade varied, and both warfare among the competing city-states and periodic drought may have caused considerable fluctuations in population, Kano and Katsina, two of the largest and most important Hausa cities, probably in good times had 50,000 or more inhabitants. The capital of the Borno kingdom, Ngazargamo, probably reached a similar size, and a number of other urban centers of somewhat lesser scale also dotted the region. Among the major products of long-distance commerce in the Chad Basin, besides cloth, were salt, iron, and slaves, the latter traded north across the Sahara, with the principal traders in slaves coming from Borno and some of its peripheral states.

The political and commercial relations of one such state, Wandala, with its southern neighbors in the Mandara Mountains illustrate one of the ways in which independent small, nonstate societies could still persist in West Africa, even when often at enmity with neighboring large kingdoms. The relations in this case rested on a terrible irony, though. A long-existing, Chadic-speaking state, Wandala was situated south of Lake Chad at the north edge of the Mandara Mountains. Its origins go back to the first half of the second millennium CE; its rulers adopted Islam in the early eighteenth century. Wandala had two major products to offer, iron goods and slaves, and here is where the irony comes in. Both commodities came ultimately from the numerous independent, non-Muslim peoples, also Chadic in language, who lived in the Mandara

FIG. 75 Brass currency

This ladle-shaped currency comes from Chadic societies of the Jos Plateau. The Jos Plateau, to the west of the Mandara Mountains, was similarly a highland area located at the southern edges of the Chad Basin and inhabited by small-scale societies. These societies, like those in the Mandara Range, engaged in trading relations with the larger-scale societies to the north of them, in this case the Hausa city-states, but they also were raided by those states for slaves and other booty.

range to the south of Wandala. The Mandara mountaineers carried iron ore as well as unforged iron ("bloom") from their smelting furnaces to the market at Mora, the capital of Wandala, exchanging these products for essential goods unavailable in the mountains, especially fish from Lake Chad and salt. The Wandala smiths then forged the iron into a variety of implements, including weapons for the very Wandala armies that raided the mountain communities for slaves all through the seventeenth and eighteenth centuries. Protected by the ruggedness of their lands, the societies of the Mandara Mountains lost battles and people to Wandala, but not their independence, all the while depending on trade with the same people who made war on them.

Peasants, Clerics, and Warlords in Senegambia

Much farther west, in the Senegambia region, the effect of the new commercial pressures was to make the later seventeenth and the eighteenth centuries a period of increased warfare and political fragmentation. The kings of the Baol, Waalo, and Kajoor states still held a nominal authority in their territories, but the *ceddo,* the local nobility of those areas, often acted as autonomous warlords and frequently fought among themselves. Trade commonly continued through the turmoil; in fact, the fighting produced large numbers of captives to be sold either at the coast, and then transported to America, or northward across the Sahara to North Africa. The chief sufferers at all times were the peasantry of these lands.

A different kind of peasant suffering took place in nearby Futa Toro, along the middle Senegal River. There the landholding noble class, established under Tengela at the end of the fifteenth century, had increasingly subordinated and dispossessed the peasants of their lands. In the early seventeenth century, a new ideology of the oppressed began to be preached in this region, using the Islamic idea of the brotherhood of believers as a rallying point for opposition to the existing state of affairs. The preachers of this new direction in Senegambian intellectual history came from the Jakhanke merchant group, who had already had a long history behind them of being proselytizers of Islam in the region. In the 1670s, Nasir ad-Din, one of these preachers, led a jihad that overthrew the power of the Denyanke dynasty in Futa Toro. By the 1680s another such leader, Malik Si, took over as the ruler of the neighboring territory of Bundu, claiming the religious title of *imam.*

The new type of state failed to fulfill its initial promise, as the leadership of the rebellions gradually turned into a new landholding class, ruling over states much like the old Futa Toro kingdom. But the jihads left a lasting intellectual legacy. For the first time, the common people of the region were attracted in large numbers to Islam, and for many people in Senegambia, it now became a thinkable idea that Islam might offer viable alternatives to the rule of the old indigenous nobility.

In the first half of the eighteenth century, this kind of outlook led to another jihad in the nearby Jallon Mountains in the Susu kingdom. Previously, from the mid-fifteenth century to the early seventeenth century, the Fula cattle herders of that region had been important supporters of the Susu rulers, providing cavalry forces to back up the infantry contingents of the Susu army. Sometime before the mid-1600s that relationship changed, and a situation of recurrent warfare between the Susu and the Fula minority then took its place. In the late seventeenth and early eighteenth centuries, the ideas of Islam and of a Muslim state, which had taken hold in Futa Toro, spread south to the previously non-Muslim Fula of the Jallon Mountains. Inspired by these ideas and led by Fula Muslim clerics, the Fula revolted against the Susu kingdom in the early 1720s, seizing control over its central territories and setting up in its place a new state, Futa Jallon, based on Islamic ideas. The Susu kings continued to hold on to a much-reduced territory in the southern parts of their former kingdom, but the era of Susu as a major power was over.

In the later decades of the eighteenth century, Fula clerics and teachers became the main spreaders of the new political ideas all across the western and central Sudan. At the close of the century, a prime exemplar of this intellectual ferment was Usuman dan Fodio, a Fula cleric living in the Hausa kingdom of Gobir. In 1804, he declared a jihad against the old Hausa ruling order. His campaigns attracted a large following among Fula in the region and among Hausa disaffected with their lot in life. Out of his jihad, there arose the major nineteenth-century empire of the central Sudan region, known as the Caliphate of Sokoto. His example then led to other jihads in the western Sudan, as a new age of empires, based on Muslim beliefs, took form in the first half of the nineteenth century. But that is a story that belongs to later times and that other books must tell.

Between Ocean and Savanna: Small-Scale Societies on the Guinea Coast

In the belt of rainforest between the Jallon Mountains and the coast lay another West African region, Guinea, in which small-scale societies persisted in the seventeenth and eighteenth centuries despite disruptions and attacks from larger

FIG. 76 Mende mask

The Mende people, although speakers of a Mande Niger-Congo language, inhabited areas just inland from the Guinea Coast and in most respects, in the seventeenth and eighteenth centuries, fit into the same cultural and smaller-scale political world as their neighbors, whose languages belonged to the West Atlantic branch of the Niger-Congo family.

polities, or perhaps because of these very factors. The small societies of the Guinea Coast and hinterland originally all spoke languages of the West Atlantic branch of the Niger-Congo family. From the late fifteenth century onward, the chiefdoms and tiny states of southern Senegambia as well as Guinea began to supply the growing Atlantic commerce as well as continuing to participate in trade relations of more ancient standing with the Susu kingdom and other states, such as Kaabu, in the interior. Large canoes, fashioned from great rainforest trees, provided the principal means of transport of goods and people through these forested areas, unhealthful to the donkeys and horses used in the savannas to the north.

African rice was the staple of the diet everywhere. As we already learned in chapter 5, the West Atlantic peoples living near the coast had earlier developed a special technology of rice growing, adapted to the environments along the estuaries of the rivers. It was captive Africans from just these areas who brought this technology for growing rice along the river estuaries across the Atlantic Ocean in the late seventeenth and the eighteenth centuries to colonial South Carolina.

The many small polities of the Guinea Coast and its hinterland faced a new scale of warfare and insecurity after the mid-seventeenth century, as the Atlantic demand for slaves began to take off. Even in the sixteenth and early seventeenth centuries, the forces of the Kaabu kingdom and its allies frequently raided the areas extending southward from the Gambia River, garnering captives for the Atlantic trade as well as the trans-Saharan commerce in slaves to Morocco. Similarly, farther south in Guinea, periods of warfare in the later sixteenth and early seventeenth centuries had deeply unsettled political and economic relationships among the chiefdoms and small kingdoms of that region. After the 1720s a new threat came from Futa Jallon, which raided for slaves in the middle parts of the Guinea Coast, previously part of the trading sphere of the Susu kingdom. The peoples of the coasts and coastal hinterlands still followed many of the beliefs of Niger-Congo religion, and so the slaving campaigns from Futa Jallon often took the guise of religious jihads against non-Muslims. In response, many of the small Atlantic polities set themselves on a more continually ready military footing; and despite the recurrent loss of people to slave capture, they maintained their independence from the large states and participated actively in commerce right on through the eighteenth century.

Coastal Communities in Two Cultural Worlds

By the early eighteenth century, the growing involvement of Europeans in the affairs of the coastal societies lent new prominence to an old feature of the Atlantic coastal commerce, the existence of communities with roots in both the African and European cultural worlds. In the sixteenth and seventeenth centuries, such communities had been primarily Afro-Portuguese, as we have discovered for the Kongo kingdom and in Angola. Afro-Portuguese populations, similarly involved as agents of the overseas trade, could be found in those centuries in the southern Senegambian ports and as far south as Sierra Leone. Now in the eighteenth century, at the French trading centers of Gorée and St. Louis along the northern Senegambian coast, there grew up a small local population acculturated to French ideas and social practices. In addition, farther southeastward along the Guinea Coast, a number of European adventurers from such countries as England newly established themselves in the coastal trading centers, becoming rich through their participation in the Atlantic trade. Marrying the daughters of important local chiefly families, they established influential new family lines and sometimes new chiefdoms, ruled by their offspring.

With their wealth from the trade, they could often send their children to Europe for their education.

In the commercial towns of the Gold Coast, still farther east, the access of a few Africans to European education led gradually to the emergence of a small group of individuals and families who, in varying degrees, blended African and European experiences and knowledge systems. A notable example from the mid-eighteenth century was Philip Quaque, the African Christian pastor for both British merchants and African townspeople in the town of Cape Coast, who trained for the ministry in Britain. An even more interesting case is that of William Amo, who studied for a Ph.D. in European philosophy in the late 1730s and early 1740s in Germany. After receiving his degree, he returned to the Gold Coast and remained throughout his life a man greatly respected for his knowledge and varied experiences.

Central Africa: The Expanding Impact of Atlantic Commerce

West-Central Africa after 1640: Commerce and Society

The western equatorial rainforest and the savannas to the south in modern-day Angola were regions, too, in which the abruptly growing volume of trade in people and in goods in the mid-seventeenth century brought about significant social and political transformation. In the inland commerce, the most striking consequence was the realigning of the commercial networks in the 1640s and 1650s, and this realignment severely affected the vitality of the Kongo kingdom.

To the immediate north of Kongo, the Vili people of the Loango kingdom rapidly grew into the dominant carriers of the interior trade to the coast during the early and mid-seventeenth century. Loango, located along the Atlantic shore north of the mouth of the Congo River, was one of the cluster of several small kingdoms that had arisen before the fourteenth century along the lower Congo River—the same cluster of small states to which the Kongo kingdom traced its origins. Already in the sixteenth century, Vili merchants carried on a brisk trade in ivory with nearby BaTwa gatherer-hunters and in iron and ivory with the Teke areas farther inland. In the first half of the seventeenth century, Vili began operating in Kongo itself. Then, in the 1640s and 1650s, they opened a new interior trade connection leading from the capital city of Loango inland via the Teke country to the Malebo Pool and from there southward up the Kwango River to the Imbangala kingdom.

As we have already seen, the Portuguese by the 1620s had established trade

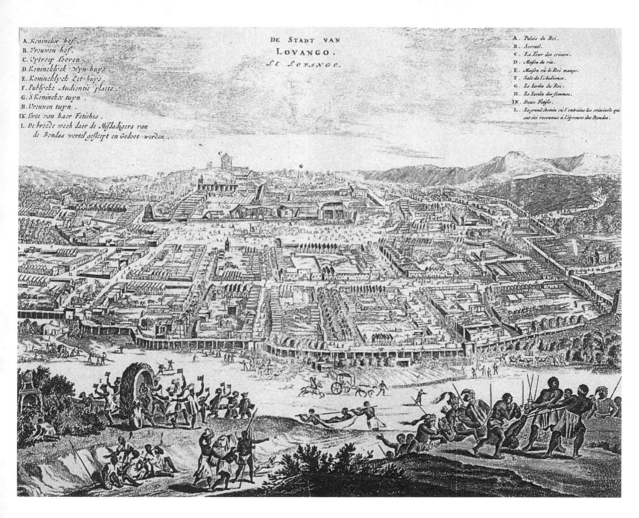

FIG. 77 Loango, capital city of the Loango kingdom

From this city, pictured here in the seventeenth century, the Vili merchants traveled far inland to tap into the commerce of the Congo Basin in the sixteenth through eighteenth centuries.

and military links of their own with the Imbangala, following routes that passed to the south of Kongo. The merchants along these routes, the *pombeiros*, were of mixed Afro-Portuguese parentage. By the second half of the seventeenth century, the Ovimbundu, who inhabited the southern highland areas of today's Angola, became involved in this trade too. In particular, they began to organize trading caravans to travel still farther inland, to the newly emerging Lunda empire.

The central government of Kongo by the 1640s and 1650s also faced a growing internal competition from its own provincial lords, most significantly those of the province of Nsoyo. Located at the coast on the south side of the Congo River, Nsoyo was able to gain its own direct access by river to the trade passing downstream from the Malebo Pool and by sea to European merchant ships traversing the Atlantic. The Dutch-Portuguese commercial rivalry was the key to the timing of this change. The Dutch gained a major stake in the trade of the region with their seizure of Luanda from the Portuguese in 1642. When they gave Luanda back to Portugal in 1649, they maintained their economic stake by shifting the main focus of their commercial activities back to Nsoyo and to Loango and, like the Vili, by beginning to operate directly within the territories of Kongo.

The upshot of these commercial shifts was that Kongo rapidly lost the commercial profits that had underpinned the power of the capital, Mbanzakongo, over the provincial towns. The Vili, with their trade route in the interior, bypassed Kongo to the east by carrying goods north from the Imbangala to the Malebo Pool and then overland from there to Loango at the coast. The rise of Nsoyo's own commerce meant, in addition, that goods that had formerly traveled through Mbanzakongo now passed directly downriver from the Malebo Pool to the coast, leaving the central governing region of Kongo out of the loop.

Through the 1640s and 1650s, the rapid debilitation of the revenue-capturing abilities of the central Kongo government was masked by the political skills of the king during those two decades, Garcia II. But a combined attack by the Imbangala of Kasanje and the Portuguese on the Kongo kingdom in 1665, four years after Garcia's death, brought this problem out into the open. The invasion killed the reigning king, Antonio I, and for the next forty years competing provincial lords battled to control the succession to the kingship. The provinces devolved into small independent states, and the kingship of Kongo, into a ceremonial position of little practical power. By the early eighteenth century, the kingdom of Kongo had ceased to exist as a significant polity, although the kings long continued to be installed and recognized at the now small town of Mbanzakongo.

In the second half of the seventeenth century and in the eighteenth century, the impact of trade at the coast spread farther and farther inland. To the north

FIG. 78 Kuba raffia cloth

The Kuba kingdom in the eighteenth century was a major producing area for especially fine and valued raffia cloth. Shown here are two twentieth-century examples of that craft.

of the Loango kingdom, the old Ogowe River route of interregional African trade, by which ironworking had spread from the deep interior to the coast 2,000 years earlier, now became the way by which coastal imports, such as guns and cloth, could spread far inland, and by which inland products, such as ivory, reached the newer and much more lucrative markets of the Atlantic trading system. Along the Congo River, a growing volume and a new variety of goods now passed both upstream and downstream. Unfortunately, the commodity that most grew in importance was enslaved people. By the close of the seventeenth century, the Congo River routes reached more than 1,000 kilometers into the interior. The Bobangi people, who inhabited the key juncture of trade routes at the confluence of the Ubangi and Congo Rivers, became the major carriers of goods between there and the Malebo Pool. They built large canoes from the trees of the rainforest and traveled hundreds of kilometers along the rivers to carry on their commerce.

At the southern margins of the rainforest, the areas along the lower Kasai River also became a center of expanding economic relations in the seventeenth century and of new state formation as well. Settlers from the Mongo regions farther north had filtered south into those areas before and during the middle centuries of the second millennium CE and, together with the Western-Savanna Bantu peoples resident there ever since the first millennium BCE, became part of a culturally and economically varied cluster of matrilineal communities. In about the sixteenth century, chiefs with earlier cultural ties to the Bolia kingdom and small sister states of the Lake Mai Ndombe area (described in chapter 6) moved into the lower Kasai region and begin to build up larger chiefdoms. The foundation of the Kuba kingdom around the 1620s then united these chiefdoms into a larger state that was to persist down to the colonial era. As important manufacturers and suppliers of raffia cloth, the various peoples of the kingdom, located as they were near the transition from rainforest to woodland savanna, became intermediaries in the exchange of forest and savanna products as well as the beneficiaries of trade westward along the Kasai and Kwa Rivers to the Congo River.

We cannot leave this topic without saying something about its social costs. In the rainforest regions, the increased demands at the coast for forest products, such as tropical woods, and products of hunt and collecting, such as ivory and wax, at first must have increased the importance of the gatherer-hunter BaTwa as primary producers. But the merchants of the trade came from the farming and fishing communities and were not themselves the BaTwa. The struggle to gain better access to the forest products seems to have resulted in many areas in a subordination of the previously independent gatherer-hunter BaTwa to the neighboring non-gatherer-hunter communities.

The growth of wealth from trade also enhanced social differences within the farming and fishing societies. The old *-kumu, the lineage heads, changed into wealthy "big men," whose leadership of a ward in a large village was legitimized more by the wealth they could accumulate and the number of wives they could marry than by their ritual functions. The process of social redefinition of the *-kumu role may indeed, as some historians believe, have begun centuries earlier, especially in areas along the old interior routes of interregional trade. But the wider spread and establishment all across the western equatorial rainforest of this kind of social stratification within the villages and towns of the region, and of local oligarchic rule by such "big men," surely belong to the era of the great expansion of trade in the seventeenth and eighteenth centuries.

Commercial Expansion in the Southern Savannas

South of the kingdom of Kongo, in what is today the country of Angola, the period from the 1640s through the 1700s was similarly a time of both political realignment and new kinds of commercial activities.

Following the collapse of the Ndongo kingdom in the 1630s and 1640s (described in chapter 8), a variety of claimants to chiefly and royal titles began to scatter out, seeking new bases of power in different areas of Angola. The new titleholders traced their political legitimacy back to the Kasanje kingdom or to the earlier Kinguli rulers of the Imbangala, and they adopted Imbangala military tactics and discipline to conquer existing kingdoms or to establish new states. Between 1650 and the early 1700s, rulers of this type replaced the earlier ruling lines in a majority of the small Ovimbundu kingdoms of the Benguela Highlands. The largest and most powerful state founded as a consequence of this political diaspora, Humbe, emerged in the lower countries to the south of the Ovimbundu. In the second half of the seventeenth century, Humbe made itself the dominant power all across the lands north of the lower Kunene River and west of the middle Kunene. Its forces destroyed the previously powerful Mataman kingdom (described in chapter 8) of the lower Kunene Basin. In the aftermath of the Humbe conquest, satellite ruling families of the Humbe state seized lasting power in the kingdoms of the Ovambo and other Southwest-Bantu peoples, located on both sides of the lower Kunene River. These smaller states appear to have previously been constituents of the Mataman state. Their new royal families continued to recognize Humbe overlordship down to the nineteenth century.

African merchant caravans from the Angolan regions also traveled farther and farther into the interior as the eighteenth century proceeded. The Portuguese contributed indirectly to the expanding interior networks by building their seventeenth-century coastal town of Benguela into a new regular outlet for the trade from the highland territories of the Ovimbundu kingdoms. The Ovimbundu responded by developing their own commercial system to tap into the products of the deeper interior. By the late eighteenth century, Ovimbundu caravans seeking ivory and human cargo traveled overland not only to the Lunda empire but also into the areas of the upper Zambezi where the Chinyama kings had formerly been influential. There they established relations with the various chiefs of the Luvale and Luchazi, who claimed political descent from the Chinyama. These relations helped to set off a turbulent period, during which, for many decades, the chiefs of the various Luvale chiefdoms and their followers raided neighboring peoples to take captives to sell to the Ovimbundu.

East-Central Africa: Realignments in Economy and Polity

Across the continent at the other end of the southern savanna belt, in Malawi, Zambia, Mozambique, and Zimbabwe, a more mixed picture of the effects of the changing commercial pressures can be drawn.

On the Zimbabwe Plateau, the intrusion of Portuguese adventurers and merchants into the affairs of the Mutapa kingdom was eventually countered, late in the seventeenth century, by a highly successful African reaction against the intrusive influences from outside the continent. It all began in the northeastern part of the Zimbabwe Plateau between 1660 and 1680 with the conversion of a previously small subordinate state, whose rulers bore the title Changamire, into a major power. The transformation came about under the leadership of the Changamire Dombo, whose military campaigns in that period brought an end to the Torwa kingdom of southwestern Zimbabwe. The new state created under Dombo is known to us as the Rozvi empire. Called upon in 1692 by the ruler of the Mutapa kingdom for assistance against the Portuguese, Dombo responded by sending his forces into the Mutapa territories, where they routed the Portuguese and their allies and finally drove them from the country by 1694. The unintended consequence for the Mutapa state was that Dombo incorporated most of the highland parts of that kingdom into his own empire. The Mutapa kingdom survived as a much shrunken state occupying the far north edge of the Zimbabwe Plateau and adjacent parts of the Zambezi River Valley.

Having chased the Portuguese traders, officials, and missionaries out of Zimbabwe, Dombo and his successor kings confined them to a few designated towns along the Zambezi outside of the Rozvi kingdom proper. At these locations, the Portuguese were allowed to carry on trade, still a valuable source of wealth for the state.

Within the bounds of the Rozvi kingdom, the power of the rulers rested on three pillars. One was the close relation of the kings with the Mwari oracular shrine and its priests in the Matopos hills of southern Zimbabwe, a connection that gave the rulers added moral and spiritual legitimacy in the eyes of the general populace. The shrine probably began as the ritual site of a territorial spirit, but by the time of the Rozvi rulers its priests claimed it as a shrine of the Creator God of Niger-Congo religion, called Mwari in the Shona language of Zim-

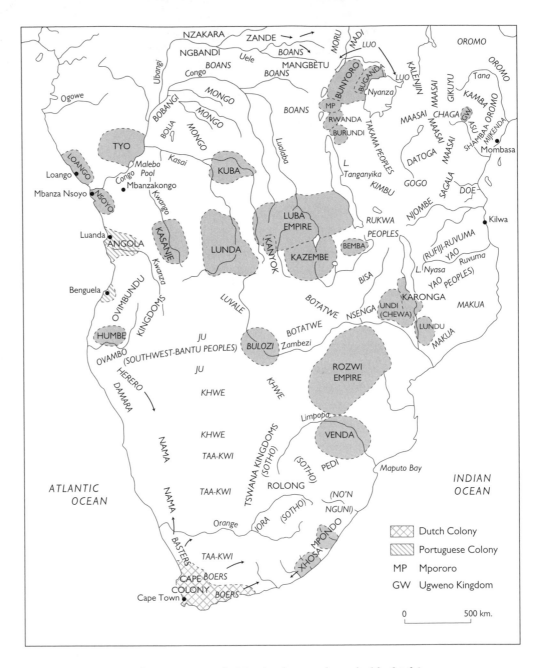

MAP 24 Peoples, states, and cities in the southern half of Africa, ca. 1725–1775

babwe. The second pillar of royal power, and a primary element in the material basis of the state, was the king's possession of enormous herds of cattle and the practice of loaning out such cattle to loyal subject chiefs in distant parts of the kingdom. The third pillar was the king's use of the moral and material attractions of the first and second pillars to field a large army and send it out to squelch rebellion in distant parts of the country.

South across the Limpopo River lay the lands of another fairly large state, the Venda kingdom, which came into being in the seventeenth century. In the later seventeenth and early eighteenth centuries, the Venda polity had the characteristics of a small empire. Its territories, which covered the greater part of the modern-day northern and eastern Transvaal, encompassed not only the central and directly governed areas, in which the Venda people themselves resided, but also a large number of subject chiefdoms and small kingdoms, whose peoples spoke dialects of a separate Bantu language, Sotho.

Ever since the time of the Mapungubwe kingdom in the twelfth century, the Venda region had been strongly influenced culturally by developments to the north in Zimbabwe. The Venda kings of the seventeenth and eighteenth centuries, according to the oral traditions, had arrived in the region as royal migrants from Zimbabwe. Clearly, the prestigious claim of Zimbabwean royal ancestry greatly helped in legitimizing their position as rulers.

Much of the power of the Venda state was probably built around controlling interior access to the kinds of trade goods that were in demand at the Indian Ocean coast. The main routes of this commerce passed along the Limpopo Valley and had their outlets at Maputo Bay, where European ships, usually Dutch or Portuguese, regularly stopped to trade. The prime item that drew the Europeans to this location was ivory, from the then abundant elephants of the Limpopo Valley and other parts of the Venda domains.

To the north of Zimbabwe, in Malawi in the late seventeenth and the eighteenth centuries, the former Malawi empire had devolved into several lesser kingdoms ruled by Phiri kings. The most important of these by the eighteenth century was the Chewa kingdom of the Undi, as the rulers of that state were titled. The Chewa kings benefited materially from the fact that trade routes leading coastward as well as deeper into the interior passed through their territories.

The areas around the north end of Lake Nyasa and between Lake Nyasa and the coast, on the other hand, were divided into hundreds of small chiefdoms and clan territories. Here the factor of rising importance was the Yao. Before

1500 inhabiting the middle reaches of the Ruvuma River, the Yao began in the late 1500s to find a special economic niche for themselves as the transporters of inland commodities to the coast and of coastal imports into the interior. In the 1600s and 1700s, Yao merchants began to travel regularly to such ports on the Indian Ocean seaboard as the Swahili town of Kilwa and the Portuguese port of Mozambique Island. The early important product they sold was ivory, but in the late 1700s, especially as the French began plantation agriculture on the Indian Ocean islands of Reunion and Mauritius, the Yao turned more and more to supplying slaves to the coastal ports.

It was the wars of the Chewa state in Malawi and a situation of recurrent small-scale warfare in eastern Zambia that, we suspect, provided many of the captives transported to the coast by the Yao in the late eighteenth century. The wars establishing the kingdom of the Kazembe in the 1760s through the 1790s probably added a further source of captives. A people of the Sabi Bantu group, the Bisa, were the intermediate carriers of trade in people as well as in copper, ivory, and other products. Bisa merchants brought goods and people to the Lake Nyasa region, and from there Yao merchants took them to the coast, along with additional commodities the Yao had acquired along their own routes of travel. In return, imported cloth and beads, among other wares, traveled far inland.

Interestingly, the Malawi region and several surrounding areas remained important producers of indigenous cotton cloth, and this cloth also figured strongly in the interregional commerce. An important insight to be gained from this knowledge is that it is easy for non-Africans to be so aware of the evil side of this trading system as to miss the fact that much more complex relations and a much more varied array of products drove commerce in these regions. Slave trade in the nineteenth century did eventually greatly distort human values and the goals of commercial enterprise. In east-central Africa in the eighteenth century, however, the trade in human beings was still just one thread in the web of the African economic relationships.

Empire Building in the Central Parts of the Southern Savannas

Far inland, the heartlands of the southern savanna belt, between 1640 and 1800, were the scene of the expansion and consolidation of two large states. To the west, in the far upper watershed of the Kasai and Lulua Rivers, the Rund kings turned their Lunda kingdom into the chief power within a wider cluster of associated independent states. One scholar, Jan Vansina, has aptly called this group of kingdoms the "Lunda Commonwealth." The Rund kings expanded their own domains especially through the conquest of stateless peoples to the north and west of the Rund heartland. To the south and east, on the other hand, they laid the basis for the wider Lunda Commonwealth of independent kingdoms by judiciously bestowing the prestigious Lunda chiefship on aspiring leaders from far-off locales who came as supplicants to the court.

The most notable extension of the Lunda Commonwealth into a distant area belongs to the eighteenth century. It began with the migration of a Lunda titleholder, the Kazembe, and his followers to the Copper Belt and then a further movement east by his son to the Luapula River around the mid-eighteenth century. In short order, the settlement on the Luapula became the center of a large new state, called the kingdom of the Kazembe after the title held by its monarchs. Strongly tied by its history and ideology to the Lunda Commonwealth, this kingdom was able to impose its authority over a territory extending from the Copper Belt on the west almost to the south end of Lake Tanganyika on the east during the last four decades of the eighteenth century.

A different kind of empire building took shape just north of the Kazembe kingdom. There a new major Luba state was established in the seventeenth century, after a two-century interregnum following the end of the Upemba kingdom (see chapter 6). The royal towns and the ritual centers of this kingdom, interestingly, lay not in the Upemba Depression itself, as had those of the earlier Upemba state, but in the hilly areas to the west of the depression. The history of the earliest era of the new Luba kingdom is obscure, but the efforts of its rulers in the mid- and late eighteenth century turned the kingdom into the largest empire yet seen south of the Sudan regions of Africa. At the close of the eighteenth century, the territories tributary to the Luba kings stretched from Lake Tanganyika on the east to the Kanyok kingdom on the west and from the edge of the Copper Belt in the south almost to the rainforest in the north.

The old material bases of the earlier Upemba state, such as the production of iron and salt, and the control over access to the copper of the Copper Belt re-emerged in the Luba empire of the eighteenth century. By the late eighteenth century, tenuous and indirect trade links also had begun to connect the outlying parts of the Luba empire with the Atlantic on one side and the Indian Ocean on the other.

The ideology of rule in the Luba empire had a unique new aspect to it. Local authority all across its domains was tied to membership in the Bambudye association, to which chiefs and leading men had to belong if they were to exercise power and influence in the Luba society. We do not know of the Bambudye institution before the Luba empire, and so it may well be an innovation of the seventeenth century, instituted during the early rise of the state. It proved to be a highly successfully instrument for political and cultural integration.

As the Luba rulers conquered new areas in the eighteenth century, their usual policy was to co-opt the previous leadership of the conquered areas by admitting them to the Bambudye association. In this way, the ability of such leaders to retain their positions after conquest became dependent on their commitment to a Luba political institution with branches all across the empire and on their acceptance of the legitimizing rituals associated with that organization. At the same time, however, membership in the Bambudye association, because of its ritual and political salience in the new social order, acted as a check against despotic rule. It gave the regional and local authorities a forum through which they could shape the directions of change in their areas and act as the intermediaries in the relations of their region with the distant authority of the Luba kings.

A third, lesser area of state building in the seventeenth and eighteenth centuries lay to the south of the Luba empire, in modern-day eastern Zambia. There a new larger political formation, the Bemba kingdom, first began to coalesce in the late seventeenth century, under the aegis of an immigrant chiefly clan from the Luba country, the Bena-Ng'andu. At first very small, and always a relatively loosely held-together state, the Bemba kingdom became a powerful factor in regional history only in the later parts of the eighteenth century, during the same period as the establishment of the kingdom of the Kazembe in the nearby Luapula Valley.

Along the northern fringes of the Kalahari region, one additional notable kingdom, Bulozi, also took shape in the seventeenth and eighteenth centuries. The old heartland of the kingdom lay among the Luyana people of the interior floodplain of the Zambezi. The Luyana language belongs to its own distinctive branch of Savanna Bantu. The ancestral Luyana-speaking community moved into the interior floodplain of the Zambezi in the early centuries of the first millennium CE. The region around the floodplain comprised a considerable variety of environments, and this factor made the floodplain the centerpiece in a multifaceted exchange of products. The floodplain itself, with its moist soils and high water table, had long been an area of greater agricultural productivity and greater concentration of population than the steppe and dry savanna regions all around it. From the river itself and from its tributaries came fish, while

FIG. 79 Luba sculpture

The old Niger-Congo tradition of wood sculpture has remained strong right down to recent centuries in many areas of West Africa and in the Congo Basin. The various Luba-related peoples, both those incorporated directly into the Luba empire of the eighteenth century and those who remained outside it, were particularly important in the preserving and developing of new versions of that artistic tradition, as this sculpture of a female figure shows us.

the Southwest-Bantu and the Khwe peoples living west of the floodplain kept large numbers of livestock. In addition, hunting still provided a major source of food, leather, and other products both for the Bantu-speaking communities and for the Ju and Khwe (Khoisan) peoples of the wider region.

The fact that the floodplain lay at the hub of the local exchange of a varied array of products may well have given some kind of economic prominence to the Luyana and their local chiefs even in earlier centuries. But why the larger

Bulozi kingdom should have emerged to prominence at this particular period is not yet understood. Perhaps the key difference in the seventeenth and eighteenth centuries was that the long-distance routes of trade connection to the distant eastern, western, and southern coasts had all finally begun to reach as far inland as Bulozi. But just how that new element in economic relations might have been connected to the social and political changes that produced the Bulozi kingdom remains to be investigated by historians.

Outside of the kingdoms of the Bemba, the Kazembe, and Bulozi, the rest of modern-day eastern and central Zambia continued right into the nineteenth century to be a region of small independent chiefdoms and tiny kingdoms. The Nsenga, a Sabi-speaking people who resided around and to the east of the confluence of the Luangwa and Zambezi Rivers, were organized, for instance, in clan-based chiefdoms. In the eighteenth century some of these chiefdoms aligned themselves in a loose larger grouping under the leadership of the Mburuma chiefdom, which had become particularly wealthy and powerful from the Zambezi River trade of that period. The Ila and Tonga descendants of the Botatwe who established themselves centuries earlier in central Zambia (see chapter 6), remained divided, however, into a great number of wholly independent clan chiefdoms very much like those we believe to have been characteristic of their Savanna-Bantu ancestors of the first millennium BCE (see chapter 5).

Political and Economic Change in the Northern Congo Basin

Far to the north, at the other side of the Congo Basin in the Ubangi, Uele, and Bomu River regions, the political trends already evident in the mid-seventeenth century (see chapter 8) gave rise to a new emerging political force, the Zande. The idea of the "spoils of the leopard" and the military innovations that went along with that ideology had already set in motion the expansion of the Nzakara and Ngbandi kingdoms by around 1600, as we learned in chapter 8. Living east of the Bomu-Uele confluence, the Vungara rulers of the Zande in the eighteenth century launched a long-lasting series of campaigns that slowly, decade by decade, advanced their power eastward up the Bomu River as far as the southwestern edges of the Middle Nile Basin, as well as southeastward toward the upper Uele River. The Zande kings set in motion an ongoing process of military conquest and cultural incorporation of numerous previously distinct Ubangian peoples. By this means, stage by stage, they expanded a single Zande ethnicity across hundreds of kilometers of woodland savanna.

In the late eighteenth century, the possibility of further Zande expansion southward may have been diverted by the rise of the Mangbetu kingdom near the upper sources of the Uele River, at the northern edge of the rainforest. The Mangbetu kings, themselves of Medje-Lombi Central Sudanian ancestry, united a diverse set of forest farming peoples of Boan (Bantu) and Central Sudanic background in a strong multi-ethnic state. The Mangbetu kingdom had a highly productive manufacturing sector. It included a sophisticated forging technology, known for producing fine copper ornaments and a wide range of iron tools and weapons, including throwing knives. The copper, as in earlier times in the region, was imported from the north, ultimately from Darfur. Raffia cloth weaving and barkcloth making were other important manufacturing activities. The poison for the *benge* ordeal, made by the nearby Boan peoples, was used in the kingdom and passed in trade farther north to the Zande. The staple of Mangbetu agriculture was the banana, raised in many varieties. In addition, a significant population of BaTwa people contributed forest gathering and hunting products to the overall mix of trade.

The most spectacular accomplishment of the Mangbetu kings was their

FIG. 80 Great palace of Mangbetu king

The scene presented here (drawn by the nineteenth-century European traveler Schweinfurth) depicts the Mangbetu king Mbunza of the 1860s and 1870s dancing before his seated wives inside his enormous wooden palace.

building of huge wooden palaces, rivaling certain Japanese temples as the largest wooden structures ever built. The examples of such royal palaces we have certain knowledge of belong to the heyday of Mangbetu power in the nineteenth century. We cannot yet be sure that this kind of architecture actually goes back to the earliest years of the kingdom in the eighteenth century.

Southern Africa: New Pastoral and Trading Frontiers

The Establishment of the Cape Colony

At the far south of Africa, the commerce of the middle Atlantic Age had a strikingly different kind of consequence than anywhere else on the continent—it led to the creation by the Dutch of the first European *settler* colony in Africa. In 1652, the Netherlands East India Company, needing a secure place from which to resupply its ships with food and water on the long journey to the East Indies, took the step of founding a station at Cape Town on Table Bay just north of the Cape of Good Hope.

Table Bay was a place at which European ships had been stopping in large numbers for the preceding seventy years (see chapter 8). From the point of view of the local Khoekhoe people, the initial Dutch settlement of about seventy people must have seemed little different from the even larger numbers of European sailors who came each year and camped ashore for several weeks at a time, while they bargained for meat and collected water from the local streams before sailing on.

But that understanding rapidly changed. Within the next five years, the Dutch began to bring in the first few permanent settlers from Europe, intending that these people would grow vegetables for the passing ships. At the same time, the company began to build up its own herds of cattle, seeking to lessen its dependence on trade with the Khoekhoe to supply its needs for meat. The Netherlands East India Company continued to bring in settlers in small numbers through the rest of the seventeenth century, but the settlers soon discovered that raising cattle was easier and more profitable for them than planting vegetables. Of Dutch, German, and French Huguenot ancestry and Calvinist Christian in religion, these Europeans progressively insinuated themselves into more and more of the grazing lands of the Khoekhoe.

During two periods of desultory mutual raiding between the Dutch and Khoekhoe, sometimes called the First and Second Khoekhoe Wars, the local people sought to stem this settlement of Europeans. The first conflict, between

1656 and 1658, affected the small Khoekhoe subchiefdoms within about 30 kilometers of the Dutch settlement at Cape Town. The second, between 1673 and 1677, engaged the larger Chochoqua kingdom, whose territories extended from 60 to 150 kilometers east of Cape Town. Too deeply tied economically by this time to the trade in cattle and sheep with the Europeans, and too decentralized politically to mount a concerted military campaign, the Khoekhoe in both periods of conflict eventually gave way to Dutch expansion. After 1677, the Chochoqua kingdom gradually ceased to form an effective political unit.

By the close of the seventeenth century, the Cape Colony of the Netherlands East India Company stretched for about 100 kilometers east and north from Cape Town. Its lands interspersed the holdings of European settlers with those of several still autonomous Khoekhoe bands. The culminating disaster for the indigenous societies of the colony came in 1713, when a great smallpox epidemic killed a large proportion of the Khoekhoe, who seem to have lacked a previous experience of that disease and so lacked any immunity to it.

Creating a New Social Formation

By that time, a new social formation had begun to take shape in the then still tiny Cape Colony. At the top were patriarchal landholding families of largely, but not entirely, European ancestry. By the late eighteenth century, around 8 percent of the genetic makeup of this upper stratum appears to have been African. Their descendants in later times called themselves Afrikaners; another name they have been given is Boers. Under this dominant stratum of society came people of Khoekhoe and mixed European-Khoekhoe ancestry. They formed a caste of free persons who worked sometimes for themselves in skilled occupations but more often as herders for the landowning upper caste. Still lower on the social scale came slaves, imported at first from the East Indies and then increasingly from other parts of Africa, including Mozambique and West Africa, as well as from Madagascar.

Because of the very high birth rate of the upper stratum of mostly European descent, land soon became scarce, and many men of this ancestry began to turn to hunting and semi-nomadic herding, following the example of Khoekhoe culture in these respects. With this economy, they and their families expanded rapidly eastward at the expense of Khoekhoe societies, which had been devastated and disorganized by the disastrous smallpox epidemic of 1713 and by recurrences of that epidemic several years later. The pastoralism of these expanding Boers ("farmers") differed in several key respects from that of the

Khoekhoe, however. For one, the Boers traveled by wagon and often lived in these wagons. They also had guns with which they could kill animals at long distance, and this led to a fairly rapid decline of wild game wherever the Boers settled. The Boers also possessed the military advantage, if fighting took place, of having horses. With horses they could ride in close to their enemies and fire their single-shot muskets, ride quickly away from danger to reload, and then ride in close to shoot again.

The Boers differed significantly as well in their social ideas and practices. They believed in individual ownership of land, and they adhered to a hierarchical social order, run by men. In earlier Khoekhoe history, those who had suffered the loss of their herds could seek to rebuild their fortunes by offering their service to chiefs or other men wealthy in cattle. In return for service, they received cattle with which to rebuild their own herds and eventually regain their economic independence. But when, after the disastrous epidemics of the early eighteenth century, many Khoekhoe sought similarly to attach themselves to the expanding Boer families, rich in livestock, the only position allowed to them in Boer society was one of continuing servant status. Even when they were able to build up small herds of their own, the land was now claimed by the Boers, and the Khoekhoe could graze their cattle on it only by continuing to give service to the Boer families.

Two kinds of society emerged out of these developments. In the areas close to Cape Town, with good access to passing ships, a countryside divided up into a large number of farms of varying size, owned by Boers, took shape by the early eighteenth century. Besides raising cattle, the farmers grew wheat and grapes, crops adapted to the cool growing season of the Cape's subtropical Mediterranean climate. From the juice of the grapes the farmers made wine and brandy. The lowest stratum of society were slaves, imported by the farmers and well-to-do townspeople, sometimes from West Africa but more often from the East Indies and Madagascar, to work on their lands and in their houses. A third, intermediate stratum consisted of a free people of Khoekhoe and mixed descent, who worked as herders or in menial occupations in town. On the frontiers of the colony, in contrast, a different social formation arose, with an upper caste comprising the landholding Boer families and the lower caste consisting of their retainers of Khoekhoe and mixed ancestry. Only occasionally did the upper-caste frontier families own slaves before the nineteenth century.

Boers and Basters: Expanding an Economic and Cultural Frontier

The East India Company's government lacked the resources and usually the inclination to restrain the expansion of the frontier segment of this new society. Through the practice of granting large loan-farms to the Boers of the frontiers, typically of around 2,500 hectares, in return for a very small yearly payment in money, the government created loose ties between it and individual family heads living hundreds of kilometers from Cape Town. At the same time, however, this practice legitimized Boer claims to land and further encouraged their expansion. The company government, unwilling to spend money on military forces of its own, also frequently authorized and helped arm Boer-led commandos in the eighteenth century.

While one arm of the rapid eastward expansion of Boer pastoralist and caste society proceeded along the southern coast of Africa, a second arm of this expansion passed farther inland along the series of mountain ranges that extend eastward through the interior Cape regions. In those areas, the gatherer-hunter Khoisan peoples had been relatively untouched by the smallpox epidemics. Their societies still successfully held to the older ways, and in the second half of the eighteenth century they fought back against the incursions of the Boers and against the destruction that Boer guns brought to the animal life and that the grazing of Boer livestock brought to the plants on which the Khoisan depended for food.

Organizing commandos, usually but not always with the sanction of the distant company government at Cape Town, the Boers of the interior and their Khoekhoe servants began a long series of campaigns. Lasting from the 1760s to the early 1790s, these campaigns brought about a genocidal destruction of the still independent Khoisan communities of the interior regions of today's Cape Province. The Khoisan adults were slaughtered, but the children were frequently captured and apprenticed to European masters until they had become adults. With no homes to return to, these children grew up to be new members of the growing lower caste of free people of color in the Cape Colony.

Still a third direction of frontier expansion moved initially more directly northward from the Cape Town region into the very dry steppes of the lower Orange River. The leaders of this expansion were men of mixed ancestry, some of them escaped slaves and others belonging to the emerging lower caste of freemen. Not accepted by the upper caste of the Cape and rarely tolerated on the Boer frontier to the east, these people, called Basters, found scope for their ambitions among the still unconquered Khoekhoe and Khoisan gatherer-hunters of the lower Orange River region.

The society they created in that region greatly resembled that of the Boer pastoralists. It depended on livestock raising for its livelihood and used guns, wagons, and horses to support that livelihood. The Basters, like the Boers, thought of themselves as somehow Christian whether they had ever seen a church or not, simply because they saw themselves as having a European cultural ancestry. The Baster society, in its formative stages in the second half of the eighteenth century, consisted of a ruling stratum of Baster families and a much larger client stratum of people of purely Khoekhoe herder or Khoisan gatherer-hunter ancestries. But as developments in the early nineteenth century would later reveal, the Baster society was much less rigidly stratified. People of the lower stratum in time could and did gain wealth in cattle and come to be accepted as leaders of society alongside the older leading Baster families. In the Boer society they could not have done so.

By the 1770s, the farthest eastern frontier of Boer pastoral expansion had reached all the way to the Sundays and Fish Rivers. On the Orange River frontier, some of the mixed ancestry pastoralists of the same period began to settle across the river in far southern Namibia. A few others had moved upstream along the Orange River. By the 1790s the advancing edge of the eastward spread of the Basters reached the good grazing lands of the confluence of the Orange and Vaal Rivers.

To the south, the northern arm of Boer expansion pressed into the upper Sundays River region through the 1780s and 1790s. But still farther south, between the lower Sundays and the Fish Rivers, the southern arm of the Boer expansion came to an abrupt halt at the end of the 1770s in the face of the countervailing westward spread of the Xhosa society. In the late seventeenth century, the Xhosa, a Bantu-speaking people of the Nguni group, still formed a small kingdom centered just east of the Kei River. Then, during the more than fifty-year rule of Phalo, who died in 1760, the Xhosa tripled the size of their lands, spreading from the Kei River to the Fish, in large part by incorporating former Khoekhoe chiefdoms into their society. Between 1720 and 1770, the best known eastern Khoekhoe chiefdom, Gqona, whose territories included areas west of the Fish, was assimilated as a new division within the Xhosa, called the AmaGqunukwebe.

In the thirty years following the death of Phalo, the Xhosa kingdom broke

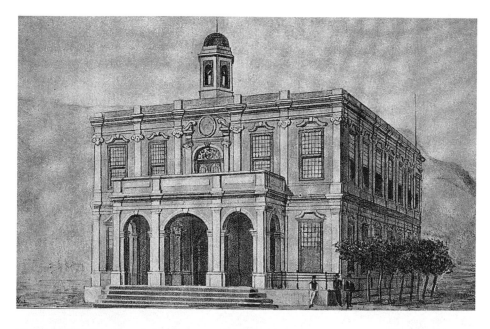

FIG. 81 Old Burgher Watch-House, Cape Town

The establishment of the Dutch Colony at the Cape of Good Hope introduced new building styles into the region. This structure, built between 1750 and 1770, followed contemporary European models for such buildings.

up into several smaller kingdoms, each still owing a nominal allegiance to a paramount king living east of the Kei River, but each in practice increasingly independent of the others. This divergence of interests did not lessen the westward push of Xhosa settlement beyond the Fish River. If anything, the competition between different Xhosa kingdoms probably increased the pressures for expansion. As a result, by the 1790s the country between the lower Sundays and Fish Rivers was a contested land, with a few Boer settlers, especially in the west, but most of it controlled by different Xhosa kings and their people.

The expansion of the Boer and Baster frontiers did not bring an end to the old trade networks of farther southern Africa but enhanced them by adding new commodities and, eventually, by changing the ways in which goods traveled. In the second half of the eighteenth century, wagons and horses increasingly became the load carriers of trade into the interior, displacing the older reliance on foot travel and pack oxen. Oxen, used indigenously as pack animals among the Khoekhoe and the Sotho of the interior for many centuries, continued to be important in the new era of trade, but now most often as draft animals, pulling wagons. The wagon trade greatly increased the quantity of goods that could be carried, and it brought into being a new occupational specialization, that of wagon driver, as European merchants in the Cape Colony began to hire people of the mixed-race caste to act as their agents in the commerce to the interior.

On the Orange River frontier, many of the Basters carried the wagon trade still deeper into the interior. By the 1790s, commerce of the new kind began to be extended north toward the center of Namibia. There the Nama Khoekhoe and their northern neighbors, the Southwest-Bantu-speaking Herero, both vied to gain better access to the new kinds of goods coming into their region. For the first time also, the wagon trade reached the capital towns of the small Tswana kingdoms along the eastern side of the Kalahari steppe, north of the

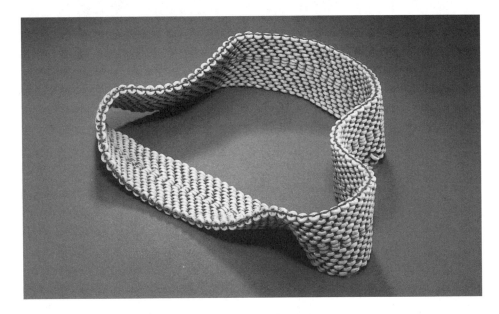

FIG. 82 Ju ostrich-eggshell decorated headband

This item, from the Ju Khoisan people, exemplifies a style of head adornment, of some antiquity among the Southern Khoisan, which also spread to some of the Kusi Bantu communities of southeastern Africa over the past 2,000 years. The Ju were one of the Khoisan peoples of the Kalahari region who in the eighteenth century (and even more so in the nineteenth century) became suppliers of the products of the hunt, especially various kinds of skins, to the growing trade of the southern African interior.

confluence of the Vaal and Orange Rivers. Goods such as guns and cloth were transported northward; cattle and sheep were among the most important products traded west and south toward Cape Town. By the close of the century, ivory and skins from the Tswana areas and from the Khoisan gatherer-hunters of the Kalahari were passing as well along the new roads of trade.

Eastern Africa: States and Stateless Societies

Eastern Africa in the 1640s and 1650s included many areas as yet untouched by the expansion of seagoing commerce in the Indian Ocean. In some regions, the most important historical themes of the later seventeenth and the eighteenth centuries had to do with shifting balances of power among states; in other, stateless regions, with changing ethnic and cultural distributions; and in still other areas, with agricultural innovation. Nonetheless, it is clear from a variety of indirect indicators that a revitalizing of commerce at the coast was underway in the eighteenth century, and that the penetration of commercial influences from the coast far into the interior had begun already by the end of the seventeenth century.

Central East Africa: Social Change in Stateless Societies

In the central interior of East Africa lay a large area where time and again the expansions of the pastoral Maasai deeply affected the course of change. The Maasai began as an offshoot of the Maa peoples resident since the eighth century in the Laikipia and Lorogi Plateaus north of Mount Kenya. As we previously discovered (in chapter 8), by sometime in the sixteenth century they had moved south and established themselves through the central parts of the Kenya Rift Valley. In the seventeenth and eighteenth centuries, various Maasai communities aggressively expanded their presence farther southward and also west of the rift, into the Uasingishu Plain, the Mau Range, and Mara Plains.

Already in the late sixteenth century, the Kamba of Kilimanjaro came under attack from the Maasai. In the seventeenth century, in the face of this recurrent threat, a goodly number of the Kamba sought refuge among the Chaga of the forested eastern and southern slopes of Kilimanjaro and were assimilated into their society. Other Kamba instead moved 150 kilometers southward, settling for perhaps a generation or two in tsetse fly–infested areas between the Chyulu Hills and the Athi River. Some Kamba continued to reside there into later times, but by the late seventeenth century the majority had moved into the then wooded highlands north of the Chyulu Hills, called by them Mbooni. Drawing on the agricultural knowledge gained during their Kilimanjaro sojourn, the Kamba created an irrigation-based agriculture that eventually came to include terraced fields.

The success of the Kamba settlement in Mbooni contributed to a rapidly growing population. In the first quarter of the eighteenth century, as available land for crops and livestock became scarce, many Kamba began to move out from Mbooni and take up other kinds of livelihoods. A considerable number crossed the Athi River to the east, settling in dry hilly areas where irrigation was not possible, but where extensive grazing of livestock could be combined with the raising of crops suited to drier conditions, such as pearl millet and certain varieties of sorghum. Still other Kamba moved south into the coastal hinterland and established themselves in the first quarter of the eighteenth century as middlemen in the trade of interior goods at the coast. We will have more to say later about these Kamba.

As Maasai expansion continued southward around Mount Kilimanjaro, it dislodged another people, the Ma'a, from their grazing lands. Cattle-raising specialists like the Maasai but speakers of a Southern Cushitic language, the Ma'a fled north in the middle of the seventeenth century to the South Pare Mountains, the Taita hills, and the Usambara Mountains. In the Pare and Taita regions, they were eventually assimilated into the local Bantu-speaking populations, but in Usambara they found good grazing areas in the highest, coolest parts of the mountains and have remained a distinct population down to the present.

Toward the close of the eighteenth century, the Shambaa kingdom was founded in the Usambaras. The founding of this state came about surely in part as a response to the problems of conflict over land and resources between the Shambaa people, who were of Northeast-Coastal Bantu antecedents and were long-time residents of the mountains, and newer immigrants. These included the Ma'a and also the Daiso, a Thagiicu people who arrived from Mount Kenya in about the seventeenth century ("Daiso" is actually a dialect version of the old name "Thagiicu"). The Shambaa king and court formed a set of institutions that maintained the peace and mediated between the divergent interests of different segments of the population. Royal power drew on the imagery of the king as provider of prosperity and rested also on the performance of yearly rituals that gave the Ma'a as well as the Shambaa essential roles in the ideology of the state. In place of the clan chiefs of the older Niger-Congo civilization, still important in the seventeenth and early eighteenth centuries in Usambara, the Shambaa kings delegated authority over various localities to different sons and other close relatives.

West of the rift valley lay another set of regions across which Maasai expansion was powerfully felt in the seventeenth and eighteenth centuries. In the areas occupied today by the famous game reserves of Serengeti, Manyara, and Ngorongoro Crater, the last quarter of the seventeenth century was the time of the Il-Tatua wars, as they are known in Maasai historical tradition. In a series of attacks, the Maasai drove the Datoga, a Southern Nilotic people, southward and westward and seized a lasting control over the vast grasslands of the Mara and Serengeti regions. Farther north, at about the same time, another grouping of Maasai communities, the Il-Uasinkishu, struck northward into the Uasingishu Plain, which bears their name today. By the early eighteenth century, they had scattered the Kalenjin-speaking Sirikwa from the region. The Sirikwa mostly found refuge among nearby Kalenjin communities, who farmed the montane forest areas all around the Uasingishu Plain.

The last stage of the Maasai expansion carried the Kisonko Maasai alliance far southward over the course of the eighteenth century, almost to what is today central Tanzania. There the Kisonko defeated and absorbed into their society the former South Kalenjin pastoral inhabitants of this region, which is today called the Maasai Steppe.

By the 1790s, the Maasai had the ability to upset the peace and to influence cultural change over 50,000 square kilometers of East African interior. In the Mount Kenya region, in the second half of the eighteenth century, the prestige of Maasai culture played a central role in development of new military tactics and weaponry in the Gikuyu society. At same time, the Maasai were key actors in the expanding market relations of Mount Kenya and Mount Kilimanjaro. As raisers of a majority of the cattle in central East Africa and of very large numbers of goats and sheep, the Maasai were the chief providers of leather at the marketplaces. They were important consumers of the iron produced on Mount Kenya and in Ugweno and were also buyers of gourd containers, which they used in great numbers and variety but did not usually plant themselves.

A new kind of influential leader appeared among the Maasai in the 1780s, the *ol-oibon*. The word originally described local prophetic figures, influential because of their repute as seers and their ability to invoke the sanctions of Divinity in the affairs of men and women. In the closing decades of the eighteenth century, one such prophet, Supet, took on a key role in successfully mediating relations between several of the Maasai alliances. So great was Supet's prestige in the aftermath of these events that he was able to gain a following and reputation across many of the central parts of the Maasai territories. After his death, his authority and prestige were passed down to one of his sons, and in this way a new kind of *ol-oibon* came into being, whose prophecies and pronouncements could greatly affect the decisions reached by the elders of communities even 200 kilometers away.

The Great Lakes Region: New States Emerge

Developments in the African Great Lakes region followed a quite different trajectory in the period between 1640 and 1800. Bunyoro remained through the period the most powerful state of the region, but its power was no longer uncontested.

On the eastern margins of the Bunyoro hegemony, in the wooded lands along the northwestern shores of Lake Nyanza, the chief new challenge came from the slowly growing power of the once tiny kingdom of Buganda. A subordinate unit of Bunyoro in the sixteenth century, Buganda by the 1640s and 1650s appears to have slipped from Bunyoro control. In the second half of the seventeenth century, its kings engaged in wars that added several new areas to the kingdom. In the eighteenth century, further conquests and the movement of Buganda settlers into these areas had consolidated a state that stretched for 200 kilometers around the northern and western sides of Lake Nyanza.

More important for social and political history, these conquests ushered in a new era in the politicization of Buganda life. The kings from the later seventeenth century onward put into effect a policy of placing all newly conquered territories under the authority of appointed chiefs. When later kings in the eighteenth century doubled and redoubled again the size of Buganda with further wars of conquest, they continued the policy of establishing appointive chiefships in all the new lands. By time of King Semakokiro and his son Junju in the second half of the eighteenth century, the local authority through most of Buganda was in the hands of the king's men, appointed to office by him and dependent on him for staying in office. Semakokiro and Junju had a degree of personal authority over their kingdom and subjects unmatched anywhere else in the Great Lakes region or perhaps anywhere else in sub-Saharan Africa. Their country had, as well, interior routes of communication by boat on Lake Nyanza that gave them an unmatched ability to move forces rapidly between the center and the periphery of the state. Accompanying the creation of a more and more authoritarian and centralized Buganda state came a decline in the position of women both in government and in society in general and an increase in male authority within the households of the country.

Along the southern peripheries of the Bunyoro sphere of power between the 1640s and the 1790s, a still different range of social and political changes was under way. In the second half of the seventeenth century, numerous tiny subordinate states on the southern marches of Bunyoro still recognized the suzerainty of the Bunyoro kings. But the era of the great Bunyoro military campaigns that might reach as far south as Rwanda appears by then to have been over. Two notable long-term trends in the history of this region became increasingly apparent over the course of the later seventeenth and early eighteenth centuries. One of these was a new growth in power and self-assertion among the rulers of the tiny southern polities. The other was an ideological ferment centering around the idea that the cattle-keeping specialist communities of the region were people "born to rule." This is an idea, of course, that we have already encountered in chapter 8 in reading about Rwanda and Burundi.

The Nkore kingdom under Ntare IV in the early eighteenth century provides a particularly provocative case of the new assertiveness of the southern statelets. On the military side, Ntare IV instituted a new kind of military force, a contingent of bowmen, an idea he may have adopted from the nearby small kingdom of Buhweju. He also sought to better tie his subjects to the state by establishing new offices at court, which he filled with persons from different clans and localities, thus giving the people from the different areas of the kingdom a kind of representation at court.

One new large state in this region was the short-lived kingdom of Mpororo. Put together under King Kahaya ya Murari in the last quarter of the seventeenth century, Mpororo remained powerful for another generation under Kahaya's son. The key to holding this state together appears to have been the kings' reliance on the specialized pastoralists of the region, who were given important chiefly positions and allowed to seize cattle as booty and so enlarge their herds by participating in Mpororo's wars.

With the collapse of the kingdom in the early eighteenth century, the pastoralist groups lost their special political position, and many of them shifted their support southward to the then expanding kingdom of Rwanda, where a special higher status for pastoralists was part of an already emerging caste system. They and their descendants became a key element in Rwanda's wars of expansion in the middle and late eighteenth century. Their participation in those wars helped bring to an end the independence of several small, non-pastoralist-ruled BaHutu kingdoms in what became the northern areas of Rwanda. The Rwandan conquest of the rival BaTutsi-ruled states of Gisaka and Ndorwa in the late eighteenth century completed the early era of Rwanda's rise to power and consolidated the caste system in that country (already discussed in chapter 8).

Trade and Political Change in the East African Interior, 1640–1800

In several parts of East Africa, it is apparent that, at least from the end of the seventeenth century, a new growth of commercial activities was underway. In the coastal hinterland of today's northeastern Tanzania, Kamba immigrants from the north struggled with the Doe people in the 1720s over who was to control the carrying of trade goods between the inland areas of the Wami and Ruvu Rivers and the small Swahili merchant towns at the coast. The Doe eventually won this struggle, and the Kamba ceased to be a factor in the region.

Other more indirect evidence suggests that overland trade links had begun to stretch far inland, as far almost as Lake Tanganyika, even before 1700. A large number of new chiefdoms were founded among the Takama Bantu peoples in western Tanzania, especially the Kimbu and Nyamwezi, in the late seventeenth and early eighteenth centuries. Two features are striking about the chiefly families of these new polities. Several of them came from the east, from Usagara, a region adjacent to the upper Wami and Ruvu Rivers, and they brought with them chiefly regalia of coastal origin, notably conus shells and carved wooden horns, resembling the *siwa* horns symbolic of ruling status in the coastal Swahili cities and towns. These facts tell us that, already in the late seventeenth century, the East African coast and its trade products must have exerted a powerful draw on the cultural imaginations of peoples living as many as 800 kilometers inland from the coast. Only in that way can we explain how symbols connected with the coast could have had such political salience for interior communities. The chiefs who came from Usagara, we suspect, must originally have been intermediaries in the interior trade links. As traders, they would have had been able to obtain items from the coast. By trading with the inland areas, they would have acquired sufficient knowledge of the contemporary currents of thought in the Takama societies to use their possession of the regalia to gain recognition as chiefs.

In the second half of the eighteenth century, the coastal trading links expanded still farther inland, all the way to Lake Nyanza. The sign in Buganda of

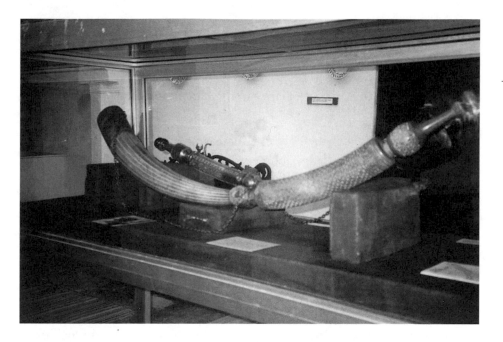

FIG. 83 *Siwa* horn

Horns like this magnificent, almost four-meter-long instrument, here made of ivory but more usually carved from wood, had long been emblems of the rulers of Swahili city-states. Horns of a similar style were introduced as chiefly paraphernalia to the Takama societies of interior East Africa by the Usagara immigrants in the later seventeenth and early eighteenth centuries.

the new economic connections was the first arrival of cups and saucers at the court of Junju sometime around the 1770s or 1780s. Just how this trade was carried over the hundreds of kilometers between the coast and the Great Lakes is not yet clear to historians. Long-distance caravans, organized by the Nyamwezi of western Tanzania, certainly followed the routes of trade between Lake Tanganyika and the Indian Ocean by the start of the nineteenth century. But it seems probable that, before the 1790s, goods were still transmitted by stages: carried by small, less formal trading parties traveling between Usagara and the coast; transported by other traders traversing the dry plains of central Tanzania between Usagara and the Takama communities of western Tanzania; and carried by still other traders following the land and lake routes between western Tanzania and Buganda.

Northeastern Africa: An Age of Political and Cultural Realignment

Political Power and Social Allegiance in the Horn of Africa

In the Horn of Africa, as in many other parts of the continent, new directions of social and political change became increasingly evident beginning in the 1640s. But contrasting with developments in West Africa, the external factor of relations with Europeans had little to do with what took place. Instead, the regional ethnic and political disruptions of the sixteenth and early seventeenth centuries, and the choices made by communities and leaders in response to the troubles of that time, set the historical agenda of the ensuing age. If any outside factors did shape the course of change, they were ones connected to economic relations with the Muslim Middle East.

Within the Solomonic kingdom, the choice by Fasiladas in the 1630s to establish a fixed capital greatly weakened the abilities of subsequent kings to intervene in the affairs of distant areas. Nevertheless, the great regional lords, called by the title *ras* (roughly equivalent to a duke in medieval Europe), continued for the next century and a half to recognize the overall authority of the kings at Gondar. Their own legitimacy as feudal lords, after all, was tied to that of their overlord, the "king of kings," as the Solomonic rulers were styled.

An illustration of how crucial it still was for the regional feudal lords to claim allegiance to the Solomonic kings is provided by developments in Showa. Although Showa had been part of the home region of Yekunno-Amlak, the founder of the Solomonic dynasty, by the mid-sixteenth century it lay beyond the southeastern margins of the feudal state. Rarely in touch with events in Gondar and with large parts of it now Oromo in culture and language, Showa also contained areas that hung on to the feudal Christian political economy. In the 1680s, an ambitious local lord, Negussie, who claimed a distant familial connection to the Solomonic rulers, traveled to Gondar to seek the sanction of the king to act as the governor of Showa. Armed with this moral claim to legitimacy, Negussie and his descendants in the eighteenth century sought with gradually increasing success to unite the Showa region into a new kingdom, subordinate in name to the Solomonic state but in practice an independent Christian feudal state.

In the late seventeenth and early eighteenth centuries, the Solomonic court at Gondar became a place of political intrigue, as the *rases* struggled among themselves for preeminent position. The king of kings, no longer able to effectively intervene militarily in the provinces, tried to maintain power by playing off the great lords against one another. In these struggles, the *rases* whose lands lay closest to Gondar tended most often to have the advantage. In the 1760s and 1770s, this competition finally broke down, as Ras Michael of Begemder, the region to the east of Gondar, became the most powerful figure in the kingdom, able to depose and install new holders of the Solomonic office almost at will. After the 1780s, Solomonic kings continued be named at Gondar, but their legitimacy was no longer recognized by the society as a whole. What Ethiopians call the Era of the Princes, in which the great lords became independent rulers in fact as well as in the perceptions of society, had truly begun.

All around the remaining Solomonic domains, in the lands of the now numerous Oromo, a characteristic feature of historical change between 1640 and the 1790s was the re-emergence, in new forms, of the social and political patterns of earlier times. In the Wollo region, which lay along the edge of the highlands not much more than 200 kilometers to the east of Gondar, feudal relations gradually displaced the age-grade-based institutions of the *gada* republic, brought in by the Oromo in the late sixteenth century (see chapter 8). A number of Oromo leaders became strongly involved in the political struggles at the Solomonic court in the late seventeenth century and were sometimes appointed by the kings to the feudal position of *ras* in the eighteenth century.

Farther east, most of the people of the old central territories of the Adal state had adopted Oromo ethnic identity by the middle of the seventeenth century. Only in the walled city of Harar, an important entrepot in the continuing commercial activities of the region, and in a few rural areas did the local Ethiopic Semitic languages, Harari and Argobba, continue to be spoken. The remnant of the Adal state survived only around the oasis of Ausa in the Danakil Depression. The institutions of the *gada* republic took hold as part of the Oromoization of the general populace. At the same time, one older kind of cultural feature of the region, adherence to Islam, gradually reasserted its importance among the rural population, both Oromo and non-Oromo.

A still more striking revival of the institutions of earlier times took place in Wollega in the second half of the eighteenth century. Wollega is the name given the extensive region of the Ethiopian Highlands that lay between the Omotic states of the southwest, such as Kafa, and the Solomonic state to the north of the Abbai River. The cultural expansion of the Oromo all across that region took place, as we have seen (chapter 8), between the late 1500s and 1650. The age-grade-based institutions of the *gada* republic provided the governing structure of the period of conquest. The indigenous majority of the region was not at first integrated into these institutions but given a subordinate status.

As the social distinction between Oromo and subject peoples broke down in Wollega in the late seventeenth and early eighteenth centuries, the older ideas of Omotic sacral kingship began again to be part of the regional political discourse. Between 1750 and 1800, several ambitious Oromo leaders adapted these older ideas to the situation of the times. They established themselves as the kings of new Oromo-speaking states, the foremost of these kingdoms being Abu Jimma Jafar. Throughout the greater part of Wollega, though, the *gada* republic remained the accepted pattern of government right on through the eighteenth century.

The increased political fragmentation of the times did not bring commerce to a halt. The Omotic and Highland Eastern Cushitic peoples of the Ethiopian Rift Valley and the Omotic peoples in the southwestern kingdoms continued to

FIG. 84 Maria Theresa dollar

In the late eighteenth century, as the Era of the Princes got fully under way in Ethiopia, a new kind of currency began to be imported via the Red Sea coasts, a silver coin minted in the Austro-Hungarian Empire in central Europe and known by the name of the Austrian empress, Maria Theresa, whose visage appeared on the front side of the coin. The back of the coin is shown here. An older Ethiopian currency, important ever since the Aksumite kings ceased to mint coins of their own back in the seventh century, was the *amole*. The *amole* was a block of salt, mined at a certain locale in the desert below the northeastern edge of the Ethiopian Highlands. It continued to be used for everyday trade through the nineteenth century. But high-value, long-distance trade in the region, as well as the power and wealth of the feudal lords, came to depend more and more, from the close of the eighteenth century onward, on the availability of large quantities of Maria Theresa dollars.

produce civet, coffee, and a variety of other commodities for export. If anything, the political situation may have increased productivity, both because many producers competed to supply the trade and because the retreat of Solomonic power removed the hindrances of taxation and regulation to the flow of goods.

The volume of one kind of exported commodity, enslaved human beings, in fact, greatly increased in this period. European demand played no part in this development. Instead, this trade in people went to the oldest slaveholding part of the world, the Middle East. In the late eighteenth century, the main areas of supply lay in the southwest Ethiopian Highlands, in such places as Kafa and Abu Jimma Jafar. The kings of Showa, whose territories were adjacent to the main routes to the coast, faced a moral dilemma because an important school of thought in Ethiopian Christianity held that Christianity was incompatible with slave trade. But their economic interests generally overcame their scruples, and they facilitated that trade through their territories and sometimes contributed to it themselves.

Trade, Class, Kings, and Religion in the Eastern Sudan Region

To the west of the Ethiopian Highlands, in the Middle Nile Basin, several recurrent themes can be discerned in the events of the period between 1640 and the 1790s. For one thing, merchants and their commercial activities penetrated progressively deeper and in more intricate fashion into the daily lives of people in more and more parts of the region. Among the unfortunate consequences was an enormous growth in the scale of slave trade, especially in western parts of the Middle Nile Basin, supplying Egypt and, through Egypt, other parts of the Middle East. A second trend was a widening adoption of the Arabic language and of the ethnic label of Arab by many of the indigenous people of the region. A third theme was the growing establishment of Islam as a replacement for the earlier Sudanic religion.

In the Sinnar kingdom and along the stretches of the Nile north of Sinnar, all three themes came together. The Sinnar kingdom continued to follow a policy throughout the seventeenth century of requiring foreign merchants to come to the court and display their wares, so that the king would get first choice before allowing the traders to proceed further. A new set of developments, beginning in the seventeenth century, eventually brought this system to an end in the eighteenth century and opened the Middle Nile Basin to much more open expressions of merchant capitalist enterprise.

The changeover had its roots inauspiciously enough along the Nubian-speaking Dongola Reach of the Nile. In the seventeenth century, farmable lands in that region fell more and more into the hands of large landowners. Again the majority of the population became poor tenants, much as their forebears had been four centuries earlier under the Nubian Christian kings. But by that time a different worldview had come into being, an Islamic one in which the occupation of merchant was both respected and encouraged. Many Dongolawi Nubians moved south of the desert in the late seventeenth and early eighteenth centuries, escaping an increasingly impoverished farming life by becoming small-scale traders, especially in the western parts of the Sinnar domains. In the first half of the eighteenth century, these Danagla, as they were called, became part of an expanding indigenous merchant class in the kingdom, spreading their activities southward into regions where commerce had rarely touched before, such as the Nuba Mountains.

The new merchant class, not unlike their counterparts in the Protestant parts of Europe, favored the traits of frugality and restraint, in contrast to the ostentatious displays of the traditional ruling class. They saw to the education of their children by pious Muslim teachers, and in this way they imbibed a bookish and more straitlaced kind of Islam, in conflict with the easygoing coexistence of Islamic and older Sudanic religious beliefs among the peasantry and the ruling stratum of society. Islam also gained new footholds in the countryside, in the form of religious settlements, established by religious teachers. These colonies, exempted from the variety of taxes, duties, and tribute imposed by the state and by the increasingly autonomous regional notables and lords of Sinnar, attracted many adherents, who sought relief from the growing capriciousness with which such impositions seemed to be collected.

By the middle of the eighteenth century, the economic importance of the commercial class had grown so great, and the new intellectual currents of the time had become so strong, that the kings of Sinnar began to eschew the customs of sacral kingship and to accommodate the views of the merchants and the religious teachers. But in doing so, they undercut their legitimacy in the eyes of the many rural folk to whom the ideas of sacral kingship were still meaningful. The Sinnar kingdom entered the last quarter of the eighteenth century a much weakened power. In the 1770s, the forces of the Darfur kingdom invaded and successfully wrested away the tributary lands of Sinnar in the Nuba Mountains, for a while disrupting trade. The Danagla merchants, however, were soon back in business in the now eastern territories of Darfur.

The Darfur state first took shape in the mid-seventeenth century in the regions surrounding the Marra Mountains. The military conquests of the early kings of Darfur joined together many of the same territories that had belonged to the earlier Tunjur state in the fifteenth and sixteenth centuries. As members of the Keira ruling clan of the Marra region, these kings based their authority on ideas derived from the Sudanic sacral tradition.

In its early years the state ruled by the Darfur kings consisted of a collection of smaller tributary territories, which after their conquest often continued to be administered by their old ruling families. In the late seventeenth century and the early eighteenth century, the Keira rulers instituted a new class of estate-holding lords as a way of lessening the potential for revolt by the subordinate chiefs and kings. An estate-holder was granted an area of land, his to administer free from intervention by the chief of the larger territory in which the estate was located. The estate-holders were required to provide military contingents for the Darfur army when called upon. Over the course of the eighteenth century, they took on an additional role of growing importance for their own fortunes and for those of the state: they began to regularly send their armed contingents southward beyond the southern borderlands of Darfur to raid for slaves in the many small independent, Central Sudanic and Ubangian-speaking communities of the woodland savanna zone.

The demand for slaves to which Darfur responded was not European, but Arab and Egyptian. The northward trade in human beings opened up a newly important trans-Saharan route, passing to the west of the Nile through the Kharga Oasis to Egypt. The conquest of the Nuba Mountains from Sinnar in the 1770s strengthened Darfur's stake in the trade links crossing eastward to the Nile and the Red Sea, but the Kharga route northward continued to be the most important overall.

Darfur even in the later seventeenth century was sharply stratified. The king and other members of the Keira group formed the top layer of the system. A second stratum of subordinate notables rested their claim to authority and position on the historical background of their families as the former independent rulers of the territories they governed. Below them came the great majority of the population, most of whom were rural cultivators or raisers of livestock. These vertical distinctions of class extended horizontally across a great variety of distinct ethnic groups.

In the eighteenth century the new political class of estate-holders became generally established, and a growing slave class took shape as well. Merchants from other areas also traveled in greater numbers to Darfur, involved in the trans-Saharan commerce or in the trade with Sinnar to the east or the Chad Basin to the west. In the eighteenth century, too, an ethnic and economic element of increasing importance, the Baggara Arabs, cattle nomads in their economic pursuits, spread widely across the plains between the Nuba Mountains and the Marra Mountains, especially into areas previously inhabited by Daju cattle raisers. Standing outside the usual stratification of the society, the Baggara proved to be a difficult element for the state to control.

The kings of Darfur from the outset claimed to be Muslim in religion, but they never faced the kind of challenges to the ideology of sacral kingship that the Sinnar rulers did. In part, a policy of royal patronage of Muslim teachers assured that such individuals were beholden to the kings for their livelihoods. It appears, as well, that a truly indigenous class of merchants, with different economic interests and different worldviews from those of royalty and able to offer an alternative source of patronage for learning, did not emerge in Darfur until later times. In the eighteenth century in Darfur, merchants were mostly travelers from other lands.

North Africa: The Decline of Ottoman Over-rule

All across North Africa as far west as present-day western Algeria, the power of the Ottoman Empire faded in the late seventeenth and the eighteenth centuries. The officials who governed different parts of this region in the name of the empire increasingly became, in fact, independent rulers. Even in Egypt, where the Ottoman influence remained strongest, the local administration was largely autonomous of Ottoman oversight. The realms of the various polities that divided up the regions extending from Tripoli to Morocco tended to center on particular cities, usually located along the Mediterranean coast, and on the surrounding areas. The Berber societies of the mountains remained largely autonomous of these governments and independent of each other as well.

The shift of the balance of Mediterranean sea power back to the Italian city-states and Spain after the 1570s greatly weakened the ability of the North Africa territories, such as Algiers, Tunis, and Tripoli, to benefit from trade in the Mediterranean. What the rulers of those areas continued to do after the sixteenth century, however, was to raid seaborne commerce. Pirates from the island of Malta, allied to European states, raided the North African ports; but more often it was ships and crews from the North African cities, from Tripoli to Algiers, that attacked European merchant craft during the seventeenth and eighteenth centuries. (An American retaliatory raid against the "Barbary pirates" of Tripoli, undertaken in 1803 by a force of marines, accounts for the phrase, "to the shores of Tripoli," which appears in the U.S. Marine anthem.)

In Morocco the receding power of the Sa'di dynasty in the first half of the seventeenth century left the way open to the rise of a new dynasty, the Alawi, who unified the country once again by mid-century. The fifty-year reign by the Alawite ruler Isma'il (1672–1727) built a seemingly strong base for Moroccan unity and established a claim of Moroccan hegemony over the western Sahara to the south of Morocco. But Isma'il also founded his own power on the recruitment of a slave army from the western Sudan. After his death real power fell for a time into the hands of the leaders of this army, before being finally regained by the Alawite dynasty during the later decades of the eighteenth century.

South of Morocco, the ethnic expansion of the Hasaniya Arabs continued apace, with gradually more and more of the earlier Znaga and other Berber populations of the western Sahara being absorbed, as a nonnoble stratum, into Hasaniya society. The trans-Saharan trade through the west side of the Sahara continued unabated, linking Senegambia in a two-directional system of trade: at the Atlantic coast with Europeans, after the seventeenth century especially with the French, and simultaneously northward, overland to Morocco. Slaves and gold passed north in this system; slaves, hides, and gum went to the Europeans at the coast; and horses and other products moved south both from the Sahara fringes and from Morocco to the Senegambian kingdoms and principalities.

The Close of the Eighteenth Century: A New Era Begins

By the close of the eighteenth century, a quickening of commerce and a deepening of the ties of Africans to an emerging world economy had begun to be felt almost everywhere in Africa. The trade in human cargoes from the western coasts of the continent continued at a high rate for another fifty years, but gradually and slowly the struggle against this trade gained the upper hand.

Out of the campaigns against the slave trade came a new kind of European cultural impact in West Africa, through the establishment of colonies populated at first by manumitted, or freed, former slaves from North America and, after 1807, by people freed from captured slave ships. The British founded the earliest such colony, Sierra Leone, along the Guinea Coast, already in the eighteenth century, in 1787, by bringing in settlers of African descent from Nova Scotia. In the nineteenth century, as the British freed numerous captives from slave ships and resettled them in Sierra Leone, the colony grew into a center of new cross-cultural influences, and its citizens spread their new mixture of African and European culture to a number of towns and cities along the coasts of West Africa.

Far across the continent, from the eastern Sudan and interior East Africa, growing numbers of Africans continued to be exported as slaves to the Middle East until the close of the nineteenth century. But in many areas of the continent, a new kind of external demand grew for the oils of Africa. In the end it would surpass the demand for people and ivory. In the rainforests and savannas of West Africa, states such as Dahomey as well as smaller societies, such as the Krobo, turned to the export of palm oil, responding to the needs of the Industrial Revolution in Europe for lubricants, soaps, and lamp oil. Along the Senegal River, the oil export of growing importance became, in contrast, peanuts, a crop that had come to Africa from the New World three centuries earlier.

Whenever European adventurers set out to "explore" the continent in the nineteenth century, they traveled along routes of trade pioneered centuries earlier by the Africans. The rights to pass along such routes were granted them, whether they acknowledged it or not, by the African authorities of the regions through which the routes passed. And when Europeans, advantaged by their own recent inventions in military technology such as repeating rifles and early forms of the machine gun, began their scramble to colonize Africa in the 1880s and 1890s, the already integral connection of most African economies to those of the Atlantic world, the Middle East, and the Indian Ocean aided immeasurably in the establishment of European political control.

NOTES FOR READERS AND TEACHERS

Issues and Questions

A problem that readers of African history of the seventeenth and eighteenth centuries must always grapple with is the temptation to turn the story of those times into a monolithic tale of the trans-Atlantic slave trade and its consequences. We cannot and must not neglect this fundamental topic. But at the same time, we must not lose sight of the still vibrant and independent agency of Africans in the events of that age.

We must do justice also to all of the other and varied courses of historical change taking place across the continent. The questions we ask ourselves should reflect the variety of this history.

- Commerce along many coastal areas in Africa in the later seventeenth and the eighteenth centuries underwent a massive rebalancing of demand, with slaves becoming the chief export and manufactured goods from other parts of the world becoming the major imports. What kinds of political and social effects did this pattern of trade have in Senegambia? In the Gold Coast? In the areas that today comprise Nigeria? In Angola and the Congo Basin? In east-central Africa and the Zambezi River regions?
- What kinds of social and economic transformations did the founding of the first European settler colony at the Cape of Good Hope in the 1650s bring about over the next 150 years?
- What particular change increasingly took hold in the technology of warfare in Africa in the seventeenth and especially eighteenth centuries?
- How did the policies of the seventeenth- and eighteenth-century Solomonic kings in Ethiopia help in setting off the period of political disunity, beginning in the later eighteenth century, known as the Era of the Princes?
- Even though the Maasai belonged to a decentralized, nonstate society, in the seventeenth and eighteenth centuries they were the most powerful people in all the regions around the Eastern Rift. Why was this so?
- At a number of points in this book, we have encountered explicit instances of the gendering of social, economic, and political roles in society. European colonial rulers of Africa in the late nineteenth century came from societies in which political and economic authority was a male prerogative, and so they assumed that the same prerogatives had previously existed among the Africans they conquered. Were they right? (The reader may wish to draw illustrative examples from several different chapters in considering this question.)
- At a number of points in the last two chapters we have considered the plight of smaller societies bordered by expansive states, especially in West Africa. What kinds of tactics or historical circumstances enabled such small-scale polities and communities to persist?

Further Reading

As in the notes to chapter 8, here in chapter 9 I have also chosen just a few works to cite—works that seem to me to present especially original, thought-provoking, or intellectually engaging perspectives on one or another aspect of African history between 1640 and 1800. Once again, too, the time spans of these books may be wider than the time period covered by the chapter.

Bay, Edna G. *Wives of the Leopard: Gender, Politics, and Culture in the Kingdom of Dahomey.* Charlottesville: University Press of Virginia, 1998.

Elphick, Richard. *Kraal and Castle.* New Haven: Yale University Press, 1977.

Kimambo, Isaria. *A Political History of the Pare of Tanzania.* Nairobi: East African Publishing House, 1969.

Manning, Patrick. *Slavery and African Life.* Cambridge and New York: Cambridge University Press, 1990.

Miller, Joseph C. *Kings and Kinsmen.* Oxford: Clarendon Press, 1976.

Spaulding, Jay. *The Heroic Age of Sinnar.* East Lansing: African Studies Center, Michigan State University, 1985.

Index

Illustration Credits

Figs. 1, 3, 4, 5, 9, 10, 15, 17, 18, 41, and 67: Drawn or photographed by the author.

Figs. 2, 6, 7, 8, 11, 13, 14, 16, 23, 25, 28, 30, 32, 33, 44, 45, 46, 47, 50, 52, 53, 54, 56, 58, 60, 61, 62, 63, 64, 66, 69, 70, 71, 72, 73, 74, 75, 78, 79, 82, and 84: © UCLA Fowler Museum of Cultural History; photographs by Don Cole.

Fig. 12: From James Bruce, *Travels to Discover the Source of the Nile in the Years 1768, 1769, 1770, 1771, 1772, and 1773*, 6 vols., 1790–91; photograph by Don Cole.

Fig. 19: Luo Cultural Museum, Kisumu, Kenya. Photograph by Patricia Ehret.

Figs. 20, 29, 34, 48, and 76: Courtesy of the Field Museum, Chicago; photographs by Dr. Chapurukha Kusimba.

Fig. 21: Photograph by Michael Goe, Institut für Nutztierwissenschaften, Zurich.

Fig. 22: Photograph by Dr. William Cahill.

Fig. 24: Photograph by Frances Cahill.

Figs. 26 and 27: By permission of Dr. Marie-Claude Van Grunderbeek.

Fig. 31: From *The Last Journals of David Livingstone*, vol. 1, 1874; photograph by Don Cole.

Fig. 35: From D. Krencker, *Ältere Denkmäler Nordabessiniens*, Tafeln, Deutsche Aksum-Expedition, 1912; photograph by Don Cole.

Fig. 36: Provided by Professor Merrick Posnansky; photograph by Don Cole.

Figs. 37 and 59: Photographs by Professor Michael Morony.

Fig. 38: From E. A. Wallis Budge, *The Egyptian Sudan*, vol. 2, 1907; photograph by Don Cole.

Figs. 39, 42, 55, 57, and 65: Photographs by Professor Merrick Posnansky.

Fig. 40: By permission of the South African Museum, Cape Town.

Fig. 43: By permission of Professor David Lewis-Williams and the Rock Art Research Unit, University of the Witwatersrand.

Fig. 49: Photographs by Lahra Smith.

Fig. 51: From E. A. Wallis Budge, *The Egyptian Sudan*, vol. 1, 1907; photograph by Don Cole.

Fig. 68: Photograph by Don Cole.

Fig. 77: From O. Dapper, *Description of Africa*, 1686; photograph by Don Cole.

Fig. 80: From G. Schweinfurth, *In the Heart of Africa*, vol. 2, 1874; photograph by Don Cole.

Fig. 81: From George McCall Theal, *South Africa*, 1894; photograph by Don Cole.

Fig. 83: Lamu Museum, Lamu, Kenya; photograph by the author.